Developing Microsoft Office Solutions

Developing Microsoft Office Solutions

Answers for Office 2003, Office XP, Office 2000, and Office 97

Ken Bluttman

✦✦Addison-Wesley

Boston • San Francisco • New York • Toronto • Montreal
London • Munich • Paris • Madrid
Capetown • Sydney • Tokyo • Singapore • Mexico City

The publisher offers discounts on this book when ordered in quantity for bulk purchases and special sales. For more information, please contact:

U.S. Corporate and Government Sales
(800) 382-3419
corpsales@pearsontechgroup.com

For sales outside of the U.S., please contact:

International Sales
(317) 581-3793
international@pearsontechgroup.com

Visit Addison-Wesley on the Web: www.awprofessional.com

Library of Congress Cataloging-in-Publication Data
Bluttman, Ken.
  Developing Microsoft Office solutions : answers for Office 2003,
Office XP, Office 2000, and Office 97 / Ken Bluttman.
      p. cm.
Includes bibliographical references and index.
  ISBN 0-201-73805-8 (pbk. : alk. paper)
 1. Microsoft Office. 2. Business—Computer programs. I. Title.

  HF5548.4.M525B555 2004
  005.5—dc22

                                        2003020382

ISBN: 0-201-73805-8
Text printed on recycled paper
1 2 3 4 5 6 7 8 9 10—CRS—0706050403
First printing, December 2003

For Gayla, my rainbow

Brief Contents

Contents

Preface

Walk into any business office in the world, and odds are you'll see Microsoft Office running on everyone's desktop—from assistants to managers, from directors to corporate officers. The majority of these workers depend on Office for many of their daily tasks. And yet many of them use Office in the basic off-the-shelf fashion: Word for writing documents and Excel or PowerPoint for creating spreadsheets and presentations.

There is so much more power behind these Office products. Under the hood are sophisticated technologies that, when applied, elevate Office to unprecedented custom, productive uses. But why use Office at all? Why not just use traditional development tools such as Visual Basic or C++? Isn't developing with Office just an easy way out?

Not one bit! In fact, the opposite case can be made. Why use a generic programming tool to duplicate what is already native in Office! If users need to manipulate numbers that are queried from a database, then putting some custom muscle into an Excel workbook meets their need—and rather quickly at that. Using Visual Basic for Applications (VBA) and other programming languages available to Office makes it possible to create killer apps in just a fraction of the time it takes with traditional programming tools. Time is money, and users want results. There simply is no point duplicating the functionality already built into Office.

The position and power of Office in the business world is not something that came about by luck or by accident. The functionality offered by each core Office product—Word, Excel, Access, PowerPoint, and Outlook—is based on the experience of millions of users over several years. These products are mature, stable, and feature-rich. Building solutions on top of such a foundation makes for sophisticated applications that do not share the distribution problems or incompatibility issues associated with traditional tool-based solutions. In the end, a satisfied user community is the best measure of success.

My Background in Office Development

Through the 1980s I was a sales manager in book publishing. During that time, PCs hit the market. At work, we acquired x386-processor-based computers for desktop use. I received monthly sales reports, generated from mainframe computers, that often were missing important sales data or were full of errors. I recall seeing once that an order from a bookstore went through the system with the ISBN (International Standard Book Number) mistakenly entered as the quantity. If you're not familiar with what an ISBN is, just look at the back cover of this book. All books have a unique number; the one for this book is 0-201-73805-8. Imagine if your local bookstore were to one day receive 201,738,058 copies of this book!

This example sounds humorous, but in retrospect it is clear that the order-processing system did not have built-in validation. This sort of issue led me to develop a custom application built with Lotus 1-2-3 to track my department's sales figures. Quickly I was able to deliver better reports from my PC than those coming out of the mainframes. I spent more and more time with that PC until eventually I was programming more than anything else.

And that led to a career change. The next decade or so I spent as a contract programmer. My specialty was customization of Office products. The early versions of Microsoft Office products were being used in business. Access was just at version 1 and then had a long run as version 2. VBA was introduced in Excel 5. That single action caused Excel to leapfrog all the other competitive spreadsheet products.

I worked for many companies, large and small—from mom-and-pop shops to Fortune 500 firms. In the midst of all this, Microsoft Office just grew and grew. I've worked on numerous solutions involving Office, often with Oracle, SQL Server, Sybase, and other database products. I have programmed, trained, and managed developers on all sorts of interesting projects.

About This Book

The focus of this book is to demonstrate how to create custom solutions built on the Microsoft Office products. Programming using VBA, XML, and other technologies is key to how solutions are put together. The style of this book may seem a bit different from that of other programming books: I do not attempt to explain all there is to know about programming Office. Even if it were possible to do so in one book, such a broad approach would limit each subject area to just minuscule coverage.

Instead, I have modeled this book on my years of business experience. Subjectively, I have culled what I feel are the key things to know within the focus of each chapter. I am not trying to teach Visual Basic for Applications in this book; I assume you are familiar enough with Visual Basic or with VBA to follow along. Sometimes I will use typical programming techniques, such as implementing an error trap; other times I will not. My naming conventions may differ from yours. Teaching programming is not the point of the book. Teaching how to program *Office* is the point of the book. Take what is explained in the book and combine it with what you already know. And in the areas for which you need further information, the Appendix lists additional resources.

XML is a key technology used in the book. XML is also not something that can be taught here. I suggest that readers not already familiar with XML technologies acquaint themselves with the topic through additional study. The concepts and syntax can be difficult to learn at first, especially for schemas and transformations, but the knowledge is key to using the new XML features in Office 2003.

Which leads me to discuss the different versions of Office. Most of this book applies to any version of Office. Office 97 and Office 2000 are similar, whereas Office XP is more of a departure from Office 2000. XP had the introduction of the task pane, an updated mail merge interface, and the introduction of some XML functionality. A few areas of the book, of course, are unique to the latest version, Office 2003. In particular, Chapter 9, "XML and Office," and Chapter 11, "Introduction to InfoPath," are completely based on Office 2003. Where applicable, you will find a notice about version limitations.

Also, I must mention that I wrote the book using a beta version (Beta 2) of Microsoft Office 2003. Most of the screen shots are from the beta version. Odds are that some functionality and some screens have changed in the release of the final product.

This book is segregated into three parts. Part I devotes a chapter each to what I subjectively call the core Office products. These chapters introduce the key objects and how to program them using their particular properties and methods. Useful programming examples are given throughout to demonstrate how the objects can be used in reasonable and solution-oriented ways. Nearly all of Part I applies universally to any version of Office.

A particular comment about Access belongs here. Access holds a unique place within the Office product family. Word, Excel, PowerPoint, and Outlook have a default usage path; that is, each of these can be used without any customization. For example, a user can start typing a document in Word simply by starting up Word. A blank document is ready for entry.

In contrast, Access cannot be used until customization has been implemented. There is no default blank Access database. Even the simplest Access database is the work of customization. The nature of this book, in which each product receives a piece but not all of the spotlight, led me to include a discussion of key Access objects while avoiding coverage of any general Access or database design fundamentals.

Part II of the book delves into the technologies that are integrated with Office. In particular, Chapter 7, "Common Microsoft Office Objects," explains the workings of search features, dialogs, and customized command bars that can be applied to any of the Office products. Chapter 8, "Microsoft Forms," covers a great supportive technology available to all Office products and all versions of Office.

Chapter 9, "XML and Office," gives a detailed overview of the new XML features in Office 2003. Chapter 10, "Smart Tags," demonstrates using simple smart tags in Office XP and Office 2003. And to complete this part of the book, Chapter 11, "Introduction to InfoPath," gives an overview of this exciting new Microsoft Office product.

Part III of the book presents five case studies, each designed to demonstrate particular techniques. Some case studies are built upon real projects I have been assigned over the years, and others are hypothetical, to showcase how new Office 2003 technologies are likely to be integrated into future solutions.

Finally, the book ends with an appendix that lists further resources for the various technologies and products.

Code Listings and Conventions

Plenty of programming code is included in the book, and some is rather lengthy. The code samples are available as a download from the Office

VBA Developer Web site at *www.officevbadeveloper.com*. Check there, too, for corrections and updates to the book.

Many examples in the book simulate real business information, such as a customer list. All personal and business names and addresses and phone numbers are fictitious. Any similarity to real people or companies is not intentional. Over the years I have so often had to create test data for database projects that I have built a utility, called Records2Go, to easily generate such test records. All test data has been created with this tool. Please visit *www.records2go.com* if you are interested in this tool. I am preparing Records2Go for commercial release in the near future.

Acknowledgments

Loving thanks to my wife, Gayla, and son, Matthew, for all the times the noisy clickety-clack of the keyboard and the whirring of the printer sounded throughout the house at rather odd late-night and early-morning hours. Writing this book has given me countless opportunities to watch the sun rise.

My thanks go out to the reviewers of the book. There have been many, and the following list is *not* exhaustive, but here are the names I am able to include: Janis Archer, Richard Banks, Scott Bechtold, Maggie Biggs, Nancy Birnbaum, Shauna Kelly, Will Kelly, Beth Melton, Peter O'Kelly, and Deepak Sharma.

Thanks to Neil Salkind and the staff of StudioB—a great agency to work with!

Thanks to Chris Keane for his excellent editing and production skills—even as he scrambled to work around a power outage from Hurricane Isabel.

Finally, thanks to the fine staff at Addison-Wesley. Stephane Thomas and Mike Mullen must have the patience of saints, as I have missed many promised deadlines. Thanks, too, to Patrick Peterson, Curt Johnson, Heather Mullane, Elizabeth Ryan, and the rest of the team. All have been great to work with.

Your comments are welcome! Please write to me at *ken@logicstory.com*. Thanks and enjoy!

Ken Bluttman
October 2003

PART I

Office Development

Using Microsoft Office to Create Custom Solutions

What's New for Developers in Office 2003

Each release of Microsoft Office has introduced new features and new ways of working. User-level enhancements are the norm for each release. For developers, this is typically mirrored with new programmable objects, methods, and properties that complement the new user features. Microsoft Office 2003 continues in this tradition, and new programmable objects are appropriately covered within the product-specific chapters of the book.

Office 2003 embraces the robust set of XML (Extensible Markup Language) standards as the basis for many of the new features. This is an interesting fact because XML is not proprietary: XML-centric features are based on open standards. The result of working with XML is pure available open data. For example, in previous versions a Word document could be opened with Word or with a robust product that could interpret the proprietary Word document format. Now with Word 2003, documents can be saved in an XML format. So, Word documents can remain proprietary or be saved in one of two XML formats. One is the "plain vanilla" XML data format—without formatting information. The other is a new XML-based format called WordML. WordML allows saving the information *and* the formatting from a Word document—all as XML data.

Increased XML Support

New XML functionality has been incorporated into Word, Excel, and Access. Each of these products embraces XML usage to a differing degree and with a product-specific approach. This makes sense because the *experience* of using each individual product should remain similar to that of earlier versions.

Incorporating XML with daily work activities is exciting, because now the Office products can easily communicate with each other, as well as with any number of external systems, such as Web services. With XML serving as a structured storage medium, business data can be moved in and out of applications with less effort and no issues of proprietary limitations. With this shift, the Office products are primed as a platform for new business initiatives limited only by imagination.

Chapter 9 of the book is devoted to the new Office 2003 XML features. Many examples show how developers can use the new XML features in custom applications. Here briefly is a product-specific overview.

XML in Word 2003

Word has been given the biggest XML boost of all the core Office products. New objects, properties, methods, and collections support dynamic use of schemas, namespaces, and transformations. When working with XML, the actual element tags are visible in the document, as shown in Figure 1.1.

Word supports XML within the typical document paradigm that users are familiar with. This is no small feat, because XML forces structure on information, and most Word documents are unstructured. That is, documents do not typically have the strict structuring found in worksheets or database tables.

The placement of XML element tags in a Word document is flexible. They can be moved around and mixed with text entered with the keyboard. As stated previously, Word provides options on how to save documents with regard to XML structure.

XML in Excel

The approach for XML usage in Excel is to use a schema as a bridge between the data and the worksheet. This functionality depends on the new Map object. Figure 1.2 shows the schema provided by the map in the XML Source task pane, and the associated data in the worksheet.

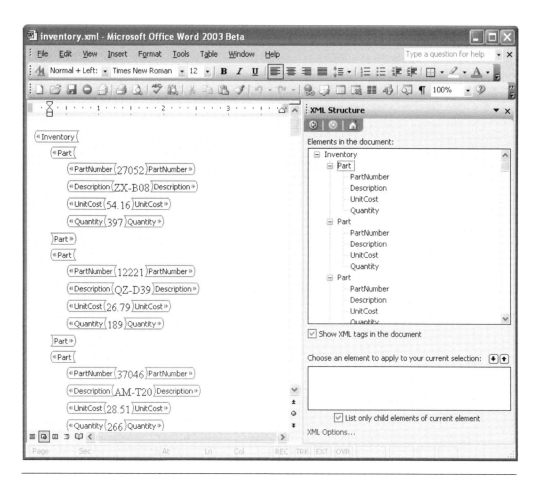

Figure 1.1 Working with XML in Word

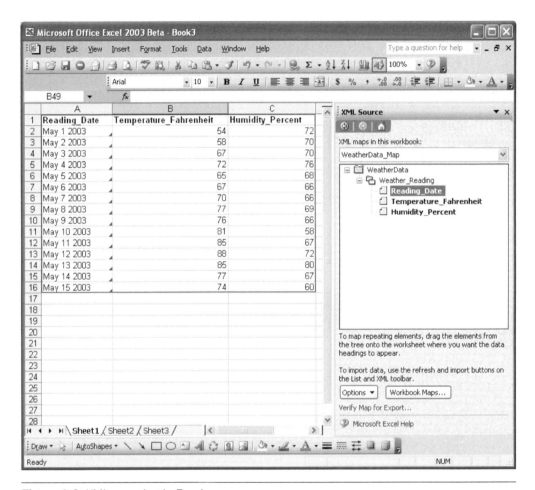

Figure 1.2 XML mapping in Excel

Elements from a schema in the XML Source task pane can be dragged onto the worksheet. Another new Excel object—the List—is used in conjunction with XML data. Lists are dynamic structured ranges. Placing XML data on a worksheet results in a list (this actually depends on the rules in the schema).

The weather data on the worksheet in Figure 1.2 is actually a list. When the active cell falls inside the list area, the list expands one row to accept new input. Figure 1.3 shows the list with the active cell present. The list is ready to accept new data in the row indicated by the asterisk.

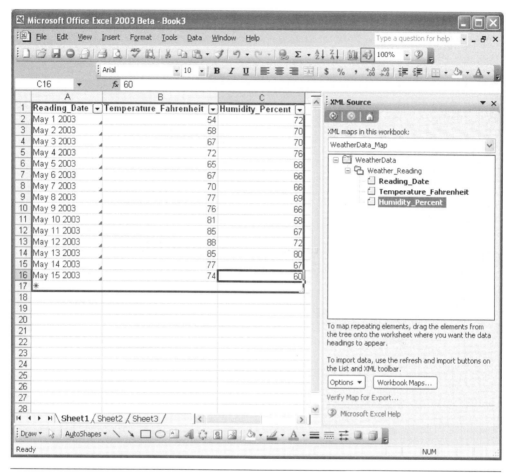

Figure 1.3   An XML-based list is ready for additional input

XML in Access

A major enhancement in XML support in Access 2003 is the ability to export related tables. In Access 2002, XML exporting was limited to a base object: one table or query, for example. Access 2003 allows data related objects to be included in an export. Figure 1.4 shows a set of related tables and the options for including the related information on an XML export.

Access also features improved XSLT (Extensible Style Sheet Transform) processing. A transform can be applied on both import and export, and transforms can be custom developed. This is an enhancement over Access 2002, in which the transformations were limited to a single built-in one.

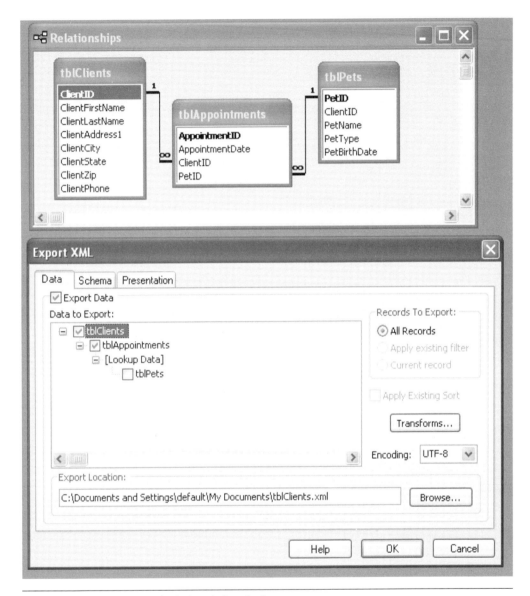

Figure 1.4 XML export of relational data in Access

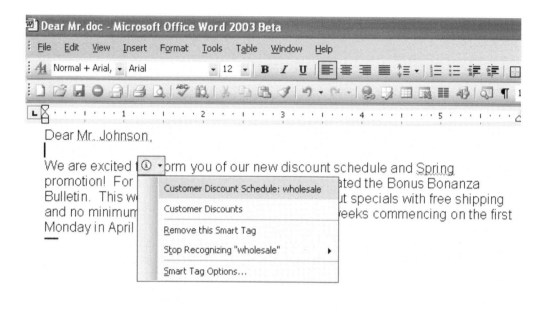

Figure 1.5 A custom smart tag in Word provides a list of actions

Enhanced Smart Tags

Smart tags were introduced in Office XP. Some smart tags operate based on user activity, such as helping with typing errors. These smart tags are supplied with the products, and are not programmable. For developers, though, there is the ability to create *custom* smart tags.

In Office XP, custom smart tags could work only in Word and Excel (also in Outlook with Word as the e-mail editor). Office 2003 extends smart tags to work in PowerPoint and Access. Smart tags work by providing a list of possible actions a user can take based on a list of recognized terms. In other words, when a term is typed in, the smart tag will appear and the user can choose from a list of actions. Figure 1.5 shows this feature in Word.

The approach for smart tags in Access differs because Access smart tags offer the list of actions without regard to any predetermined list of recognizers. This approach is explained in Chapter 10.

A distinction must be made about custom smart tag development. Extensive smart tag functionality can be delivered with a dynamic link library (DLL). DLL creation requires using a programming language such as Visual Basic or C#. However, Visual Studio programming is not the focus of this book, so this avenue of development is not included. Programming resources are listed in the Appendix.

The alternative to full DLL interaction is to create simple smart tags that offer hyperlinks. This is also a sophisticated approach. The hyperlinks can carry the recognized term to the target Web site. There, the term can be used to return dynamic information. Chapter 10 demonstrates creating and using hyperlink-based smart tags.

Smart Documents

Smart documents are a completely new feature that enhances work productivity by delivering needed functionality directly into the product workspace. Smart documents are used to control a new Document Actions task pane. This pane sits within the work area and can provide dynamic help and functionality in step with user actions.

For example, a worker might be preparing a business proposal. As the worker tackles portions of the document, the Document Actions task pane will update to give the worker vital information to finish the task at hand.

Smart documents are supported in Word and Excel. Figure 1.6 shows a smart document in Excel. The worksheet is set up to accept information about a sales call. The active cell is the entry point for the Company Name, and the Document Actions task pane, on the right, offers help based on the active cell. The content in the task pane is dynamic. The content changes as other cells receive focus.

As with smart tags, comprehensive smart documents incorporate DLL functionality. It is possible to make limited smart documents without using a DLL, but the benefit is minor. Since the scope of this book does not include programming DLLs, as previously mentioned, smart documents are not covered. However, check the Appendix for resources.

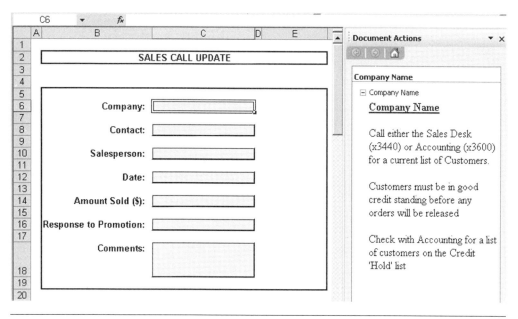

Figure 1.6 A smart document in Excel

InfoPath

InfoPath is a new standalone product that ensures data integrity from entry through delivery. InfoPath operates through a forms paradigm. As a form generator, InfoPath has the expected controls: text box, list, checkbox, and much more. However, there are new aspects of form creation that are unseen in other Office products. One feature is the inherent power of InfoPath to make forms conform to an XML schema. A schema describes the requirements and constraints of data. InfoPath flows the schema rules into the form, thereby forcing conformity of data at the point of entry. Figure 1.7 shows an InfoPath form being designed.

InfoPath is an XML generator. Forms are first designed and then distributed to workers. When a worker fills in a form, the entries are stored as XML. As XML, the data is available for reuse. InfoPath is extensible and provides more features than just creating simple forms to gather data. Other options include database integration and communication with Web services. For example, an InfoPath form can serve as a front end to Access or SQL Server. In this configuration, data can be read from and written to the database from the InfoPath form. InfoPath is explored in Chapter 11.

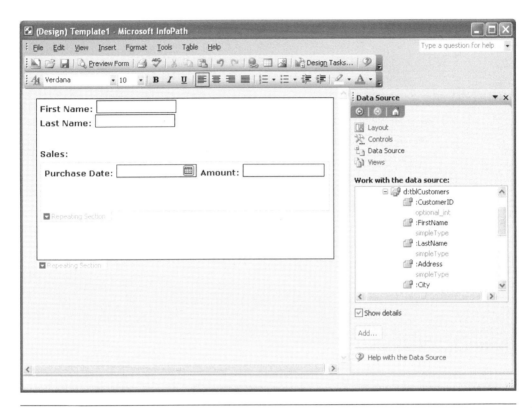

Figure 1.7 A form in InfoPath conforms to its underlying schema

The Research Task Pane

A new Research task pane is introduced in Office 2003. The task pane leads to external sources that deliver results based on a keyword or phrase search. Figure 1.8 shows the Research task pane delivering results based on a phrase.

By default, the task pane lists search engines and other similar resources to search using the keywords. For developers, the process exists to add to this list with custom internal or external Web services. Creating custom resources requires the use of Visual Studio.Net and therefore is not covered in the book. See the Appendix for resources.

Figure 1.8 Using the Research task pane

Other New Office Enhancements for Developers

There are tools that allow interaction with Visual Studio.Net. Office XP and .Net interaction is supported with the Office XP Primary Interop Assemblies. The new Visual Studio Tools for Office continues this trend by integrating the power of the .Net CLR (Common Language Runtime) with the extensive features of Word 2003 and Excel 2003. This allows the creation of Office-based solutions that benefit from incorporating external functionality not found in Office.

Team development is supported with Windows SharePoint Services (WSS). While not strictly a development tool, team services create new ways for developers to work together. The Appendix lists resources on Windows SharePoint Services.

Summary

Office 2003 embraces the latest trends affecting developers. The XML enhancements alone are bound to spawn many new solution approaches. In the near future, typical Office developer chat will likely focus on schemas and XML-based forms as much as on traditional VBA issues.

Smart client solutions will continue to grow. This thrust began with smart tags for Word 2002 and Excel 2002. Support has now been increased, and the new smart documents enhance this dynamic interaction.

InfoPath is an exciting addition to the Office family. InfoPath provides the means to gather, edit, and store data all within the confines of the XML structure.

Many of these new development roads are covered in this book. Chapter 10 is devoted to creating and using smart tags. XML usage (Chapter 9) and InfoPath development (Chapter 11) have dedicated chapters and are also featured in case studies. Many new solution approaches will be crafted based on the latest functionality. All in all, Office 2003 is an exciting version upgrade!

CHAPTER 2

Word Solution Development

VERSION NOTE: This material works for all versions of Word, except where noted. XML use in Word is covered in Chapter 9, "XML and Office."

Word, long recognized as the best in its class of word processors, is a great tool for custom application development. Word sports a very rich object model with unique methods and abilities that support many standard business needs. Coupled with the fact that it is one of the most widely used desktop applications, there is very little reason not to consider Word as a shell for custom solutions. Companies that have recognized Word as an entity in which to add customization have reaped great rewards of increased productivity.

Let's tackle the key objects, properties, and methods in Word.

Objects, Properties, and Methods

The `Application` Object

The `Application` object is the highest-level object, and it relates to Word itself. Properties of the `Application` object typically set or return information that affects any particular file or document, or Word itself. For example, the `ActivePrinter` property returns (or sets) the name of the printer. The `ScreenUpdating` property turns the screen refresh off or on. The `StatusBar` property sets messages in the status bar:

```
MsgBox "The active printer is " & Application.ActivePrinter
Application.ScreenUpdating = False
Application.StatusBar = "Reading Data..."
```

Methods of the `Application` object are more global in purpose. The `NewWindow` method opens a new window on the active document. The `Printout` method prints all or part of a document, or an envelope or mailing label. The `Quit` method of the `Application` object exits Word itself:

```
Application.NewWindow
Application.Quit
```

`ActiveDocument` and the `Documents` Collection

The main working object is the document. Documents come in a collection, which is the group of open document files. In most situations, only one document is open. When one or more documents are open, only one is the `ActiveDocument` at any given time, although which document has this distinction can be changed either programmatically or by actions in the user interface.

The example in Listing 2.1 reports on the number of paragraphs and the number of words within all open documents. The `Documents` collection is cycled through, and then the paragraph and word counts are returned from their respective collections within each document. See Figure 2.1.

Listing 2.1 Cycling through the `Documents` collection and returning paragraph and word counts

```
Dim doc As Document
Dim msg As String
For Each doc In Application.Documents
  msg = "There are " & doc.Paragraphs.Count
  msg = msg & " paragraphs and "
  msg = msg & "there are " & doc.Words.Count
  msg = msg & " words in the "
  msg = msg & doc.Name & " document."
  MsgBox msg
Next
```

Documents have methods and properties that for the most part are synchronous with user interface activities. For example, a document has paragraphs, sections, sentences, and the like. All facts about a document can be addressed in code.

Figure 2.1 Information about a document is returned

This line will report the total number of sentences in the document:

```
MsgBox ActiveDocument.Sentences.Count & " sentences"
```

The following two lines of code will report the number of sentences in just the fourth paragraph. Note that the `Paragraph` object does not contain a `Sentence` property, so another method is used. A `Range` is established to represent the paragraph and then the count of sentences is returned, as shown in Figure 2.2. (The `Range` object is explored further later in this chapter.)

```
Set myRange = ActiveDocument.Paragraphs(4).Range
MsgBox myRange.Sentences.Count
```

Consider a business letter you may type into Word. Attributes of this correspondence include characters, words, sentences, paragraphs, fonts, and alignment. That is the very least. Further features could include sections, a header or footer or both, page orientation, tab settings, graphics, and much more. All of these are addressable in VBA code. For example, the business letter may appear left justified throughout. However, alignment is not a property of the document of the whole, but rather of each individual paragraph. The `Paragraph` object is programmable. These two lines set and return the alignment of paragraph 5:

```
ActiveDocument.Paragraphs(5).Alignment = _
    wdAlignParagraphCenter
MsgBox ActiveDocument.Paragraphs(5).Alignment
```

Figure 2.2 Counting sentences

`Activate`, `Printout`, `Save`, and `Close` are commonly used methods of the `Document` object. Here is an example of a document being activated, printed, saved, and closed:

```
Documents(2).Activate
With ActiveDocument
    .PrintOut
    .Save
    .Close
End With
```

The `Selection` Object

The `Selection` object represents the selected portion of a document (see Figure 2.3), including the possibility of representing an entire document. In the absence of a selected area in a document, the `Selection` object represents the character to the right of the insertion point. This may be an actual character, but it could be a paragraph mark, a tab, or another nonprintable character.

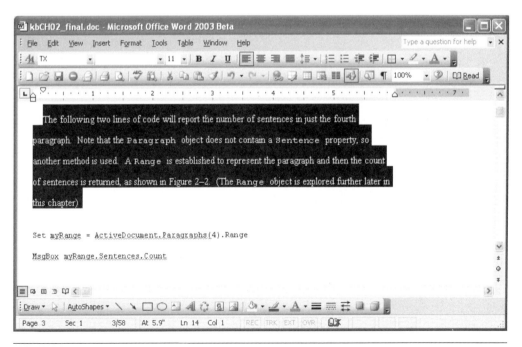

Figure 2.3 The `Selection` object represents the selected area

When working within the user interface, it is often necessary to select a part of a document prior to performing a further action. In code this is accomplished with the `Select` method. The `Select` method returns the `Selection` object. Note that there is only one `Selection` object ever available.

This simple line displays the contents of the selection in a message box. The message box will appear blank if the entire selection consists of nonprintable characters, such as tabs:

```
MsgBox Selection
```

The `Selection` object has numerous properties and methods. Some property examples:

```
With Selection
  MsgBox .Font.Name ' the font used in the selection
  MsgBox .Characters.Count ' character count of selection
  MsgBox .Document ' name of document holding selection
  MsgBox .Start ' start position of selection
  MsgBox .End ' end position of selection
  MsgBox .StoryType ' the part of the document the selection is in
  MsgBox .StoryLength ' length of the story
End With
```

The `Start, End, StoryType,` and `StoryLength` properties are based on a *story*. `StoryRanges` represent distinct areas of a document such as the main body, headers, footers, and so on. The `Start` and `End` properties return values based on the count of characters of the story that contains the selection. `StoryRanges` are discussed later on in this chapter.

The `Selection` object has dozens of methods. Table 2.1 lists several of them.

Listing 2.2 demonstrates using properties and methods of the `Selection` object.

Listing 2.2 starts by accessing the count provided by the `Sentences` collection. Then a loop is established to address each sentence. In the loop each successive sentence is selected by applying the `Select` method.

Next, using a `With...End With` construct, properties of the `Selection` object are put to use to change font attributes. Incidentally, the `Font` and `Characters` properties of the `Selection` object in turn make use of their own properties.

Table 2.1 Methods of the `Selection` object

Methods	Comments
`Collapse` `Collapse (direction)`	Removes the extended area of selection. This insertion point can be directed to land at the beginning or the end of the extended selection with the optional `direction` parameter. For example, `Selection.Collapse (wdCollapseStart)`. Two settings are available: `wdCollapseStart` or `wdCollapseEnd`. The default is to collapse to the start.

`Copy`
`Cut`
`Paste`
	Both `Copy` and `Cut` place the selection on the clipboard. `Paste` replaces whatever is selected in the document.

`Delete` `Delete (unit, count)`	Deletes the selection. Optional parameters can be set for the `unit` and `count`. For example: `Selection.Delete wdWord, 4`. This deletes four words from the beginning of the selection.
`Expand` `Expand (unit)`	Expands the selection by a specified unit. For example, `Selection.Expand wdSentence` expands the selection to include the full sentence. The default `unit` is Word (`wdWord`).
`Extend` `Extend (character)`	Extends the selection by a fixed progression of units—word, sentence, paragraph, and so on. More useful however is to supply a character to extend to. For example, `Selection.Extend "C"` will extend the selection to the next occurrence of the letter *C*. This parameter is case sensitive.
`Move` `Move (unit, count)`	Collapses the selection and moves it. The default for `unit` is character. The default for `count` is 1.

Table 2.1 *(continued)*

Methods	Comments

`MoveLeft`
`MoveLeft (unit, count, extend)`
`MoveRight`
`MoveRight (unit, count, extend)`
`MoveDown`
`MoveDown (unit, count, extend)`
`MoveUp`
`MoveUp (unit, count, extend)`
	These methods move the selection in the indicated direction. Unit, count, and extend are optional parameters.
	  The default for `unit` is character. The default for `count` is 1.
	  `Extend` is a Boolean flag that sets whether or not to extend the selection while moving. `Extend` has two possible settings: `wdMove` or `wdExtend`. The default is `wdMove` (no extension).

`InsertBefore (text)` `InsertAfter (text)`	Text is a required parameter. These methods insert the text before or after the selection and extend the selection with the inserted text.
`TypeText (text)`	Text is a required parameter. This method will either insert the text before the selection or replace the selection with the inserted text, depending on the "Typing Replaces Selection" setting in the Edit tab of Tools … Options.

Listing 2.2 Setting the first letter in each sentence to a larger font size, then copying the first sentence to the header

```
sentence_count = ActiveDocument.Sentences.Count
For this_sentence = 1 To sentence_count
  ActiveDocument.Sentences(this_sentence).Select
  With Selection
    .Font.Name = "Arial"
    .Font.Size = "12"
    .Characters(1).Font.Size = "16" ' enlarge first letter
  End With
Next this_sentence
ActiveDocument.Sentences(1).Select
Selection.Copy
ActiveDocument.StoryRanges(wdPrimaryHeaderStory).Select
Selection.Paste
```

After the loop completes, the first sentence is selected. Then the `Copy` method is applied. The first sentence goes on the clipboard. Next the header of the document is selected. Finally the `Paste` method is applied. At this last step, the first sentence is on the clipboard but is no longer the selection. The selection is in the header. The `Paste` method pastes the first sentence into the header, replacing anything that may already be there. The results are shown in Figure 2.4.

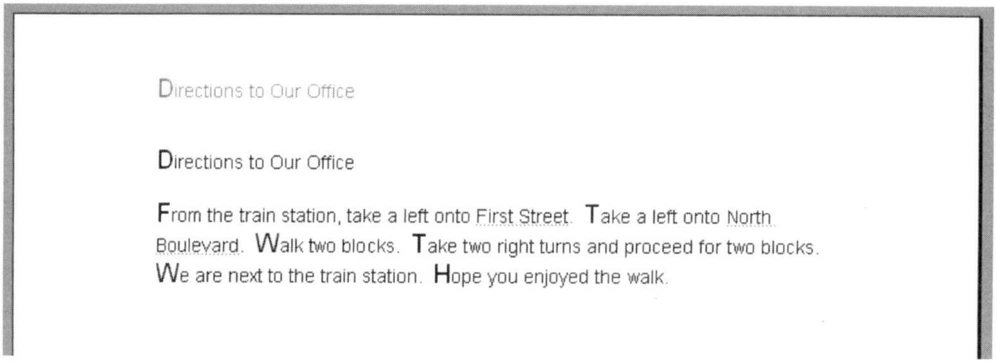

> Directions to Our Office
>
> Directions to Our Office
>
> From the train station, take a left onto First Street. Take a left onto North Boulevard. Walk two blocks. Take two right turns and proceed for two blocks. We are next to the train station. Hope you enjoyed the walk.

Figure 2.4 Working with the `Selection` object to alter sentence structure

The Range Object

The `Range` object represents a contiguous area of a document. Multiple ranges can be established. On the other hand, there is no default range. Until one or more ranges are established, the number of ranges is zero.

Similar to the `Selection` object, a `Range` can represent some or all of a document. Unlike the `Selection` object, establishing a `Range` does not "select" anything. There is no visible counterpart to establishing a range. In this respect ranges are geared toward programmable purposes. In fact ranges exist just within code procedures. Their scope is limited to the running procedure. A range cannot outlive the termination of the procedure in which it was created.

Ranges are created with the use of either the `Range` method or the `Range` property. The `Range` method belongs to the `Document` object. The `Range` property is available to many objects in Word. In Listing 2.3, four variables are dimensioned as ranges, then they are set to areas of the document. Range1 is set by using the Range method. Range2, Range3, and Range4 are set using the Range property of objects in Word.

The Range method used to set Range1 takes start position and end position parameters. Range2 and Range4 are set to fixed portions of the document. Range3 is set to the Selection object, wherever it may be.

Listing 2.3 Setting ranges

```
Dim Range1 As Range
Dim Range2 As Range
Dim Range3 As Range
Dim Range4 As Range
With ActiveDocument
  Set Range1 = .Range(0, 25)
  Set Range2 = .Paragraphs(3).Range
  Set Range3 = Selection.Range
  Set Range4 = .StoryRanges(wdPrimaryFooterStory)
End With
```

The properties and methods of the Range object are similar to those of the Selection object, but there are a few differences. For example, the Range object has the Duplicate and ShowAll properties, and the CheckGrammar and CheckSpelling methods. For the most part though, the Selection object and a Range object can be used in the same way. The key differences between the Selection object and Range object are:

- The Selection object has a visible counterpart in the user inter-face—the selected area of the document.
- There can be multiple Ranges, but there is only one Selection object (per windowpane).
- Selections remain after a code procedure terminates; ranges do not.

Ranges are better suited for manipulation in code. By virtue of being named, the use of ranges provides for more readable code. Manipulation of the Selection object affects which part of a document is visibly selected. Using ranges has no such effect. Ranges are independent of the Selection object.

StoryRanges

StoryRanges is a collection of specific ranges that represent areas of the document. These areas are the main body, footers, headers, and the like. In other words, stories are nonsubjective, standard parts of a document.

The StoryRanges collection can contain up to 11 members, as this is the total number of stories that are available. StoryRanges are not created directly either programmatically or through user-interface actions, but rather they exist as parts of a document. For example, a simple document has one StoryRange: *wdMainTextStory*. Adding a footer causes the StoryRanges collection to have a second member: *wdPrimary-FooterStory*.

The StoryRanges collection belongs to the Document object. In contrast the StoryType property is available to the Range, Selection, and Bookmark objects. The 11 types of stories are:

wdCommentsStory

wdEndnotesStory

wdEvenPagesFooterStory

wdEvenPagesHeaderStory

wdFirstPageFooterStory

wdFirstPageHeaderStory

wdFootnotesStory

wdMainTextStory

wdPrimaryFooterStory

wdPrimaryHeaderStory

wdTextFrameStory

To make use of story ranges, apply the StoryType property. The code in Listing 2.4 will change the header to Arial, size 9, if the selection (or just the insertion point) is currently in the header.

Navigating Through a Document

Often there is a need to work with different areas of a document. Depending on the purpose, either the desired area needs to be represented as a range or the insertion point must actually be at the area.

Listing 2.4 Using the `StoryType` property to determine where the `Selection` object is in a document

```
If Selection.StoryType = wdPrimaryHeaderStory Then
  ActiveDocument.StoryRanges(wdPrimaryHeaderStory).Select
  With Selection.Font
    .Name = "Arial"
    .Size = 9
  End With
End If
```

The `GoTo` method is used to meet either need. The `GoTo` method is available to the `Document`, `Range`, and `Selection` objects. The syntax for the `GoTo` method is:

```
expression.GoTo(What, Which, Count, Name)
```

`Expression` is either a document, an established `Range` object, or the `Selection` object. If the document or a range is used, a new range is set to the area indicated by the parameters of the `GoTo` method. For the `Selection` object, the insertion point actually travels to the indicated area. The syntax is a bit different for the document or range versus the selection:

```
Dim Range1 As Range
Set Range1 = ActiveDocument.Paragraphs(1).Range
Range1.GoTo wdGoToPage, wdGoToAbsolute, 2
Selection.GoTo wdGoToPage, wdGoToAbsolute, 2
```

In the preceding code, the first three lines are used to set a range to an area of the document. The last line actually moves the insertion point to the new area. This occurs because the `GoTo` method is applied as a member of the `Selection` object.

The `What` parameter is a constant that is available from a limited list. The list includes items such as *wdGoToLine*, *wdGoToPage*, *wdGoToTable*, and *wdGoToGraphic*. Noticeably missing from the list are other common document objects such as paragraphs. However, these are addressable using their collections. A little perseverance is needed in making the best of Word's programming rules. It's all there, but what you need just may not be where you first thought it was.

The `Which` parameter is set to one of these six constants: *wdGo-ToAbsolute*, *wdGoToFirst*, *wdGoToLast*, *wdGoToNext*, *wdGo-ToPrevious*, or *wdGoToRelative*.

The settings for absolute and relative work together with the `Count` parameter. In the following code sample, the insertion point is first moved to page two. The text "This is the start of page 2" is entered at the top of page two. Then the insertion point is moved two pages farther to page four. This is accomplished by using the relative setting for the `Which` parameter and 2 for the `Count` parameter. The text "This is the start of page 4" is entered at the top of page four. The `TypeParagraph` method is used to improve readability. After the text is inserted, the `TypePara-graph` method serves the same function as pressing the Enter key.

```
With Selection
   .GoTo wdGoToPage, wdGoToAbsolute, 2
   .TypeText "This is the start of page 2"
   .TypeParagraph
   .GoTo wdGoToPage, wdGoToRelative, 2
   .TypeText "This is the start of page 4"
   .TypeParagraph
End With
```

The last parameter of the `GoTo` method, `Name`, is useful for items that have a name, such as a bookmark. The following line moves the insertion point to a bookmark:

```
Selection.GoTo What:=wdGoToBookmark, Name:="Date"
```

The `Move` method, available to the `Range` and `Selection` objects, is an alternative way to navigate around a document. `Move` has two optional parameters, `Unit` and `Count`. The defaults for these, respectively, are character (`wdCharacter`) and 1. The `Move` method is similar to the `GoTo` method; however, `Move` takes only the two parameters, whereas `GoTo` takes up to four.

The `Move` method collapses the selection or range. If there currently is an extended selection, the `Move` method will collapse the selection down to the insertion point prior to the move. The result is that the insertion point has been relocated. These two lines of code move the insertion point up three paragraphs, then ahead two words, respectively:

```
Selection.Move wdParagraph, -3
Selection.Move wdWord, 2
```

A move can be tested to see if it was successful. The following code snippet attempts to move the selection down five sections, but there may not be five sections below the insertion point. The `move_result` variable receives the count of the specified unit the operation was able to find. The test here is to see if the result is less than the indicated count. If it is less, then the operation failed:

```
move_result = Selection.Move(wdSection, 5)
If move_result < 5 Then
    MsgBox "Move operation failed"
End If
```

For a `Range` object, the area the range represents will change although nothing visibly moves. However, the range is collapsed. This may produce an unintended result. In this example a range is set to a given sentence. When the `Move` method is applied, the range is set to the start of another sentence, but it no longer represents the entire sentence itself. The last line selects the `mySentence` range, but all that appears is the insertion point:

```
Set mySentence = ActiveDocument.Sentences(3)
mySentence.Move wdSentence, -2
mySentence.Select
```

Word has several variations of the `Move` method, such as `MoveLeft`, `MoveRight`, `MoveUp`, `MoveDown`, `MoveStart`, and `MoveEnd`. There are even conditional move methods such as `MoveUntil` and `MoveWhile`.

The `MoveLeft`, `MoveRight`, `MoveUp`, and `MoveDown` methods apply only to the `Selection` object. Here is an example of each:

```
With Selection
    .MoveLeft wdCharacter, 1 '1 character left, no extend
    .MoveRight wdWord, 1, wdExtend '1 word right with extend
    .MoveUp wdLine, 2, wdMove '2 lines up, no extend
    .MoveDown wdParagraph, 3, wdExtend '3 down, with extend
End With
```

In the preceding example, the insertion point is moved one character to the left. Next the selection is extended to include one word to the right. Next the selection is collapsed and the insertion point is moved two lines up. Finally, the selection is extended downward to include a total of three paragraphs. Note that the extend mode parameter can be either wdMove or wdExtend. The default is wdMove, which results in the selection being collapsed and the insertion point being moved.

The MoveStart and MoveEnd methods are available to both the Range and the Selection objects. The extend mode parameter is not available for these methods; only unit and count can be indicated. These methods change the start or end position of the range or selection. Some examples:

```
' move the start of the selection back 2 sentences,
' which increases the size of the selection
Selection.MoveStart wdSentence, -2

' move the start of the selection ahead 3 lines,
' which decreases the size of the selection
Selection.MoveStart wdLine, 3

' move the end of the selection ahead 5 characters,
' which increases the size of the selection
Selection.MoveEnd wdCharacter, 5

' move the end of the selection back 1 paragraph,
' which decreases the size of the selection
Selection.MoveEnd wdParagraph, -1

' Initially myRange represents just the second table.
' After the MoveStart method, MyRange represents
' the first table through the second table, including
' anything in between the tables
Dim myRange As Range
Set myRange = ActiveDocument.Tables(2).Range
myRange.MoveStart wdTable, -1
```

The MoveWhile, MoveStartWhile, MoveEndWhile, Move-Until, MoveStartUntil, and MoveEndUntil methods are available to both the Range and Selection objects. These methods make use of a test to determine the extent of processing. The test is a set of one or more characters. This set of characters appears to be a single text string, but actually each character in it is treated separately. The following two lines of code perform a move operation as long as any number is successfully found during the move. The difference between these two lines is that MoveWhile collapses the selection and moves the insertion point, and MoveEndWhile extends the selection. The second parameter, Count, can take a number or a directional constant:

```
Selection.MoveWhile "1234567890", wdForward
Selection.MoveEndWhile "1234567890", wdForward
```

When the `Count` parameter is fixed to a number, then the move only occurs through that number, even if the test would continue to be successful. This next line moves the insertion point two characters to the right, provided the characters are numbers. However, it will not move any farther even if more numbers follow the first two:

```
Selection.MoveWhile "1234567890", 2
```

The `MoveWhile` method collapses the selection and moves the insertion point while the test is true. The `MoveStartWhile` and `MoveEndWhile` methods extend the selection while the test is true. For these "While" methods, the test is true as long as successive encountered characters match any characters in the character set supplied as a parameter to the method.

The `MoveUntil` method collapses the selection and moves the insertion point while the test is true. The `MoveStartUntil` and `MoveEndUntil` methods extend the selection while the test is true. For these "Until" methods, the test is true as long as successive encountered characters do *not* match any characters in the character set supplied as a parameter to the method.

When applied to a range, the size of the range will change. The `MoveUntil` and `MoveWhile` methods effectively collapse the range, similar to how these methods affect the `Selection` object. `MoveStartWhile`, `MoveEndWhile`, `MoveStartUntil`, and `MoveEndUntil` all increase or decrease the size of the range as well.

Note that the `MoveStartWhile`, `MoveEndWhile`, `MoveStartUntil`, and `MoveEndUntil` methods can take either the `wdForward` or `wdBackward` constant in place of an actual count. These constants ensure that the test will continue until there is either a definitive success or a failure to the test. It is possible that the necessary count parameter value will not be known; therefore, these constants are valuable in this regard. For example, you may need to extend the selection until a given character is found, but there is no way of knowing how many characters to search through to find it.

Here are examples of the conditional Move and While methods:

```
' Initially myRange represents the first paragraph.
' The end of the range is increased until the first
' uppercase T or G is found. The range does not include
```

```
' the T or G. If a T or G is not encountered, then
' the range is not altered.
Dim myRange As Range
Set myRange = ActiveDocument.Paragraphs(1).Range
myRange.MoveEndUntil "TG", wdForward

' move the insertion to the right while 0's are encountered
Selection.MoveWhile "0"

' extend the selection while 0's are encountered,
' working backward through the document
Selection.MoveStartWhile "0", wdBackward
```

Tables

Word tables provide great functionality. Their ability to organize information into visually pleasing structures is excellent and serves many needs. Tables consist of rows and columns, just as a spreadsheet or a database table does. However, tables in Word sport some interesting settings that differ from a spreadsheet or a database table.

Each cell in a Word table can contain text and graphics. The background shading and coloring of each cell is individually addressable. A cell can contain multiple paragraphs. Then within the cell, each paragraph can contain individual formatting. Each paragraph in a cell can be assigned a different background color, and the cell itself yet another color. Figure 2.5 illustrates the flexibility of cell-level formatting in a Word table.

Product Code	Details
AV202	Cost per Unit: $85.00 Stock on Hand: 17
AV288	Cost per Unit: $120.00 **Stock on Hand: 0** *(out of stock)*
CD125	Cost per Unit: $60.00 Stock on Hand: 24

Figure 2.5 Multiple formatting in a Word table

Rows, Columns, Borders, Shading, and Spacing are just some of the properties available to tables. Some properties, such as Rows, return collections. Cell, ConvertToText, Delete, Sort, and Split are some methods available. Note that Cell is a method of the Table object that returns a single cell at a specified row and column junction. Cells is a property of a Row, Column, Selection, or Range object. The Cells property returns a Cells collection.

To programmatically create a table, the Add method is used to add a new table to the Tables collection. The method requires at least three parameters: where, the number of rows, and the number of columns. In the following two examples, the first simply inserts a table at the insertion point. The second example establishes a variable to a new table:

```
ActiveDocument.Tables.Add Range:=Selection.Range, _
    numrows:=4, numcolumns:=3

Set myTable = ActiveDocument.Tables.Add _
    (Range:=Selection.Range, NumRows:=12, NumColumns:=12)
```

Tables have rows and columns, and the intersection of a row and a column is a cell. These are all available objects in code. This next example sets a reference to the first table in the document, then returns the number of columns, adds a row, returns the contents of the cell where the second row and second column intersect, and finally changes the background of the first cell to yellow:

```
Set myTable = ActiveDocument.Tables(1)
MsgBox myTable.Columns.Count
myTable.Rows.Add
MsgBox myTable.Cell(2, 2)
myTable.Cell(1, 1).Shading _
   .BackgroundPatternColor = wdColorYellow
```

Listing 2.5 contains a procedure that makes use of tables to present a crossword puzzle. Because a crossword puzzle layout consists literally of rows, columns, and cells, a table is the ideal vehicle for displaying one. With the use of the shading property, the cells that are blank in the crossword are set to black.

NOTE: Creating a crossword puzzle is an ideal way to learn how to program tables in Word. By necessity, the design of a crossword requires individual addressing of columns, rows, and cells. This example serves as a foundation for applying tables to diverse business needs.

Listing 2.5 Creating a crossword puzzle, with questions and an answer key

```
Public Sub make_crossword()
' set variables
Dim crossword As Table
Dim questions As Document
Dim questions_arr()
Dim questions_count As Integer
Dim question_text
Dim question_split
Dim split_count As Integer
Dim questions_loop As Integer
Dim start_row As Long
Dim start_col As Long
Dim cell_text As String
Dim char_loop As Integer
Dim answer_length As Integer
Dim cw_row As Integer
Dim cw_col As Integer
Dim question_num As String
' set error trap
On Error GoTo error_end

' questions and answers are stored in separate file
' the file structure is:
'    Question Number
'    Direction (A for across, D for down)
'    Question
'    Answer
'    Row
'    Column

' set variable and open the Questions file
Set questions = Application.Documents.Open _
   (ActiveDocument.Path & "\Questions.doc")

With questions
  ' get the paragraph count, which is
  ' the number of questions plus one for the header row
  questions_count = .Paragraphs.Count
  ' size the array to questions_count, 6 is the field count
  ReDim questions_arr(6, questions_count)
```

Listing 2.5 *(continued)*

```
' loop through questions(paragraphs) and split them
' using the tab character as the delimiter - chr(9)
' populate questions_arr from the array that holds
' the split paragraph
For questions_loop = 0 To questions_count - 1
  question_text = .Paragraphs(questions_loop + 1)
  question_split = Split(question_text, Chr(9))
  For split_count = 0 To 5
    questions_arr(split_count, questions_loop) _
      = question_split(split_count)
  Next split_count
Next questions_loop
End With
' done with the Questions file, close it
questions.Close savechanges:=False
' delete existing document content, if any
Selection.WholeStory
Selection.Delete

' prepare three blank pages
' page 1 will hold crossword
' page 2 will hold clues
' page 3 will hold crossword filled in

' The three pages are separated by the insertion of
' section breaks.  Page 2 requires double-column
' formatting, pages 1 and 3 do not.
With Selection
  ' single-column setup for page 1
  With .PageSetup.TextColumns
    .SetCount 1
  End With
  ' section break for start of page 2
  .InsertBreak Type:=wdSectionBreakNextPage
  ' double-column setup for page 2
  With .PageSetup.TextColumns
    .SetCount 2
    .EvenlySpaced = True
  End With
```

Listing 2.5 *(continued)*

```
  ' section break for end of page 2
  .InsertBreak Type:=wdSectionBreakNextPage
  ' single-column setup for page 3
  With .PageSetup.TextColumns
      .SetCount 1
  End With
End With

' create new table, named crossword
' it is created at the insertion point, now on page 3
Set crossword = ActiveDocument.Tables.Add _
    (Range:=Selection.Range, NumRows:=12, NumColumns:=12)
With crossword
  .Select
  With Selection
    ' set column widths to half inch
    .Columns.SetWidth _
    ColumnWidth:=InchesToPoints(0.5), _
    RulerStyle:=wdAdjustNone
    ' set row heights to half inch
    .Rows.SetHeight _
    RowHeight:=InchesToPoints(0.5), _
    HeightRule:=wdRowHeightExactly
    ' set borders
    With .Borders
      .InsideLineStyle = wdLineStyleSingle
      .InsideLineWidth = wdLineWidth100pt
      .OutsideLineStyle = wdLineStyleSingle
      .OutsideLineWidth = wdLineWidth100pt
    End With
  End With
End With

' now new table is created, populate it from the array
' skip element 0 - it has the headings
For questions_loop = 1 To questions_count - 1
  answer_length = Len(questions_arr(3, questions_loop))
  start_row = questions_arr(4, questions_loop)
  start_col = questions_arr(5, questions_loop)
```

Listing 2.5 *(continued)*

```
Select Case questions_arr(1, questions_loop)
  Case "A" ' for Across
    ' for across column is incremented, but row stays same
    For char_loop = 0 To answer_length - 1
      crossword.Cell(start_row, start_col + char_loop) _
      .Range.Text = _
      Mid(questions_arr(3, questions_loop), _
      char_loop + 1, 1)
    Next char_loop
  Case "D" ' for Down
    ' for down row is incremented, but column stays same
    For char_loop = 0 To answer_length - 1
      crossword.Cell(start_row + char_loop, start_col) _
      .Range.Text = _
      Mid(questions_arr(3, questions_loop), _
          char_loop + 1, 1)
    Next char_loop
  End Select
Next questions_loop
' now darken empty cells
For cw_row = 1 To 12
  For cw_col = 1 To 12
    cell_text = crossword.Cell(cw_row, cw_col).Range.Text
    If Len(cell_text) < 3 Then
      crossword.Cell(cw_row, cw_col).Shading _
      .BackgroundPatternColor = wdColorBlack
    End If
  Next cw_col
Next cw_row
' copy the table, go to start of document, and paste
ActiveDocument.Tables(1).Select
Selection.Copy
Selection.GoTo wdGoToLine, wdGoToFirst
Selection.Paste

' reset the crossword variable to represent the table
' just pasted at the start of the document
Set crossword = ActiveDocument.Tables(1)
```

Listing 2.5 *(continued)*

```
' loop through the table on page 1 and remove all contents
' however, the shading formatting stays intact
For cw_row = 1 To 12
  For cw_col = 1 To 12
    crossword.Cell(cw_row, cw_col).Range.Text = ""
  Next cw_col
Next cw_row

' put the question numbers followed by a period
' into the table on page 1
For questions_loop = 1 To questions_count - 1
  question_num = questions_arr(0, questions_loop)
  start_row = questions_arr(4, questions_loop)
  start_col = questions_arr(5, questions_loop)
    crossword.Cell(start_row, start_col).Range.Text = _
    question_num & "."
Next questions_loop

' insert questions on page 2
' loop twice - once inserting Across questions,
' once inserting Down questions
' in between Across and Down, insert a column break
' this page is already formatted to display 2 columns
Selection.GoTo wdGoToPage, wdGoToAbsolute, 2
With Selection
  .TypeText "ACROSS"
  .TypeParagraph
  For questions_loop = 1 To questions_count - 1
    If questions_arr(1, questions_loop) = "A" Then
      .TypeText questions_arr(0, questions_loop) & ". " & _
        questions_arr(2, questions_loop)
      .TypeParagraph
    End If
  Next questions_loop
  ' insert the column break
  Selection.InsertBreak Type:=wdColumnBreak
  .TypeText "DOWN"
  .TypeParagraph
```

Listing 2.5 *(continued)*

```
  For questions_loop = 1 To questions_count - 1
    If questions_arr(1, questions_loop) = "D" Then
      .TypeText questions_arr(0, questions_loop) & ". " & _
        questions_arr(2, questions_loop)
      .TypeParagraph
    End If
  Next questions_loop
End With

' set font sizes
ActiveDocument.Range.Font.Size = 12
ActiveDocument.Tables(1).Range.Font.Size = 9
' format the answer key table on page 3
' to be centered horizontally and vertically
Set crossword = ActiveDocument.Tables(2)
crossword.Select
With Selection
  .ParagraphFormat.Alignment = wdAlignParagraphCenter
  .Cells.VerticalAlignment = wdCellAlignVerticalCenter
End With

' last - leave user on page 1
Selection.GoTo wdGoToPage, wdGoToAbsolute, 1
MsgBox "done"
Exit Sub

error_end:
MsgBox Err.Description
End Sub
```

Listing 2.5 contains several programming approaches unique to Word. To start, a number of variables are defined and a simple error trap is set. An external Word document contains structured data used for creating the crossword. This data consists of six fields, delimited by tabs. The fields are for the question number, the direction ("A" for across or "D" for down), the question itself, the answer, the row number, and the column number. The row and column numbers indicate where the answer belongs in the crossword grid. Figure 2.6 shows how the data appears in the external Word document.

Question#	Direction	Question	Answer	Row	Column
1	A	The long and short of it	RULER	1	1
1	D	Not well done	RARE	1	1
2	D	-- and behold	LO	1	3
3	D	Love	EROS	1	4
4	D	Tyrannosaurus ---	REX	1	5
5	A	Opportunity ------	KNOCKS	1	7
5	D	Type of energy	KINETIC	1	7
6	D	Looks over another's shoulder	CHEATER	1	10
7	D	Compass point	SE	1	12
8	A	Iron	ORE	2	3
9	A	Like a mule	OX	3	4
10	A	Very big river	NILE	3	7
11	A	Breakfast food	EGGS	4	1
12	D	Southern state (abbr.)	GA	4	3
13	A	Card	ACE	4	10
14	A	Legal term	TORT	5	7
15	D	"--- to a Tree"	ODE	5	8
16	A	Sea creature	SQUID	6	4

Figure 2.6 The source of data for the crossword: six fields, tab delimited

The external file is opened and set to the variable name `questions`. The file, Questions.doc, must be in the same directory, because the `Path` property of the active document is used to locate it:

```
Set questions = Application.Documents.Open _
    (ActiveDocument.Path & "\Questions.doc")
```

The data is read from the questions file and stored in the `questions_arr` array. In order to make use of the data, the records must be parsed into separate data entities. In the external file, the number of questions is determined using the `Paragraphs.Count` property:

```
With questions
    ' get the paragraph count, which is
    ' the number of questions plus one for the header row
    questions_count = .Paragraphs.Count
```

This returns the number of records, because each is one paragraph. The number of fields is already fixed at six. The `questions_arr` array is redimensioned to these numbers:

```
ReDim questions_arr(6, questions_count)
```

Next a loop is set to cycle through the records of the questions file, parsing the data in the process, and filling in the `questions_arr` array. The VBA `Split()` function is used to accomplish this:

```
For questions_loop = 0 To questions_count - 1
  question_text = .Paragraphs(questions_loop + 1)
  question_split = Split(question_text, Chr(9))
  For split_count = 0 To 5
    questions_arr(split_count, questions_loop) _
      = question_split(split_count)
  Next split_count
Next questions_loop
```

Now that the array is filled, the questions file is closed. The main document is cleared using the `WholeStory` and `Delete` methods of the `Selection` object:

```
questions.Close savechanges:=False
' delete existing document content, if any
 Selection.WholeStory
 Selection.Delete
```

At this point all the necessary data is stored in the `questions_arr` array, and the main document is empty. Three pages must be set up: one for the blank crossword, one for the questions, and one for the answer key (the crossword filled in). Page two, which will hold the questions, will have a double-column format. To accomplish this, page two must be a separate section. As a separate section, the formatting will not affect or be affected by pages one or three. The following snippet sets page one as a single column, inserts a next page section break, sets page two to have two columns, inserts another next page section break, then sets page three to a single column format.

The `InsertBreak` method is used to insert the next page section breaks, and the `TextColumns` property sets the number of columns for each page. With page two, the `EvenlySpaced` property is used to balance the columns:

```
With Selection
  ' single-column setup for page 1
  With .PageSetup.TextColumns
    .SetCount 1
  End With
```

```
' section break for start of page 2
.InsertBreak Type:=wdSectionBreakNextPage
' double-column setup for page 2
With .PageSetup.TextColumns
   .SetCount 2
   .EvenlySpaced = True
End With
' section break for end of page 2
.InsertBreak Type:=wdSectionBreakNextPage
' single-column setup for page 3
With .PageSetup.TextColumns
   .SetCount 1
End With
End With
```

Even though page two is now set to display two columns, there is no apparent change until page two has a column break inserted in it. This occurs farther down in the code when the text for page two is being read out of the questions_arr array.

A table is created, 12 rows by 12 columns. Using nested With...End With constructs, the table's row height, column width, and borders are set:

```
Set crossword = ActiveDocument.Tables.Add _
   (Range:=Selection.Range, NumRows:=12, NumColumns:=12)
With crossword
  .Select
  With Selection
    ' set column widths to half inch
    .Columns.SetWidth _
    ColumnWidth:=InchesToPoints(0.5), _
    RulerStyle:=wdAdjustNone
    ' set row heights to half inch
    .Rows.SetHeight _
    RowHeight:=InchesToPoints(0.5), _
    HeightRule:=wdRowHeightExactly
    ' set borders
    With .Borders
      .InsideLineStyle = wdLineStyleSingle
      .InsideLineWidth = wdLineWidth100pt
      .OutsideLineStyle = wdLineStyleSingle
      .OutsideLineWidth = wdLineWidth100pt
    End With
  End With
End With
```

Next the table is seeded with the answers. This table is actually the answer key for the crossword; that is, it is the crossword grid with the answers filled in. This is accomplished with a loop based on the number of questions, and then a `Select Case` construct further drives the processing based on whether an across or down answer is being inserted into the table. The row and column numbers are used here to determine the cells that receive the entries.

Within the outer loop based on the question count, and the `Select Case` construct, an inner loop based on the count of characters in the answer is used. The variable `char_loop` holds the current character position. The `Select Case` construct is used to implement different processing dependent on whether a question's direction is across or down. The difference is whether the value of the `char_loop` variable is added to the column (for across questions) or the row (for down questions):

```
For questions_loop = 1 To questions_count - 1
  answer_length = Len(questions_arr(3, questions_loop))
  start_row = questions_arr(4, questions_loop)
  start_col = questions_arr(5, questions_loop)
  Select Case questions_arr(1, questions_loop)
    Case "A" ' for Across
      ' for across column is incremented, but row stays same
      For char_loop = 0 To answer_length - 1
        crossword.Cell(start_row, start_col + char_loop) _
        .Range.Text = _
        Mid(questions_arr(3, questions_loop), _
        char_loop + 1, 1)
      Next char_loop
    Case "D" ' for Down
      ' for down row is incremented, but column stays same
      For char_loop = 0 To answer_length - 1
        crossword.Cell(start_row + char_loop, start_col) _
        .Range.Text = _
        Mid(questions_arr(3, questions_loop), _
            char_loop + 1, 1)
      Next char_loop
  End Select
Next questions_loop
```

At this point the table on the third page is filled with the answers but is not yet formatted, as shown in Figure 2.7.

Section Break (Next Page)
Section Break (Next Page)

R	U	L	E	R		K	N	O	C	K	S
A		O	R	E		I			H		E
R			O	X		N	I	L	E		
E	G	G	S			E			A	C	E
		A				T	O	R	T		
			S	Q	U	I	D		E	L	F
H	A	T		U		C	E		R	A	M
I			W	I	N				R		
	C	H	I	N	A		G	A	U	G	E
H		A		C	T		A	N		E	
A	I	R		Y			S	T	A	R	T
M	A	D	E				E	L			

Figure 2.7 The crossword puzzle answers are filled in

Next a loop with a nested loop (one for rows, one for columns) is used to test if each cell has one or more characters. If it does not, then the cell's background color is set to black. The test for a cell's length being less than 3 (see why below) determines whether to set the background color:

```
For cw_row = 1 To 12
  For cw_col = 1 To 12
    cell_text = crossword.Cell(cw_row, cw_col).Range.Text
    If Len(cell_text) < 3 Then
      crossword.Cell(cw_row, cw_col).Shading _
      .BackgroundPatternColor = wdColorBlack
    End If
  Next cw_col
Next cw_row
```

NOTE: Paragraph and cell marks take up physical space and must be considered when working with string lengths in Word. Using the word "hello" as the string whose length is being returned, PowerPoint and Excel return a length of 5.

If the word "hello" stands alone as an entire paragraph and we are not careful to avoid the paragraph mark, Word will return a value of 6. The length of the paragraph is not the length of the word. The same word in a cell inside a Word table would have a length of 7. Cell marks have a length of two. Consider the following examples:

```
' PowerPoint returns a length of 5 from a text box
hello_length = Len(ActivePresentation.Slides(1).Shapes(1) _
    .TextFrame.TextRange.Text)
MsgBox hello_length ' returns 5

' Excel returns a length of 5 from a worksheet cell
hello_length = Len(Sheets(1).Cells(1, 1))
MsgBox hello_length ' returns 5

' Word returns a length of 6 from a paragraph
hello_length = Len(ActiveDocument.Paragraphs(1).Range.Text)
MsgBox hello_length ' returns 6

' Word returns a length of 7 from a table cell
hello_length = Len(ActiveDocument.Tables(1).Cell(1, 1) _
    .Range.Text)
MsgBox hello_length ' returns 7
```

Next, the completed table, which is on the third page, is copied and pasted on the first page. The Copy, GoTo, and Paste methods of the Selection object are used here:

```
' copy the table, go to start of document, and paste
ActiveDocument.Tables(1).Select
Selection.Copy
Selection.GoTo wdGoToLine, wdGoToFirst
Selection.Paste
```

Now the table on the first page needs to be cleared of all letters. To clear the cells, an outer and an inner loop are again used to set each cell to an empty text string. Note that just text is being cleared, but formatting remains intact. This means that cells that are now shaded black will remain so:

```
For cw_row = 1 To 12
  For cw_col = 1 To 12
    crossword.Cell(cw_row, cw_col).Range.Text = ""
  Next cw_col
Next cw_row
```

Next the question numbers must be inserted into the appropriate cells. The `questions_arr` array contains the row and column where each question number belongs. As each question number is entered, it is followed by a period:

```
For questions_loop = 1 To questions_count - 1
  question_num = questions_arr(0, questions_loop)
  start_row = questions_arr(4, questions_loop)
  start_col = questions_arr(5, questions_loop)
    crossword.Cell(start_row, start_col).Range.Text = _
    question_num & "."
Next questions_loop
```

Next the guide to the crossword is entered on page two. The `GoTo` method is used to get to the page. Then successive loops, one for across and one for down, are used to enter the questions. In between the two loops, the needed column break is inserted using the `InsertBreak` method. This forces the page to display a column with the across questions and a column with the down questions. This page has already been formatted to display two columns. The column break inserted here indicates where column one ends and column two begins:

```
Selection.GoTo wdGoToPage, wdGoToAbsolute, 2
With Selection
  .TypeText "ACROSS"
  .TypeParagraph
  For questions_loop = 1 To questions_count - 1
    If questions_arr(1, questions_loop) = "A" Then
      .TypeText questions_arr(0, questions_loop) & ". " & _
        questions_arr(2, questions_loop)
      .TypeParagraph
    End If
  Next questions_loop
```

```
' insert the column break
Selection.InsertBreak Type:=wdColumnBreak
.TypeText "DOWN"
.TypeParagraph
For questions_loop = 1 To questions_count - 1
  If questions_arr(1, questions_loop) = "D" Then
    .TypeText questions_arr(0, questions_loop) & ". " & _
        questions_arr(2, questions_loop)
    .TypeParagraph
  End If
Next questions_loop
End With
```

Next comes some final formatting. The font size is set to 12 for the entire document, then just the first table is reset to font size 9. The purpose here is to make the numbers in the empty crossword grid small, while the questions on page two and the answer key on page three are easy to read. Finally, the answer key table is formatted to have the letters in each cell appear centered horizontally and vertically:

```
' set font sizes
ActiveDocument.Range.Font.Size = 12
ActiveDocument.Tables(1).Range.Font.Size = 9
' format the answer key table on page 3
' to be centered horizontally and vertically
Set crossword = ActiveDocument.Tables(2)
crossword.Select
With Selection
  .ParagraphFormat.Alignment = wdAlignParagraphCenter
  .Cells.VerticalAlignment = wdCellAlignVerticalCenter
End With
```

The final action is to leave the insertion point at the start of the document:

```
Selection.GoTo wdGoToPage, wdGoToAbsolute, 1
```

After the code has completed running, three pages are present. The first has the crossword ready to be filled in, the second is the list of questions, and the third is the crossword filled in with the answers and formatted. Figures 2.8, 2.9, and 2.10, respectively, show these pages.

Figure 2.8 The empty crossword grid

ACROSS
1. The long and short of it
5. Opportunity ------
8. Iron
9. Like a mule
10. Very big river
11. Breakfast food
13. Card
14. Legal term
16. Sea creature
18. Small magical person
21. Goes on your head
22. Microsoft Windows for handhelds
23. Aries the ---
24. Opposite of "lose"
26. Large Asian country
28. Measures things
31. New England state (abbr.)
32. Common English language particle
33. "--- on a G String", by J.S. Bach
35. Off to a good -----
37. ---- in the shade
38. -- Dorado

DOWN
1. Not well done
2. -- and behold
3. Love
4. Tyrannosaurus ---
5. Type of energy
6. Looks over another's shoulder
7. Compass point
12. Southern state (abbr.)
15. "--- to a Tree"
17. City in Massachusetts
19. ------ than life
20. Radio band
21. Shorter than "hello"
24. Northern state (abbr.)
25. --- King Cole
27. Not soft
28. Natural ---
29. In cards, up the ----
30. Goes with item in 11 Across
34. Midwestern state (abbr.)
36. First name of VP who lost 2000 election

Figure 2.9 The questions for the crossword

46

Figure 2.10 The answer key is filled and formatted

Mail Merge

Mail merge functionality has always been a standard feature in Word. Mail merge was updated with the release of Word 2002. The Mail Merge Wizard in Word 2002 replaced the retired Mail Merge Helper in earlier versions of Word. The Mail Merge Wizard is a user-interface improvement, providing a clear set of steps for users to create mail merges.

VERSION NOTE: The Mail Merge Wizard is available in Word 2002 and Word 2003. Earlier versions of Word use the Mail Merge Helper. However, the automated mail merge demonstration in Listing 2.6 *will* run in all versions of Word.

The `MailMerge` object is used for programmatically manipulating the Mail Merge Wizard. The Mail Merge Wizard contains six successive steps, presented in the task pane. The `ShowWizard` method of the `MailMerge` object is used to call up the Mail Merge Wizard, and it also allows setting which step appears first, and which steps appear at all. This example displays the wizard already set to Step 2, and indicates to skip Step 4:

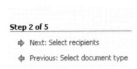

Figure 2.11 The Mail Merge Wizard displayed to show only five of six steps

```
With ActiveDocument.MailMerge
  .ShowWizard InitialState:=2, ShowWriteStep:=False
End With
```

Without manipulation, the wizard would start with Step 1 and display the caption "Step 1 of 6." The preceding example opens the wizard set to Step 2 and contains the caption "Step 2 of 5," as shown in Figure 2.11.

Providing a customized Mail Merge Wizard to users will further improve their productivity providing that any skipped steps are accounted for in your code. This next example sets the wizard to display starting with Step 2; however, the `MainDocumentType` property is used to set the merge type for envelopes. The users do not make the choice, it's established in code:

```
With ActiveDocument.MailMerge
  .MainDocumentType = wdEnvelopes
  .ShowWizard InitialState:=2
End With
```

Mail merge functionality can be implemented without the use of the Mail Merge Wizard. A complete custom implementation of a mail merge can be run without any interaction with the user interface.

Listing 2.6 is an implementation of an automated mail merge. An SQL string is sent to Access to pull records that match particular criteria. The document body text and merge fields are set using methods of the `Selection` object. Two custom subroutines, `add_field` and `insert_paragraphs`, are used to insert repetitive entries. An additional routine, `initialize_MergeEvents`, is called once in the code just before the merge is performed. This sets up an event handler for the merge. (Mail merge events are explained later in this chapter, in "Events.") The merge is finally run with the `Execute` method.

Listing 2.6 An automated mail merge

```
Dim myWord As New modWordEvents
Public Sub client_billing()
On Error GoTo error_end
' set document as a mail merge document
ActiveDocument.MailMerge.MainDocumentType = wdFormLetters
' variable to Access database with clients
client_path = ActiveDocument.Path & "\Clients.mdb"
' SQL statement to select only clients with balance
sql_string = "SELECT * FROM [tblClients] WHERE "
sql_string = sql_string & "[tblClients].Balance > 0"

' first clear the document
Selection.WholeStory
Selection.Delete
' initialize merge event
initialize_MergeEvents
With ActiveDocument.MailMerge
  ' open the data source
  .OpenDataSource Name:=client_path, SQLStatement:=sql_string
  With Selection
    .Font.Size = "16"
    .TypeText "MONTHLY BILLING STATEMENT"
    insert_paragraphs 6
    .Font.Size = "12"
    add_field "FirstName"
    .TypeText " "
    add_field "LastName"
    .TypeParagraph
    add_field "Address"
    .TypeParagraph
    add_field "City"
    .TypeText ", "
    add_field "State"
    insert_paragraphs 5
    .TypeText "Dear "
    add_field "FirstName"
    .TypeText " "
```

Listing 2.6 *(continued)*

```
   add_field "LastName"
   .TypeText ", "
   .TypeParagraph
   .TypeText "Your current balance is "
   .Font.Bold = True
   .TypeText "$"
   add_field "Balance"
   .Font.Bold = False
 End With ' End With Selection

 .Destination = wdSendToNewDocument
 .Execute
End With ' End With ActiveDocument.MailMerge
Exit Sub

error_end:
MsgBox "Error: " & Err.Description
End Sub

Public Sub add_field(field_name As String)
   Selection.Fields.Add Range:=Selection.Range, _
   Type:=wdFieldMergeField, Text:="" & field_name & ""
End Sub

Public Sub insert_paragraphs(paragraph_count As Integer)
   For insert_para = 1 To paragraph_count
   Selection.TypeParagraph
   Next insert_para
End Sub

Public Sub initialize_MergeEvents()
  Set myWord.objWord = Word.Application
End Sub
```

In detail, here is how it works:

The active document is set to be a mail merge document. A document can be set to any of the following merge types: *wdCatalog*, *wdDirectory*, *wdEMail*, *wdEnvelopes*, *wdFax*, *wdFormLetters*, *wd-*

FirstName	LastName	Address	City	State	Balance
Val	Alford	Lark Avenue	Milford	OH	450
Theodore P	Bachar	116 Pennsylvania Avenue	New London	WI	125
Yuny	Balkin	Oakwood Road	Inman	SC	65
Kathleen M	Ballard	158 Lemona Avenue	Morgan Hill	CA	225
Talli	Banning	153 Ashfield Blvd	Palos Hills	IL	225
Talib	Beare	Dunsmere Way	Ukiah	CA	80
Andrea	Behling	160 Bechelli Street	Melville	NY	0
Natasha	Bevens	Pearlman Street	Neenah	WI	100
Rima	Borowitz	5 Globe Street	Farmington	MO	25
Hugo	Boshak	149 Apache Blvd	Parsippany	NJ	225
Venessa	Bray	177 Timberlane Avenue	Webb City	MO	75
Marjorie	Brightman	8 Bakker Blvd	Chesapeake	VA	0
Bali	Byrne	30-C Stetler Blvd	Rochester	MN	0
Simon	Callicoatt	145 18th Road	Waynesville	NC	225
Sarae	Castor	Fieldcrest Blvd	Columbia	TN	80
Belinda	Cecil	High Avenue	Manchester	MA	50

Figure 2.12 The tblClients table that contains the source data for the mail merge

`MailingLabels`, or `wdNotAMergeDocument`. In this case the type is set to form letters:

```
ActiveDocument.MailMerge.MainDocumentType = wdFormLetters
```

In this example the data source for the merge is an Access database that resides in the same directory as the active Word document. The `client_path` variable is set to the `Path` property of the active document concatenated with the database name:

```
client_path = ActiveDocument.Path & "\Clients.mdb"
```

In the Clients.mdb database is a table named tblClients. See Figure 2.12. This table contains the names and address of clients, as well as a field named Balance. An SQL statement is created to pull records from the tblClients table where the balance is greater than zero:

```
sql_string = "SELECT * FROM [tblClients] WHERE "
sql_string = sql_string & "[tblClients].Balance > 0"
```

The document is cleared:

```
Selection.WholeStory
Selection.Delete
```

The data source is opened. This means that all records in the database that match the criteria are now available for the mail merge:

```
With ActiveDocument.MailMerge
   ' open the data source
   .OpenDataSource Name:=client_path, SQLStatement:=sql_string
```

Before the merge is run, however, the document is prepared. At this point it is empty. Several methods and properties of the Selection object are used to create the merge document:

```
With Selection
    .Font.Size = "16"
    .TypeText "MONTHLY BILLING STATEMENT"
    insert_paragraphs 6
    .Font.Size = "12"
    add_field "FirstName"
    .TypeText " "
    add_field "LastName"
    .TypeParagraph
    add_field "Address"
    .TypeParagraph
    add_field "City"
    .TypeText ", "
    add_field "State"
    insert_paragraphs 5
    .TypeText "Dear "
    add_field "FirstName"
    .TypeText " "
    add_field "LastName"
    .TypeText ", "
    .TypeParagraph
    .TypeText "Your current balance is "
    .Font.Bold = True
    .TypeText "$"
    add_field "Balance"
    .Font.Bold = False
  End With ' End With Selection
```

Two subroutines have been created for some of this effort. The insert_paragraphs subroutine takes a single numeric argument, which indicates the number of times to use the TypeParagraph method of the Selection object:

```
Public Sub insert_paragraphs(paragraph_count As Integer)
   For insert_para = 1 To paragraph_count
   Selection.TypeParagraph
   Next insert_para
End Sub
```

The `add_field` subroutine takes a string argument, which is the name of the mail merge field. It then inserts the field into the document:

```
Public Sub add_field(field_name As String)
   Selection.Fields.Add Range:=Selection.Range, _
   Type:=wdFieldMergeField, Text:="" & field_name & ""
End Sub
```

The `Destination` property is used to force the merge to create new documents. The options for destination are: *wdSendToFax*, *wdSend-ToPrinter*, *wdSendToEmail*, or *wdSendToNewDocument*. Finally, the merge is run with the `Execute` method:

```
.Destination = wdSendToNewDocument
.Execute
```

Figure 2.13 shows the result of the mail merge. Note that the `After-Record` merge event (see the next section, "Events") is used to insert an extra line into any created merge letters if the state field is TX (Texas). The billing statement shown in Figure 2.13 shows this message because the recipient's state is Texas.

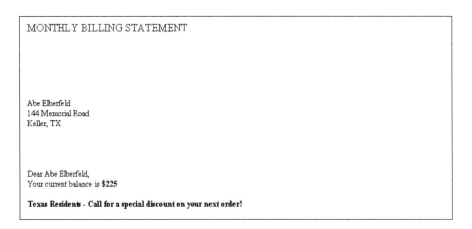

Figure 2.13 A letter created from an automated mail merge

NOTE: Chapter 12, "Mail Merge Magic," demonstrates how to program mail merge features to solve a business problem.

Events

Word provides useful events for the Application, Document, and MailMerge objects. The application and mail merge events need to be created in class modules. Document events do not require a class module.

Document Events

The Document object provides six events: New, Open, Close, Sync, XMLAfterInsert, and XMLBeforeDelete. (The latter three are available only in Word 2003.) The implementation of these differs depending on whether they are applied to an individual document or to a template, including Normal (Word's default template).

Event procedures for documents belong to the ThisDocument object. The ThisDocument object is found in the VBE Project Explorer. To access the events, either select the object in the Project Explorer and use the View...Code menu, or just right-click on the object and select View Code from the shortcut menu. See Figure 2.14.

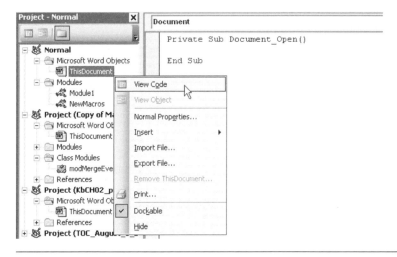

Figure 2.14 Accessing the document events

Table 2.2 Implementation of `New`, `Open`, and `Close` events

Event	Occurs . . .
Template—**New**	When a new document is created based on the template
Template—**Open**	When the template itself is opened, or a document based on the template is opened
Template—**Close**	When the template itself is closed, or a document based on the template is closed
Document—**New**	Never
Document—**Open**	When the existing document is opened
Document—**Close**	When the existing document is closed

Note that there are multiple `ThisDocument` objects. Normal has one, as do any open documents. Be sure to select the correct object for the task at hand. Entering code into the event procedures of Normal's `This-Document` object will affect all documents. This may or may not be the intention.

Once the code module opens, select `Document` from the list of objects, and the events are listed in the procedure list. The `New` event has no effect for a document. Clearly, any existing document will never have a `New` event happen (again). Table 2.2 provides an overview of the `New`, `Open`, and `Close` events.

`Application` **Events**

The `Application` object provides the following events:

DocumentBeforeClose

DocumentBeforePrint

DocumentBeforeSave

DocumentChange

DocumentOpen

DocumentSync

EPostageInsert

```
EPostageInsertEx
EPostagePropertyDialog
NewDocument
Quit
WindowActivate
WindowBeforeDoubleClick
WindowBeforeRightClick
WindowDeactivate
WindowSelectionChange
WindowSize
XMLSelectionChange
XMLValidationError
```

(The *DocumentSync*, *EPostageInsertEx*, *XMLSelectionChange*, and *XMLValidationError* events are available only in Word 2003.)

There are several application events that apply to mail merges. These are described in the following section, on mail merge events.

Application events are not available until the events are established in a class module and then initialized. Following are the steps to accomplish this.

First insert a class module. The name of the class module is later referenced in the declaration and initialization routine in a standard module, so optionally rename the class module using the properties page. In this example the class module is renamed to modWordEvents. In the class module, enter this declaration:

```
Public WithEvents objWord As Application
```

Note that *objWord* is a name to be supplied by you. Once the declaration is entered, events for the Application object are available. First select the object, *objWord*, from the object drop-down list on the left side of the code window, then access the various events in the procedure drop-down list on the right side of the code window. Enter code as needed into event procedures.

Here is a routine that fires on the BeforePrint event. In other words, anytime a document is printed, this routine runs just before printing starts. Although this code may be entered into the class module of a single particular document, once initialized it will run when any document is printed because it is the `Application` object that it is hooked into. Here is the code:

```
Public WithEvents objWord As Application
Private Sub objWord_DocumentBeforePrint _
    (ByVal Doc As Document, Cancel As Boolean)
If Selection _
    .Information(wdNumberOfPagesInDocument) > 50 Then
        MsgBox "Put more paper in the printer."
End If
End Sub
```

The preceding routine causes the display of a message box whenever a document greater than 50 pages is printed. The routine must be initialized. In any standard module, enter this declaration and routine:

```
Dim myWord As New modWordEvents
Public Sub initialize_appEvents()
  Set myWord.objWord = Word.Application
End Sub
```

Note that *myWord* is a name to be supplied by you. Run the initialization routine to enable the event procedure created in the class module. Figure 2.15 displays what the class module and standard module must contain to enable the event procedure.

Mail Merge Events

Mail merge events are enabled as events of the `Application` object. There are two groupings of the events: events that follow actions in the Mail Merge Wizard and events that follow the mail merge process as it executes. The events for the Mail Merge Wizard are:

> *MailMergeWizardSendToCustom*
>
> *MailMergeWizardStateChange*

The events for the mail merge process are:

> *MailMergeAfterMerge*
>
> *MailMergeAfterRecordMerge*
>
> *MailMergeBeforeMerge*
>
> *MailMergeBeforeRecordMerge*

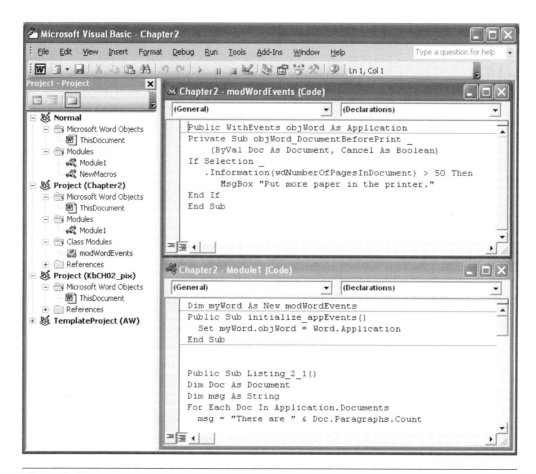

Figure 2.15 A class module and a standard module contain event and initialization procedures

```
MailMergeDataSourceLoad
MailMergeDataSourceValidate
```

The mail merge events are created in the same manner as other application events. (See the preceding section, on application events, for more details.) First, a class module must contain the declaration with the `With-Events` keyword and any event procedures.

For this example, a class module is inserted and renamed to `mod-MergeEvents`. Listing 2.7 contains the declaration and event procedures. Two event procedures are set up: one to fire after each record is merged, and one to fire when the entire merge is complete. These event procedures are set to run with the client_billing routine presented in Listing 2.6 (on page 49).

The AfterRecord merge event is used to insert a message into merged letters only when a recipient's state is Texas (as we already saw in Figure 2.13). The AfterMerge event updates a log table in an Access database. The log table stores the SQL string that was used to pull records for the merge, the number of merged records, and the date of the merge.

Listing 2.7 Declaration and event procedures for the mail merge events

```
Public WithEvents appMerge As Application
Private Sub appMerge_MailMergeAfterRecordMerge _
    (ByVal Doc As Document)
' Texas clients are offered a discount on their next order.
' The State field is checked here, after each record
' merge to see if the state is Texas.
' If yes, then a message is inserted into the
' end of their invoice
With Documents("MailMerge_Demo.doc").MailMerge.DataSource
  If .DataFields("State") = "TX" Then
    With Selection
        .EndKey Unit:=wdStory, Extend:=wdMove
        .Move wdLine, -1
        .TypeParagraph
        .TypeParagraph
        .TypeText "Texas Residents - Call for a special "
        .TypeText "discount on your next order!"
    End With
  End If
End With
End Sub


Private Sub appMerge_MailMergeAfterMerge _
    (ByVal Doc As Document, ByVal DocResult As Document)
' after a mail merge, the query string,
' number of returned records, and the date/time
' of the merge are stored in Access
Dim ssql As String
Dim record_count As Integer
Dim query_string As String
Dim db_path As String
```

Listing 2.7 *(continued)*

```
Dim conn As New ADODB.Connection
' get path of the database
db_path = _
  Documents("MailMerge_Demo.doc").Path & "/clients.mdb"
' get number of merged records, which equals
' the number of sections minus 1
record_count = ActiveDocument.Sections.Count - 1
' get the query string from the mail merge object
With Documents("MailMerge_Demo.doc").MailMerge
    query_string = .DataSource.QueryString
End With
' SQL insert into database table
conn.Provider = "Microsoft.Jet.Oledb.4.0"
conn.Open db_path
ssql = "INSERT INTO tblMergeLog Values ("
ssql = ssql & """" & query_string & ""","
ssql = ssql & record_count & ", "
ssql = ssql & "#" & Now & "#);"
conn.Execute ssql
' close database connection
conn.Close
Set conn = Nothing
End Sub
```

In the class module, the needed declaration is entered:

```
Public WithEvents appMerge As Application
```

The `appMerge_MailMergeAfterRecordMerge` event procedure occurs once for each record in the data source. The State field is tested to see if its value is "TX". If so, then the insertion point is relocated using methods of the `Selection` object to be at the end of the letter. The special message for Texas residents is inserted into the letter. Note that the test for the data source field must occur based on the mail merge document. This is no longer the active document. At this point the active document is the new merged document created by the mail merge process:

```
With Documents("MailMerge_Demo.doc").MailMerge.DataSource
  If .DataFields("State") = "TX" Then
    With Selection
       .EndKey Unit:=wdStory, Extend:=wdMove
```

```
        .Move wdLine, -1
        .TypeParagraph
        .TypeParagraph
        .TypeText "Texas Residents - Call for a special "
        .TypeText "discount on your next order!"
    End With
  End If
End With
```

The `appMerge_MailMergeAfterMerge` event procedure fires once at the end of the merge. During a merge sent to a document, each merge record ends with a section break. Therefore, the total number of records used in the merge operation equals the number of sections in the created document, minus one for the last section break. The query string is the constructed SQL statement used to pull selected records from the database. This query is available as a property of the `MailMerge` object:

```
record_count = ActiveDocument.Sections.Count - 1
' get the query string from the mail merge object
With Documents("MailMerge_Demo.doc").MailMerge
    query_string = .DataSource.QueryString
End With
```

The query string, the record count, and the date/time of the merge are stored in the same database that holds the client records. Using ActiveX Data Objects (ADO), an SQL Insert is executed to put the data into the tblMergeLog table:

```
ssql = "INSERT INTO tblMergeLog Values ("
ssql = ssql & """" & query_string & ""","
ssql = ssql & record_count & ", "
ssql = ssql & "#" & Now & "#);"
conn.Execute ssql
```

NOTE: A reference to an ADO library must be made in order for the ADO code to work.

Connectivity to the Access database is accomplished via ADO. Therefore, a reference must be set to the ADO library. See Figure 2.16. To do this:

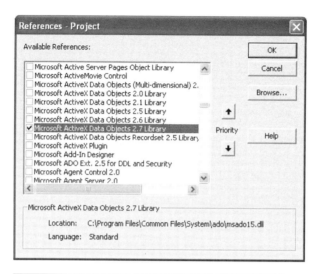

Figure 2.16 Setting a reference to ADO

1. In any code module within Word, use the Tools ... References menu to display the References dialog.
2. Select the Microsoft ActiveX Data Objects (2.x) Library (the version doesn't matter for this example).

In order for the event procedures to work, they must be initialized. In Listing 2.6, the initialization occurs when the `client_billing` routine calls the `initialize_MergeEvents` procedure. This procedure enables the event procedures just prior to the merge execution. See the code for the `initialize_MergeEvents` procedure in Listing 2.6. Figure 2.17 displays the VBE showing the class and standard modules used in the mail merge.

Summary

Word is a great host for document-centric custom solutions. The ability to manipulate the numerous objects with programming code makes it possible to create applications that are just not possible via the functionality of the user interface. The robust features of mail merge, tables, and other

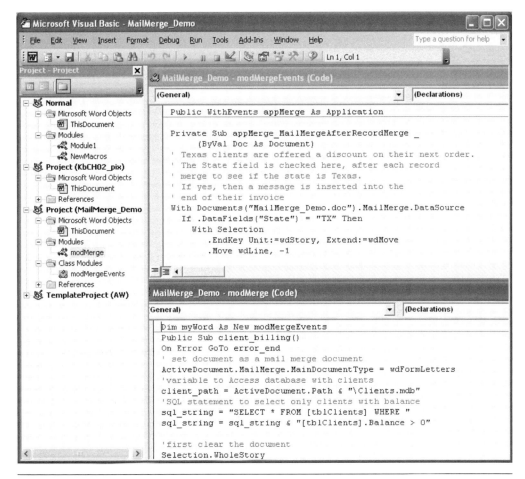

Figure 2.17 Class and standard modules used in the mail merge operation

Word features can be integrated with other systems, as demonstrated in this chapter with Access.

The `Selection` and `Range` objects provide all the means to work with any portion of a document. Events allow implementing functionality at many different processing steps. Taken all together, custom solutions built in Word are able to address many purposes beyond typical document creation. Chapter 9, "XML and Office," demonstrates the robust features of XML in Word 2003. Chapters 12 and 15 show how custom development built on Word is used to solve real business problems.

CHAPTER 3

Excel Solution Development

VERSION NOTE: This material works for all versions of Excel, except where noted. XML use in Excel, including List technology, is covered in Chapter 9, "XML and Office."

Excel applications generally cover three basic tasks: data entry, analysis, and reporting. Data entry is simple in Excel; navigating through its structure of cells, rows, and columns is straightforward. As an alternative to manual entry, Excel is often populated with data from other external sources, such as databases, text files, or XML files.

For analysis and reporting, Excel offers a sophisticated set of mathematical and statistical functions, a fully developed set of charting methods, and many formatting options. Excel contains a robust set of objects. Even within a subset of Excel's functionality, such as charts, there are dozens of child objects. This chapter explores several key objects, methods, and properties of Excel.

Objects, Properties, and Methods

The `Application` Object

The `Application` object refers to Excel itself and is manipulated for tasks that affect the overall use of Excel. Some examples of this are the `DisplayAlerts` property, the `ScreenUpdating` property, the `Cursor` property, and the `Quit` method. The routine in Listing 3.1 gives an example of using the `Application` object. Other Excel objects, methods, and properties that are in this routine are explained in the appropriate sections of this chapter.

Listing 3.1 Setting application properties, deleting and adding sheets, copying and pasting data

```
With Application
  .ScreenUpdating = False
  .DisplayAlerts = False
  On Error Resume Next
  Sheets("Working Data").Delete
  On Error GoTo error_end
  ActiveWorkbook.Worksheets.Add
  ActiveSheet.Name = "Working Data"
  Sheets("Download Data").Activate
  Cells(1, 1).Activate
  ActiveCell.CurrentRegion.Select
  Selection.Copy
  Sheets("Working Data").Activate
  Cells(1, 1).Select
  ActiveSheet.Paste
  Cells(1, 1).Select
  Sheets("Download Data").Delete
  ActiveWorkbook.Save
  .Quit
  Exit Sub
error_end:
  .ScreenUpdating = True
  .DisplayAlerts = True
  MsgBox Err.Description
End With
```

Listing 3.1 turns off the screen refresh and turns off warnings, using the ScreenUpdating and DisplayAlerts properties of the Application object. The value of setting these properties becomes apparent as the code accomplishes further tasks. Sheets will be activated, data will be copied and pasted, and sheets will be deleted.

Unless planned for, this activity leaves the actions visible as they are occurring. Setting the ScreenUpdating property to false hides the actions from the screen. When sheets are deleted in this routine, unless DisplayAlerts is set to false, the system will prompt for confirmation. See Figure 3.1.

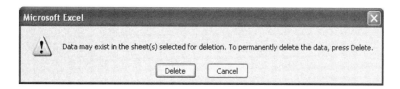

Figure 3.1 A warning appears before a sheet is deleted if the `DisplayAlerts` property is not set to false

This type of warning will certainly disturb many users, because they will not know what action to take. Setting the `DisplayAlerts` property to false forces these warnings not to appear.

Prior to the first sheet deletion in Listing 3.1, there is an error trap. In this routine, because a worksheet is added and named, it is good practice first to attempt to delete a sheet with the intended name, in case it already exists. Sheets in a workbook must have unique names. Trying to give a sheet the same name as an existing sheet will cause an error. Therefore, an attempt is made to delete the sheet first. However, this creates another problem. Attempting to delete a sheet that doesn't exist also causes an error. The workaround for this is to precede the delete with an error trap that steps to the next line of code if the delete causes an error. Once the delete is either accomplished or skipped with the help of the `On Error Resume Next` statement, the error trap is reset to go to the `error_end` code section. Then a new sheet is added, and properly named:

```
On Error Resume Next
Sheets("Working Data").Delete
ActiveWorkbook.Worksheets.Add
ActiveSheet.Name = "Working Data"
```

The next several lines take data from the Download Data sheet and paste it on the new Working Data sheet. The particulars of working with sheets and cells are discussed later in this chapter. Once the data is pasted on the Working Data sheet, the Download Data sheet is to be deleted. The `DisplayAlerts` property is still set to false, so the delete will occur without any pause. Finally, the workbook is saved and the `Quit` method of the application is used to close Excel itself:

```
Sheets("Download Data").Delete
ActiveWorkbook.Save
.Quit
```

If an error occurs that causes execution to jump to error_end, the DisplayAlerts and ScreenUpdating properties are flipped to true. Normally these properties are flipped back at the end of successful execution as well. In this case though, successful execution ends with Excel being closed. Therefore, resetting the properties serves no purpose.

The Application object has a useful property named Caller. This property returns the name of the object that called a procedure. For example, three buttons are on a worksheet. Each, when clicked, activates a procedure named who_called. The procedure simply reports back the name of which button was clicked:

```
Public Sub who_called()
  MsgBox Application.Caller
End Sub
```

How is this useful? The effect is similar to passing an argument to a procedure, but without having to set the procedure up to accept arguments. So in this example, each button calls the procedure directly and the procedure knows what to do based on the Caller property. Normally each button would call a separate routine, which in turn would call the procedure with a passed argument. By using the Caller property, the three intermediate routines can be skipped.

Here is a typical way to take an action based on a passed argument. Each button runs a separate routine, which in turn calls the who_called_now routine. So a total of four routines are needed here:

```
Public Sub who_called_now(caller As String)
   MsgBox caller & " Called"
End Sub
Public Sub Button_1_Calling()
   who_called_now "Button 1"
End Sub
Public Sub Button_2_Calling()
   who_called_now "Button 2"
End Sub
Public Sub Button_3_Calling()
   who_called_now "Button 3"
End Sub
```

Using the Caller property boils this down to a single routine, presented here in Listing 3.2.

Listing 3.2 Using the `Caller` property of the `Application` object

```
Public Sub who_called()
 Select Case Application.caller
   Case "Button 1"
      MsgBox "Button 1 Called"
   Case "Button 2"
      MsgBox "Button 2 Called"
   Case "Button 3"
      MsgBox "Button 3 Called"
 End Select
End Sub
```

The following routine uses properties and methods discussed so far, with the addition of the `StatusBar` property. This member of the `Application` object writes information to the lower-left corner of the application, an area known as the status bar. This is helpful in conjunction with setting the `ScreenUpdating` property to false. Turning off the screen updating speeds up execution, which is useful for large, repetitive tasks. However, if no visible activity is seen, a user may think his or her computer has crashed or is hung up in a process. Even though the cursor changes to an hourglass, this only indicates a busy state and does not show progress. Writing to the status bar alleviates this problem. The information in the status bar changes, but the main workbook window does not update. The user can see that activity *is* occurring.

In the example shown in Listing 3.3, a worksheet has several thousand rows of inventory data in column A. The data is a concatenation of date, product number, and quantity. The data in each row is 14 characters long. The first 6 characters are month, day, year, then 5 characters for the product number, and 3 characters for the quantity. This data shows the quantity of a given product on a certain date. For example, "031599R3T44150" indicates that on March 15, 1999, there were 150 units of product number R3T44.

The task is to parse the data into columns B, C, and D. Depending on the performance of the computer running this task, it could take a noticeable amount of time.

Listing 3.3 Parsing data in column A into three other columns

```
Public Sub Inventory_Parse()
On Error GoTo error_end
```

Listing 3.3 *(continued)*

```
Dim row_count As Integer
Dim parse_inv As Integer
Dim loop_count As Integer
loop_count = 0
Application.Cursor = xlWait
Application.ScreenUpdating = False
Sheets("Inventory").Activate
Cells(1, 1).Activate
row_count = ActiveCell.CurrentRegion.Rows.Count
For parse_inv = 1 To row_count
  With ActiveCell
    .Offset(0, 1) = Left(ActiveCell, 6)
    .Offset(0, 2) = Mid(ActiveCell, 7, 5)
    .Offset(0, 3) = Right(ActiveCell, 3)
  End With
  ActiveCell.Offset(1, 0).Activate
  loop_count = loop_count + 1
  Application.StatusBar = "Row " & loop_count & _
    " of " & row_count
Next parse_inv
Application.ScreenUpdating = True
Application.Cursor = xlDefault
Application.StatusBar = ""
Exit Sub
error_end:
Application.ScreenUpdating = True
Application.Cursor = xlDefault
MsgBox Err.Description
End Sub
```

Although this routine barely involves the `Application` object, its effect is major on the performance and the experience. A loop is used in this routine to attend to each successive row. With thousands of rows, this takes a noticeable amount of time. Turning off the screen refresh significantly cuts the amount of processing time, but it does not make it instantaneous. Writing feedback to the status bar gives visual reassurance to the user that the procedure is running, since the screen will look frozen and may be regarded as a system crash.

When writing to the status bar, it is helpful to have the message inform the user of the progress of the process. This is accomplished not only by keeping a running count of records completed, but also by indicating the total number of records involved. The total number of records that will be parsed is obtained by getting the row count of the current region:

```
row_count = ActiveCell.CurrentRegion.Rows.Count
```

A loop counter, named `loop_count`, has been initialized to zero. With each iteration of the loop, the counter is incremented and the message is written to the status bar. The message takes the form "Row (current row) of (total rows)". For example, "Row 4500 of 9000" gives a clear indication that the process is 50 percent complete. See Figure 3.2.

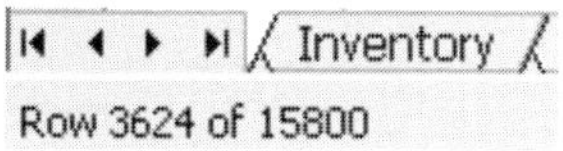

Figure 3.2 Feedback in the status bar

An alternative way of performing this parsing routine is presented in Listing 3.11, later in this chapter.

The `Workbook` Object and the `Workbooks` Collection

The workbook is the main working object in Excel. There is a `Workbooks` collection, which represents all open workbooks. One workbook is always the *active* workbook.

The `Workbooks` collection provides the methods to add, open, and close workbooks. The singular `Workbook` object has `Save` and `SaveAs` methods. Listing 3.4, run from the current, active workbook, demonstrates these methods.

Listing 3.4 Working with workbooks

```
Dim this_book As Workbook
Dim sales_data As Workbook
Dim new_book As Workbook
Set this_book = ActiveWorkbook
```

Listing 3.4 *(continued)*

```
Set sales_data = Workbooks.Open("C:\Baker\SalesData.xls")
  ' SalesData.xls is now the active workbook
Set new_book = Workbooks.Add
  ' new unsaved workbook is now the active workbook
new_book.Worksheets(1).Range("A1") = _
  sales_data.Worksheets(3).Range("A1")
sales_data.Close SaveChanges:=False
new_book.SaveAs "C:\Baker\SalesData_2.xls"
new_book.Close
```

Three workbook variables are defined. One is set to the current active workbook. One is set to the existing SalesData.xls file in the Baker directory. The variable is set to the workbook as it is opened:

```
Set sales_data = Workbooks.Open("C:\Baker\SalesData.xls")
```

Immediately after the Open method is used, the `sales_data` workbook is the active workbook. Next the `new_book` variable is set to a new workbook, created by using the Add method. Once added, the new, unsaved workbook is the active workbook:

```
Set new_book = Workbooks.Add
```

The data in the first cell of sheet three in the `sales_data` workbook is inserted into the first cell of the first sheet of the `new_book` workbook. Then the `sales_data` book is closed without saving changes, since no changes were made. Finally, the `new_book` is saved for the first time using the SaveAs method:

```
new_book.Worksheets(1).Range("A1") = _
    sales_data.Worksheets(3).Range("A1")
sales_data.Close SaveChanges:=False
new_book.SaveAs "C:\Baker\SalesData_2.xls"
```

As shown in Listing 3.4, multiple workbooks can be used in custom solutions. Assigning meaningful named variables to the workbooks helps keep track of them throughout the code.

The `Sheet` and `Worksheet` Objects and the `Sheets` and `Worksheets` Collections

Within a workbook, there are one or more sheets. All sheets are named, with the name appearing on the tab at the bottom of the sheet. Each sheet name must be unique.

The `Sheets` collection is a superset of the `Worksheets` collection and the `Charts` collection. There are individual `Worksheet` and `Chart` objects; however, there is only a `Sheets` collection. There is no single `Sheet` object. A "sheet" must be either a worksheet or a chart. Note that *chart* in this respect refers to a chart that is contained on its own dedicated sheet—not to be confused with charts that sit on regular worksheets (which are chart objects). Charts are discussed in more detail in a later section.

The number of worksheets can be either equal to or less than the number of sheets. The number of charts can be either equal to or less than the number of sheets. Last, the number of worksheets plus the number of charts must equal the total number of sheets. This code snippet reports the count of each collection:

```
With ActiveWorkbook
  MsgBox .Worksheets.Count & " Worksheet(s)"
  MsgBox .Charts.Count & " Chart(s)"
  MsgBox .Sheets.Count & " Sheet(s)"
End With
```

As with all collections, an item can be addressed by its name or its index number in the collection. Assuming the third sheet in a workbook is named "Sales," any of the following activates the sheet:

```
Sheets(3).Activate
Sheets("Sales").Activate
Worksheets(3).Activate
Worksheets("Sales").Activate
```

However, as sheets are added or deleted, using the index position becomes haphazard. If a new sheet (a worksheet or a chart) is added to the beginning of the workbook, then Sales is no longer the third sheet. Therefore, addressing sheets by name guarantees the intended result.

A few key methods applicable to all sheets are `Add`, `Copy`, `Delete`, and `Printout`, as described in Table 3.1.

Table 3.1 Methods applicable to sheets

Method	Usage

`Add`	The full syntax is `Sheets.Add(Before, After, Count, Type)`. All the parameters are optional. For example, `Sheets.Add` inserts a new worksheet before the active sheet. If needed, use either the `Before` or the `After` parameter, but not both. The default for `Count` is 1. The default for `Type` is a worksheet. The type can be indicated with these constants: `xlWorksheet` or `xlChart`.
	
	The following example inserts a new worksheet after the existing Working Data sheet:
	
	`ActiveWorkbook.Sheets.Add After:=Sheets("Working Data")`
	
	This next example inserts two charts before the existing Summary sheet:
	
	`ActiveWorkbook.Sheets.Add _`
	`  Before:=Sheets("Summary"), Count:=2, Type:=xlChart`

`Copy`	The full syntax is `Sheet.Copy(Before, After)`. The two parameters are optional. Without either parameter, the `Copy` method will copy the active sheet to a new workbook. This provides a useful approach to distributing an Excel-based report. However, consideration must be given to whether the individual sheet has any formulas that reference other sheets. This situation is discussed further in the section on formulas later in this chapter.
	
	This line will place a copy of the active sheet into a new, unsaved workbook:
	
	`ActiveSheet.Copy`
	
	With either the `Before` or the `After` parameter, a sheet is copied to another place in the active workbook:
	
	`Sheets("Summary").Copy After:=Sheets("Sales")`
	
	The preceding example places a copy of the Summary sheet after the Sales sheet. Note that the resultant sheet is named Summary (2), because each sheet name must be unique.

`Delete`	The full syntax is `Sheet.Delete`. This deletes the Sales worksheet: `Sheets("Sales").Delete`
`Printout`	The full syntax is `Sheet.Printout`. This prints the Sales worksheet: `Sheets("Sales").Printout`

By establishing an array of sheets, the methods in Table 3.1 can be applied to multiple sheets in a single operation. For example, the following copies three sheets into a new workbook:

```
Sheets(Array("Inventory", "Sales", "Summary")).Copy
```

Worksheets have `Rows`, `Columns`, and `Cells` properties, which provide significant worksheet management. Each of these properties establishes a range that has an assortment of further properties and methods. Listing 3.5, for example, shows a few lines of code that place a copy of the contents of the second column into the fourteenth column.

Listing 3.5 Copying data from one column to another

```
With Worksheets("Inventory")
  .Columns(2).Select
  Selection.Copy
  .Columns(14).Select
  .Paste
End With
Application.CutCopyMode = False
```

Note that in Listing 3.5 the `Select` method is used to select the second column and the `Copy` method is then applied to the `Selection` object. The `Paste` method works a bit different. The destination, column 14, is selected. However, the `Paste` method belongs to the worksheet, not to the `Selection` object.

In Table 3.1, the `Copy` method is shown as it applies to an entire sheet. In Listing 3.5, the `Copy` method is applied to a selection, or a portion of the sheet, rather than to the sheet itself. The `Copy` method for a sheet does not use a `Paste` method. But when copying a part of a sheet, the `Paste` method of the worksheet is used.

When an area of worksheet is selected, it appears "highlighted" as expected, but it also receives a marquee around the area. Column two receives the marquee when the `Copy` method is applied. The last line in Listing 3.5 sets the `CutCopyMode` property to false. This removes the marquee. See Figure 3.3.

Multiple rows or columns can be selected prior to an operation. This snippet shows selecting rows five through ten and then changing their font to bold:

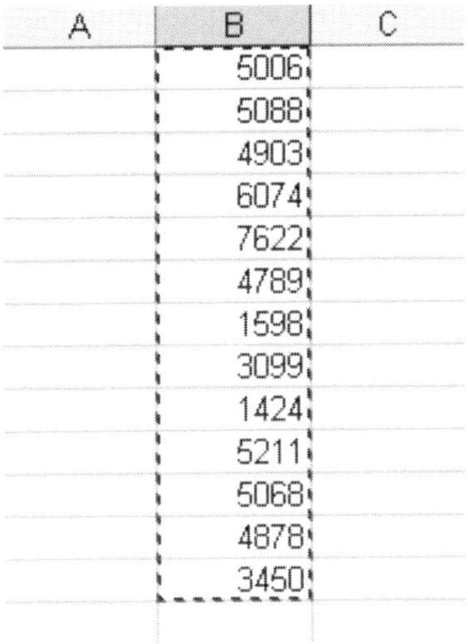

Figure 3.3 After a copy operation, a visible marquee remains

```
Rows("5:10").Select
Selection.Font.Bold = True
```

The Range Object

Ranges are used to represent areas on a worksheet. Particular needs determine what a range will represent. There can be multiple ranges. For example, different ranges may be used to represent total assets, total liabilities, and owner equity on a balance sheet.

Ranges are established by applying the Range property. As applied to worksheets, ranges can represent a single cell, a contiguous area, or multiple noncontiguous areas.

Listing 3.6 Setting ranges

```
Public Sub make_ranges()
Dim range_one As Range
Dim range_two As Range
Dim range_three As Range
With Worksheets(1)
  Set range_one = .Range("B2")
  Set range_two = .Range("B2:D12")
```

Listing 3.6 *(continued)*

```
   Set range_three = .Range("B4:B8, D4:D8, F4:F8")
End With
range_three.Select
End Sub
```

Listing 3.6 creates three ranges. The first represents the single cell B2. The second range represents an area. The third range represents three noncontiguous areas. The third range is selected at the end of the routine. Figure 3.4 shows the result on the worksheet when the third range is selected. Note there is always an active cell, even when there is a selection. The active cell here is B4. It is a part of the selection, but it stands out from the other cells by having a border and not appearing selected.

Note that though the routine in Listing 3.6 results in visible selected areas on the worksheet, the ranges themselves no longer exist. That is, ranges are not persistent. They perish when code execution is complete.

The following example sets a range, `sales_totals`, to represent an area on the Sales worksheet, then sets the range to bold:

```
Dim sales_totals As Range
Set sales_totals = Worksheets("Sales").Range("C5:G15")
sales_totals.Font.Bold = True
```

Ranges can be used in a number of ways. This next example sets four ranges, then uses the `Max()` function to determine which contains the highest value.

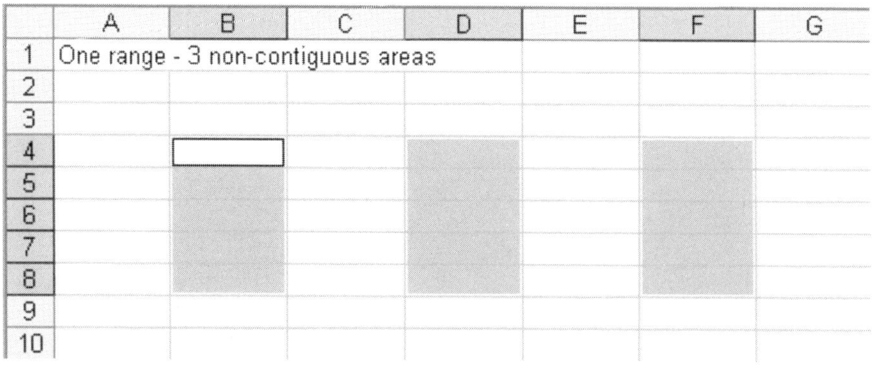

Figure 3.4 A selected noncontiguous range

Listing 3.7 Determining which range has the maximum value

```
Public Sub max_value_range()
  Dim r_1 As Range
  Dim r_2 As Range
  Dim r_3 As Range
  Dim r_4 As Range

  Set r_1 = Worksheets("Summary").Range("B5")
  Set r_2 = Worksheets("Summary").Range("D22")
  Set r_3 = Worksheets("Summary").Range("H36")
  Set r_4 = Worksheets("Summary").Range("AD82")

  MsgBox Application.Max(r_1, r_2, r_3, r_4)
End Sub
```

Ranges can also be set with the use of the `Cells` property. Within the `Range` construct, two successive `Cells` constructs are inserted. For example:

```
Set returned_units = Range(Cells(12, 5), Cells(18, 5))
```

You may not know the exact coordinates of a range as it is being established. Using the `Cells` property provides a way to work around this. Consider the routine in Listing 3.8. Successive cells going down the third column from row 10 through row 50 are tested for the occurrence of a value greater than 999. If found, a range named `exceeded` is established, and execution jumps out of the loop with the `Exit For` statement.

Listing 3.8 Using the `Cells` property to create a range

```
Dim exceeded As Range
For test_value = 10 To 50
   If Cells(test_value, 3) > 999 Then
      Set exceeded = _
         Range(Cells(test_value, 3), Cells(test_value, 5))
      Exit For
   End If
Next test_value
```

Names

Ranges exist only as long as the routine that establishes them. However, Excel provides a way to give permanent names to areas of a workbook. The named areas, once established, are available in the user interface. Named areas can be created, edited, or deleted both through the user interface and programmatically. In the user interface, they are found in the View...Names menu.

The routine shown in Listing 3.9 establishes two Name objects.

Listing 3.9 Setting up named ranges

```
Sub named_ranges()
  ' select area and name it US_Sales
  Range("A9:D9").Select
  With Selection
    ActiveWorkbook.Names.Add Name:="US_Sales", _
        RefersTo:="=" & .Parent.Name & "!" & .Address
  End With
  ' select area and name it Intl_Sales
  With Selection
  Range("A14:D14").Select
    ActiveWorkbook.Names.Add Name:="Intl_Sales", _
        RefersTo:="=" & .Parent.Name & "!" & .Address
  End With
  ' goto US_Sales, set as italic
  Application.Goto Reference:="US_Sales"
  Selection.Font.Italic = True
  ' select A1
  Range("A1").Select
End Sub
```

The actual syntax to establish a named area is:

```
Names.Add Name:="your_name", RefersTo:="=sheet name!range"
```

Names are added to a Names collection, which can belong to the application or to the active workbook. Each Name object must have a name and must refer to one or more cells on a worksheet. The code in Listing 3.9 uses a method of first selecting an area of cells. Then the RefersTo

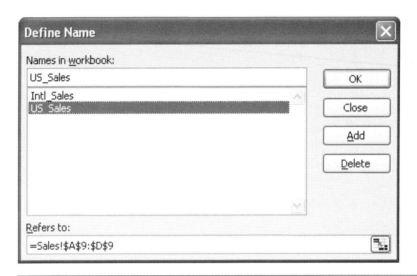

Figure 3.5 The Define Name dialog

property is set by providing the `Parent.Name` and `Address` properties of the selection. These return the required sheet name and area.

The `Goto` method of the `Application` object makes use of a named area:

```
Application.Goto Reference:="US_Sales"
```

As names are established, they are also available in the user interface in the Define Name dialog. Figure 3.5 shows the result of Listing 3.9.

The `Cells` Property and the Current Region

The `Application` object, `Worksheet` object, and `Range` object all have a `Cells` property that returns a `Range` object. For the application or worksheet, the `Cells` property can return a range of cells or an entire worksheet. For a range, the `Cells` property returns a range of cells within the range.

Using the `Cells` property to return an entire worksheet is useful when all cells on the sheet are to be handled in a similar manner. For example, changing the font in all cells of the worksheet is easily accomplished by using the `Cells` property of the worksheet:

```
With Worksheets("Inventory").Cells.Font
    .Name = "Arial"
    .Size = 11
End With
```

In the preceding example, the `Cells` property is used without any further qualification, and therefore it represents all cells on the worksheet. The alternative is to qualify the `Cells` property with row and column parameters. This isolates the returned range object to one or more cells. Consider these:

```
' select the cell at E4
ActiveSheet.Cells(4, 5).Select
' select the first 25 cells on the worksheet
ActiveSheet.Range(Cells(1, 1), Cells(5, 5)).Select
```

The syntax when using row and column indicators with the `Cells` property is `Cells(row, column)`. Therefore, the preceding example of `Cells(4, 5)` returns the cell at the intersection of the fifth column and the fourth row, or E4.

The `CurrentRegion` property provides a way of returning a range of contiguous cells. The current region is a property of a given range. The current region is an area that includes the range itself and extends until a blank row, a blank column, or both are encountered. The size of a current region is not known (at least not to the running code) until its size is determined with the rows and columns properties. This example selects the current region of a named area, then returns the row count and column count of the current region.

```
Application.Goto "Departments"
ActiveCell.CurrentRegion.Select
row_count = Selection.Rows.Count
column_count = Selection.Columns.Count
MsgBox "The current region is " & row_count & _
   "row(s) by " & column_count & "column(s)."
```

Navigating Around a Workbook

At any given moment, there is always an active workbook and an active sheet. There are likely to be other active objects as well. If the active sheet is a worksheet, then an active cell is present. There may be an active range, chart object, or control, window, or pane.

The `Activate` method is used to set an object as active and to navigate to the object. The following line activates the Inventory worksheet and navigates to it. In the user interface, this action sets the Inventory worksheet as the visible sheet. Because Inventory is a worksheet, the second line activates the cell at E2. If the second line were absent, the active cell on the Inventory worksheet would be whatever cell previously was active:

```
Sheets("Inventory").Activate
Cells(2, 5).Activate
```

The `Offset` method provides a very useful *relative* addressing method. Often it is necessary to address a cell or range based on its position relative to another given cell or range.

`Offset` is a method of the `Range` object that accepts a number of rows to offset and a number of columns to offset from the cell or range itself. As such, the row and column parameters can be negative numbers—provided that the result does not address a row or column that is less than the absolute first row or column of the worksheet. For example, `Range("D2").Offset(-1, -2)` returns cell B1. Note that an offset of 0,0 is legal but does nothing—it indicates no row or column offset.

When applied to a range, the offset is based on the active cell within the range. Consider the examples presented in Table 3.2.

Table 3.2 Use of the `Offset` method

Example	Returned Range
`Range("D6").Offset(0, 0).Address`	D6
`Range("D6").Offset(1, 1).Address`	E7
`Range("D6").Offset(0, 1).Address`	E6
`Range("D6").Offset(1, 0).Address`	D7
`Range("A3:C5").Offset(1, 1).Address`	B4:D6
`Cells(5, 5).Offset(-4, -4).Address`	A1
`Cells(5, 5).Offset(-5, -4).Address`	Error—attempts to address nonexistent row

The Goto method is used to navigate to ranges or named areas of a workbook. In the following code, the first line goes to an area on the Inventory worksheet. The second line goes to a previously named area: US_Sales:

```
Application.Goto Worksheets("Inventory") _
    .Range("B2:D12")
Application.Goto Reference:="US_Sales"
```

A powerful enhancement to the standard Goto method is the SpecialCells method of the Selection object. The SpecialCells method provides a way to address useful cells, ranges, or areas, such as all cells with a formula in them. In the user interface, the Go To Special dialog is used to perform these actions. This dialog is found under the Edit...Go To menu. See Figure 3.6.

The find_cell_source routine in Listing 3.10 accepts two arguments: a worksheet name and a cell address. Using these values, a range is created based on all cells in the passed worksheet that contain a formula. Then, for each cell that does contain a formula, its precedents' addresses

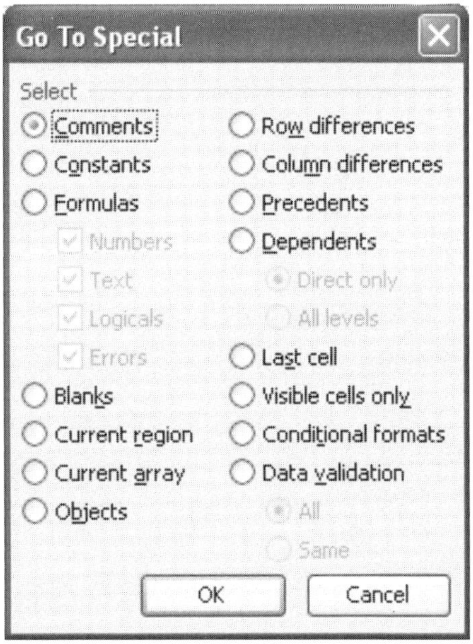

Figure 3.6 The Go To Special dialog box

are tested to see if any match the passed cell address. When there is a match, the cell address and formula are returned. The `which_cell` routine calls the `find_cell_source` routine, sending it the two arguments.

Listing 3.10 Using the `SpecialCells` method to identify cells with a formula

```
Sub which_cell()
  find_cell_source "Summary", "$B$5"
End Sub
Sub find_cell_source(wrksht As String, find_cell As String)
' routine accepts passed worksheet name and cell address
Dim this_cell As Range
Dim this_precedent As Range
' set range to all cells on worksheet that have formulas
With Sheets(wrksht)
Set formula_cells = _
   .Cells.SpecialCells(xlCellTypeFormulas)
End With
' cycle through each cell in range
For Each this_cell In formula_cells
  ' cycle through each precedent for this_cell
  For Each this_precedent In this_cell.Precedents
    If this_precedent.Address = find_cell Then
      MsgBox "The formula in " & this_cell.Address _
          & " is:  " & this_cell.Formula
    End If
  Next
Next
```

Formulas and Worksheet Functions

The `Formula` property is used to set or return the formula in a cell or range of cells. Formulas are always preceded with an equal sign. The following sets a formula in cell A20:

```
Range("A20").Formula = "=SUM(A10:A19)"
```

It is possible to enter a formula in a range of cells with a single statement:

```
ActiveSheet.Range("A5:C5").Formula = "=Average(A1:A4)"
```

The preceding code line may or may not produce the intended effect. The formula in cell A5 becomes =Average(A1:A4), the formula in cell B5 becomes =Average(B1:B4), and the formula in cell C5 becomes =Average(C1:C4). It may be the intention to have all cells receive the exact same formula, without any update of row or column references. To do this, prefix rows, columns, or both with dollar signs ($). This forces rows/columns to be fixed to an absolute value.

The previous example, modified to achieve this, is:

```
ActiveSheet.Range("A5:C5").Formula = "=Average($A$1:$A$4)"
```

In this case, all three cells, A5, B5, and C5 have the formula =Average($A$1:$A$4).

Without dollar signs, Excel considers references to be *relative*. In the case of relative references, Excel adjusts the references as actions are implemented in the worksheet. The inserting of the formula into multiple cells, without using dollar signs, causes the adjustment. This is normal Excel behavior and *is* often the desired outcome.

Relative references also adjust with the insertion or deletion of rows and columns. Consider if cell E10 has the formula =Sum(E6:E9). What happens if columns A and B are deleted? All columns shift two positions to the left. Column E is now column C. The formula now in cell C10 is =Sum(C6:C9).

Dollar signs are used to indicate *absolute* references. When cell E10 has the formula =Sum($E$6;$E$9), the deletion of columns A and B causes cell E10 to shift to C10; however, the formula does not change.

Absolute addressing can be indicated for just the row or just the column. For example, Range("$G24") will always reference column G, but the row reference is relative and can change.

Often relative formulas need to be inserted into numerous cells going down a column or across a row. An efficient way of doing this is to use the AutoFill method of the Range object. AutoFill copies from a specified source to a specified destination. In the next example, column C needs to be filled with formulas that reference columns A and B. As long as there is data in column A, each cell in column C receives a formula. This routine enters the first instance of the formula into cell C1, determines the size of the data range in column A, then uses AutoFill to fill successive rows in column C:

```
Range("C1").Formula = "=IF(B1>0, A1/B1,1)"
Range("A1").CurrentRegion.Select
```

```
last_row = Selection.Rows.Count
Range("C1").Select
Selection.AutoFill Destination:=Range("C1:C" & last_row)
```

It may be beneficial to replace formulas with their calculated values. Once a worksheet is "complete," meaning that no further changes are expected, converting the formulas to values is an option. Earlier in this chapter we discussed using the `Copy` method of a worksheet, which puts a copy of the worksheet into a new workbook. The new workbook then may have links to the original workbook, depending on whether the formulas on the copied worksheet reference any worksheets other than itself. If so, those references point to the original workbook. This is likely an undesirable situation. If the original workbook is removed, the new workbook will have errors.

The `PasteSpecial` method provides a way to convert formulas into values. This method of the `Range` object pastes data into a range in a manner indicated in the `Paste` parameter. For the purpose here, the parameter is `xlPasteValues`. For example, cells B1 through B4 have formulas. These next few lines of code select the cells, copy them, and then paste the calculated values back into the cells. The result is the removal of formulas and therefore the removal of problematic references. The cells are left filled with actual values:

```
Range("B1:B4").Select
Selection.Copy
Selection.PasteSpecial (xlPasteValues)
Application.CutCopyMode = False
Range("B1").Select
```

Earlier, Listing 3.3 presented a solution for parsing thousands of rows of inventory data. In Listing 3.3, this was accomplished with a loop that cycles for as many rows of data as are present. Listing 3.11 revisits this problem with a different approach. Now the inventory data is parsed by inserting formulas in the first row and using `AutoFill` to fill the rest of the rows. This approach runs much faster. At the end of the routine, the `PasteSpecial` method is used to remove the formulas and just leave calculated data.

Listing 3.11 Parsing multiple rows of data using `AutoFill`, then using `PasteSpecial` to remove formulas

```
Public Sub Inventory_Parse_with_Formulas()
On Error GoTo error_end
Dim row_count As Integer
Application.Cursor = xlWait
Application.ScreenUpdating = False
Sheets("Inventory").Activate
Cells(1, 1).Activate
row_count = ActiveCell.CurrentRegion.Rows.Count
ActiveCell.Offset(0, 1).Formula = "=Left(" & _
   ActiveCell.Address(RowAbsolute:=False, _
      columnabsolute:=False) & ", 6)"
ActiveCell.Offset(0, 2).Formula = "=Mid(" & _
   ActiveCell.Address(RowAbsolute:=False, _
      columnabsolute:=False) & ", 7,5)"
ActiveCell.Offset(0, 3).Formula = "=Right(" & _
   ActiveCell.Address(RowAbsolute:=False, _
      columnabsolute:=False) & ", 3)"
Range("B1:D1").Select
Selection.AutoFill Destination:=Range("B1:D" & row_count)
' paste special to values
Range("B1:D" & row_count).Select
Selection.Copy
Selection.PasteSpecial (xlPasteValues)
Application.CutCopyMode = False
Range("A1").Select
Application.ScreenUpdating = True
Application.Cursor = xlDefault
Exit Sub
error_end:
Application.ScreenUpdating = True
Application.Cursor = xlDefault
MsgBox Err.Description
End Sub
```

Excel has dozens of built-in functions. These are not native VBA functions, yet they can be employed in VBA routines with the use of the `WorksheetFunction` object. This object is called as a property of the `Application` object in the form of `Application.Worksheet-Function.(Function)`. Examples are shown in Listing 3.12.

Listing 3.12 Examples of using the `WorksheetFunction` object

```
Dim a_units(5)
Dim b_units(5)
a_units(0) = 16
a_units(1) = 11
a_units(2) = 46
a_units(3) = 42
a_units(4) = 22

b_units(0) = 14
b_units(1) = 18
b_units(2) = 35
b_units(3) = 31
b_units(4) = 31

max_units_a = Application.WorksheetFunction.Max(a_units)

standard_dev_b = _
   Application.WorksheetFunction.StDev(b_units)

permutations = _
   Application.WorksheetFunction.Permut _
      (a_units(0), b_units(0))

correlation = Application.WorksheetFunction.Correl _
   (a_units, b_units)
```

Worksheet Protection

VERSION NOTE: The discussion here about protection applies to Excel 2002 and Excel 2003 only.

Several types of protection are applicable to worksheets. It is possible to protect an entire worksheet—including the protection of contents and the disabling of destructive actions such as formatting and deletion. Worksheets can also maintain protection of certain designated areas of a worksheet—each with its own password. The advantage of this feature is to allow only responsible parties to edit data. See Figure 3.7.

Worksheets themselves are protected with or without a password. Either way, the items and actions that are protected are indicated by using

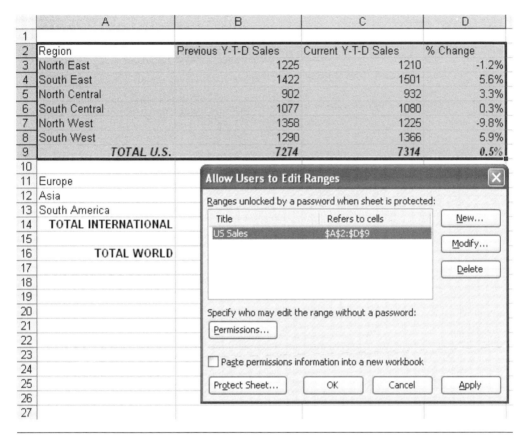

Figure 3.7 Protecting a range on a worksheet

the `Protect` method to set necessary properties of the worksheet's `Pro-tection` object. The following example protects the Data worksheet from the deletion of columns or rows but does allow either to be inserted. The optional password parameter is used as well:

```
Sheets("Data").Protect _
    Password:="mountain", _
    AllowDeletingColumns:=False, _
    AllowDeletingRows:=False, _
    AllowInsertingColumns:=True, _
    AllowInsertingRows:=True
```

As vital to protecting worksheets is the ability to remove protection. The `Unprotect` method serves this function. To reverse the actions in the preceding example, apply the `Unprotect` method, in this case with the optional password:

```
Sheets("Data").Unprotect Password:="mountain"
```

Note that it is the worksheet's `Protect` method that sets the protection properties. However, the `Protection` object maintains the state of the individual properties. The `Protection` object offers read-only information about the properties. For example, this line returns true or false depending on the setting:

```
MsgBox Sheets("Data").Protection.AllowInsertingRows
```

The `AllowEditRange` object is used to password-protect an area of a worksheet. There is an `AllowEditRanges` collection. Each member of the collection maintains a separate name and password. An `Allow-EditRange` overrides the protection of the worksheet. In other words, when both an area of a worksheet and the worksheet itself are password-protected, edits can be made in the `AllowEditRange` area once the password for the area is supplied. Listing 3.13 demonstrates setting `AllowEditRanges`.

Listing 3.13 Protecting worksheet ranges with `AllowEditRanges`

```
Public Sub Protection_Demo()
   Dim edit_rng As AllowEditRange
   Sheets("Protect_Demo").Activate
   With ActiveSheet
      .Unprotect ' in case already protected
      ' clear any existing AllowEditRanges
      For Each edit_rng In .Protection.AllowEditRanges
         edit_rng.Delete
      Next
      ' create three AllowEditRanges
      .Protection.AllowEditRanges.Add Title:="Bread", _
         Range:=Range("A1:C8"), Password:="butter"
      .Protection.AllowEditRanges.Add Title:="Salt", _
         Range:=Range("D1:F8"), Password:="pepper"
      .Protection.AllowEditRanges.Add Title:="Coffee", _
         Range:=Range("A6:F12"), Password:="milk"
```

Listing 3.13 *(continued)*

```
    ' protect sheet
    .Protect AllowFormattingCells:=True, _
        AllowFormattingColumns:=True, _
        AllowFormattingRows:=True
  End With
End Sub
```

The `Protection_Demo` routine in Listing 3.13 creates three ranges each with a separate name and password. Note that the third range intersects individually with the first and second ranges. In this situation, either password can unlock cells in the intersection.

Charts

Charts are supported in Excel with two types of objects: the `Chart` and the `ChartObject`. The distinction is that charts exist on separate chart sheets and chart objects sit on worksheets. Other than that, usage is identical. For the purpose of this discussion the terms *chart* and *charts* may refer to either.

The object model for charts is extensive. There are many objects within a chart, and many properties for each. A simple chart has at least a chart area, a plot area, and a series. There may be additional series and one or more axes. Then there are dozens of formatting options. Just a single series alone has settings for area color, border color, error bars, and data labels. An axis takes settings for tick mark types, tick mark labels, scale parameters, number formatting, font formatting, and more.

There are many chart types: line, bar, pie, scatter, and more. Some are flat in appearance and some are three-dimensional. The latter then have additional properties such as viewing angles. See Figure 3.8.

VBA fully supports all chart actions and settings. Charts are added by using the `Add` method and indicating the type of chart (chart sheet or object). Once the chart is added, the numerous properties set to defaults. The task at hand will likely be to override some defaults in order to customize the chart.

Listings 3.14 and 3.15 work together to add a chart and set many properties and formats. The options for the chart are selected from choices in a form. (Microsoft Forms are discussed in Chapter 8.)

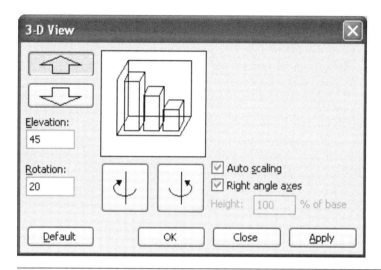

Figure 3.8 There are many ways to format charts, such as adjusting the 3-D angle

Listing 3.14 contains the routine that prepares the form and displays it. The form presents the choice of two series to plot, from a pool of the three stock indices: the Dow Jones Industrial Average, the NASDAQ Composite, and the S&P 500. The closing values of each index for the year 2001 are stored in an Access database. In the database is a single table, tbl-Stocks, which has four fields: Date, DJIA, Nasdaq, and SP500.

NOTE: A reference to an ActiveX Data Objects (ADO) library must be made in order for the routine to work.

Connectivity to an Access database is required. A reference must be set to the ADO library for this to work. See Figure 3.9. To do this:

1. In any code module within Excel, use the Tools . . . References menu to display the References dialog.
2. Select the Microsoft ActiveX Data Objects (2.x) Library (the version doesn't matter for this example).

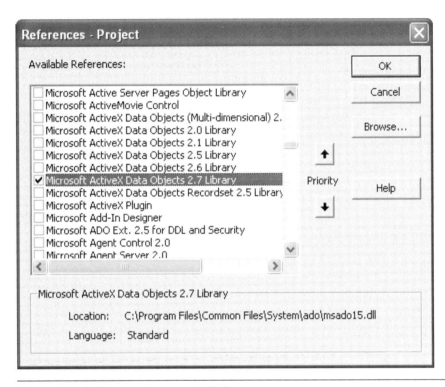

Figure 3.9 Setting a reference to ADO

The `fill_and_view_form` procedure runs first. Its purpose is to prepare the form and display it (see Figure 3.10). This procedure is not connected to the form. It exists in a module of the workbook.

Listing 3.14 Preparing and displaying a form

```
Public Sub fill_and_view_form()
' before showing the form,
' fill the two list boxes with
' available dates from the database

Dim ssql As String
On Error GoTo error_end
' connect to database
Dim conn As New ADODB.Connection
Dim rsDates As New ADODB.Recordset
```

Listing 3.14 *(continued)*

```
conn.Provider = "Microsoft.jet.oledb.4.0"
conn.Open ActiveWorkbook.Path & "/stocks.mdb"
rsDates.ActiveConnection = conn

' get dates from database
ssql = "Select Date From tblStocks"
ssql = ssql & " Order by tblStocks.Date"
rsDates.Open ssql

' load list boxes
' first clear them out
With frmCreateChart
  .lstStartDate.Clear
  .lstEndDate.Clear
  Do Until rsDates.EOF
    .lstStartDate.AddItem rsDates(0)
    .lstEndDate.AddItem rsDates(0)
    rsDates.MoveNext
  Loop
  ' initialize option groups on form
  .optD1 = True
  .optN2 = True
  .optWorksheet = True

  ' initialize colors for series
  .bar_red_1 = 255
  .bar_green_1 = 0
  .bar_blue_1 = 0

  .bar_red_2 = 0
  .bar_green_2 = 0
  .bar_blue_2 = 255

  ' show the form
  .Show
End With
Exit Sub
error_end:
MsgBox Err.Description
End Sub
```

Prior to display, the two list boxes on the form must be filled. These list boxes contain the available data dates found in the database. Therefore, the first action is to query the database for dates. A connection is made to the database and a recordset is opened with an SQL statement:

```
Dim conn As New ADODB.Connection
Dim rsDates As New ADODB.Recordset
conn.Provider = "Microsoft.jet.oledb.4.0"
conn.Open ActiveWorkbook.Path & "/stocks.mdb"
rsDates.ActiveConnection = conn

' get dates from database
ssql = "Select Date From tblStocks"
ssql = ssql & " Order by tblStocks.Date"
rsDates.Open ssql
```

Next the list boxes are cleared and populated based on the recordset. The list boxes serve to offer the selection of the start and end dates, respectively, for the chart data. They are named `lstStartDate` and `lstEndDate`:

```
With frmCreateChart
  .lstStartDate.Clear
  .lstEndDate.Clear
  Do Until rsDates.EOF
    .lstStartDate.AddItem rsDates(0)
    .lstEndDate.AddItem rsDates(0)
    rsDates.MoveNext
  Loop
```

The form offers options of which index is represented in each of the two data series in the chart. Defaults are set by selecting the DJIA for series one and the NASDAQ for series two. The form offers the choice of putting the chart on the same worksheet with the data or as a separate chart sheet. The choice defaults to chart on worksheet:

```
  .optD1 = True
  .optN2 = True
  .optWorksheet = True
```

The form offers the selection of color for each series line in the chart. This is accomplished by two sets of three scroll bars, one set per chart series. For each set, there is a scroll bar for red, green, and blue. Taken together, these values are mixed using the RGB() function. This occurs later,

after the form is visible. For now, the colors are set to red for series one
and blue for series two.

```
' initialize colors for series
.bar_red_1 = 255
.bar_green_1 = 0
.bar_blue_1 = 0

.bar_red_2 = 0
.bar_green_2 = 0
.bar_blue_2 = 255
```

The routine ends by displaying the form with the Show method. Figure
3.10 shows the form.

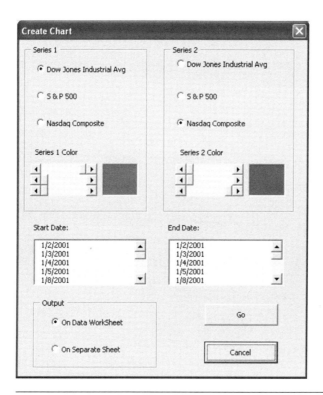

Figure 3.10 The Create Chart form

The code in Listing 3.15 belongs to the form itself—it's the "Code Behind the Form." A detailed explanation follows.

Listing 3.15 The various routines involved in creating the chart

```
Sub change_color(series_num As Integer)
  Select Case series_num
    Case 1
      Me.txtSeries1Color.BackColor = _
        RGB(Me.bar_red_1, Me.bar_green_1, Me.bar_blue_1)
    Case 2
      Me.txtSeries2Color.BackColor = _
        RGB(Me.bar_red_2, Me.bar_green_2, Me.bar_blue_2)
  End Select
End Sub
Private Sub bar_red_1_Change()
  change_color 1
End Sub
Private Sub bar_green_1_Change()
  change_color 1
End Sub
Private Sub bar_blue_1_Change()
  change_color 1
End Sub
Private Sub bar_red_2_Change()
  change_color 2
End Sub
Private Sub bar_green_2_Change()
  change_color 2
End Sub
Private Sub bar_blue_2_Change()
  change_color 2
End Sub
Private Sub cmdCancel_Click()
  Me.Hide
End Sub
Private Sub cmdGo_Click()
' validation
' do not allow same index in both series
If (Me.optD1 = True And Me.optD2 = True) Or _
   (Me.optN1 = True And Me.optN2 = True) Or _
   (Me.optS1 = True And Me.optS2 = True) Then
```

Listing 3.15 *(continued)*

```
    MsgBox "Cannot have same index in both series"
  Exit Sub
End If
' dates validation
If IsNull(Me.lstStartDate) Or IsNull(Me.lstEndDate) Then
    MsgBox "Must supply a start and end date"
    Exit Sub
End If
If CDate(Me.lstStartDate) > CDate(Me.lstEndDate) Then
    MsgBox "Start Date cannot be later than End Date"
    Exit Sub
End If
' end of validation
On Error GoTo error_end
Dim ssql As String
Dim ch As Chart
Dim stock_chart As Variant
Dim conn As New ADODB.Connection
Dim rsStocks As New ADODB.Recordset
' open connection to Access
conn.Provider = "Microsoft.Jet.OleDB.4.0"
conn.Open ActiveWorkbook.Path & "/stocks.mdb"
rsStocks.ActiveConnection = conn
' build SQL statement based on form selections
ssql = "SELECT tblStocks.Date, "
' get value from Frame 1
If Me.optD1 = True Then
  series_1 = "DJIA"
  ssql = ssql & " tblStocks.DJIA, "
End If
If Me.optN1 = True Then
  series_1 = "Nasdaq"
  ssql = ssql & " tblStocks.Nasdaq, "
End If
If Me.optS1 = True Then
  series_1 = "S & P 500"
  ssql = ssql & " tblStocks.SP500, "
End If
```

Listing 3.15 *(continued)*

```vb
' get value from Frame 2
If Me.optD2 = True Then
  series_2 = "DJIA"
  ssql = ssql & " tblStocks.DJIA "
End If
If Me.optN2 = True Then
  series_2 = "Nasdaq"
  ssql = ssql & " tblStocks.Nasdaq "
End If
If Me.optS2 = True Then
  series_2 = "SP500"
  ssql = ssql & " tblStocks.SP500 "
End If
ssql = ssql & "FROM tblStocks "
ssql = ssql & "WHERE tblStocks.Date BETWEEN #"
ssql = ssql & Me.lstStartDate & "# AND #"
ssql = ssql & Me.lstEndDate & "#"
ssql = ssql & " ORDER BY tblStocks.Date"
rsStocks.Open ssql
If Not rsStocks.EOF Then
    ' turn off screen refresh, turn off warnings
    Application.ScreenUpdating = False
    Application.DisplayAlerts = False
    ' delete any chart sheets
    For Each ch In Charts
       ch.Delete
    Next
    ' each time a chart is made,
    ' the existing sheet is deleted, then created new
    On Error Resume Next ' in case the sheet is not there
    Sheets("Stock_Chart").Delete
    ' reset error routine
    On Error GoTo 0
    Worksheets.Add
    ActiveSheet.Name = "Stock_Chart"
    ' put headings in row 1
    Cells(1, 1) = "Date"
    Cells(1, 2) = series_1
    Cells(1, 3) = series_2
    Cells(2, 1).Activate
```

Listing 3.15 *(continued)*

```
' as long as there is data...
Do Until rsStocks.EOF
   ActiveCell = rsStocks.Fields(0) ' date
   ActiveCell.Offset(0, 1) = rsStocks.Fields(1) ' s. 1
   ActiveCell.Offset(0, 2) = rsStocks.Fields(2) ' s. 2
   ' activate the next row, column 1
   ActiveCell.Offset(1, 0).Activate
   ' move to next record
   rsStocks.MoveNext
Loop
' data now on worksheet, close connection to database
rsStocks.Close
conn.Close
Set rsStocks = Nothing
Set conn = Nothing
' format dates, may have landed in serial date format
Columns("A:A").Select
Selection.NumberFormat = "m/d/yyyy"
' establish data size as number of rows
' columns are already known as three
Cells(1, 1).Activate
ActiveCell.CurrentRegion.Select
row_count = Selection.Rows.Count
Cells(1, 1).Select
   ' determine 10% floor room and head room
   ' the value and secondary axis scales may not
   ' default to a useful range - this technique
   ' will force them to show 10% head room and floor room
   ' -  change the formula to have more or less room
series_1_data = Worksheets("Stock_Chart") _
   .Range(Cells(2, 2), Cells(row_count, 2))
series_1_min = _
   Application.WorksheetFunction.Min(series_1_data)
series_1_max = _
   Application.WorksheetFunction.Max(series_1_data)
series_1_size = series_1_max - series_1_min
series_1_floor = series_1_min - (series_1_size * 0.1)
series_1_ceiling = series_1_max + (series_1_size * 0.1)
series_2_data = Worksheets("Stock_Chart") _
   .Range(Cells(2, 3), Cells(row_count, 3))
```

Listing 3.15 *(continued)*

```
series_2_min = _
   Application.WorksheetFunction.Min(series_2_data)
series_2_max = _
   Application.WorksheetFunction.Max(series_2_data)
series_2_size = series_2_max - series_2_min
series_2_floor = series_2_min - (series_2_size * 0.1)
series_2_ceiling = series_2_max + (series_2_size * 0.1)
' Excel will treat the chart as a separate window
' so first save a reference to the current window
this_window = ActiveWindow.Caption
Set stock_chart = Charts.Add
' chart sheet or chart object on worksheet?
If Me.optChartSheet = True Then
   ' create a new chart sheet
   stock_chart.Location Where:=xlLocationAsNewSheet
Else
   ' create as a chart object on worksheet
   ' note - this worksheet also has the data on it, so
   ' use the Top and Left properties to avoid placing
   ' the chart over the data
stock_chart.Location Where:=xlLocationAsObject, _
   Name:="Stock_Chart"
' place and size the chart object
' based on the useable area of the application
' to do this must reactivate the worksheet
Windows(this_window).Activate
' select the chart object
Worksheets("Stock_Chart").ChartObjects(1).Select
width_3_cols = (Columns(1).Width * 3)
Selection.Top = 10
Selection.Left = width_3_cols
Selection.Width = _
   ActiveWindow.UsableWidth - (width_3_cols + 40)
Selection.Height = ActiveWindow.UsableHeight - 40
' reactivate the chart object
Worksheets("Stock_Chart").ChartObjects(1).Activate
End If ' If Me.optChartSheet
```

Listing 3.15 *(continued)*

```
With ActiveChart
' the data is on the Stock_Chart sheet, columns 1-3
' row_count is the row number of the bottom of the data
.SetSourceData Source:=Sheets("Stock_Chart") _
    .Range("A1:C" & row_count), _
    PlotBy:=xlColumns
' set chart type
' this particular chart is to have two vertical axes -
' one for each series, plotted against common dates
' in the category (horizontal) axis -
.ApplyCustomType ChartType:=xlBuiltIn, TypeName:= _
    "Lines on 2 Axes"
' add a title to the chart using the series_1 and
' series_2 variables, and the range of dates
chart_title = series_1 & " vs. " & series_2 & Chr(10)
chart_title = chart_title & Me.lstStartDate & _
    " through " & Me.lstEndDate
' set this property to make the title visible...
.HasTitle = True
' assign the text string to the title
.ChartTitle.Text = chart_title
' set properties for Category (X) Axis
With .Axes(xlCategory)
    .HasTitle = False
    .CrossesAt = 1
    .TickLabelPosition = xlNone
    If row_count < 200 Then
        .TickMarkSpacing = (row_count / 10) + 1
    Else
        .TickMarkSpacing = row_count / 5
    End If
End With
' set properties for Primary Value Axis
With .Axes(xlValue, xlPrimary)
    .HasTitle = True
    .AxisTitle.Text = series_1
    .MinimumScale = series_1_floor
    .MaximumScale = series_1_ceiling
    .MajorUnit = series_1_size / 4
    .TickLabels.NumberFormat = "0"
End With
```

Listing 3.15 *(continued)*

```
    ' set properties for Secondary Value Axis
    With .Axes(xlValue, xlSecondary)
        .HasTitle = True
        .AxisTitle.Text = series_2
        .MinimumScale = series_2_floor
        .MaximumScale = series_2_ceiling
        .MajorUnit = series_2_size / 4
        .TickLabels.NumberFormat = "0"
    End With
    ' set properties for series 1 line
    With .SeriesCollection(1)
        .Border.Weight = xlThin
        .Border.LineStyle = xlAutomatic
        .MarkerStyle = xlNone
        .Smooth = False
        .Border.Color = _
            RGB(Me.bar_red_1, Me.bar_green_1, Me.bar_blue_1)
    End With
    ' set properties for series 1 line
    With .SeriesCollection(2)
        .Border.Weight = xlThin
        .Border.LineStyle = xlAutomatic
        .MarkerStyle = xlNone
        .Smooth = False
        .Border.Color = _
            RGB(Me.bar_red_2, Me.bar_green_2, Me.bar_blue_2)
      End With
      Windows(this_window).Activate
End With ' with active chart
Else ' rsStocks is empty
    rsStocks.Close
    conn.Close
    Set rsStocks = Nothing
    Set conn = Nothing
    MsgBox "No data found - chart creation canceled"
End If ' If Not rsStocks.EOF
Me.Hide
Exit Sub
error_end:
Me.Hide
MsgBox Err.Description
End Sub
```

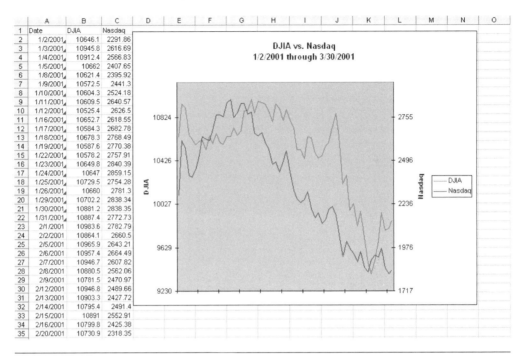

	A	B	C
1	Date	DJIA	Nasdaq
2	1/2/2001	10646.1	2291.86
3	1/3/2001	10945.8	2616.69
4	1/4/2001	10912.4	2566.83
5	1/5/2001	10662	2407.65
6	1/8/2001	10621.4	2395.92
7	1/9/2001	10572.5	2441.3
8	1/10/2001	10604.3	2524.18
9	1/11/2001	10609.5	2640.57
10	1/12/2001	10525.4	2626.5
11	1/16/2001	10652.7	2618.55
12	1/17/2001	10584.3	2682.78
13	1/18/2001	10678.3	2768.49
14	1/19/2001	10587.6	2770.38
15	1/22/2001	10578.2	2757.91
16	1/23/2001	10649.8	2840.39
17	1/24/2001	10647	2859.15
18	1/25/2001	10729.5	2754.28
19	1/26/2001	10660	2781.3
20	1/29/2001	10702.2	2838.34
21	1/30/2001	10881.2	2838.35
22	1/31/2001	10887.4	2772.73
23	2/1/2001	10983.6	2782.79
24	2/2/2001	10864.1	2660.5
25	2/5/2001	10965.9	2643.21
26	2/6/2001	10957.4	2664.49
27	2/7/2001	10946.7	2607.82
28	2/8/2001	10880.5	2562.06
29	2/9/2001	10781.5	2470.97
30	2/12/2001	10946.8	2489.66
31	2/13/2001	10903.3	2427.72
32	2/14/2001	10795.4	2491.4
33	2/15/2001	10891	2552.91
34	2/16/2001	10799.8	2425.38
35	2/20/2001	10730.9	2318.35

Figure 3.11 The completed stock chart

> **NOTE:** The following explains how VBA code creates and manipulates the chart. It is beneficial to refer to the completed chart in Figure 3.11 while reading the explanation.

Each scroll bar on the form has been set to have a minimum value of zero and a maximum value of 255. Each scroll bar has a change event that calls the change_color routine. The change_color routine updates the back color of two text boxes on the form—one for each series. These text boxes do not display any text, but simply serve to display the mixture of colors selected in the scroll boxes. As any scroll bar changes, its associated text box updates its back color property. When the chart is completed, these are the colors of the two series lines.

The RGB() function mixes varying amounts of red, green, and blue. When red, green, and blue are all set to zero, the resultant color is black.

When they are all set to 255 the resultant color is white. Here are the handful of routines that manage the color selections:

```
Sub change_color(series_num As Integer)
  Select Case series_num
    Case 1
       Me.txtSeries1Color.BackColor = _
         RGB(Me.bar_red_1, Me.bar_green_1, Me.bar_blue_1)
    Case 2
       Me.txtSeries2Color.BackColor = _
         RGB(Me.bar_red_2, Me.bar_green_2, Me.bar_blue_2)
  End Select
End Sub
Private Sub bar_red_1_Change()
    change_color 1
End Sub
Private Sub bar_green_1_Change()
    change_color 1
End Sub
Private Sub bar_blue_1_Change()
    change_color 1
End Sub
Private Sub bar_red_2_Change()
    change_color 2
End Sub
Private Sub bar_green_2_Change()
    change_color 2
End Sub
Private Sub bar_blue_2_Change()
    change_color 2
End Sub
```

In the displayed form, choices were preset for which index is represented in each series. These choices can be overridden. As option groups, only one choice can be made for each series. Once the Go button is clicked, however, a validation is done to make sure that the same index is not selected for both series. Validation also checks that both a start date and an end date are selected, and that the start date is not greater than the end date.

```
If (Me.optD1 = True And Me.optD2 = True) Or _
   (Me.optN1 = True And Me.optN2 = True) Or _
   (Me.optS1 = True And Me.optS2 = True) Then
```

```
    MsgBox "Cannot have same index in both series"
    Exit Sub
End If
' dates validation
If IsNull(Me.lstStartDate) Or IsNull(Me.lstEndDate) Then
    MsgBox "Must supply a start and end date"
    Exit Sub
End If
If CDate(Me.lstStartDate) > CDate(Me.lstEndDate) Then
    MsgBox "Start Date cannot be later than End Date"
    Exit Sub
End If
```

If validation is successful, then the database is once again accessed to pull data just for the two indexes, for the selected range of dates:

```
' open connection to Access
conn.Provider = "Microsoft.Jet.OleDB.4.0"
conn.Open ActiveWorkbook.Path & "/stocks.mdb"
rsStocks.ActiveConnection = conn

' build SQL statement based on form selections
ssql = "SELECT tblStocks.Date, "
' get value from Frame 1
If Me.optD1 = True Then
  series_1 = "DJIA"
  ssql = ssql & " tblStocks.DJIA, "
End If
If Me.optN1 = True Then
  series_1 = "Nasdaq"
  ssql = ssql & " tblStocks.Nasdaq, "
End If
If Me.optS1 = True Then
  series_1 = "S & P 500"
  ssql = ssql & " tblStocks.SP500, "
End If
' get value from Frame 2
If Me.optD2 = True Then
  series_2 = "DJIA"
  ssql = ssql & " tblStocks.DJIA "
End If
```

```
If Me.optN2 = True Then
  series_2 = "Nasdaq"
  ssql = ssql & " tblStocks.Nasdaq "
End If
If Me.optS2 = True Then
  series_2 = "SP500"
  ssql = ssql & " tblStocks.SP500 "
End If
ssql = ssql & "FROM tblStocks "
ssql = ssql & "WHERE tblStocks.Date BETWEEN #"
ssql = ssql & Me.lstStartDate & "# AND #"
ssql = ssql & Me.lstEndDate & "#"
ssql = ssql & " ORDER BY tblStocks.Date"
rsStocks.Open ssql
```

Screen refresh and warning messages are turned off. The procedure now deletes any existing chart sheets, and it deletes the datasheet, Stock_Chart. A new worksheet is added and renamed Stock_Chart. An alternative to deleting and adding a new worksheet is to clear all contents of the Stock_Chart. Either way achieves the same result. Headings are put in the first row on the worksheet:

```
Application.ScreenUpdating = False
Application.DisplayAlerts = False
' delete any chart sheets
For Each ch In Charts
  ch.Delete
Next
' each time a chart is made,
' the existing sheet is deleted, then created new
On Error Resume Next ' in case the sheet is not there
Sheets("Stock_Chart").Delete
' reset error routine
On Error GoTo error_end
Worksheets.Add
ActiveSheet.Name = "Stock_Chart"
' put headings in row 1
Cells(1, 1) = "Date"
Cells(1, 2) = series_1
Cells(1, 3) = series_2
```

The sheet is populated with data from the recordset. To accomplish this, the first cell in each successive row is activated. The date (the first field in the recordset) is put into the active cell. Within the same row, the price data for the two indices is put into the two columns to the right. The `Off-set` property is used for this purpose. For the two lines placing price data, the row indicator of the offset is set to zero, which means no offset, or use the same row. Next, though, the offset is used to activate the cell below it. In this case the row indicator is set to one and the column indicator is set to zero. This relates to the cell directly below the active cell—which is itself activated. In this manner the active cell keeps moving down column A.

```
        Cells(2, 1).Activate
        ' as long as there is data...
        Do Until rsStocks.EOF
           ActiveCell = rsStocks.Fields(0) ' date
           ActiveCell.Offset(0, 1) = rsStocks.Fields(1) ' s. 1
           ActiveCell.Offset(0, 2) = rsStocks.Fields(2) ' s. 2
           ' activate the next row, column 1
           ActiveCell.Offset(1, 0).Activate
           ' move to next record
           rsStocks.MoveNext
        Loop
End If ' If Not rsStocks.EOF
```

NOTE: An alternative method for placing recordset data onto a worksheet is to use the `CopyFromRecordset` method of the `Range` object. In this example, this single line:

```
        Range("A2").CopyFromRecordset rsStocks
```

replaces these lines:

```
        Do Until rsStocks.EOF
           ActiveCell = rsStocks.Fields(0) ' date
           ActiveCell.Offset(0, 1) = rsStocks.Fields(1) ' s. 1
           ActiveCell.Offset(0, 2) = rsStocks.Fields(2) ' s. 2
           ActiveCell.Offset(1, 0).Activate
          rsStocks.MoveNext
        Loop
```

It is likely that the dates in column A are in serial date format. For example, March 15, 2001, will be the number 36965. Therefore, column A receives a format:

```
Columns("A:A").Select
Selection.NumberFormat = "m/d/yyyy"
```

It is necessary to know how much data there is. Using the `Current-Region` and `Rows` properties, this is determined. The number of columns is already known to be three:

```
Cells(1, 1).Activate
ActiveCell.CurrentRegion.Select
row_count = Selection.Rows.Count
```

The system-supplied default scale settings for the two vertical axes may not be visually pleasing. The series lines may be squeezed into a band of the available chart area that leaves a noticeable empty portion above or below the series. Using the `Min()` and `Max()` worksheet functions to calculate the smallest and largest data points, these next several lines determine useful minimum and maximum scale values. For each series, calculations are used to set the maximum scale value as the sum of the maximum data point plus 10 percent of the difference of the data points. The minimum scale values are set as the minimum data point minus 10 percent of the difference of the data points. Ten percent is a subjective choice:

```
series_1_data = Worksheets("Stock_Chart") _
    .Range(Cells(2, 2), Cells(row_count, 2))
series_1_min = _
    Application.WorksheetFunction.Min(series_1_data)
series_1_max = _
    Application.WorksheetFunction.Max(series_1_data)
series_1_size = series_1_max - series_1_min
series_1_floor = series_1_min - (series_1_size * 0.1)
series_1_ceiling = series_1_max + (series_1_size * 0.1)
series_2_data = Worksheets("Stock_Chart") _
    .Range(Cells(2, 3), Cells(row_count, 3))
series_2_min = _
    Application.WorksheetFunction.Min(series_2_data)
series_2_max = _
    Application.WorksheetFunction.Max(series_2_data)
series_2_size = series_2_max - series_2_min
series_2_floor = series_2_min - (series_2_size * 0.1)
series_2_ceiling = series_2_max + (series_2_size * 0.1)
```

When a chart is added to a sheet and selected, it is considered a separate window. Later in the code we will need to return to the worksheet—as a window. The `this_window` variable stores the current window name before working with the chart itself. Up until now only the data has been addressed:

```
this_window = ActiveWindow.Caption
```

Next the chart is added to the workbook using the `Add` method. The `stock_chart` variable is set to the chart. Then, the `Location` property sets the location of the chart, based on the option on the form either as a new chart sheet or as an object on the Stock_Chart worksheet.

If the chart is an object on the worksheet, then further processing sets the position of the chart. First the worksheet is reactivated by activating the window. The point is that for the chart to be positioned on the worksheet, it is necessary to treat the chart as on object from the perspective of the worksheet.

The pricing data is in the first three columns. The total width for the three columns is calculated by taking the width of the first and multiplying by three. Whether the three columns have different widths is not a concern here because the worksheet has just been created. No opportunity has been available to change the widths, so right now they are all the same. The total width of the three columns is stored in the `width_3_cols` variable.

With the chart selected as an object, its `Left` property is set to the `width_3_cols` value. When the chart is complete, its left side will sit on the border of the third and fourth columns. The `Top` property is set to a fixed value of 10. There is no conflict of positioning concerning where the top of the chart is.

However, the width and height of the chart are another matter. Using the `UsableWidth` and `UsableHeight` properties of the active window, the width and height of the chart are set such that they will nearly fill the available space. This addresses the differences between varying screen sizes and whether or not Excel is maximized. The purpose of using the values 40 and –40 is to adjust for the row and column headers, scroll bars, and menu bars, which take up some of the window space. After all this is done, the chart itself is reactivated:

```
Set stock_chart = Charts.Add
' chart sheet or chart object on worksheet?
If Me.optChartSheet = True Then
    ' create a new chart sheet
    stock_chart.Location Where:=xlLocationAsNewSheet
Else
```

```
' create as a chart object on the Stock_Chart worksheet
' note - this worksheet also has the data on it, so
' use the Top and Left properties to avoid placing
' the chart over the data
stock_chart.Location Where:=xlLocationAsObject, _
     Name:="Stock_Chart"

' place and size the chart object
' based on the useable area of the application
' to do this must reactivate the worksheet
Windows(this_window).Activate

'select the chart object
Worksheets("Stock_Chart").ChartObjects(1).Select
width_3_cols = (Columns(1).Width * 3)
Selection.Top = 10
Selection.Left = width_3_cols
Selection.Width = _
   ActiveWindow.UsableWidth - (width_3_cols + 40)
Selection.Height = ActiveWindow.UsableHeight - 40
' reactivate the chart object
Worksheets("Stock_Chart").ChartObjects(1).Activate
End If
```

At this point the chart exists but remains empty until certain properties are set. First the `Source` parameter of the `SetSourceData` method tells the chart where to find the data. The range is set to the data pulled from the database, now on the Stock_Chart worksheet.

Next the type of chart is set. There are many types of charts available: line, bar, pie, and so on. The chart is set to a custom type called a combination chart. A combination chart displays each value axis on its own scale, instead of on a shared one. The primary axis is on the left side of the chart and the secondary is on the right side. The two series do share the category axis—which sits horizontally along the bottom of the chart.

There are variations of combination charts. The one used here is aptly named "Lines on 2 Axes." The `ChartType` and `TypeName` parameters of the `ApplyCustomType` method are used in setting the chart.

```
With ActiveChart
.SetSourceData Source:=Sheets("Stock_Chart") _
   .Range("A1:C" & row_count), _
   PlotBy:=xlColumns
```

```
.ApplyCustomType ChartType:=xlBuiltIn, TypeName:= _
   "Lines on 2 Axes"
```

A title for the chart is created from concatenating the two series names and the range of dates. The `HasTitle` property and the `Text` property of the `ChartTitle` object are used here:

```
chart_title = series_1 & " vs. " & series_2 & Chr(10)
chart_title = chart_title & Me.lstStartDate & _
   " through " & Me.lstEndDate
' set this property to make the title visible...
.HasTitle = True
' assign the text string to the title
.ChartTitle.Text = chart_title
```

For the horizontal category axis, tick mark spacing is set to a tenth or a fifth of the number of dates in the data. If there are fewer than two hundred dates, then tick mark spacing is set to the number of dates divided by ten, plus one. One is added to ensure at least of value of one is supplied, otherwise an error occurs.

Tick mark labels are set to none. The labels, if made visible, are dates found in column A. Depending on the size of the source data, this could make for a quite crowded chart. Therefore, subjectively, these are left out. The dates represented by the chart are in the chart title.

```
   With .Axes(xlCategory)
   .HasTitle = False
   .CrossesAt = 1
   .TickLabelPosition = xlNone
   If row_count < 200 Then
      .TickMarkSpacing = (row_count / 10) + 1
   Else
      .TickMarkSpacing = row_count / 5
   End If
End With
```

The properties for the two vertical axes are set in identical fashion. Each receives a title, which is the respective index name. The scales are set to minimum and maximum values as previously determined. The `Major-Unit` property is set to a fourth of the numerical range of the data points, previously determined. The `NumberFormat` is set to zero to avoid showing any decimals;

```
   With .Axes(xlValue, xlPrimary)
   .HasTitle = True
   .AxisTitle.Text = series_1
   .MinimumScale = series_1_floor
   .MaximumScale = series_1_ceiling
   .MajorUnit = series_1_size / 4
   .TickLabels.NumberFormat = "0"
End With
   With .Axes(xlValue, xlSecondary)
   .HasTitle = True
   .AxisTitle.Text = series_2
   .MinimumScale = series_2_floor
   .MaximumScale = series_2_ceiling
   .MajorUnit = series_2_size / 4
   .TickLabels.NumberFormat = "0"
End With
```

The properties for the two series lines are set. Each line is set to not show markers, to not smooth out the line, and to set the color as determined with the scroll bars in the Create Chart form:

```
With .SeriesCollection(1)
   .Border.Weight = xlThin
   .Border.LineStyle = xlAutomatic
   .MarkerStyle = xlNone
   .Smooth = False
   .Border.Color = _
      RGB(Me.bar_red_1, Me.bar_green_1, Me.bar_blue_1)
End With
With .SeriesCollection(2)
   .Border.Weight = xlThin
   .Border.LineStyle = xlAutomatic
   .MarkerStyle = xlNone
   .Smooth = False
   .Border.Color = _
      RGB(Me.bar_red_2, Me.bar_green_2, Me.bar_blue_2)
End With
```

The creation and formatting of the chart are complete. The worksheet window is reactivated:

```
Windows(this_window).Activate
```

Finally the form itself is dismissed:

```
Me.Hide
```

As Figure 3.11 shows (on page 104), the completed stock chart sits as an object on the Stock_Chart worksheet. Note that the chart borders the third column and just fits within the screen area.

Events

Several useful events exist for the Workbook, Worksheet, and Chart sheet objects. To access these events, start the VBE and open the Project Explorer pane if it isn't already open. Then either select the object and use the View…Code menu, or just right-click on the desired object and select View Code from the shortcut menu.

In the Code window, select the object from the object drop-down list. The procedure drop-down list will now contain the available events in which to place code routines. Figure 3.12 shows the results of these steps.

Workbook Events

There are more than twenty workbook events. See Table 3.3 for a complete list. Workbook events are available in the procedure drop-down list when the selected object in the Project Explorer is "ThisWorkbook". ThisWorkbook sits in with the sheet objects but is unique in that it represents the workbook itself. (See Figure 3.12.) Listing 3.16 shows a handful of workbook event procedures.

Listing 3.16 A selection of workbook events

```
Private Sub Workbook_Activate()
  MsgBox "Workbook Activate Event"
End Sub
Private Sub Workbook_BeforePrint(Cancel As Boolean)
  MsgBox "Workbook Before Print Event"
End Sub
Private Sub Workbook_BeforeSave _
    (ByVal SaveAsUI As Boolean, Cancel As Boolean)
  MsgBox "Workbook Before Save Event"
End Sub
```

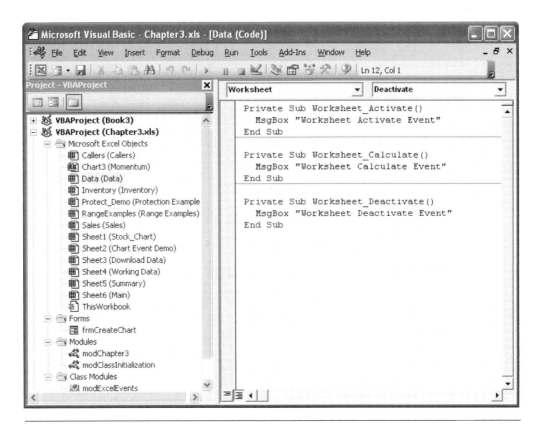

Figure 3.12 Accessing event procedures in the Visual Basic Editor

Listing 3.16 *(continued)*

```
Private Sub Workbook_NewSheet(ByVal Sh As Object)
  MsgBox "Workbook New Sheet Event"
End Sub
Private Sub Workbook_Open()
  MsgBox "Workbook Open Event"
End Sub
Private Sub Workbook_PivotTableOpenConnection _
    (ByVal Target As PivotTable)
  MsgBox "Workbook Pivot Table Open Connection Event"
End Sub
```

Worksheet and Chart Events

In the Project Explorer are listed all worksheets and charts (separate chart sheets) in the workbook. (See Figure 3.12.) Each worksheet and chart maintains its own events. Listing 3.17 shows a few event procedures for a worksheet. See Table 3.3 for the full list of events.

Listing 3.17 A selection of worksheet events

```
Private Sub Worksheet_Activate()
  MsgBox "Worksheet Activate Event"
End Sub
Private Sub Worksheet_Calculate()
  MsgBox "Worksheet Calculate Event"
End Sub
Private Sub Worksheet_Deactivate()
  MsgBox "Worksheet Deactivate Event"
End Sub
```

Table 3.3 Workbook, worksheet, and chart events

Object	Events
Workbook	Activate, AddinInstall, AddinUninstall, AfterXmlExport (Excel 2003 only), AfterXmlImport (Excel 2003 only), BeforeClose, BeforePrint, BeforeSave, BeforeXmlExport (Excel 2003 only), BeforeXmlImport (Excel 2003 only), Deactivate, NewSheet, Open, PivotTableCloseConnection, PivotTableOpenConnection, SheetActivate, SheetBeforeDoubleClick, SheetBeforeRightClick, SheetCalculate, SheetChange, SheetDeactivate, SheetFollowHyperlink, SheetPivotTableUpdate, SheetSelectionChange, Sync (Excel 2003 only), WindowActivate, WindowDeactivate, WindowResize
Worksheet	Activate, BeforeDoubleClick, BeforeRightClick, Calculate, Change, Deactivate, FollowHyperlink, PivotTableUpdate, SelectionChange
Chart	Activate, BeforeDoubleClick, BeforeRightClick, Calculate, Deactivate, DragOver, DragPlot, MouseDown, MouseMove, MouseUp, Resize, Select, SeriesChange

Chart Object Events

Dedicated charts (separate chart sheets) have a selection of available events; however, chart objects (on worksheets) do not. With the use of a class module and an initialization routine, it is possible to create events for chart objects.

First create a class module. The name of the class module is referenced in the initialization routine, so optionally rename the module using the properties page. Figure 3.13 (on page 119) shows a class module aptly named modExcelEvents with event procedures for both the Chart object and the Application object. In the class module, enter a declaration of this form:

```
Public WithEvents objChart As Chart
```

Note that objChart can be a different name supplied by you. Once the declaration is entered, events for the type of object specified above (Chart in this case) are available. First select the object from the object drop-down list on the left side of the Code window, then access the various events in the procedure drop-down list on the right side of the Code window.

Enter code as needed into the event procedures. Here are two routines that prevent a chart from being resized or moved on its parent worksheet. The routines fire on the chart's Deactivate and Resize events, respectively:

```
Private Sub objChart_Deactivate()
With ActiveSheet.ChartObjects(1)
  .Top = 50
  .Left = 50
End With
End Sub

Private Sub objChart_Resize()
With ActiveSheet.ChartObjects(1)
  .Height = 200
  .Width = 200
End With
```

The Deactivate routine repositions the chart. The effect may be nil—there is no test to see if the top or left properties are not equal to fifty. However, if the chart had been moved, this would put it back in place. Likewise, the Resize routine resizes the chart back to a fixed size.

The events need to be initialized. To accomplish this, create or activate a standard code module and enter this declaration:

```
Dim myChart As New modExcelEvents
```

Note that `myChart` can be a different name supplied by you. The class module name following the `New` keyword must match the name of the class module in which the event procedures are stored. Finally, create a procedure that effectively links the desired chart with the code in the class module. Here are the declaration and initialization procedures together:

```
Dim mychart As New modExcelEvents
Sub initialize_chart()
  Set myChart.objChart = _
    Worksheets("Sheet1").ChartObjects(1).Chart
End Sub
```

Note that `objChart` is the name of the object reference created in the class module, and note that the event procedures created in the class module can be accessed only by one given chart object. The initialization routine set the particular event procedure to a particular chart object. For event procedures to be attached to additional chart objects, they need to have their own object names, such as `myChart2`, and be initialized with separate statements.

Application Events

Events for the `Application` object need to be created within a class module and initialized. The steps are identical to the setup of `Chart-Object` events just listed. In a class module, a declaration must be written:

```
Public WithEvents objApp As Application
```

In the declaration, the name `objApp` can be a different name supplied by you. Once the declaration is entered, the created object reference and available events are listed in the object and procedure drop-down lists, respectively. For this example, a routine is set to fire whenever a new worksheet is inserted into the workbook. The code goes in the `Work-bookNewSheet` event handler:

```
Private Sub objApp_WorkbookNewSheet _
(ByVal Wb As Workbook, ByVal Sh As Object)
  ActiveSheet.Name = "Baker Company " & _
    ActiveWorkbook.Sheets.Count
End Sub
```

When a new worksheet is entered, it is renamed without manual intervention. The event procedure must be initialized. In a standard module, enter this declaration and initialization routine:

```
Dim myApp As New modExcelEvents
Sub initialize_app()
  Set myApp.objApp = Application
End Sub
```

Note that `objApp` is the name of the object reference created in the class module. Figure 3.13 shows the class module set up with event procedures.

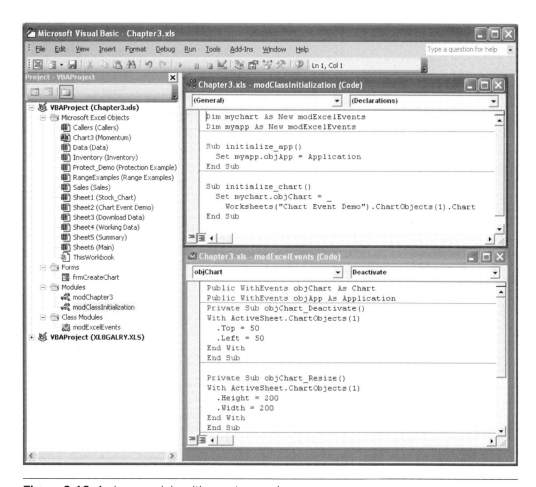

Figure 3.13 A class module with event procedures

Summary

Excel is an enormously powerful desktop application. Countless initiatives in the workplace rely on Excel in some form. Entire departments thrive on Excel—just think of the accounting or finance group in your place of work.

This chapter demonstrated how to program many facets of Excel. There are a vast number of objects in Excel, and exponentially more properties and methods to manipulate. Chapter 9, "XML and Office," demonstrates the XML and List features in Excel 2003. Chapters 13 and 14 illustrate using Excel to solve specific business needs.

CHAPTER 4

Access Solution Development

VERSION NOTE: This material works for all versions of Access, except where noted. XML use in Access is covered in Chapter 9, "XML and Office."

By its nature, Access requires a formal approach to development. The other Office products work on two levels: the standard user interface and the optional development environment. In contrast, Access use is synonymous with complete custom development. Some customization must be done before any activity can be accomplished with an Access database. The minimum in this regard is the creation of a table to hold data.

Solutions built with Access often differ from the development approaches used for the other Office products. Custom solutions for Word, Excel, PowerPoint, and Outlook all typically interact with the inherent object model—and VBA is needed to do so. With Access it is often the case that a solution relies more on SQL and ADO, and less on VBA.

However, with Access, it is useful to tap the object model with VBA as part of either creating or modifying the solution.

To clarify, since much of the core database functionality is embedded in the Jet database engine, ADO objects, such as the `Recordset`, are used in a custom solution. The majority of Access solutions also use SQL. This may not be apparent to the "power user" or the novice developer, because many choose to assemble queries using the query grid. The query grid allows easy creation of simple-to-sophisticated SQL statements. Yet its use does not require any interaction or knowledge of the actual SQL that is generated. See Figure 4.1. Of course, some query types—such as a Union—can only be written with SQL.

On the other hand, if changes to the *design* of the custom solution are needed, especially if they involve multiple objects, VBA and the collections

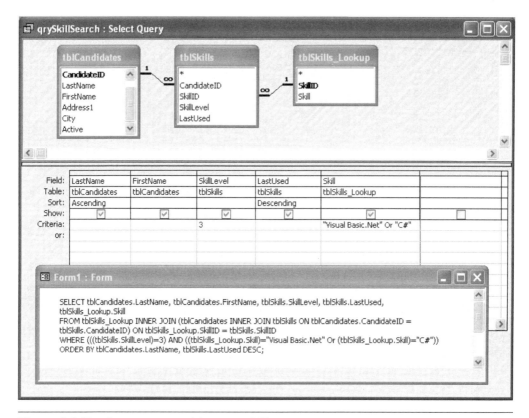

Figure 4.1 The Access query grid creates SQL statements

available in the object model are used to accomplish the task. Performing these mass updates with Access collections is the focus of this chapter.

Consider the following code example. Most of the functionality is based on ADO objects (such as `Connection` and `Recordset`) and SQL (such as `Select * From`):

```
Dim conn As ADODB.Connection
Set conn = CurrentProject.Connection
Dim rs As ADODB.Recordset
Set rs = New ADODB.Recordset
rs.Open "Select * From tblCandidates Where CandidateID=" & _
    Me.txtCandidateID, conn
If Not rs.EOF Then
    MsgBox "There already is a candidate with an ID of " & _
        Me.txtCandidateID & ". Must enter a unique Candidate ID"
```

```
      DoCmd.CancelEvent
      Exit Sub
   End If
```

This preceding code is typical of an Access solution's functionality. In contrast, a developer may need to update all controls on a form. Such a routine will make use of the `Controls` collection and use VBA to manipulate it. For example, the following code shows a routine that takes the name of a form as an argument and then updates the `Tag` property for all controls on the form. This routine consists completely of VBA and Access objects:

```
Sub update_controls(form_name As String)
   Dim ctl As Control
   For Each ctl In Forms(form_name).Controls
      ctl.Properties("Tag") = "ABC"
   Next
End Sub
```

This chapter does not give instruction in either database fundamentals or basic Access development. These subjects themselves fill up books. See the Appendix for resources on Access development. The coverage in this chapter mostly shows how to work with a few key objects and collections in Access.

Objects, Properties, and Methods

The Database Window

When Access is started up, users have two options: to work on an existing database or to start a new one. If the user chooses to work on a new database, the first action required is to save it. This workflow directly contrasts with the start-up procedure of the other Office products, in which users can immediately start to work and then save or discard their work later.

Once a name and directory are selected and the database is saved, the Database window is available. See Figure 4.2.

The Database window is the "plain vanilla" interface with the database. Depending on your purpose, the Database window may be adequate for use. It offers access to the tables, queries, and other major objects inherent in an Access database.

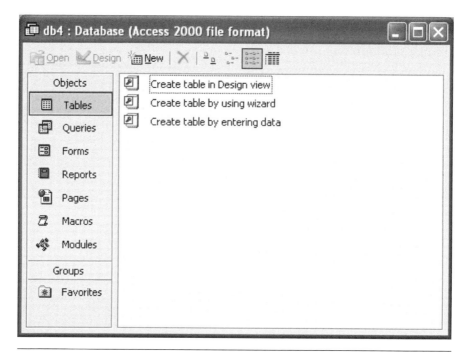

Figure 4.2 The Access database window

Access Database Structure

Note that an Access database contains the components of both the "front end" and the "back end" of a solution. In particular, as shown in Figure 4.2, Access has form and report design capabilities (there are Forms and Reports tabs). Forms and reports are elements of a database solution front end.

Tables are the core objects of a database. Tables hold data. Tables and the data within are the core back end in a database solution.

Forms provide a way to interact with data in a purposeful way. In other words, forms are a bridge between functionality and raw data. Forms help control the viewing, editing, and other manipulation of data.

Reports are used strictly for output. Like forms, they provide a helpful way of viewing and summarizing the data, but they are not considered part of the back end itself.

The Application Object

The Application object effectively serves as Access itself. The properties and methods that belong to the Application object allow manipulation of the Access objects seen in the Database window. Functionality at the application level also offers "domain-level" summaries. These are functions that provide typical summarization, such as averaging, that are applied to a set of specified records, called a *domain*.

Finally, the Application object has the methods that create, open, and close databases, as well as quit Access itself.

Table 4.1 displays some useful properties and methods of the Application object.

Table 4.1 Selected properties and methods of the Application object

Name	Type	Comment
CurrentData	Property	Returns the CurrentData object, which contains data-centric collections such as AllTables and AllQueries
CurrentProject	Property	Returns the CurrentProject object, which contains functional collections such as AllForms and AllReports
DoCmd	Property	Returns the DoCmd object, which supports many useful methods
Forms	Property	Returns collection of all "open" forms
Modules	Property	Returns collection of all "open" modules
Printers	Property	Returns collection of all "available" printers (Access 2002 and Access 2003 only)
Reports	Property	Returns collection of all "open" reports
Quit	Method	Closes the database and exits Access
RunCommand	Method	Used to initiate many useful database functions
SysCmd	Method	Used mainly to control the status bar

The CurrentData Object

The CurrentData object returns a few key collections: AllDatabase-
Diagrams, AllFunctions, AllQueries, AllStoredProcedures,
AllTables, and AllViews. Using these collections, useful database information can be attained. For example, running this code returns the information shown in Figure 4.3:

```
Dim msg As String
With Application.CurrentData
  msg = "There are " & .AllQueries.Count & " queries and " & _
    .AllTables.Count & " tables in the current database."
  MsgBox msg
End With
```

Figure 4.3 Using collections to return the count of tables and queries

The AllTables and AllQueries collections report back on the tables and queries in a standard Access database. The other four collections
involve using Access with SQL Server and are not discussed in this book.

Note that the routine just shown will report that there are more tables
than may be apparent. Access keeps a handful of system tables in a database that are used for internal purposes to manage the database. These tables are not meant to be accessed directly by any user activity or code
functionality.

However, system tables can be viewed. Within the Options dialog
(under the Tools menu) is a tab named "View". On the tab is a setting to
display system objects, shown in Figure 4.4.

Selecting to display system objects results in a number of tables appearing in the Tables tab of the Database window. The names of these tables all start with "MSys", as shown in Figure 4.5.

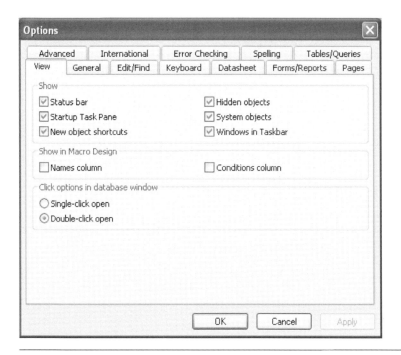

Figure 4.4 Selecting to display system objects

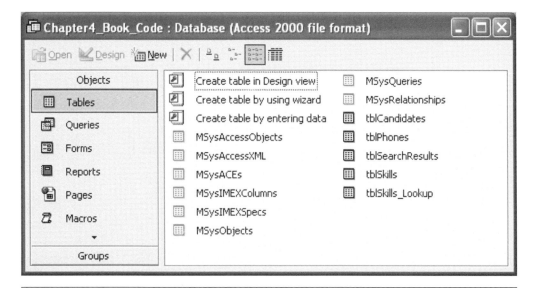

Figure 4.5 System tables appear under the Tables tab

Luckily, the consistent naming scheme of the system tables allows an easy alteration to the previous code routine to skip counting them in the sum of database tables. Listing 4.1 shows the enhanced routine.

Listing 4.1 Returning a true count of solution tables and queries

```
Sub explore_currentdata_collections_not_msys()
Dim msg As String
Dim tbl As Integer
Dim table_count As Integer
table_count = 0
With Application.CurrentData
  msg = "There are " & .AllQueries.Count & " queries and "
  For tbl = 0 To .AllTables.Count - 1
    If Left(.AllTables(tbl).Name, 4) <> "MSys" Then
      table_count = table_count + 1
    End If
  Next tbl
  msg = msg & table_count & " tables in the current database."
  MsgBox msg
End With
End Sub
```

Figure 4.6 now displays a different table count compared to that shown in Figure 4.3. The system tables are not included in the count shown in Figure 4.6.

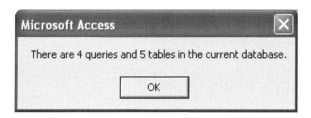

Figure 4.6 Returning the table and query counts, excluding the system tables

AllTables **and** AllQueries

By applying an item index to the AllTables or AllQueries collections, pertinent information can be found for a particular table or query.

The properties available to tables or queries within these collections are the same, so the following routines can be used with either an individual table or an individual query.

The following routine loops through the `AllTables` collection and tests each table to see if it is loaded (that is, to see if it is open in either design or datasheet view). For each table that passes the test, a message is returned with the name and view of the table (see Figure 4.7):

```
Dim msg As String
With Application.CurrentData
  For find_table = 0 To .AllTables.Count - 1
    If .AllTables(find_table).IsLoaded = True Then
      msg = .AllTables(find_table).Name & " is loaded"
      Select Case .AllTables(find_table).CurrentView
        Case 0
          msg = msg & " in design view"
        Case Else
          msg = msg & " in datasheet view"
      End Select
      MsgBox msg
    End If
  Next find_table
End With
```

Figure 4.7 If a table is loaded, its name and view state are returned

The following example returns the name of a query if it was created in May 2003 or later (see Figure 4.8):

```
With Application.CodeData
  For find_query = 0 To .AllQueries.Count - 1
    If .AllQueries(find_query).DateCreated > "4/30/03" Then
      MsgBox .AllQueries(find_query).Name & " created: " & _
             .AllQueries(find_query).DateCreated
```

Figure 4.8 If a query was created after a certain date, its name and the date created are returned

```
   End If
  Next find_query
End With
```

The `DateCreated` property is used for the test. This type of routine is helpful when you have a great number of queries or tables to sift through.

The `CurrentProject` Object

The `CurrentProject` object returns these collections: `AllData-AccessPages`, `AllForms`, `AllMacros`, `AllModules`, and `All-Reports`. These collections can be tapped for their counts. For example, this routine returns the message shown in Figure 4.9:

```
Dim msg As String
With Application.CurrentProject
  msg = "There are " & .AllDataAccessPages.Count & _
    " data access pages, " & .AllForms.Count & " forms, " & _
    .AllMacros.Count & " macros, " & .AllModules.Count & _
    " modules, and " & .AllReports.Count & _
    " reports in the current database."
  MsgBox msg
End With
```

Using the `AllForms` Collection

By applying an item index to the `AllForms` collection, pertinent information can be returned per individual form. Listing 4.2 shows a routine that cycles through the `AllForms` collection and tests each form to see if it is

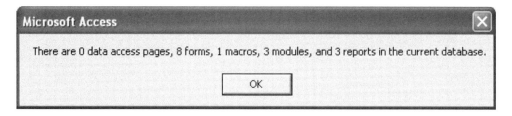

Figure 4.9 Information returned from the `CurrentProject` collections

loaded. A form is loaded if it is open in any possible state: design, form, datasheet, or pivot. For each loaded form, the `CurrentView` property is accessed to determine its state.

Listing 4.2 Testing each form in the `AllForms` collection

```
Sub explore_forms()
Dim msg As String
Dim find_form As Integer
With Application.CurrentProject
  For find_form = 0 To .AllForms.Count - 1
    If .AllForms(find_form).IsLoaded = True Then
      msg = .AllForms(find_form).Name & " is loaded"
      Select Case .AllForms(find_form).CurrentView
        Case acCurViewDesign ' 0
          msg = msg & " in Design view"
        Case acCurViewFormBrowse ' 1
          msg = msg & " in Form view"
        Case acCurViewDatasheet ' 2
          msg = msg & " in Datasheet view"
        Case acCurViewPivotTable ' 3
          msg = msg & " in Pivot Table view"
      End Select
      MsgBox msg
    End If
  Next find_form
End With
End Sub
```

Figure 4.10 The current view of a loaded form is returned

The `explore_forms` routine in Listing 4.2 returns a message such as the one shown in Figure 4.10.

Using the `AllReports` Collection

By applying an item index to the `AllReports` collection, information can be returned per individual report. Listing 4.3 shows a routine that cycles through the `AllReports` collection and returns the current view for each report that is loaded. Reports will be in only one of two current view states: design or print preview.

Listing 4.3 Testing each report in the `AllReports` collection

```
Sub explore_reports()
' return current view state of loaded reports
Dim msg As String
Dim find_report As Integer
With Application.CurrentProject
  For find_report = 0 To .AllReports.Count - 1
    If .AllReports(find_report).IsLoaded = True Then
      msg = .AllReports(find_report).Name & " is loaded"
      Select Case .AllReports(find_report).CurrentView
        Case acCurViewDesign ' 0
          msg = msg & " in Design view"
        Case acCurViewPreview ' 5
          msg = msg & " in Print Preview view"
      End Select
      MsgBox msg
    End If
  Next find_report
End With
End Sub
```

NOTE: All the collections contained within the `CurrentData` and `CurrentProject` objects have a uniform set of properties and methods that are applicable to individual items in the collection. The properties are `CurrentView`, `DateCreated`, `DateModified`, `FullName`, `IsLoaded`, `Name`, `Parent`, `Properties`, and `Type`. The methods are `GetDependencyInfo` and `IsDependentOn`.

In contrast, the `Forms`, `Modules`, and `Reports` collections offer a much greater degree of interaction with individual items. These collections, which belong directly to the `Application` object, allow interaction with specific object type properties, methods, and event procedures.

The one caveat of these collections is that `Forms`, `Modules`, and `Reports` contain only open objects.

Using the `Forms` Collection

Access provides a `Forms` collection, which consists just of loaded forms. This differs from the `AllForms` collection, which contains all forms in the database regardless of loaded state.

By cycling through the `Forms` collection, information can be read or applied to each member. For example, this code loops through the `Forms` collection and reports back each form's name and record source, as shown in Figure 4.11.

```
Dim frm As Form
For Each frm In Forms
  MsgBox frm.Name & ": " & frm.RecordSource
Next
```

Taking this a step further, the following `explore_forms_col-lection_2` routine searches for all open forms that are bound to the

Figure 4.11 Information about a form is returned

tblCandidates table. When a form passes the test, its code module receives a comment line:

```
Sub explore_forms_collection_2()
Dim frm As Form
For Each frm In Forms
  If InStr(1, frm.RecordSource, "tblCandidates") Then
    frm.Module.InsertLines 1, "' uses the Candidates table"
  End If
Next
End Sub
```

NOTE: Working programmatically with modules is explained later in this chapter.

The results of the explore_forms_collection_2 are shown in Figure 4.12.

The Forms collection provides an efficient way to tap the properties and methods of multiple forms. By cycling through the collection, it is possible to read from or update several forms at once. However, there is a limitation: the Forms collection contains only open forms.

By combining the utility of the AllForms collection with that of the Forms collection, all forms can be addressed to have properties (or methods) read or manipulated. This next example in Listing 4.4 makes use of both collections to update the Caption property on all forms.

```
(General)
   ' uses the Candidates table
   Option Compare Database
   Private Sub cmbCandidates_AfterUpdate()
      On Error Resume Next
      DoCmd.RunCommand acCmdSaveRecord
      Me.cmbCandidates.Requery
      Me.CandidateDetail.Visible = True
      Me.txtCandidateID.Visible = True
      DoCmd.GoToControl "txtCandidateID"
      DoCmd.FindRecord cmbCandidates
```

Figure 4.12 A comment line has been inserted into a form's code module

The Caption property is not directly accessible to individual forms in the AllForms collection; however, the property *is* available to any forms in the Forms collection. The explore_forms_collection routine taps into both collections.

Listing 4.4 Using both the AllForms and the Forms collections to update a property on all forms

```
Sub explore_forms_collection()
Dim form_count As Integer
Dim close_forms As Integer
Dim frm As Form
' close any open forms
For close_forms = Forms.Count To 1 Step -1
  DoCmd.Close acForm, Forms(close_form).Name, acSaveNo
Next close_forms
' now no forms are open,
' reopen one by one in design view, and update caption
With Application.CurrentProject
  For form_count = 0 To .AllForms.Count - 1
    DoCmd.OpenForm .AllForms(form_count).Name, acDesign
    ' update caption
    If InStr(1, Forms(0).Caption, "In Development") = 0 Then
      Forms(0).Caption = "In Development " & Forms(0).Caption
    End If
    DoCmd.Close acForm, Forms(0).Name, acSaveYes
  Next form_count
End With
MsgBox "done"
End Sub
```

In the explore_forms_collection routine, first all open forms are closed. This is done by applying the Close method of the DoCmd object to any members of the Forms collection:

```
For close_forms = Forms.Count To 1 Step -1
  DoCmd.Close acForm, Forms(close_form).Name, acSaveNo
Next close_forms
```

NOTE: The DoCmd object is explained later in this chapter.

Next a loop construct is sized to the count of the `AllForms` collection:

```
With Application.CurrentProject
   For form_count = 0 To .AllForms.Count - 1
```

One by one, each form is opened in design view and the caption is tested for the phrase "In Development". If the phrase is *not* found, the phrase is inserted at the beginning of the caption:

```
DoCmd.OpenForm .AllForms(form_count).Name, acDesign
' update caption
If InStr(1, Forms(0).Caption, "In Development") = 0 Then
    Forms(0).Caption = "In Development " & Forms(0).Caption
End If
```

Only one form is open at a time. Therefore, just using the first element in the `Forms` collection, `Forms(0)`, is guaranteed to address the correct form. At each end of the loop, the form is saved and closed. The form is saved even if the caption was not changed. A further test and code could be added to apply the save only to updated forms. Either way, the form needs to be closed:

```
DoCmd.Close acForm, Forms(0).Name, acSaveYes
```

Figure 4.13 displays a form with the updated caption.

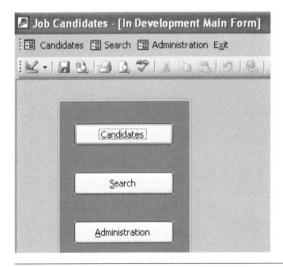

Figure 4.13 A form has received a new caption

Using the `Reports` Collection

The `Reports` collection is similar to the `Forms` collection, in that reports are similar to forms. Many properties are common to these object types, such as size attributes, view attributes, events, binding, and more. Of course, some properties and methods are unique. For example, reports have a `Group-Level` property and a `Circle` method. Forms have neither of these.

The `explore_reports_collection` routine in Listing 4.5 makes use of both the `AllReports` and the `Reports` collections to update any report that meets a certain criterion. In this case, if the word "Summary" is in the name of a report, then the `Visible` property of the detail section is set to false. This serves a likely need that summarized data should not display details. A routine such as this can update the designs of many reports in one process.

Listing 4.5 Using both the `AllReports` and the `Reports` collections to update a property on all reports

```
Sub explore_reports_collection()
Dim rpt_count As Integer
Dim close_rpt As Integer
Dim rpt As Report
' close any open reports
For close_rpt = Reports.Count - 1 To 0 Step -1
  DoCmd.Close acReport, Reports(close_rpt).Name, acSaveNo
Next close_rpt
' now no reports are open,
' reopen one by one in design view
With Application.CurrentProject
  For rpt_count = 0 To .AllReports.Count - 1
    DoCmd.OpenReport .AllReports(rpt_count).Name, acViewDesign
    ' if "Summary" is in the name, then
    'hide the detail section
    If InStr(1, Reports(0).Name, "Summary") > 0 Then
       Reports(0).Section("Detail").Visible = False
    End If
    DoCmd.Close acReport, Reports(0).Name, acSaveYes
  Next rpt_count
End With
MsgBox "done"
End Sub
```

The `explore_reports_collection` routine is nearly identical to the `explore_forms_collection` routine shown in Listing 4.4. `AllReports` and `Reports` replace `AllForms` and `Forms` in the routine.

Using the `Modules` Collection

Just as with forms and reports, there are `AllModules` and `Modules` collections. The `Modules` collection contains only open modules. The `explore_modules_collection` routine in Listing 4.6 is similar to the routines in Listings 4.4 and 4.5, however, working with modules requires a different approach.

Listing 4.6 Using both the `AllModules` and the `Modules` collections to add a declaration line to each module

```
Sub explore_modules_collection()
Dim mdl_count As Integer
Dim close_mdl As Integer
Dim mdl As Module
Dim mdl_name As String
Dim declare_lines As Integer
Dim opt_explicit_flag As Boolean
Dim current_module_flag As Boolean
' close all modules except the one running this code
For close_mdl = Modules.Count - 1 To 1 Step -1
  If Modules(close_mdl).Name <> "modChapterCode" Then
    DoCmd.Close acModule, Modules(close_mdl).Name, acSaveNo
  End If
Next close_mdl
With Application.CurrentProject
  For mdl_count = 0 To .AllModules.Count - 1
    mdl_name = .AllModules(mdl_count).Name
    current_module_flag = True
    If .AllModules(mdl_count).IsLoaded = False Then
      current_module_flag = False
      DoCmd.OpenModule mdl_name
    End If
      opt_explicit_flag = False
      For declare_lines = 1 To _
        Modules(mdl_name).CountOfDeclarationLines
```

Listing 4.6 *(continued)*

```
        If InStr(1, Modules(mdl_name) _
          .Lines(declare_lines, 1), "Option Explicit") > 0 Then
          opt_explicit_flag = True
        End If
      Next declare_lines
      If opt_explicit_flag = False Then
        ' insert the "Option Explicit" line
        Modules(mdl_name).InsertLines _
          declare_lines, "Option Explicit"
      End If
      If current_module_flag = True Then
        DoCmd.Save acModule, mdl_name
      Else
        DoCmd.Close acModule, mdl_name, acSaveYes
      End If
    Next mdl_count
End With
MsgBox "done"
End Sub
```

Both the `explore_forms_collection` and the `explore_re-ports_collection` routines closed *all* respective forms or reports early in their routines. This cannot be done when working with modules. The one module that contains the running `explore_modules_collec-tion` routine cannot be closed while running, or else the routine will stop running!

Therefore, this piece of the routine:

```
For close_mdl = Modules.Count - 1 To 1 Step -1
  If Modules(close_mdl).Name <> "modChapterCode" Then
    DoCmd.Close acModule, Modules(close_mdl).Name, acSaveNo
  End If
Next close_mdl
```

tests for the name of the module running the routine. Only modules that are not named `modChapterCode` are closed.

A loop cycles through all members of the `AllModules` collection, which includes the single open module and all the closed modules. With each module in turn, the name is stored in the `mdl_name` variable.

The `current_module_flag` Boolean variable is used to indicate if the module being processed in the loop is the open module. The flag's value is determined by testing the `.IsLoaded` property. If the module is not loaded, it is opened using the `OpenModule` method of the `DoCmd` object:

```
For mdl_count = 0 To .AllModules.Count - 1
    mdl_name = .AllModules(mdl_count).Name
    current_module_flag = True
    If .AllModules(mdl_count).IsLoaded = False Then
      current_module_flag = False
      DoCmd.OpenModule mdl_name
    End If
```

The purpose of this routine is to add the "Option Explicit" statement to every module's declaration section. Part of this process, though, is to make sure this line is not already in the declaration section.

To test this condition, a loop is sized to the number of declaration lines in the module. This value is returned by the `.CountOfDeclaration-Lines` property. The loop uses the `InStr()` function to test each line of the declaration section for "Option Explicit". The `opt_explicit_flag` Boolean variable holds the true or false results of the test. After the short loop, if the flag is false, the `InsertLines` method is used to insert "Option Explicit" as the new last line of the declaration section.

The `declare_lines` variable is used to indicate where the new line should go, since this variable is now equal to the number of current declaration lines plus one. The `declare_lines` variable has this value because it was just used for the short loop (a loop counter variable ends up containing the loop's top value plus one, assuming the loop was incrementing by one):

```
opt_explicit_flag = False
For declare_lines = 1 To _
  Modules(mdl_name).CountOfDeclarationLines
  If InStr(1, Modules(mdl_name) _
    .Lines(declare_lines, 1), "Option Explicit") > 0 Then
    opt_explicit_flag = True
  End If
Next declare_lines
```

```
If opt_explicit_flag = False Then
  ' insert the "Option Explicit" line
  Modules(mdl_name).InsertLines _
    declare_lines, "Option Explicit"
End If
```

Finally, each module is saved. If a module is not the modChapter-Code module, it is saved and closed. If it is the modChapterCode module, it is just saved and remains open:

```
If current_module_flag = True Then
  DoCmd.Save acModule, mdl_name
Else
  DoCmd.Close acModule, mdl_name, acSaveYes
End If
```

NOTE: The Modules and AllModules collections recognize standard and class modules as defined in the Modules tab of the Database window. Form and report modules belong to Forms and Reports, respectively.

The DoCmd Object

The DoCmd object is used to run standard Access actions. There are many methods available through the DoCmd object, as shown in Figure 4.14. The methods mirror the actions available in Access macros.

A particular method, RunCommand, leads to dozens of further actions that mirror most standard menu items. See Figure 4.15.

Dependencies

VERSION NOTE: Dependencies are new in Access 2003. Also, note that in Access 2003 Beta, the Dependants property of GetDependencyInfo is incorrectly spelled; it should be "Dependents". The code that follows in this section maintains the misspelling—otherwise it wouldn't have worked in the Beta. This misspelling may be corrected in the final release of Access 2003.

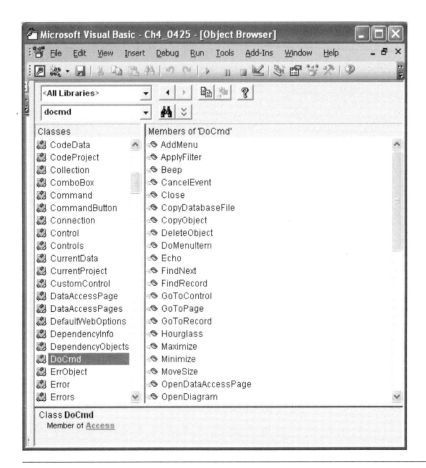

Figure 4.14 Many useful methods are available via the `DoCmd` object

```
Sub docmd_example()
  With DoCmd
    .RunCommand(
  End RunComm: ⊟ acCmdSaveRecord
End Sub           ⊟ acCmdSelectAll
                  ⊟ acCmdSelectAllRecords
                  ⊟ acCmdSelectDataAccessPage
                  ⊟ acCmdSelectForm
                  ⊟ acCmdSelectRecord
                  ⊟ acCmdSelectReport
```

Figure 4.15 The `RunCommand` method leads to many actions

An object can depend on other objects, or have other objects depend on it. For example, a bound form *depends on* the table or tables of its record source. A form may have a subform. Here too, the form *depends on* the subform. However, from the perspective of the subform, it has a dependency: the parent form.

Access provides a pair of methods to address these dependencies. These methods, GetDependencyInfo and IsDependentOn, are always taken from the perspective of a single object. The object may be a member of one of the CurrentData or CurrentProject collections discussed before, or the object can be accessed via the AccessObject object, which is returned by these collections to represent individual members.

The explore_dependents routine in Listing 4.7 uses the Get-DependencyInfo method to return the names of objects that depend on individual members of a given collection, in this case AllForms.

Listing 4.7 Creating a set of dependent objects for each member of AllForms

```
Sub explore_dependents()
Dim a_obj As AccessObject
Dim tbl_loop As Integer
Dim dep_loop As Integer
With Application.CurrentProject
  For Each a_obj In .AllForms
    ' report on dependents
    For dep_loop = 0 To _
      a_obj.GetDependencyInfo.Dependants.Count - 1
      Debug.Print _
        a_obj.Name & " HAS THIS DEPENDENT: " & _
        a_obj.GetDependencyInfo.Dependants(dep_loop).Name
    Next dep_loop
  Next
End With
Debug.Print "done"
End Sub
```

In the explore_dependents routine, the a_obj variable is set as an AccessObject object. It is used in a For...Each...Next loop that addresses the AllForms collection:

```
With Application.CurrentProject
  For Each a_obj In .AllForms
```

An inner loop is sized to the count of dependents. This count is re-turned by the `Dependants` property of `GetDependencyInfo`. For each dependent object found in the loop, a line is written to the Debug (Immediate) window:

```
For dep_loop = 0 To _
  a_obj.GetDependencyInfo.Dependants.Count - 1
  Debug.Print _
    a_obj.Name & " HAS THIS DEPENDENT: " & _
    a_obj.GetDependencyInfo.Dependants(dep_loop).Name
Next dep_loop
```

The routine returns information as shown in Figure 4.16.

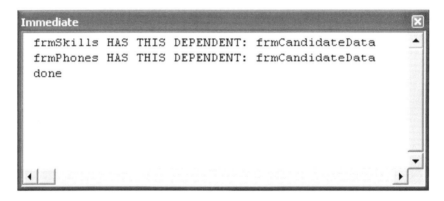

Figure 4.16 For an object, a line states another object's dependency on it

The `explore_dependencies` routine in Listing 4.8 is similar to the `explore_dependents` routine; however, there are a few key differences. This routine loops through the `AllForms` collection and looks to see which tables each form depends on. The tables are cycled through with an inner loop.

The results of the `explore_dependencies` routine are shown in Figure 4.17.

Listing 4.8 Creating a set of tables that each member of `AllForms` depends on

```
Sub explore_dependencies()
Dim a_obj As AccessObject
Dim tbl_loop As Integer
Dim dep_loop As Integer
With Application.CurrentProject
  For Each a_obj In .AllForms
    ' report on dependencies
    With Application.CurrentData
      For tbl_loop = 0 To .AllTables.Count - 1
        If a_obj.IsDependentUpon(acTable, _
          .AllTables(tbl_loop).Name) = True Then
          Debug.Print a_obj.Name & " DEPENDS ON " & _
            .AllTables(tbl_loop).Name
        End If
      Next tbl_loop
    End With
  Next
End With
Debug.Print "done"
End Sub
```

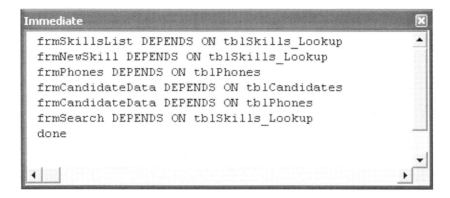

Figure 4.17 A line is written for each table that a form depends on

Summary

Access programmatic functionality generally falls into two camps: ADO/SQL for user interaction and VBA/object model manipulation during development and application enhancements. This is not a fixed division; certainly these distinctive uses overlap. However, it is rare that once in production, user activities are going to create or change the structure of forms or reports.

This chapter presented examples of manipulating forms, reports, and modules by interacting with the respective `Forms`, `Reports`, and `Modules` collections. Tables do not have a similar collection. There is no Access object collection that contains open tables. This functionality is achieved via ADO. In other words, tables are data-centric and are appropriately handled with a technology such as ADO that is intended for data access.

Chapter 9, "XML and Office," demonstrates XML functionality in Access 2003. Chapters 12 and 16 illustrate business solutions that involve Access.

CHAPTER 5

PowerPoint Solution Development

VERSION NOTE: This material works for all versions of PowerPoint, except where noted.

PowerPoint is the premier presentation software tool, used in diverse industries for presenting a broad range of information. There are two "modes" of operation: design/edit and slide show. The enhancements offered with VBA-based custom development differ depending on the mode of operation.

Design mode is used in all cases, because even when a PowerPoint file (a presentation) is used as a slide show, it first must be assembled. Design mode, however, should not be considered a preliminary step to a useful PowerPoint application. Design mode provides the same level of usefulness as do Word documents and Excel workbooks. In other words, with just the design aspect of PowerPoint, you are able to create and print slides—a slide being the equivalent of a document page or spreadsheet. Many PowerPoint-based tasks are performed at this level, to create and print slides.

Slide shows are automations of the slides in a PowerPoint file. Generally, the slides are cycled through for viewing, once or repeatedly. Many factors are controllable in a slide show, such as the presentable time of each slide, the "transition" effect as one slide is replaced with another, and the appearance and animations of text and graphics on each slide.

Programming PowerPoint has a few twists that must be considered in order to accomplish custom tasks. The first consideration is that slides do not have event procedures in which to place code. That is, slides by default do not even appear in the Project Explorer in the Visual Basic Editor (VBE). Likewise, the PowerPoint file—the presentation—is not available in the VBE. See Figure 5.1.

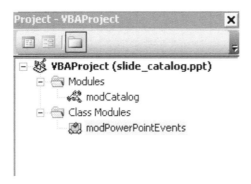

Figure 5.1 The PowerPoint development environment—just modules

Actually, a slide will appear in the VBE if controls from the toolbox are placed on it. In this case the slide will be in the VBE and will have a dedicated code module. But the code module will only show event stubs for the controls.

The second consideration in PowerPoint solution development is that events for the presentation and slide show objects are available, but not until they are set up in a class module and initialized. See the section on events, later in this chapter, for more information.

A third consideration is that events attached to controls, such as the OnClick event of command buttons, do not work in design mode. In design mode, code can be run in only one of three ways: (1) running a routine manually in the VBE, (2) incorporating a routine into a menu bar, or (3) accessing the built-in events—after they are initialized.

Functionality fired by button clicks, list box actions, and the like occurs only in slide shows. This is similar to the way a form in Access is built. In design mode, you add controls to a form and set up the associated event procedures. In Access, the functionality developed during design becomes active when the form is in Form view.

PowerPoint's set of objects includes many unique items such as shapes and animations. There are quite a number of interesting, graphic-based methods and properties that are unique to PowerPoint.

Objects, Properties, and Methods

The `Application` Object

The `Application` object represents PowerPoint itself. Much of the work in PowerPoint, though, is addressed at the presentation level. However, it is the `Application` object that maintains the `Presentations` collection. For example, the `Add` method is used to create a new presentation, which becomes a member of the `Presentations` collection. In Listing 5.1, the Folder Picker dialog box is used to target a directory, then a new presentation is added, aptly named new_presentation.ppt. If the Cancel button is clicked in the File Picker dialog box, then an error occurs and is picked up by the error routine.

Listing 5.1 A new presentation is created and saved

```
Public Sub new_presentation()
  On Error GoTo err_end
  Dim file_name As String
  Dim dlg As FileDialog
  Set dlg = _
    Application.FileDialog(msoFileDialogFolderPicker)
  dlg.AllowMultiSelect = False
  dlg.Show
  file_name = dlg.SelectedItems(1) & _
    "\new_presentation.ppt"
  Application.Presentations.Add
  ActivePresentation.SaveAs file_name
err_end:
  ' error 5 occurs when Cancel button clicked, so report
nothing
  If Err.Number <> 5 Then
    MsgBox Err.Number
  End If
End Sub
```

The routine in Listing 5.2 reports the name and slide count for all open presentations. For the sake of correct grammar, an `If` statement checks the slide count before returning the message. If the slide count is 1, then the message differs.

Listing 5.2 Cycling through open presentations and counting slides

```
Public Sub presentation_slide_counts()
On Error GoTo err_end
Dim prst As Presentation
Dim prst_name As String
Dim slide_count As Integer
Dim msg As String
For Each prst In Application.Presentations
    prst_name = prst.Name
    slide_count = prst.Slides.Count
    If slide_count = 1 Then
        msg = "There is " & slide_count & " slide in the "
    Else
        msg = "There are " & slide_count & " slides in the "
    End If
    msg = msg & prst_name & " presentation"
    MsgBox msg, vbOKOnly, prst.Name
Next
Exit Sub
err_end:
    ' error 5 occurs when Cancel button clicked
    If Err.Number <> 5 Then
        MsgBox Err.Number
    End If
End Sub
```

The `presentation_slide_counts` routine in Listing 5.2 displays a message such as the one shown in Figure 5.2.

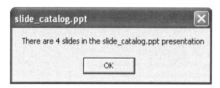

Figure 5.2 Information returned about a presentation

Presentations

A presentation is the equivalent of a single PowerPoint file. As such, there are methods that perform file-related activities. These are summarized in Table 5.1.

Table 5.1 Selected methods of the `Presentation` object

Method/Property	Example/Comments
`Save`	Saves a presentation. Does not close the presentation. Example: `ActivePresentation.Save` Note that the `Save` method will not prompt for a file name when applied to a new, unsaved presentation. The `Save` method will run using a standard enumerated file name (such as Presentation2.ppt) or will make use of the first string of text in the first slide to create a file name. For control over the file name of a new presentation, use the `SaveAs` method.

`SaveAs`	Saves a presentation. Allows setting the file name, the format, and whether to embed fonts.
	The syntax is:
	`expression.SaveAs File Name _`
	`  [,File Format, Embed Fonts]`
	Examples:
	`ActivePresentation.SaveAs "October_Sales"`
	or
	`ActivePresentation.SaveAs _`
	`  "C:\Sales\October_Sales", ppSaveAsHTML, _`
	`  msoTriStateMixed`
	
	The `File Name` parameter may include a path. If not, then the saved file is placed in the same directory.
	The settings for `File Format` and `Embed Fonts` are optional. The default for `File Format` is the current version of PowerPoint.
	The possible values are:
	`ppSaveAsHTMLv3`
	`ppSaveAsAddIn`
	`ppSaveAsBMP`
	`ppSaveAsDefault`
	`ppSaveAsGIF`
	`ppSaveAsHTML`
	`ppSaveAsHTMLDual`
	`ppSaveAsJPG`
	`ppSaveAsMetaFile`

Table 5.1 *(continued)*

Method/Property	Example/Comments

`SaveAs` *(continued)*	`ppSaveAsPNG`
	`ppSaveAsPowerPoint3`
	`ppSaveAsPowerPoint4`
	`ppSaveAsPowerPoint4FarEast`
	`ppSaveAsPowerPoint7`
	`ppSaveAsPresentation`
	`ppSaveAsRTF`
	`ppSaveAsShow`
	`ppSaveAsTemplate`
	`ppSaveAsTIF`
	`ppSaveAsWebArchive`
	
	The default setting for `Embed Fonts` is the constant `msoTriStateMixed`.
	The possible values are:
	
	`msoCTrue`
	`msoFalse`
	`msoTriStateMixed` Default.
	`msoTriStateToggle`
	`msoTrue`
	
	Note that certain file formats will force PowerPoint to save a separate file for each slide. For example, when the `ppSaveAsJPG` file format is indicated, PowerPoint will create a new subdirectory with the path indicated in the `File Name` parameter (which may just be the directory that the current presentation is in). Within the new subdirectory will be a series of files such as Slide1.jpg, Slide2.jpg, and so on.

`Close`	Closes a presentation. Note there is no warning or prompt to save work. Example: `ActivePresentation.Close`

`Export`	`Export` performs a function that is similar to the `SaveAs` method. A single slide, a range of slides, or an entire presentation may be exported. A format type is indicated, and the height and width of the exported slides are optionally set in pixels. The syntax is:
	`expression.Export Path, Filter Name _`
	`    [, ScaleWidth, ScaleHeight]`

Table 5.1 *(continued)*

Method/Property	Example/Comments

Export *(continued)*	The available Filter Names are based on the registry settings of the computer. Common graphics formats such as BMP, JPG, GIF, and PNG should be available on all computers.
	
	This next example exports the entire presentation into a specified directory. The Filter Name—BMP—is set as well as the size of the files. An individual file is created for each slide of the presentation:
	
	`ActivePresentation.Export "C:\april2002", _`
	`    "BMP", 300, 300`
	
	The next example exports a single slide. In this case, the file name must be provided:
	
	`ActivePresentation.Slides(5).Export _`
	`    "C:\april2002\slide4.gif", "GIF"`

PrintOut	Prints the presentation. The syntax is:
	
	`expression.PrintOut _`
	`    [From, To, PrintToFile, Copies, Collate]`
	
	All parameters are optional.
	The From and To parameters indicate which slide to start from and which to end with. One parameter can be supplied without the other. If not present, the From parameter is assumed to be 1. If not present, the To parameter is assumed to be the last slide number in the presentation.
	PrintToFile allows the output to go to a file rather than to the printer. Copies is used to set the number of copies to print. If left out, then one copy is printed. Collate can be set as true or false. The Collate default is false.
	This example prints the entire presentation, one page per slide:
	
	`ActivePresentation.PrintOut`
	
	This example prints three copies of slides one through four, collated:
	
	`ActivePresentation.PrintOut From:=1, To:=4, _`
	`    Copies:=3, Collate:=True`

Slides

A presentation consists of one or more slides. There is a `Slides` collection available to the `Presentation` object. The `Slides` property returns the `Slides` collection. This example returns the number of slides in the collection, then cycles through the slides and returns the name of each:

```
MsgBox ActivePresentation.Slides.Count
Dim sld As Slide
For Each sld In ActivePresentation.Slides
  MsgBox sld.Name
Next
```

Typical actions taken with the `Slides` collection are to add, copy, move, and delete. This example performs these methods:

```
Dim slide_count As Integer
With ActivePresentation
    slide_count = .Slides.Count
    .Slides.Add slide_count + 1, ppLayoutTextAndChart
    .Slides(3).Copy
    .Slides.Paste 5
    .Slides(2).MoveTo 4
    .Slides(6).Delete
End With
```

In the preceding example, the `slide_count` variable receives the count of slides from the `Count` property of the `Slides` collection. Next a new slide is added. Adding slides requires two parameters be given to the `Add` method. The first parameter indicates the position where the new slide will go. In this case it is placed at the end of the presentation simply by supplying an index number that is one greater than the current slide count.

The second parameter of the `Add` method designates the type of layout. Layouts indicate the mixture of slide items such as text boxes, charts, media clips, and org charts. Note that a layout is just a starting point for the structure of a slide. Objects on slides are easy to add, delete, and manipulate. In fact, one of the predefined layouts is `ppLayoutBlank`—just a blank slide. There are many predefined layouts. Figure 5.3 displays the list from the Object Browser.

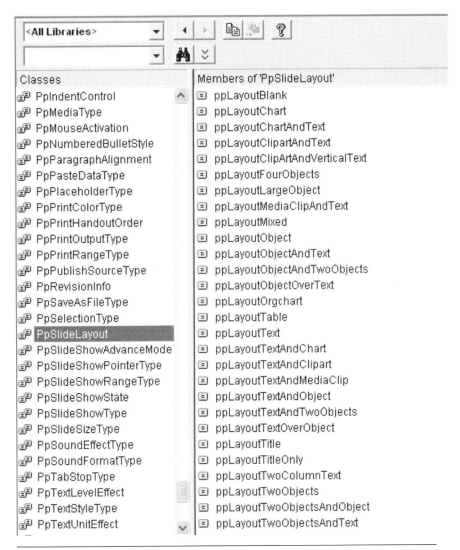

Figure 5.3 Many predefined layouts are available

The Copy method requires that the slide or range of slides to copy be supplied. In the preceding example, a single slide is indicated:

```
.Slides(3).Copy
```

A range of slides can also be indicated:

```
.Slides.Range(Array(3, 6)).Copy
```

When a slide or range of slides is pasted, the positional index number for the paste is an optional parameter. If the parameter is left out, the paste appends the slide or slides to the end of the presentation. In the preceding example, the paste occurs after the existing fifth slide:

```
.Slides.Paste 5
```

Shapes

Shapes represent the family of objects that are placed on a slide. This eclectic mix includes all items from text boxes to video clips. For example, the slide shown in Figure 5.4 contains five diverse objects—each a "shape" object.

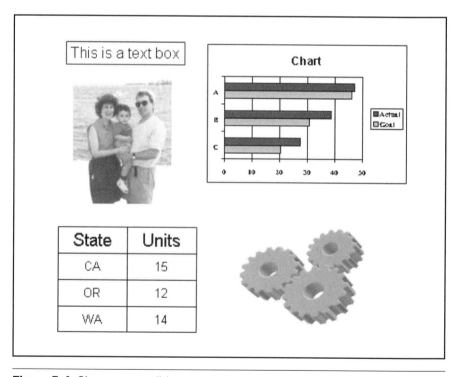

Figure 5.4 Shapes on a slide

The shape_information procedure in Listing 5.3 cycles through the shapes on a slide and returns information about each shape.

Listing 5.3 Returning the properties of shapes on a slide

```
Public Sub shape_information()
Dim shp As Shape
Dim shape_info As String
For Each shp In ActivePresentation.Slides(6).Shapes
  With shp
    shape_info = "Name=" & .Name & ", Type="
    shape_info = shape_info & Choose(.Type, _
          "Auto Shape", "Callout", "Chart", "Comment", _
          "Free Form", "Group", "Embedded OLE Object", _
          "Form Control", "Line", "Linked OLE Object", _
          "Linked Picture", "OLE Control Object", _
          "Picture", "Picture Holder", "Text Effect", _
          "Media", "Text Box", "Script Anchor", "Table")
    If .HasTextFrame = msoTrue Then _
        shape_info = shape_info & ", Text=" & _
        .TextFrame.TextRange.Text
  End With
  MsgBox shape_info
Next
End Sub
```

The shape_information procedure examines the shapes on a slide, in this case the sixth slide of a presentation. A Shape object type is declared and a For Each...Next construct is set up to cycle through the shapes.

A string is built that consists of a shape's name, type, and text, if any. To start, the name of the shape is returned from the Name property:

```
For Each shp In ActivePresentation.Slides(6).Shapes
  With shp
    shape_info = "Name=" & .Name & ", Type="
```

Then the shape type is returned. The Type property returns a number. The Choose() function is used to derive a name for the type, based on the type's number. There are more than twenty shape types, ranging from common text boxes to rarely used types such as a script anchor.

> **NOTE:** The AutoShape type—type number 1—reflects a group of more than one hundred additional shapes. AutoShapes contain items such as geometric shapes, callouts, stars, banners, and more. A dedicated property—`AutoShapeNumber`—returns the AutoShape type number. This number is unique and not related to the general shape type property. In a nutshell, all AutoShapes have a unique AutoShape type number, and all have a shape type property of 1.

At the end, the `HasTextFrame` property is used to decide whether to append the text. If there is a text frame, then the assumption is that there is text, although it is allowable to have an empty text frame:

```
If .HasTextFrame = msoTrue Then _
    shape_info = shape_info & ", Text=" & _
    .TextFrame.TextRange.Text
```

The `shape_information` routine finally returns a message box for each shape on a slide. Figure 5.5 displays the accumulated `shape_info` string.

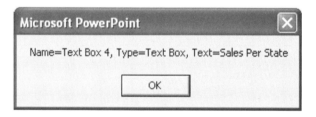

Figure 5.5 Returning shape information

Programmatically, shapes are added to slides using variations of the Add method. Table 5.2 summarizes how to add shapes to a slide.

Table 5.2 Programmatically adding shapes to a slide

Shape	Add Method	Syntax
Callout	AddCallout	AddCallout Type, Left, Top, Width, Height
Comment	AddComment	AddComment [Left, Top, Width, Height]
Connector	AddConnector	AddConnector Type, BeginX, BeginY, EndX, EndY
Curve	AddCurve	AddCurve SafeArrayOfPoints
Diagram (org. chart, pyramid, and more)	AddDiagram	AddDiagram Type, Left, Top, Width, Height
Label	AddLabel	AddLabel Orientation, Left, Top, Width, Height
Line	AddLine	AddLine BeginX, BeginY, EndX, EndY
Media Object (movie clip, sound, and others)	AddMediaObject	AddMediaObject (FileName [, Left, Top, Width, Height])
OLE Object (Word file, Excel file, control, and others)	AddOLEObject	AddOLEObject [Left, Top, Width, Height, ClassName, FileName, DisplayAsIcon, IconFileName, IconIndex, IconLabel, Link]
Picture (.bmp, .gif, and others)	AddPicture	AddPicture FileName, LinkToFile, SaveWithDocument, Left, Top [, Width, Height]
Placeholder	AddPlaceholder	AddPlaceholder Type [, Left, Top, Width, Height]

Table 5.2 *(continued)*

Shape	Add Method	Syntax
Polyline	`AddPolyline`	`AddPolyline SafeArrayOfPoints`
AutoShape (arrows, stars, flowchart symbols, and many more)	`AddShape`	`AddShape Type, Left, Top, Width, Height`
Table	`AddTable`	`AddTable(NumRows, NumColumns [, Left, Top, Width, Height])`
Text Box	`AddTextbox`	`AddTextbox(Orientation, Left, Top, Width, Height)`
Text Effect	`AddTextEffect`	`AddTextEffect(PresetTextEffect, Text, FontName, FontSize, FontBold, FontItalic, Left, Top)`
Title	`AddTitle`	`AddTitle` (**Note:** Uses the `TextFrame`, `TextRange`, and `Text` properties.)

Listing 5.4 demonstrates adding and manipulating shapes.

Listing 5.4 Adding and manipulating shapes on a slide

```
Public Sub add_shapes()
On Error GoTo err_end
Dim fso As FileSystemObject
Dim txt_stream As TextStream
Dim data_row
Dim row_num As Integer
Dim newslide As Slide
Dim sales_chart As Object
Dim sales_datasheet As Variant
Dim w_height As Single
Dim w_width As Single
```

Listing 5.4 (continued)

```
Set fso = New FileSystemObject
' test if view is a single slide
' if not then switch the view
If ActiveWindow.ViewType <> ppViewSlide Then
  ActiveWindow.ViewType = ppViewSlide
End If
' get the dimensions of the window
With ActiveWindow
  w_height = .Height
  w_width = .Width
End With
With ActivePresentation
  ' add a new slide as the first slide
  ' layout has just a title
  Set newslide = .Slides.Add(1, ppLayoutTitleOnly)
  ' goto the slide
  ActiveWindow.View.GotoSlide Index:=1
  With newslide.Shapes
    ' update the text of the title
    .Title.TextFrame.TextRange.Text = "Sales Per State"
    ' add a line just a little above the center,
    ' with a width of 400 points (500-100)
    .AddLine 100, Int(w_height / 2) - 10, _
        500, Int(w_height / 2) - 10
    ' add a chart, the top of which is halfway
    ' down the window
    Set sales_chart = .AddOLEObject(100, _
        Int((w_height / 2)), 500, 300, _
        ClassName:="MSGraph.Chart", Link:=msoFalse)
    ' open the data file, change path as needed
    Set txt_stream = _
        fso.OpenTextFile("G:\sales\sales_q3.txt")
    ' need to overwrite the chart's data with
    ' our own - the datasheet is used for this
    Set sales_datasheet = sales_chart.OLEFormat.Object. _
        Application.DataSheet
    ' insert data into datasheet
    With sales_datasheet
      For row_num = 1 To 4
        data_row = Split(txt_stream.ReadLine, Chr(9))
        .Cells(row_num, 1) = data_row(0)
```

Listing 5.4 (continued)

```
            .Cells(row_num, 2) = data_row(1)
            .Cells(row_num, 3) = data_row(2)
            .Cells(row_num, 4) = data_row(3)
            .Cells(row_num, 5) = data_row(4)
        Next row_num
      End With
      ' the datasheet is now the active window, so
      ' unselect it - which closes it
      ActiveWindow.Selection.Unselect
      ' now back on the slide, select all the objects
      .SelectAll
      ' center the objects, relative to the slide
      With ActiveWindow.Selection
        .ShapeRange.Align _
          msoAlignCenters, True
        .Unselect
      End With
  End With
End With
' close the data file
txt_stream.Close
Exit Sub
err_end:
MsgBox Err.Description
End Sub
```

The add_shapes routine in Listing 5.4 demonstrates several key approaches to working with PowerPoint. The slide and shapes created with the add_shapes routine are displayed in Figure 5.6.

After declaring variables, the first task is to test which view Power-Point is currently in. There are multiple views in PowerPoint; the one needed here is the display of a single slide. The ViewType property of the ActiveWindow is tested and changed if necessary:

```
If ActiveWindow.ViewType <> ppViewSlide Then
  ActiveWindow.ViewType = ppViewSlide
End If
```

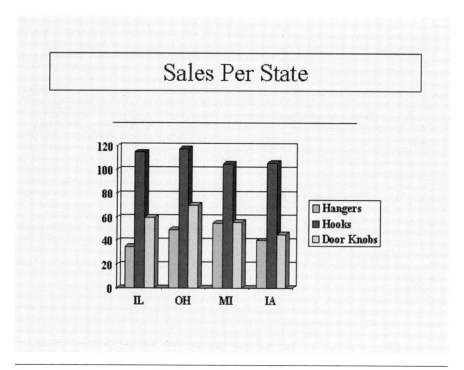

Figure 5.6 Shapes are added to a slide via VBA code

NOTE: PowerPoint offers the following view types: `ppViewHandout-Master`, `ppViewMasterThumbnails`, `ppViewNormal`, `ppView-NotesMaster`, `ppViewNotesPage`, `ppViewOutline`, `ppViewPrintPreview`, `ppViewSlide`, `ppViewSlideMaster`, `ppViewSlideSorter`, `ppViewThumbnails`, and `ppViewTitle-Master`. These represent the various display options in the PowerPoint user interface.

We need the single-slide view in this example because the window's measurements are used for placing shapes on the slide. The next snippet stores the height and width of the window:

```
With ActiveWindow
  w_height = .Height
  w_width = .Width
End With
```

Next a new slide is added to the presentation. It is inserted as the first slide. Its layout will have just a title placeholder:

```
Set newslide = .Slides.Add(1, ppLayoutTitleOnly)
```

The text of the title is updated:

```
' update the text of the title
.Title.TextFrame.TextRange.Text = "Sales Per State"
```

A line is added to the slide with the Add method. The parameter settings set the line up such that it is 400 points long: the difference between the start and end values (500 – 100 = 400). Its vertical placement is set to be 10 points above the window's middle. A chart, which is added next, uses the vertical midpoint as its Top property. Placing the line a little above the midpoint makes for a better appearance on the slide:

```
.AddLine 100, Int(w_height / 2) - 10, _
    500, Int(w_height / 2) - 10
```

NOTE: Bear in mind that the window and the slide are not the same. The document window (the active window) has height and width properties. Slides do not have these properties. When in single-slide view, the midpoints of the window's height and width can be assumed to be the same or reasonably close to the midpoints of the slide.

An OLE object is added. The class parameter sets it as a chart and the link is set as false. The chart is set to sit in the bottom half of the slide by setting the chart's Top property to be half of the window's height: Int(w_height/2).

The data for the chart sits in a text file. The File Scripting Object (FSO) is used to retrieve the data. Once the file is opened, the ReadLine method is used to get a row of data at a time. The data in each row is delimited by a tab, and the Split() function is used to separate the retrieved data into distinct parts. Split() parses the data into separate array elements. A parameter to the Split() function indicates to use the tab character (chr(9)) as the delimiter.

NOTE: See the Appendix for resources on the File Scripting Object.

The data in the sales_q3.txt file consists of a header row and then three data rows. The total number of rows to be read—four—is known, so a loop that iterates four times is used. The `data_row` array is used to hold the results of the split, and the cells of the charts datasheet are updated to the array values.

The datasheet of the chart is addressed by setting the `sales_datasheet` variable to the `OLEFormat.Object.Application.DataSheet` property construct. The activities taking place in the datasheet occur in a separate window, so when the code is finished, the focus is moved off the Datasheet window using the `Unselect` method:

```
Set sales_chart = .AddOLEObject(100, _
    Int((w_height / 2)), 500, 300, _
    ClassName:="MSGraph.Chart", Link:=msoFalse)
' open the data file
Set txt_stream = _
    fso.OpenTextFile("G:\sales\sales_q3.txt")
' need to overwrite the chart's data with
' our own - the datasheet is used for this
Set sales_datasheet = sales_chart.OLEFormat.Object. _
    Application.DataSheet
' insert data into datasheet
With sales_datasheet
  For row_num = 1 To 4
    data_row = Split(txt_stream.ReadLine, Chr(9))
    .Cells(row_num, 1) = data_row(0)
    .Cells(row_num, 2) = data_row(1)
    .Cells(row_num, 3) = data_row(2)
    .Cells(row_num, 4) = data_row(3)
    .Cells(row_num, 5) = data_row(4)
  Next row_num
End With
' the datasheet is now the active window, so
' unselect it - which closes it
ActiveWindow.Selection.Unselect
```

Finally the objects on the slide—the title, line, and chart—are centered relative to each other and relative to the slide. The objects are all selected, then the `Align` method is used with the align type parameter set to centers. The final parameter—set to true—indicates to center relative to the slide:

```
.SelectAll
' center the objects, relative to the slide
With ActiveWindow.Selection
  .ShapeRange.Align _
     msoAlignCenters, True
```

Text Frame, Text Range, and Text

Text is presented on slides within text frames. A text frame can be a text box, a title or subtitle, a bullet list, or a caption of a control. A text frame is synonymous with the control: text box or other. Within the text frame, however, is the text range. It is the text range that contains the actual text as a property. See Figure 5.7.

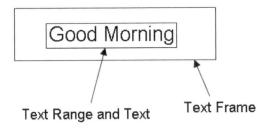

Figure 5.7 Text frame and text range

This notion differs slightly from the usual concept of a text control directly containing the Text property. In PowerPoint, the control has no direct connection to the text. Specifically, there is no Text property of the TextFrame object. The TextFrame object does offer other properties and one method that can manipulate the text. These are summarized in Table 5.3.

The TextRange object, on the other hand, offers a different set of properties and methods, summarized in Table 5.4.

Table 5.3 Selected `TextFrame` properties and method

Property/Method	Comment
`HasText`	Returns true or false
`HorizontalAnchor` `VerticalAnchor`	Returns or sets the horizontal and vertical positioning of the text within the text frame. Various settings such as `msoAnchorCenter` and `msoAnchorTop` are available.
`Orientation`	Returns or sets the orientation of the text within the text frame. Various settings such as `msoTextOrientationHorizontal` and `msoTextOrientationDownward` are available.
`WordWrap`	Returns or sets whether text can wrap within the text frame. True/False.
`DeleteText` (method)	Deletes the text in the text frame

Table 5.4 Selected `TextRange` properties and methods

Property/Method	Comment
`Font`	Returns and sets font properties such as name, size, bold, color, and so on
`Length`	Returns the character length of the text
`Text`	Returns or sets the actual text
`ChangeCase`	Sets the text to the indicated case. Can be one of: `ppCaseLower`, `ppCaseSentence`, `ppCaseTitle`, `ppCaseToggle`, `ppCaseUpper`
`Find`	Finds a string of text
`Replace`	Replaces a string of text

Events

PowerPoint provides events for presentations, slide shows, and windows. All events must be established in class modules and initialized in a standard module. All the events belong to the `Application` object. Table 5.5 summarizes the events by practical function.

The events listed in Table 5.5 are not available until established in a class module and then initialized. Following are the steps to accomplish this.

Table 5.5 Events in PowerPoint

Item	Events
Presentation	AfterNewPresentation AfterPresentationOpen ColorSchemeChanged NewPresentation PresentationBeforeSave PresentationClose PresentationNewSlide PresentationOpen PresentationPrint PresentationSave PresentationSync SlideSelectionChanged
SlideShow	SlideShowBegin SlideShowEnd SlideShowNextBuild SlideShowNextClick SlideShowNextSlide
Window	WindowActivate WindowBeforeDoubleClick WindowBeforeRightClick WindowDeactivate WindowSelectionChange

First insert a class module. The name of the class module is later referenced in the declaration and initialization routine in a standard module, so optionally rename the class module using the Properties window. In this example the class module is renamed to modPowerPointEvents. In the class module, enter this declaration:

```
Public WithEvents app As Application
```

Note that app can be a different name supplied by you. Once the declaration is entered, events for the Application object are available. First select the object, app, from the object drop-down list on the left side of the Code window, then access the various events in the procedure drop-down list on the right side of the Code window. Enter code as needed into event procedures.

Here is a routine that fires on the new slide event. When a new slide is inserted, a message box comes up asking whether to give the slide an alternate background. (Look ahead to Figure 5.9 for a preview.) If the Yes button is clicked, then the new slide receives a grayish background. The color of the background is set with the RGB() function:

```
Private Sub app_PresentationNewSlide(ByVal sld As Slide)
Dim this_slide_index As Integer
Dim slide_background As Integer
If ActiveWindow.ViewType <> ppViewNormal And _
   ActiveWindow.ViewType <> ppViewSlide Then
   ActiveWindow.ViewType = ppViewSlide
End If
this_slide_index = ActiveWindow.View.Slide.SlideIndex
slide_background = _
   MsgBox("Use Alternate Background?", vbYesNo, _
   "Slide Background")
If slide_background = vbYes Then
  ActivePresentation.Slides(this_slide_index).ColorScheme _
     .Colors(ppBackground).RGB = RGB(238, 238, 238)
End If
End Sub
```

The routine in the class module must be initialized in any standard module; enter this declaration and routine:

```
Dim ppt_app As modPowerPointEvents
Public Sub initialize_events()
  Set ppt_app = New modPowerPointEvents
  Set ppt_app.app = Application
End Sub
```

Note that `ppt_app` can be a different name supplied by you. Run the initialization routine to enable the event procedure created in the class module. Figure 5.8 displays what the class module and standard module contain to enable the event procedure.

In the `app_PresentationNewSlide` procedure, the view is changed to slide view if the current view is not slide or normal view. One of these views is necessary to get the slide index (the positional number of the slide), which is stored in the `this_slide_index` variable:

```
If ActiveWindow.ViewType <> ppViewNormal And _
    ActiveWindow.ViewType <> ppViewSlide Then
```

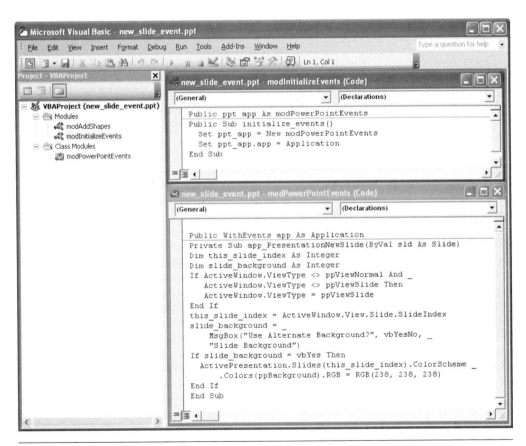

Figure 5.8 A class module and a standard module contain event and initialization procedures

```
    ActiveWindow.ViewType = ppViewSlide
End If
this_slide_index = ActiveWindow.View.Slide.SlideIndex
```

A message box is presented with a yes/no choice of whether to use an alternate background for the new slide. See Figure 5.9. If Yes is clicked, the `Colors` method of the `ColorScheme` property is used to change the color of the slide. The `RGB` property and `RGB()` function are used to set the color. (RGB is an acronym for red, green, blue.) Each of these three colors can receive a value between 0 and 255:

```
slide_background = _
    MsgBox("Use Alternate Background?", vbYesNo, _
    "Slide Background")
If slide_background = vbYes Then
  ActivePresentation.Slides(this_slide_index).ColorScheme _
      .Colors(ppBackground).RGB = RGB(238, 238, 238)
End If
```

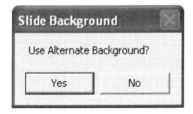

Figure 5.9 Select which background to use

Using VBA with PowerPoint in Design Mode

The likely use of VBA in design mode is to automate tasks involved with standard file or data manipulations. PowerPoint has a rich model for animations and transitions between slides too, but these come into play only during a slide show.

For working in the design environment of PowerPoint, VBA offers great increases in productivity—performing tasks involved in creating and manipulating the presentation. As an example of PowerPoint development in design mode, this section demonstrates creating a PowerPoint file catalog and generator.

Users often create new PowerPoint presentations combining slides from existing presentations. This approach leads users to look haphazardly through numerous presentations to copy just a few desired slides to a new file. In this example, this process is automated to a degree. In particular, VBA is used to open all PowerPoint files in a specified directory, then allow a user to point and click through all the slides to select which to put into a new presentation. There are five routines involved. Two are event procedures: one to run when a new slide is inserted; the other to run when the right mouse button is clicked. Therefore, there is also the initialize event procedure, as described in the preceding section on events. The other two routines handle getting slides into the active presentation file and sending them back out to a new file. First the code, as shown in Listings 5.5 and 5.6.

VERSION NOTE: The `slide_catalog` routine uses the `FileDialog` object to find PowerPoint files for the routine to open. `FileDialog` is available only in PowerPoint 2002 and PowerPoint 2003. For earlier versions, alternative coding methods can be employed to provide the file name(s).

Listing 5.5 The procedures in the `modCatalog` module

```
Public Sub tag_settings()
Dim sld As Slide
For Each sld In ActivePresentation.Slides
  With sld.Tags
    MsgBox "Slide Number = " & sld.SlideIndex & _
       "  Tag Name = " & .Name(1) & _
       "  Tag Value = " & .Value(1)
  End With
Next
End Sub
Public Sub slide_catalog()
On Error GoTo err_end
Dim slide_source As Presentation
Dim slide_target As Presentation
```

Listing 5.5 *(continued)*

```
Dim sld As Slide
Set slide_target = ActivePresentation
Dim fd As FileDialog
Dim tag_flag As Boolean
If ActiveWindow.ViewType <> ppViewSlide Then
   ActiveWindow.ViewType = ppViewSlide
End If
' configure and display the File Picker dialog
' it will show just PowerPoint presentations (.ppt)
Set fd = Application.FileDialog(msoFileDialogFilePicker)
With fd
  .ButtonName = "OK"
  .AllowMultiSelect = True
  .Filters.Clear
  .Filters.Add "PowerPoint Presentations", "*.ppt"
  .InitialFileName = slide_target.Path
  .Title = "Select Presentations"
  If .Show = -1 Then
    ' for each selected file . . .
    For selected_files = 1 To .SelectedItems.Count
      ' check that it is not "this" file, then . . .
      If .SelectedItems(selected_files) <> _
           slide_target.FullName Then
        ' open the file . . .
        Set slide_source = _
        Application.Presentations.Open _
           (.SelectedItems(selected_files))
        ' copy all the slides into "this" presentation
        For Each sld In slide_source.Slides
          sld.Copy
          slide_target.Slides.Paste
        Next
          ' close the presentation that slides were
          ' copied from
          slide_source.Close
      End If
    Next
  End If
End With
```

Listing 5.5 *(continued)*

```
' now have all slides from other presentations
' test each slide if has the Use tag
' if so leave alone, if not then add Use tag with N value
For Each sld In slide_target.Slides
  tag_flag = False
  With sld.Tags
    For check_tags = 1 To .Count
      If .Name(check_tags) = "Use" Then
        tag_flag = True
      End If
    Next
    If tag_flag = False Then
      .Add "Use", "N"
    End If
  End With
Next
Exit Sub
err_end:
MsgBox Err.Description
End Sub
Public Sub create_presentation()
On Error GoTo err_end
Dim msg As String
Dim this_presentation As Presentation
Dim new_presentation As Presentation
Dim sld As Slide
Dim tag_flag As Boolean
Set this_presentation = ActivePresentation
' first test that at least one slide has the
' Use tag set to Y (yes)
tag_flag = False
For Each sld In this_presentation.Slides
  If sld.Tags("Use") = "Y" Then tag_flag = True
Next
If tag_flag = True Then
  ' add a new presentation
  Set new_presentation = Application.Presentations.Add
  ' test the Use tag for each slide
  ' if yes copy the slide and paste in new presentation
  For Each sld In this_presentation.Slides
```

Listing 5.5 *(continued)*

```
    If sld.Tags("Use") = "Y" Then
      sld.Copy
      new_presentation.Slides.Paste
    End If
  Next
  ' finally, close this presentation without saving
  ' and leave user in the new presentation
  this_presentation.Close
Else
  ' inform user that no slides are set to copy
  msg = "No slides in current presentations have been "
  msg = msg & "set for copying to a new presentation. "
  msg = msg & "To do so, right click desired slides and "
  msg = msg & "click the Yes button in the message box."
  MsgBox msg, vbOKOnly, "No slides set for copying"
End If
Exit Sub
err_end:
MsgBox Err.Description
End Sub
```

Listing 5.6 The event procedures in the modPowerPoint events module

```
Public WithEvents app As Application
Private Sub app_PresentationNewSlide(ByVal sld As Slide)
Dim this_slide_index As Integer
If ActiveWindow.ViewType <> ppViewSlide Then
    ActiveWindow.ViewType = ppViewSlide
End If
this_slide_index = ActiveWindow.View.Slide.SlideIndex
' set the Use tag to N
ActivePresentation.Slides(this_slide_index) _
    .Tags.Add "Use", "N"
End Sub
Private Sub app_WindowBeforeRightClick _
    (ByVal Sel As Selection, Cancel As Boolean)
Dim sld_name As String
Dim use_slide As Integer
Dim msg As String
```

Listing 5.6 (continued)

```
If ActiveWindow.ViewType <> ppViewNormal And _
    ActiveWindow.ViewType <> ppViewSlide Then
  msg = "Must be in Normal View or Slide View to "
  msg = msg & "use the Use for Copy feature"
  MsgBox msg, vbOKOnly, "Change View"
  MsgBox ActiveWindow.ViewType
  Exit Sub
End If
this_slide = ActiveWindow.View.Slide.Name
use_slide = MsgBox _
    ("Insert This Slide in New Presentation?", _
    vbYesNo, "Use Slide")
If use_slide = 6 Then
  ActivePresentation.Slides(this_slide).Tags.Add "Use", "Y"
Else
  ActivePresentation.Slides(this_slide).Tags.Add "Use", "N"
End If
End Sub
```

The first step in using this custom catalog application is to initialize the event procedures. To do so, simply run the `initialize_events` procedure in the VBE, or use the Tools...Macros menu. See Figure 5.10.

An important precept of this application is that every slide has a *tag* that indicates whether to include it in a new presentation that is created at the end of processing. The scheme is that slides from various presentations are brought into the current presentation (the catalog) and then only the user-selected slides are copied into a single new presentation. See Figure 5.11.

As each slide is inserted, the `Use` tag property is tested. (`Use` is simply a defined tag name, in this case to mean "Use the slide?") If the `Use` tag is not present, then one is added with a value of N. Although the `slide_catalog` procedure, discussed later, is used to mass-input slides, there is nothing stopping a normal new slide insert. Therefore, the `app_PresentationNewSlide` event is put to use to set the `Use` tag to N for any new slides:

```
Private Sub app_PresentationNewSlide(ByVal sld As Slide)
Dim this_slide_index As Integer
```

Figure 5.10 Run the event initialization first

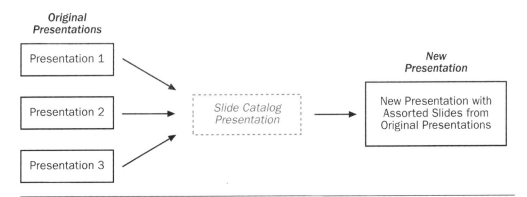

Figure 5.11 The flow of slides in and out of the catalog presentation

```
If ActiveWindow.ViewType <> ppViewSlide Then
   ActiveWindow.ViewType = ppViewSlide
End If
this_slide_index = ActiveWindow.View.Slide.SlideIndex
' set the Use tag to N
ActivePresentation.Slides(this_slide_index) _
    .Tags.Add "Use", "N"
End Sub
```

NOTE: What are tags? Tags are custom objects that are used for maintaining persistent information about a parent object. Tags have two properties: a name and a value. In this example, tags are used with each slide to maintain the yes or no value of whether to use them when creating a new presentation. The `Use` name is set to a value of either Y or N (yes or no).

The `slide_catalog` procedure is used to import slides from other presentations. The procedure starts by displaying the File Picker dialog. See Figure 5.12. The code for presenting the dialog is listed here. (See Chapter 7 for more information on using this dialog.)

```
Set fd = Application.FileDialog(msoFileDialogFilePicker)
With fd
  .ButtonName = "OK"
  .AllowMultiSelect = True
  .Filters.Clear
  .Filters.Add "PowerPoint Presentations", "*.ppt"
  .InitialFileName = slide_target.Path
  .Title = "Select Presentations"
  If .Show = -1 Then
```

Each selected file from the File Picker dialog is opened, and all slides are copied into the catalog presentation. The presentation with the slides to be copied is the `slide_source` and the catalog presentation is the `slide_target`:

```
For selected_files = 1 To .SelectedItems.Count
  ' check that it is not "this" file, then . . .
  If .SelectedItems(selected_files) <> _
      slide_target.FullName Then
```

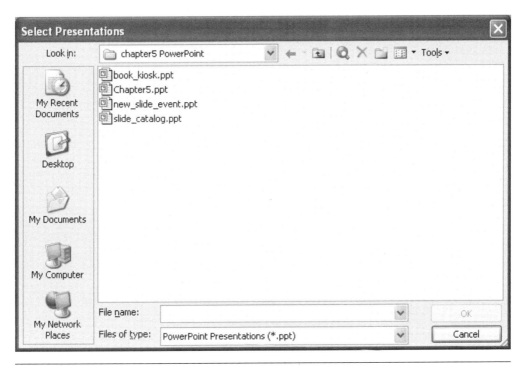

Figure 5.12 Select PowerPoint presentation files

```
' open the file . . .
Set slide_source = _
Application.Presentations.Open _
    (.SelectedItems(selected_files))
' copy all the slides into "this" presentation
For Each sld In slide_source.Slides
  sld.Copy
  slide_target.Slides.Paste
Next
  ' close the presentation that slides were
  ' copied from
  slide_source.Close
```

After all slides are inserted, each slide now in the catalog presentation is tested to see if it has the Use tag. If it does, it is left alone. If it does not, then the Use tag is added and the value is defaulted to N:

```
For Each sld In slide_target.Slides
  tag_flag = False
  With sld.Tags
    For check_tags = 1 To .Count
      If .Name(check_tags) = "Use" Then
        tag_flag = True
      End If
    Next
    If tag_flag = False Then
      .Add "Use", "N"
    End If
  End With
Next
```

In the preceding code, each slide is first tested to see if it has the `Use` tag. The `slide_catalog` routine is independent from the `app_WindowBeforeRightClick` event, which is used to set an individual slide to either Y or N. Possibly, existing slides have already been set to Y with a right-click, so these are left alone.

At this point the catalog presentation is filled with slides, each with a `Use` tag. The next step is for each slide to be manually reviewed and possibly set to be included when a new presentation is created. Slides that are desired need to have their `Use` tag set to the Y value. This is done while looking at slides in the user interface. The `app_WindowBeforeRightClick` event is used for this purpose:

```
Private Sub app_WindowBeforeRightClick _
    (ByVal Sel As Selection, Cancel As Boolean)
Dim sld_name As String
Dim use_slide As Integer
Dim msg As String
If ActiveWindow.ViewType <> ppViewNormal And _
    ActiveWindow.ViewType <> ppViewSlide Then
  msg = "Must be in Normal View or Slide View to "
  msg = msg & "use the Use for Copy feature"
  MsgBox msg, vbOKOnly, "Change View"
  MsgBox ActiveWindow.ViewType
  Exit Sub
End If
this_slide = ActiveWindow.View.Slide.Name
use_slide = MsgBox _
    ("Insert This Slide in New Presentation?", _
    vbYesNo, "Use Slide")
```

```
If use_slide = 6 Then
  ActivePresentation.Slides(this_slide).Tags.Add "Use", "Y"
Else
  ActivePresentation.Slides(this_slide).Tags.Add "Use", "N"
End If
End Sub
```

Figure 5.13 shows the message box that appears when a slide is right-clicked. Remember that every slide has a Use tag already, most or all of them set to N. In the user interface, each slide is now viewed, and if wanted, a right-click allows setting the Use tag to Y.

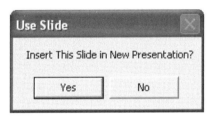

Figure 5.13 User indicates whether to include a slide in a new presentation.

The create_presentation routine creates a new presentation and copies only the slides with the Y value into it. Near the start of the routine, though, a test first sees if there any slides with a Y value:

```
tag_flag = False
For Each sld In this_presentation.Slides
  If sld.Tags("Use") = "Y" Then tag_flag = True
Next
```

If no slides have been set to Y, then a message is returned. See Figure 5.14.

Figure 5.14 A message is returned if no slides have the Use tag set to Y (yes)

If there is at least one slide with a Y value for the Use tag, then a new presentation is created:

```
If tag_flag = True Then
  ' add a new presentation
  Set new_presentation = Application.Presentations.Add
```

Each slide is tested for the Y value. If true, then the slide is copied and pasted into the new presentation:

```
For Each sld In this_presentation.Slides
    If sld.Tags("Use") = "Y" Then
      sld.Copy
      new_presentation.Slides.Paste
    End If
  Next
```

At this point both the catalog presentation and the new presentation are open. All flagged slides have been copied. The catalog presentation is closed, without changes. The new presentation is left open, although it has never yet been saved:

```
this_presentation.Close
```

The user can now save the new file, work on it more, print it, and so on. The presentation is now in the user's control.

An additional routine, tag_settings, is in the catalog presentation. This routine cycles through the slides and reports back each slide's setting of the Use tag. This is an optional routine, available just for checking the tag setting for each slide. See Figure 5.15. Here's the routine:

```
Public Sub tag_settings()
Dim sld As Slide
For Each sld In ActivePresentation.Slides
  With sld.Tags
    MsgBox "Slide Number = " & sld.SlideIndex & _
        "  Tag Name = " & .Name(1) & _
        "  Tag Value = " & .Value(1)
  End With
Next
End Sub
```

Figure 5.15 Returning the setting of the `Use` tag

Using VBA with PowerPoint Slide Shows

Controls are active when running a slide show—meaning that, for example, a command button's click event is enabled. This is in contrast to design mode in PowerPoint, in which control events are not enabled.

A common application of a PowerPoint slide show is to be interactive and informational, responding to requests and left running indefinitely. This type of application is called a *kiosk*. Setting up a kiosk with VBA functionality is explained here.

This is a demonstration of a hypothetical kiosk running in a bookstore. Customers can come to the kiosk and get suggested titles in a category of their choice. There are two "screens" in this kiosk: one where the choice is made, and one with the results. The first screen is displayed in Figure 5.16.

The second screen displays the results. Figure 5.17 shows the results of clicking on the Mystery category.

The shapes on each slide trigger assorted VBA routines when clicked. Table 5.6 summarizes the shapes and the routines, and then Listing 5.7 displays the VBA code routines. These routines sit in a single module in the PowerPoint presentation.

The shapes on the first slide, in Figure 5.16, are visible, except for one. There is a rectangle with its `Fill` property set to `No Fill`. It is sized to cover the entire slide and then it is "Sent to Back" using the Draw properties of PowerPoint.

Consider that when a PowerPoint slide show runs, normally, clicking on a slide advances the show to the next slide. Here, that is not the desired action. Instead, any clicks on the slide should either run a dedicated "category" routine (when a category is clicked on) or do nothing.

Figure 5.16 A customer selects a category

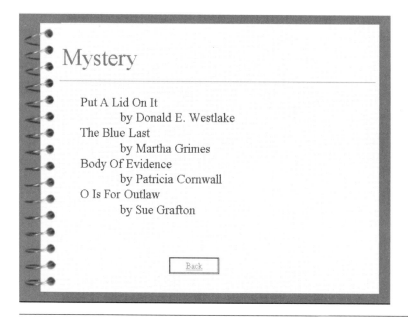

Figure 5.17 A list of suggested titles is returned to the customer

Table 5.6 Shapes and VBA routines in the bookstore kiosk presentation

Slide	Shape	Routine
One	Text Box (Mystery)	`mysteries`
One	Text Box (Science Fiction)	`sci_fi_fantasy`
One	Text Box (Romance)	`romance`
One	Text Box (Western)	`westerns`
One	Button (End Show)	`end_show`
One	Rectangle (not visible)	`do_nothing`
Two	Button (Back)	`go_home`

During design, the rectangle was sized to the slide's dimensions and was also sent to the back of the stack. This lets the category text boxes sit on top of the rectangle. In this manner, any clicks on the slide either run a category routine, or run a do-nothing routine—associated with the rectangle. The purpose of this routine is simply to catch and cancel the action of advancing to the next slide.

Listing 5.7 shows the code used in the slide show.

Listing 5.7 The code behind the slide show

```
Public Sub book_category(category As String)
On Error GoTo err_end
Dim book_db As New ADODB.Connection
Dim rsTitles As New ADODB.Recordset
Dim ssql As String
Dim book_titles As String
' open kiosk database
With book_db
  .Provider = "Microsoft.jet.oledb.4.0"
  .Open (ActivePresentation.Path & "\Kiosk.mdb")
End With
' build ssql to select top titles for supplied category
ssql = "Select Top 4 * From tblTitles Where "
ssql = ssql & "tblTitles.Category=""" & category & """;"
```

Listing 5.7 *(continued)*

```
' open recordset
With rsTitles
  .ActiveConnection = book_db
  .Open (ssql)
End With
' loop through recordset, building text to be
' displayed on slide
book_titles = ""
Do Until rsTitles.EOF
  book_titles = book_titles & rsTitles.Fields("Title") _
      & Chr(13) & Chr(9) & " by " & _
      rsTitles.Fields("Author")
  book_titles = book_titles & Chr(13)
  rsTitles.MoveNext
Loop
' update the slide title
With ActivePresentation.Slides(2).Shapes(1).TextFrame
  .DeleteText
  .TextRange.Text = category
End With

' update the slide text box
With ActivePresentation.Slides(2).Shapes(2).TextFrame
  .DeleteText
  .TextRange.Text = book_titles
End With
' view the slide
SlideShowWindows(1).View.GotoSlide 2
Exit Sub
err_end:
MsgBox Err.Description
End Sub
Public Sub mysteries()
  book_category "Mystery"
End Sub
Public Sub sci_fi_fantasy()
  book_category "Science Fiction/Fantasy"
End Sub
Public Sub romance()
  book_category "Romance"
End Sub
```

Listing 5.7 *(continued)*

```
Public Sub westerns()
  book_category "Western"
End Sub
Public Sub do_nothing()
  MsgBox "Click on a category"
End Sub
Public Sub go_home()
  SlideShowWindows(1).View.GotoSlide 1
End Sub
Public Sub end_show()
  Application.Quit
End Sub
```

The shapes and routines need to be associated. Note that the code routines are not established click events but are independent code routines. Making the connection between a shape and the code it should run is done in design mode. Right-clicking on a shape provides a shortcut menu. See Figure 5.18. One item on it is Action Settings. When this is selected, the Action Settings dialog in Figure 5.19 appears.

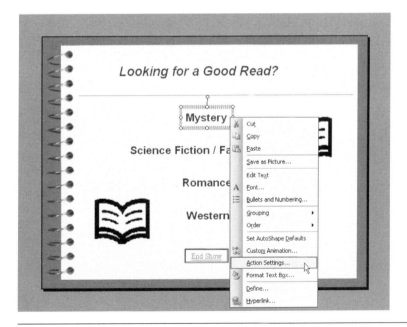

Figure 5.18 Selecting Action Settings from a shape's context menu

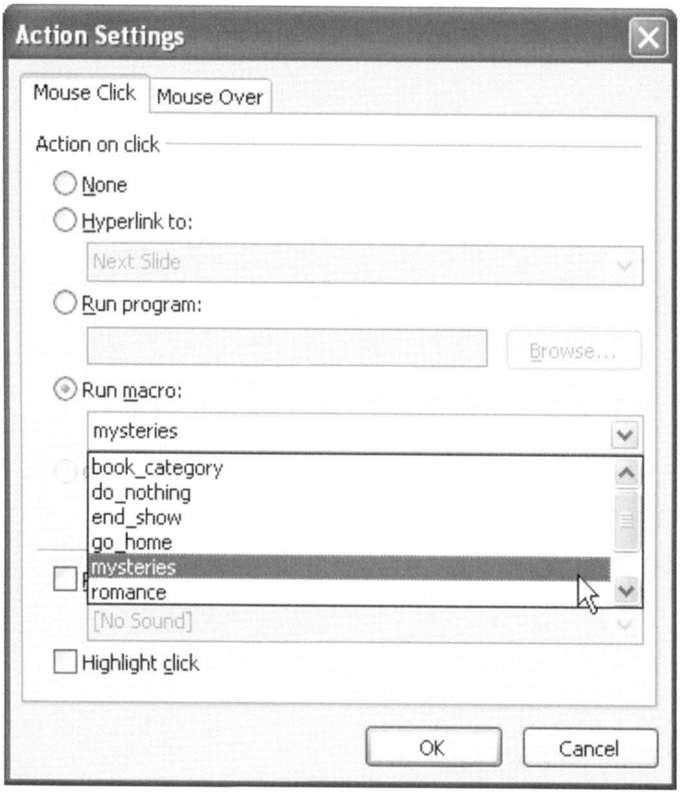

Figure 5.19 Setting a shape to run a routine when clicked

When any of the four categories—Mystery, Science Fiction/Fantasy, Romance, or Western—is clicked, the book_category routine runs, which queries an Access database for titles of the selected category. In this example, the database sits in the same directory as the PowerPoint presentation:

```
With book_db
  .Provider = "Microsoft.jet.oledb.4.0"
  .Open (ActivePresentation.Path & "\Kiosk.mdb")
End With
' build ssql to select top titles for supplied category
ssql = "Select Top 4 * From tblTitles Where "
ssql = ssql & "tblTitles.Category=""" & category & """;"
```

```
' open recordset
With rsTitles
  .ActiveConnection = book_db
  .Open (ssql)
End With
```

Using the returned records, a string is created that will fill the text box on the second slide. Embedded into the string are carriage returns (`Chr(13)`) and tabs (`Chr(9)`) to force the text box to have the desired appearance:

```
book_titles = ""
Do Until rsTitles.EOF
  book_titles = book_titles & rsTitles.Fields("Title") _
      & Chr(13) & Chr(9) & " by " & _
      rsTitles.Fields("Author")
  book_titles = book_titles & Chr(13)
  rsTitles.MoveNext
Loop
```

Finally, the slide is filled. The title box receives the category name and the text box receives the concatenated `book_titles` string, as seen in Figure 5.17. Here is the code:

```
' update the slide title
With ActivePresentation.Slides(2).Shapes(1).TextFrame
  .DeleteText
  .TextRange.Text = category
End With
' update the slide text box
With ActivePresentation.Slides(2).Shapes(2).TextFrame
  .DeleteText
  .TextRange.Text = book_titles
End With
```

The Back button on the second slide returns the slide show to the first slide:

```
SlideShowWindows(1).View.GotoSlide 1
```

NOTE: A reference to an ActiveX Data Objects (ADO) library must be made in order for the kiosk example to work.

Connectivity to an Access database is required. A reference must be set to the ADO library for this to work. See Figure 5.20. To do this:

1. In any code module within PowerPoint, use the Tools...References menu to display the References dialog.
2. Select the Microsoft ActiveX Data Objects (2.x) Library (the version doesn't matter for this example).

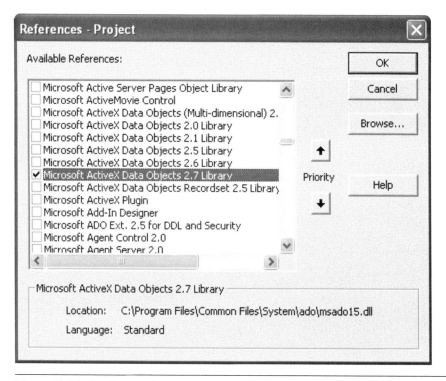

Figure 5.20 Setting a reference to ADO

Summary

PowerPoint is a powerful product that combines excellent graphics ability with controllable user interaction. The use of slides and shapes can be manipulated with VBA, and certainly more functionality is available than is apparent from typical user-level product use. Slides can act as containers for a number of objects, with which users can interact.

PowerPoint is used in two ways: for slide repositories and for slide shows. VBA can be applied to either mode to create unique applications.

In Chapter 13, a case study is presented in which data in Excel is used in the creation of charts on PowerPoint slides.

CHAPTER 6

Outlook Solution Development

VERSION NOTE: This material works for all versions of Outlook, except where noted.

Outlook serves as the e-mail/contact management/calendar utility in many businesses. Structurally, Outlook is organized as a collection of folders, which in turn store items. There are several *types* of folders: most store a certain default *type* of item, as well as being able to store other item types. The types of items are mail messages, appointments, contacts, meeting requests, journal entries, notes, and more. These are discussed further in the appropriate sections of this chapter.

Outlook is a blend of database, messaging system, and scheduler. In this regard, there are many interesting ways to apply Outlook past the standard user interface. For example, although Outlook stores contacts and e-mail messages, a custom solution could be built that checks contacts against e-mail activity and reports back on contacts with whom correspondence has not occurred within a specified amount of time.

Objects, Properties, and Methods

The `Application` Object

Development with Outlook is limited to a single project environment, and as such there are no methods to open and close files, or similar activities typical of the multiple-project environments in, say, Word or Excel.

On the other hand, the `Application` object in Outlook does offer useful methods and properties designed for unique Outlook development tasks. Some of the properties and methods are listed in Table 6.1.

Table 6.1 Selected properties and methods of the `Application` object

Property/Method	Comment
Explorers object collection **ActiveExplorer method**	An `Explorer` represents the window in which the contents of a folder is displayed.
Inspectors object collection **ActiveInspector method**	An `Inspector` represents the window in which a single Outlook item is displayed.
ActiveWindow method	Represents the topmost Outlook window, which is either an `Explorer` or an `Inspector`.
AdvancedSearch method	Performs search within specified Outlook folders for items based on supplied criteria.
CreateItem method **CreateItemFromTemplate method**	Creates new Outlook items, such as a message, an appointment, a contact, and others.
GetNamespace method **Session property**	Either of these returns the current MAPI session name.

Both `Explorers` and `Inspectors` are representations of the contents shown in a window. Under most circumstances, there is one `Explorer` and one or more `Inspectors` open. For example, the Inbox may be the current folder displayed in Outlook, and perhaps three e-mail messages are currently open. In this scenario, there are one `Explorer` and three `Inspectors`. In Figure 6.1, the Windows Taskbar shows that Outlook is open to the Inbox and three messages are open.

The count of `Explorers` and `Inspectors` can be confirmed with code such as this:

```
With Application
  MsgBox .Explorers.Count & "Explorer(s) open"
  MsgBox .Inspectors.Count & "Inspector(s) open"
End With
```

Figure 6.1 Outlook in use

The `examine_application` routine shown in Listing 6.1 reports on the state of `Explorers`, `Inspectors`, and the active window.

Listing 6.1 Properties of the `Application` object

```
Public Sub examine_application()
On Error GoTo err_end
Dim msg As String
With Application
  If .Explorers.Count > 0 Then
    If .Explorers.Count = 1 Then
      msg = "There is " & .Explorers.Count & _
        " open Explorer. "
    Else
      msg = "There are " & .Explorers.Count & _
        " open Explorers. "
    End If
    msg = msg & " The Active Explorer's Current View is "
    msg = msg & .ActiveExplorer.CurrentView & ". "
  End If
  If .Inspectors.Count > 0 Then
    If .Inspectors.Count = 1 Then
      msg = msg & "There is " & .Inspectors.Count & _
        " open Inspector. "
    Else
      msg = msg & "There are " & .Inspectors.Count & _
        " open Inspectors. "
    End If
    msg = msg & " The Active Inspector's Current Item is "
    msg = msg & .ActiveInspector.CurrentItem & ". "
  End If
  msg = msg & "The Active Window is " & .ActiveWindow & "."
  MsgBox msg
End With
Exit Sub
err_end:
MsgBox Err.Description
End Sub
```

The `examine_application` routine produces the message box shown in Figure 6.2. The results are based on the same open e-mail messages as seen in Figure 6.1.

Figure 6.2 Explorers, Inspectors, and the active window

Advanced Search

VERSION NOTE: Advanced Search is a feature available in Outlook 2002 and Outlook 2003.

Advanced Search is a powerful search tool that accepts multiple criteria and returns results in the Results property of the SearchObject object.

Using Advanced Search involves setting up a search in a separate procedure and then working with the results in the AdvancedSearch-Complete application event handler. Because the event handler is fired at the completion of a search, a first, separate procedure is needed to initiate the search.

NOTE: Application event handlers are available in the ThisOutlook-Session module. See the Project Explorer in Figure 6.3.

Here is an example of asking for user input to search the Subject field of messages in the Inbox and reporting the results via code in the event handler. Listing 6.2 shows the first routine, which initiates the search.

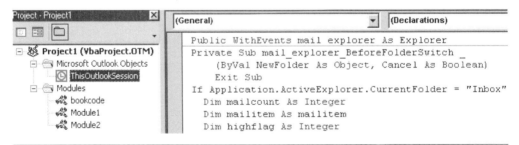

Figure 6.3 The ThisOutlookSession module contains application-level event handlers

Listing 6.2 Initiating an advanced search in Outlook

```
Public Sub advanced_search()
On Error GoTo err_end
Dim objSearch As Search
Dim search_scope As String
Dim search_crit As String
Dim search_results As Results
Dim criteria_input As String
' where to search . . .
search_scope = "'Inbox'"
' ask user what to search for . . .
criteria_input = InputBox("Enter Search String", "Search")
' use LIKE and wildcard(%) for search
search_crit = "urn:schemas:mailheader:subject LIKE '%" _
    & criteria_input & "%'"
With Application
  Set objSearch = _
      .AdvancedSearch(search_scope, search_crit, _
      True, "My Search")
End With
Exit Sub
err_end:
MsgBox Err.Description
End Sub
```

In Listing 6.2, a user is prompted to enter a string to use in the search:

```
criteria_input = InputBox("Enter Search String", "Search")
```

Then, a pseudo-SQL string is set up:

```
search_crit = "urn:schemas:mailheader:subject LIKE '%" _
    & criteria_input & "%'"
```

The criteria are assembled with DASL syntax (Distributed Authoring Search and Location—see the Appendix for resources). The LIKE keyword is used along with the percent sign (%)—used as a wildcard character. The search_crit variable ends up holding the search instruction. Figure 6.4 shows user input into the routine via the Input box.

Clicking the OK button causes the search to proceed. Here is the line of code that runs the search:

Figure 6.4 Asking for user-supplied search criteria

```
Set objSearch = _
    .AdvancedSearch(search_scope, search_crit, _
    True, "My Search")
```

At the start of the routine, the objSearch variable was established as a Search object. The AdvancedSearch method takes four parameters:

```
expression.AdvancedSearch(Scope, Filter, SearchSubFolders, Tag)
```

The parameters are used to indicate:

1. Where to search
2. What to search for
3. Whether to search in subfolders
4. A name for the search

Only the first parameter, Scope, is required. In the preceding example, these parameters have been set as:

1. Inbox
2. Any text in the Subject lines of the messages in the Inbox that have at least "Visual Basic" in them
3. False, do not search in subfolders
4. The search is named "My Search"

The search runs and the Application_AdvancedSearch-Complete routine handles the results. Listing 6.3 shows the code of the event handler.

Listing 6.3 Processing the results of a search

```
Private Sub Application_AdvancedSearchComplete _
    (ByVal SearchObject As Search)
On Error GoTo err_end
Dim show_results As Integer
Dim search_results As Results
Set search_results = SearchObject.Results
If search_results.Count = 0 Then
  MsgBox "No items found"
Else
  For show_results = 1 To search_results.Count
    open_this = MsgBox _
      (search_results(show_results).Subject & "   " & _
          search_results(show_results).SenderName _
          , vbYesNo, "Open this message?")
    If open_this = vbYes Then
      MsgBox Left(search_results(show_results).Body, 200)
    End If
  Next show_results
End If
Exit Sub
err_end:
MsgBox Err.Description
End Sub
```

NOTE: Certain programmed procedures will cause the warning dialog shown in Figure 6.5 to appear. This dialog is part of the Outlook E-Mail Security Update, which is functionality Microsoft has incorporated into Outlook to disarm malicious e-mail viruses. The dialog allows overriding its protection for up to ten minutes; however, this is only done manually via the dialog. It is not possible to override the protection programmatically.

In the event handler, a `Results` object variable holds the search object's results:

```
Dim search_results As Results
Set search_results = SearchObject.Results
```

Figure 6.5 E-mail security at work

The Count property holds the count of found items. If there are no results, a message appears stating so:

```
If search_results.Count = 0 Then
  MsgBox "No items found"
```

When there are results, further processing loops through the Results collection and displays the subject and sender of the message. With this information comes the choice of whether to see more, as shown in Figure 6.6.

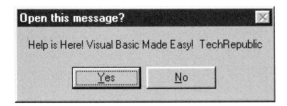

Figure 6.6 Results of the search

This is the code that displays the message box seen in Figure 6.6:

```
open_this = MsgBox _
    (search_results(show_results).Subject & "  " & _
        search_results(show_results).SenderName _
        , vbYesNo, "Open this message?")
```

Clicking Yes displays the first two hundred characters of the e-mail message in a message box. The `Left()` function is used to filter to the first two hundred characters. The text is delivered from the `Body` property of the message:

```
If open_this = vbYes Then
    MsgBox Left(search_results(show_results).Body, 200)
```

Figure 6.7 shows the first two hundred characters of the message.

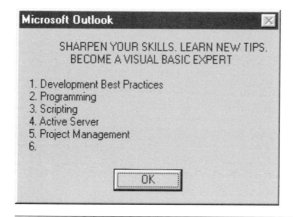

Figure 6.7 Displaying a portion of the body of an e-mail message

`AdvancedSearch` is capable of complex queries. Of importance are the values used for `Scope` and `Filter` parameters: where to search and what to search for.

This example looks in the StudioB folder for any messages from Neil about Excel:

```
search_scope = "'StudioB'"
search_filter = "urn:schemas:httpmail:fromname LIKE " & _
"'%Neil%' AND urn:schemas:httpmail:subject LIKE '%Excel%'"
With Application
  Set objSearch = _
      .AdvancedSearch(search_scope, search_filter, _
      True, "My Search")
End With
```

This next example looks in the Inbox for any messages with "XML" in the subject that were received in the last seven days:

```
search_scope = "'Inbox'"
search_filter = _
"%last7days(""urn:schemas:httpmail:datereceived"")% " & _
"AND ""urn:schemas:httpmail:subject"" LIKE '%XML%'"
With Application
  Set objSearch = _
      .AdvancedSearch(search_scope, search_filter, _
      True, "My Search")
End With
```

The `CreateItem` Method

The `CreateItem` method is used in the creation of new Outlook items. An item can be one of several available types. The `CreateItem` method is needed to create new items programmatically. The following code snippet shows how the `CreateItem` method creates items of various types:

```
With Application
  .CreateItem (olAppointmentItem) ' Appointment
  .CreateItem (olContactItem) ' Contact
  .CreateItem (olDistributionListItem) ' Distribution List
  .CreateItem (olJournalItem) ' Journal Entry
  .CreateItem (olMailItem) ' E-mail message
  .CreateItem (olNoteItem) ' Note
  .CreateItem (olPostItem) ' Post
  .CreateItem (olTaskItem) ' Task
End With
```

For example, to create a new contact, code such as this is used:

```
Dim new_contact As ContactItem
Set new_contact = Application.CreateItem(olContactItem)
With new_contact
    .FirstName ="John"
    .LastName = "Smith"
    .Save
End With
```

The `CreateItem` method is used in examples later in this chapter.

The NameSpace Object

In Outlook, the NameSpace object represents the current communication session. There is just one type available for the NameSpace object: MAPI (Mail Application Programming Interface, or Mail API). The NameSpace object either is set to a variable using the GetNamespace method or is referred to using the Session property of the Application object. Either of these two lines of code will accomplish the same thing:

```
Set OL_namespace = Application.GetNamespace(Type:="MAPI")
Set OL_namespace = Application.Session
```

The NameSpace object allows access to two useful collections: AddressLists and Folders. Other properties and methods offer pertinent information and actions.

The examine_namespace routine shown in Listing 6.4 uses some of the properties and methods of the NameSpace object.

Listing 6.4 Using properties and methods of the NameSpace object

```
Public Sub examine_namespace()
On Error GoTo err_end
' variables for NameSpace; Folder Name, and Folder ID
Dim OL_namespace As NameSpace
Dim MAPI_folder As MAPIFolder
Dim folder_id As String
' set variable to NameSpace
Set OL_namespace = Application.GetNamespace(Type:="MAPI")
' Display user, number of folders, and number of addr lists
With OL_namespace
  MsgBox .CurrentUser
  MsgBox "Folders: " & .Folders.Count
  MsgBox "Address Lists: " & .AddressLists.Count
  On Error Resume Next
  ' the PickFolder method displays a dialog box
  ' in which a folder is selected
  folder_id = .PickFolder.EntryID
  On Error GoTo err_end
  ' if a folder is selected, then display the
  ' number of items in the folder
  If Len(folder_id) > 0 Then
```

Listing 6.4 *(continued)*

```
   MsgBox .GetFolderFromID(folder_id).Items.Count & _
      " items are in the " & _
         .GetFolderFromID(folder_id) & " folder."
  Else
    MsgBox "No Folder Selected"
  End If
End With
Exit Sub
err_end:
MsgBox Err.Description
End Sub
```

In Listing 6.4, the `OL_namespace` variable is set to the `NameSpace` object:

```
Set OL_namespace = Application.GetNamespace(Type:="MAPI")
```

Certain information is returned from the `NameSpace` object. In particular, the current user name is returned, and then the counts from two collections are returned. The `Folders` collection returns the number of folders. The `AddressLists` collection encompasses various lists found in the Address Book:

```
With OL_namespace
  MsgBox .CurrentUser
  MsgBox "Folders: " & .Folders.Count
  MsgBox "Address Lists: " & .AddressLists.Count
```

Note that in this example the returned folders count is representative of just top-level folders. There are subfolders that are not accounted for here. Folders are discussed later in this chapter.

The number of address lists can vary greatly, depending on the deployment of Outlook. In a corporate environment, there may be dozens of address lists.

The `PickFolder` method of the `NameSpace` object displays a dialog of available Outlook folders, from which one can be selected. See Figure 6.8.

Folders can be identified by name or by a system ID number. In this example, the ID of the selected folder is stored in the `folder_id` variable, by accessing the `EntryID` property. Just prior to displaying the dia-

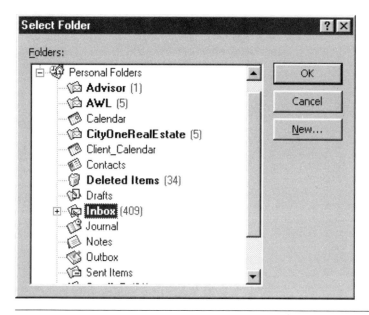

Figure 6.8 Select an Outlook folder

log, the error trap is set to Resume Next. This is done for the case where the Cancel button is clicked in the dialog.

Assuming a folder is selected, the GetFolderFromID method and the Items.Count property are used to return the number of items in the selected folder:

```
On Error Resume Next
' the PickFolder method displays a dialog box
' in which a folder is selected
folder_id = .PickFolder.EntryID
On Error GoTo err_end
' if a folder is selected, then display the
' number of items in the folder
If Len(folder_id) > 0 Then
  MsgBox .GetFolderFromID(folder_id).Items.Count & _
      " items are in the " & _
        .GetFolderFromID(folder_id) & " folder."
Else
  MsgBox "No Folder Selected"
End If
```

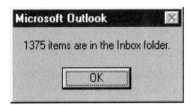

Figure 6.9 The count of items in the selected folder

The results are viewed in the message box shown in Figure 6.9.

Further methods of the `NameSpace` object are used to identify folders, as seen in the following section on folders.

Folders

In Outlook there is a set of default folders that includes standard items such as the Calendar, the Contacts list, and the Inbox. Users have the option to create additional personal and public folders.

Outlook folders are based on a different concept than typical file-based folders. For example, in a computer's file system, a folder can house any type of file. In Outlook, most folders are based on a single default item type. For example, the Calendar is a folder that holds appointment items. The Contacts folder holds contacts. By contrast, the Deleted Items folder contains a mixture of item types.

Folders are maintained in a hierarchy. There are top-level folders and then levels of subfolders underneath. See Figure 6.10.

Note the levels of folders seen in Figure 6.10. Here there are two top-level folders: Archive Folders and Personal Folders (Outlook Today). Underneath these are further folders. Going deeper, the Inbox folder has subfolders. The counts in parentheses show how many unread items are in a folder.

Listing 6.5 shows how to work with Outlook folders using VBA.

Figure 6.10 The folder structure in Outlook

Listing 6.5 Examining Outlook folders

```
Public Sub examine_folders()
Dim OL_namespace As NameSpace
Dim MAPI_folder As MAPIFolder
Set OL_namespace = Application.GetNamespace(Type:="MAPI")
' return information about top-level folders
For Each MAPI_folder In OL_namespace.Folders
  MsgBox "Name:  " & MAPI_folder.Name & _
    ", Item Count: " & MAPI_folder.Items.Count & ". " & _
    " This folder has " & MAPI_folder.Folders.Count & _
    " sub folders."
Next
' return the item count in the Inbox
Set MAPI_folder = _
  OL_namespace.GetDefaultFolder(olFolderInbox)
MsgBox "Inbox has " & _
  MAPI_folder.Items.Count & " items."
```

Listing 6.5 *(continued)*

```
' return the item count in the Calendar
Set MAPI_folder = _
  OL_namespace.GetDefaultFolder(olFolderCalendar)
MsgBox "Calendar has " & _
  MAPI_folder.Items.Count & " items."
' return the item count in Contacts
Set MAPI_folder = _
  OL_namespace.GetDefaultFolder(olFolderContacts)
MsgBox "Contacts has " & _
  MAPI_folder.Items.Count & " items."
' return the item count in the Outbox
Set MAPI_folder = _
  OL_namespace.GetDefaultFolder(olFolderOutbox)
MsgBox "Outbox has " & _
  MAPI_folder.Items.Count & " items."
' return the item count of Tasks
Set MAPI_folder = _
  OL_namespace.GetDefaultFolder(olFolderTasks)
MsgBox "Tasks has " & _
  MAPI_folder.Items.Count & " items."
End Sub
```

In the `examine_folders` routine in Listing 6.5, a `For Each...` `Next` loop returns information on each of the top-level folders:

```
' return information about top-level folders
For Each MAPI_folder In OL_namespace.Folders
  MsgBox "Name:  " & MAPI_folder.Name & _
    ", Item Count: " & MAPI_folder.Items.Count & ". " & _
    " This folder has " & MAPI_folder.Folders.Count & _
    " sub folders."
Next
```

The information returned is the name, item count, and folder (subfolder) count. See Figure 6.11.

Further in the `examine_folders` routine, the `GetDefault-Folder` method is used to reference some of the standard folders. For each of these, the item count is returned. For example, this snippet returns the item count for Contacts:

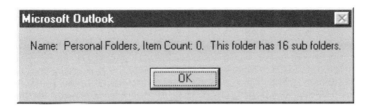

Figure 6.11 Returned information about a top-level folder

```
' return the item count in Contacts
Set MAPI_folder = _
  OL_namespace.GetDefaultFolder(olFolderContacts)
MsgBox "Contacts has " & _
  MAPI_folder.Items.Count & " items."
```

The count of folder items is returned in a message box. See Figure 6.12.

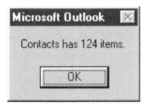

Figure 6.12 The count of folder items is displayed

The GetDefaultFolder method returns a reference to any of the standard Outlook folders. Table 6.2 lists the standard folders, along with each folder's numerical and constant identifiers, and the type of item each folder uses.

Working with E-mail

Outlook, of course, is mostly regarded as an e-mail program. Of the various Outlook item types, the Mail type is the default for four of the standard folders. Working with events in which Mail items are addressed provides ways to respond to activity that involves e-mail.

Table 6.2 Summary of default folders in Outlook

Folder	Constant	Number	Default Item Type
Inbox	`olFolderInbox`	6	Mail
Outbox	`olFolderOutbox`	4	Mail
Drafts	`olFolderDrafts`	16	Mail
Sent Items	`olFolderSentMail`	5	Mail
Calendar	`olFolderCalendar`	9	Appointment
Contacts	`olFolderContacts`	10	Contact
Tasks	`olFolderTasks`	13	Task
Notes	`olFolderNotes`	12	Note
Journal	`olFolderJournal`	11	Journal
Deleted Items	`olFolderDeletedItems`	3	All Items

Two of the `Application` event handlers are of use here: `NewMail` and `ItemSend`. Listing 6.6 shows code that is placed in the `Application_NewMail` event handler. The routine is fired as e-mail arrives.

The `Application_NewMail` procedure in Listing 6.6 is used as an e-mail routing utility. Incoming e-mails that have "Guru" in the subject are routed to the Guru folder; incoming e-mails that have "Advisor" in the subject are routed to the Advisor folder.

There are two object variable references to folders (the type is `MAPI-Folder`): `fldr` is set to the Inbox, and `personal_fldrs` is set to Personal Folders. The Guru and Advisor folders are not at the same level in the folder hierarchy and are handled slightly differently further in the routine. Refer to Figure 6.10 for the hierarchy of folders that are used in this example.

Regardless of the destination of an e-mail, it first lands in the Inbox. An assumption could be made that the last item in the `Items` collection of the Inbox is the latest message. However, this is not a guarantee. To make sure the latest e-mail is being examined, the `Items` are sorted descending by the Received timestamp. This ensures that the latest item is the first in the collection. The `True` parameter of the `Sort` method indicates to sort descending.

Listing 6.6 Using the `NewMail` event to organize incoming e-mail

```
Private Sub Application_NewMail()
Dim nmsp As NameSpace
Dim fldr As MAPIFolder
Dim personal_fldrs As MAPIFolder
Dim this_subject As String
Dim mail_items As Items
On Error GoTo err_end
Set nmsp = Application.GetNamespace("MAPI")
Set fldr = nmsp.GetDefaultFolder(olFolderInbox)
Set personal_fldrs = nmsp.Folders("Personal Folders")
With fldr
  ' sort the Inbox in descending order
  ' on the Received field
  Set mail_items = .Items
  mail_items.Sort "Received", True
  ' get the subject from the latest message
  ' the latest message just arrived . . . its arrival
  ' fired this event
  this_subject = mail_items(1).Subject
  If InStr(1, this_subject, "Guru") > 0 Then
      mail_items(1).Move fldr.Folders("Guru")
  End If
  If InStr(1, this_subject, "Advisor") > 0 Then
      mail_items(1).Move personal_fldrs.Folders("Advisor")
  End If
End With
Exit Sub
err_end:
MsgBox Err.Description
End Sub
```

```
With fldr
  ' sort the Inbox in descending order
  ' on the Received field
  Set mail_items = .Items
  mail_items.Sort "Received", True
```

The `Subject` property is tested using the `Instr()` function. If the word "Guru" is in the subject, then the e-mail is moved to the Guru folder. The Guru folder is a subfolder of the Inbox and appears in the `Folders` collection of the Inbox. The `fldr` variable is assigned as the Inbox. The `Move` method moves the first mail item:

```
this_subject = mail_items(1).Subject
If InStr(1, this_subject, "Guru") > 0 Then
    mail_items(1).Move fldr.Folders("Guru")
End If
```

If the subject has the word "Advisor", then the e-mail is moved to the Advisor folder. However, the Advisor folder is not a subfolder of the Inbox. The Advisor folder is a subfolder of Personal Folders:

```
If InStr(1, this_subject, "Advisor") > 0 Then
    mail_items(1).Move personal_fldrs.Folders("Advisor")
End If
```

Working with Contacts, Distribution Lists, and the Calendar

The `update_from_xml` routine presented in this section demonstrates adding contacts, creating a distribution list, and setting appointments. The routine reads data from an XML file. The value of the XML root element becomes the distribution list name.

Contacts are stored in the XML file as elements with a number of attributes. The attributes are for first name, last name, e-mail address, city, phone number, a flag whether to save the person as a contact in Outlook, and another flag whether to include the person in the Outlook distribution list. Last, within any person's `Contact` element, a child element, `Appointment`, *may* exist. If it does, then the Outlook Calendar is updated with the values found in the attributes of the `Appointment` element. Listing 6.7 shows the XML file.

Listing 6.7 The XML file that will be imported into Outlook

```
<?xml version="1.0"?>
<BakerCompany>
<Contact FirstName="David" LastName="Smith"
   EMail="dsmith@not-a-real-site.com"
   City="Hartford" Phone="(860)886-0656"
   set_as_contact="True"
   set_in_distribution="True"/>
```

Listing 6.7 *(continued)*

```
<Contact FirstName="Doyle" LastName="Smythe"
    EMail="dsmythe@not-a-real-site.com"
    City="Hartford" Phone="(860)886-0652"
    set_as_contact="False"
    set_in_distribution="True">
    <Appointment Start="10/16/2003 10:00:00 AM"
        End="10/16/2003 10:30:00 AM"
        Subject="Meet and Greet"/>
</Contact>
<Contact FirstName="Daryl" LastName="Southington"
    EMail="dsouth@not-a-real-site.com"
    City="New Haven" Phone="(203)508-0585"
    set_as_contact="True"
    set_in_distribution="True"/>
<Contact FirstName="Don" LastName="South"
    EMail="dsouth2@not-a-real-site.com"
    City="Hartford" Phone="(860)886-0642"
    set_as_contact="True"
    set_in_distribution="False"/>
</BakerCompany>
```

The root element contains the value "BakerCompany". This becomes the name of the distribution list. Examining the first contact, David Smith, shows that his city is Hartford. His e-mail address and phone number are included as well. David will become an individual contact, and he will be included in the distribution list, because both of these flags are true.

In contrast, the next contact, Doyle Smythe, will be in the distribution list but will not become an individual contact, because that particular flag is set to false. However, Doyle is the only contact in the XML file that has a child `Appointment` element. An appointment will be created for Doyle.

The VBA code that processes the XML is shown in Listing 6.8.

Listing 6.8 Creating contacts, distribution lists, and appointments

```
Public Sub update_from_xml()
On Error GoTo err_end
' Outlook variables
Dim OL_namespace As NameSpace
```

Listing 6.8 *(continued)*

```
Dim this_email As MailItem
Dim dist_list As DistListItem
Dim new_contact As ContactItem
Dim new_appt As AppointmentItem
' XML variables
Dim names_xml As DOMDocument
Dim node_list As IXMLDOMNodeList
Dim node_contact As IXMLDOMNode
' set the namespace
Set OL_namespace = Application.GetNamespace(Type:="MAPI")
' create mail item
' note: the mail item is used in a temporary fashion
' to build the recipient list
Set this_email = Application.CreateItem(olMailItem)
' create the distribution list item
Set dist_list = _
   Application.CreateItem(olDistributionListItem)
' Set and load the XML file
' the XML file contains data about contacts -
' name/e-mail/city/phone, and appointment info
Set names_xml = New DOMDocument
With names_xml
  .async = False
  .Load ("C:\kb\ol_add_dist.xml") ' change path as needed
End With
' put contacts into node list
Set node_list = names_xml.getElementsByTagName("Contact")
For Each node_contact In node_list
  ' attributes for each contact are . . .
  ' 0 - first name
  ' 1 - last name
  ' 2 - e-mail
  ' 3 - city
  ' 4 - phone
  ' 5 - flag to create as Outlook contact
  ' 6 - flag to include in distribution list
  With node_contact
    ' create contact flag is true . . .
    If .Attributes(5).Text = "True" Then
      Set new_contact = _
        Application.CreateItem(olContactItem)
```

Listing 6.8 *(continued)*

```
  With new_contact
    .FirstName = node_contact.Attributes(0).Text
    .LastName = node_contact.Attributes(1).Text
    .Email1Address = node_contact.Attributes(2).Text
    .BusinessAddressCity = _
      node_contact.Attributes(3).Text
    .BusinessTelephoneNumber = _
      node_contact.Attributes(4).Text
    .Save
  End With
End If
' if include in distribution flag is true . . .
If .Attributes(6).Text = "True" Then
  this_email.Recipients.Add _
    node_contact.Attributes(2).Text
End If
' if there is an appointment element . . .
If .childNodes.Length > 0 Then
' has appointment info
  ' assemble first and last name into "full name"
  prospect = _
    .Attributes(0).Text & " " & .Attributes(1).Text
  ' create new appointment item
  Set new_appt = _
    Application.CreateItem(olAppointmentItem)
  With new_appt
    .Start = _
      node_contact.childNodes(0).Attributes(0).Text
    .End = _
      node_contact.childNodes(0).Attributes(1).Text
    .Subject = _
      node_contact.childNodes(0).Attributes(2).Text
    .Location = _
      "Conference Room"
    .Body = "Meeting with " & prospect
    .Save
  End With
End If
End With
Next
```

Listing 6.8 *(continued)*

```
With dist_list
   ' copy Recipient list from mail item to distribution list
   .AddMembers this_email.Recipients
   ' distribution list is pulled from document element
   .DLName = names_xml.documentElement.baseName
   .Save
End With
MsgBox "Finished processing XML file"
Exit Sub
err_end:
MsgBox Err.Description
End Sub
```

This routine makes use of the MSXML Parser. A reference must be set to it for the routine to work. The version does not matter. See Figure 6.13.

NOTE: The `update_from_xml` routine uses both VBA and XML DOM coding. See the Appendix for resources on the MSXML Parser.

In the `update_from_xml` routine, a mail item is created. It is used in the routine to help build a recipient list, because `Recipients` is a collection that belongs to the mail item. No actual e-mail is sent; the e-mail item serves as a temporary recipient list holder. A distribution item is also created:

```
Set this_email = Application.CreateItem(olMailItem)
' create the distribution list item
Set dist_list = _
   Application.CreateItem(olDistributionListItem)
```

The XML file is set to an object variable named `names_xml`:

```
Set names_xml = New DOMDocument
With names_xml
   .async = False
   .Load ("C:\kb\ol_add_dist.xml") ' change path as needed
End With
```

The contact elements in the XML file are gathered into a "node list":

```
Set node_list = names_xml.getElementsByTagName("Contact")
```

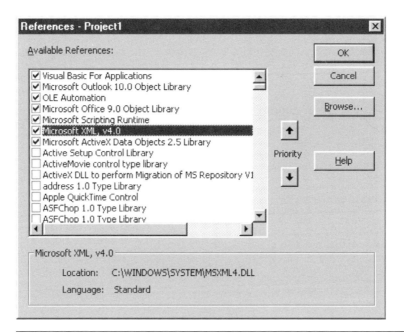

Figure 6.13 Set a reference to the MSXML Parser

Each contact is addressed within a `For Each...Next` loop. The `node_contact` variable holds each current contact through the iterations of the loop. The flag for processing the (XML) contact into an Outlook contact is tested. If true, then a new Outlook contact item is created and various properties are seeded from the XML data:

```
If .Attributes(5).Text = "True" Then
  Set new_contact = _
     Application.CreateItem(olContactItem)
  With new_contact
    .FirstName = node_contact.Attributes(0).Text
    .LastName = node_contact.Attributes(1).Text
    .Email1Address = node_contact.Attributes(2).Text
    .BusinessAddressCity = _
       node_contact.Attributes(3).Text
    .BusinessTelephoneNumber = _
       node_contact.Attributes(4).Text
    .Save
  End With
End If
```

Whether or not the XML contact became an Outlook contact, the XML contact is tested for inclusion in the Outlook distribution list. If the distribution flag is set to true, then the contact's e-mail address is added to the distribution list. The flag value, true or false, is held in the seventh attribute and the e-mail address is held in the third attribute. Attributes use a zero-based index, so the index numbers are 6 and 2, respectively:

```
If .Attributes(6).Text = "True" Then
   this_email.Recipients.Add _
      node_contact.Attributes(2).Text
End If
```

Note that when a contact is added to the distribution list, the action performed right after the flag test is to add the contact to the `Recipients` collection of the mail item. The contact is not directly added to the distribution list. Rather, at the end of the routine, the `Recipients` collection is wedded to the distribution list in one step.

Before that, though, contacts are still being processed. A third test is done to see if there is appointment information in the XML data. If there is, it sits in a child element of the contact. To check this, the presence of child elements is tested. This particular XML file will have either no children or just one child—an appointment. The count of child elements is tested. Note that in DOM syntax, the `Length` property is actually the count:

```
If .childNodes.Length > 0 Then
```

When there is appointment data in the XML file, then an appointment item is created and the appropriate data populates the properties of the item. The `Location` property, however, is hard-coded to the "Conference Room":

```
prospect = _
   .Attributes(0).Text & " " & .Attributes(1).Text
' create new appointment item
Set new_appt = _
   Application.CreateItem(olAppointmentItem)
With new_appt
   .Start = _
      node_contact.childNodes(0).Attributes(0).Text
   .End = _
      node_contact.childNodes(0).Attributes(1).Text
```

```
        .Subject = _
           node_contact.childNodes(0).Attributes(2).Text
        .Location = _
           "Conference Room"
        .Body = "Meeting with " & prospect
        .Save
     End With
```

Finally, after all XML contacts have been processed, the distribution list is completed. The individuals to be included in the list are copied en masse from the mail item `Recipients` collection to the distribution item via the `AddMembers` method. The distribution list name is assigned to the XML root element:

```
With dist_list
    ' copy Recipient list from mail item to distribution list
    .AddMembers this_email.Recipients
    ' distribution list is pulled from document element
    .DLName = names_xml.documentElement.baseName
    .Save
End With
```

In the Contacts folder, the new contacts and distribution list are found. David Smith, Daryl Southington, and Don South are new contacts. Doyle Smythe was not flagged to become an individual contact. Figure 6.14 shows the three new contacts, as well as the absence of Doyle Smythe.

Smith, David
Hartford
Business: (860) 886-0656
E-mail: dsmith@not-a-real-site.com

South, Don
Hartford
Business: (860) 886-0642
E-mail: dsouth2@not-a-real-site.com

Southington, Daryl
New Haven
Business: (203) 508-0585
E-mail: dsouth@not-a-real-site.com

Figure 6.14 New Outlook contacts

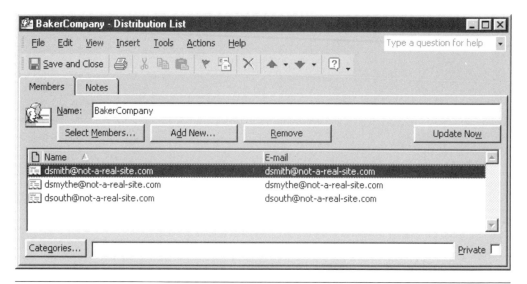

Figure 6.15 The new distribution list

The BakerCompany distribution list has also been created and populated with the e-mail addresses of David Smith, Doyle Smythe, and Daryl Southington, but not Don South—according to the flag settings in the XML file. See Figure 6.15.

Events

Application events are available by default. Outlook 2000 has these Application events: `ItemSend`, `NewMail`, `OptionPagesAdd`, `Quit`, `Reminder`, and `Startup`. Outlook 2002 adds these additional events to the list: `AdvancedSearchComplete`, `AdvancedSearchStopped`, and `MAPILogonComplete`. Outlook 2003 has one new additional event: `NewMailEx`.

Events are available for objects other than the `Application` object. Objects such as `Folders`, `Explorers`, `Inspectors`, and `Items` gain new functionality by exposing the events with the use of the `WithEvents` keyword.

To gain access to these events, a declaration must be made in a class module. This module can be either the `ThisOutlookSession` module or a class module you create. Here, for example, is a declaration to make the events available for an `Explorer` object:

```
Public WithEvents mail_explorer As Explorer
```

Once the declaration is in place, the events for the object are available in the procedure list for the object. See Figure 6.16. Note that each object type has a specific list of events, although many events are available to more than one object type.

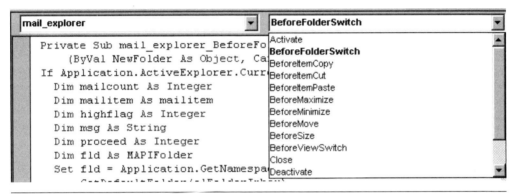

Figure 6.16 Events made available with the `WithEvents` keyword for an `Explorer` object

Listing 6.10 (on the next page) shows a routine that will fire on the Explorer's `BeforeFolderSwitch` event. Although an event handler is written, it will not run unless initialized. To initialize the event handler, the code in Listing 6.9 must be entered and run. Listing 6.9 shows both a declaration and a routine.

Listing 6.9 Initializing an event handler

```
Dim myEvents As New ThisOutlookSession
Sub initialize_events()
Set myEvents.mail_explorer = Application.Explorers.Item(1)
End Sub
```

Note that in the declaration the `New` keyword forces `myEvents` to be an instance of `ThisOutlookSession`. `ThisOutlookSession` happens to be the default class module for Outlook. Then within the `initialize_` `events` routine, the `mail_explorer` member of the class module is set to Explorer item 1. In use, this Explorer ends up containing whichever folder is current. The actual event handler is shown in Listing 6.10. Running the `initialize_events` routine in Listing 6.9 "turns on" the event handler.

Listing 6.10 The Explorer's `BeforeFolderSwitch` event handler

```
Private Sub mail_explorer_BeforeFolderSwitch _
    (ByVal NewFolder As Object, Cancel As Boolean)
If Application.ActiveExplorer.CurrentFolder = "Inbox" Then
  Dim mailcount As Integer
  Dim mailitem As mailitem
  Dim highflag As Integer
  Dim msg As String
  Dim msg_title As String
  Dim proceed As Integer
  Dim fld As MAPIFolder
  Set fld = Application.GetNamespace("MAPI") _
    .GetDefaultFolder(olFolderInbox)
  highflag = 0
  With fld
    For Each mailitem In .Items
      If mailitem.Importance = olImportanceHigh And _
        mailitem.UnRead = True Then
          highflag = highflag + 1
      End If
    Next
  End With
  If highflag > 0 Then
    msg = "There are unread messages in your Inbox " & _
     "flagged with HIGH Importance. Do you still " & _
     "wish to leave your Inbox?"
    msg_title = highflag & "HIGH IMPORTANCE Messages"
    proceed = MsgBox(msg, vbYesNo, msg_title)
    If proceed = vbNo Then
      Cancel = True
    End If
  End If
End If
End Sub
```

As a separate procedure seen here, the `initialize_events` routine runs upon some deliberate action such as a button click. However, the code within the `initialize_events` routine could also sit within another event handler. For example, the code could be contained within the `Application_Startup` event (which does not need a separate initialization). In this configuration, just starting Outlook would run the code to initialize the `BeforeFolderSwitch` event handler in Listing 6.10.

The purpose of this event handler is to see if there are messages in the Inbox that are high importance but have not been read yet. The test for this occurs when leaving the Inbox. The current folder displayed in the Explorer is tested to see if it is the Inbox. If it is, then a further test looks for high-importance, unread messages. If any are found, then the user is alerted and given the choice to stay in the Inbox.

In the routine a variable is set to the Inbox:

```
Set fld = Application.GetNamespace("MAPI") _
    .GetDefaultFolder(olFolderInbox)
```

Also a counter, `highflag`, is initialized to zero. This counter increments when high-importance, unread messages are found:

```
highflag = 0
```

All messages in the Inbox are examined. If the conditions are true for any individual message, then the `highflag` counter is incremented:

```
With fld
  For Each mailitem In .Items
    If mailitem.Importance = olImportanceHigh And _
        mailitem.UnRead = True Then
          highflag = highflag + 1
    End If
  Next
End With
```

After all messages are tested, if `highflag` is greater than zero, a message box prompts the user about the messages and whether to cancel the event of switching folders:

```
If highflag > 0 Then
  msg = "There are unread messages in your Inbox " & _
    "flagged with HIGH Importance. Do you still " & _
    "wish to leave your Inbox?"
  msg_title = highflag & "HIGH IMPORTANCE Messages"
```

```
      proceed = MsgBox(msg, vbYesNo, msg_title)
      If proceed = vbNo Then
        Cancel = True
      End If
  End If
```

The prompt the user sees is shown in Figure 6.17. If the No button is clicked, the `Cancel` argument is set to true and the folder switch does not occur.

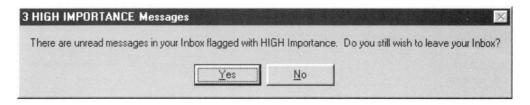

Figure 6.17 A message box prompts whether to stay in the Inbox to read important messages

Summary

The combination of uses offered by Outlook—contact management, scheduling, e-mail functionality, and more—allows great flexibility for designing custom solutions. An understanding of the key objects and methodologies used in Outlook is critical to the design of such solutions. As seen in this chapter, there are quite a few powerful and productive features beyond what is seen in the user interface. Additional solution building with Outlook is possible with the inclusion of Collaboration Data Objects (CDO). Using CDO allows interaction with the Exchange server—useful for solutions that involve companywide initiatives. See the Appendix for resources on Collaboration Data Objects.

PART II

Office Technologies

CHAPTER 7

Common Microsoft Office Objects

VERSION NOTE: The Microsoft Office Object Library is available to all versions of Office. File search and command bars are available in all versions. The `FileDialog` object is available only in Office XP and Office 2003.

File search, file dialogs, and customizable command bars are available to all Office products (but not to InfoPath). There is a `FileSearch` object and a `FileDialog` object. There are `CommandBar` objects as well as a `CommandBars` collection. Using these objects requires a reference to the Office Object Library. See Figure 7.1. The referenced library could be version 9 (Office 2000), version 10 (Office XP), or version 11 (Office 2003).

Note that although these tools are available to all Office products, the implementation may differ slightly from product to product. This variation is explained further in the following pages. The file search and command bar features are available to all versions of Office (2000 and newer). The file dialogs were introduced in Office XP.

File Search

File search is a built-in Office functionality that performs searches for files based on a number of different criteria points. File search only *identifies* files that are found based on the criteria. Further action requires further coding.

The typical expected criteria are the path to look in and the file name pattern to match (for example, "*.xls" will look for all Excel files). There are additional criteria settings that can be applied to the search.

Let's start with a simple file search routine, as shown in Listing 7.1.

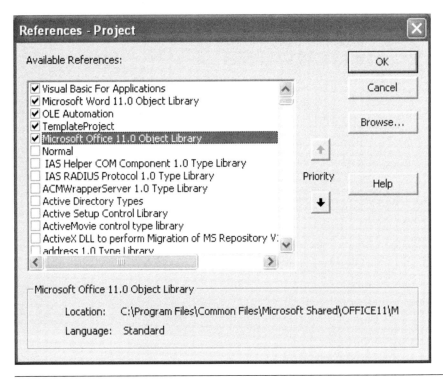

Figure 7.1 A reference to the Microsoft Office Object Library must be in place

Listing 7.1 A basic file search

```
Public Sub look_for_files_simple()
Dim myFileSearch As FileSearch
Set myFileSearch = Application.FileSearch
With myFileSearch
  .NewSearch
  .LookIn = "C:\My Documents"
  .SearchSubFolders = True
  .Filename = "*.Doc"
  If .Execute() > 0 Then
    For Each myFile In .FoundFiles
      MsgBox myFile
    Next
  End If
End With
End Sub
```

Let's pick this code apart and see what's happening. First, a variable is set to represent a `FileSearch` object. The variable name `myFileSearch` is used for this purpose. The rest of the routine makes use of `myFileSearch` with the `With...End With` construct. Within the construct the following occurs:

- **`.NewSearch`**—this informs the `FileSearch` to "let go" of any criteria from the previous search (whether there actually was one or not). The default is that searches are remembered, so unless you are sure of any criteria you wish to persist to the next search, use `.NewSearch` to clear out the criteria.

- **`.LookIn`**—this is where you indicate the path to look in. For a wider search, indicate a wider path. For example, you can just enter "C:\" to search all of a C drive.

- **`.SearchSubFolders`**—takes a true or false setting. Searching subfolders widens the search. The default is *not* to search in subfolders. So if you must widen the search into subfolders, include this setting in the code.

- **`.Filename`**—is used to set a pattern for the files being searched. The use of wildcards offers powerful and flexible ways of using the `Filename` property. For example, while a pattern of "*.doc" searches for all Word documents, a pattern of "A*.doc" returns only Word documents that start with the letter "A". A pattern of "???.doc" finds all Word documents that have a file name that is three characters long (before the .doc extension). A pattern of "A??.doc" finds all Word documents that have a file name that is three characters long (before the .doc extension), with the first of the three characters being the letter "A".

NOTE: The `Filename` property makes use of standard wildcard characters. These are an asterisk (*) to indicate any number of characters and a question mark (?) to specifically indicate any single character. A pattern of "???" returns any combination of three characters. A pattern of "*" returns any string of characters.

Wildcard pattern matching is quite helpful, too, when applied with some fixed characters. The definitive example of this is to mix a wildcard pattern with a file extension, such as "*.doc", which returns all files with the .doc extension. The flip side of this, and also quite useful, is to search for all files that have a certain name, regardless of file type. For example, "Arizona*.*" returns all files that have a name beginning with "Arizona". All of the following would be returned with the "Arizona*.*" search pattern: Arizona.doc, Arizona.xls. Arizona_trip.doc, Arizona15.jpg, and Arizona Meeting Agenda.txt.

The `Filename` property is optional. Its exclusion limits the search to only the standard Office file types (.doc, .xls, and so on). Other file types will not be returned in the search.

■ **`.Execute`**—performs the search. A number is returned indicating the number of found files. Therefore, it is typical to wrap this in a test to see if the number is greater than zero. If there are found files, then further processing can be done with them. In Listing 7.1, a few lines of code simply display the names of the found files when the number of found files is greater than zero:

```
If .Execute() > 0 Then
   For Each myFile In .FoundFiles
      MsgBox myFile
   Next
End If
```

A returned number of zero files may have just as much significance for your purposes. The absence of files may be just the condition you are looking for.

The next example is a more fully developed file search routine. This routine asks the user to input the path to search in. As such, the routine is not hard-coded to one path. Another prompt asks for a string of text (a word or phrase) to search for. This phrase can be in the body of the file or in the document properties of the file. This is accomplished with the `TextOrProperty` property. Note that this does *not* test to see if the phrase is in the actual file name. Further code must be developed to test the file name itself.

As for the file pattern to search for, the code senses which Office application it is running in and then limits the search to any files that are of the current type (for example, *.ppt if running in PowerPoint). Listing 7.2 shows the full routine; a detailed discussion follows.

Listing 7.2 A richer file search routine

```
Public Sub look_for_files_complex()
' these three variables hold user input
Dim this_path As String
Dim text_to_search_for As String
Dim search_from_date As Date
' this variable is filled from application.name property
Dim this_ext As String
' these two variables are used to prompt for a path
Dim input_prompt_path As String
Dim input_title_path As String
' these two variables are used to prompt for search phrase
Dim input_prompt_text As String
Dim input_title_text As String
' these two variables are used to prompt for search date
Dim input_prompt_date As String
Dim input_title_date As String
' this variable is used when validating the supplied path
Dim this_current_directory As String
' object variable
Dim myFileSearch As FileSearch
' error trapping
On Error GoTo err_end
' this select case statement determines the correct
' file extension to use based on which application
' this actual code is running in
Select Case Application.Name
  Case "Microsoft Access"
     this_ext = ".mdb"
  Case "Microsoft Excel"
     this_ext = ".xls"
  Case "Microsoft PowerPoint"
     this_ext = ".ppt"
  Case "Microsoft Word"
     this_ext = ".doc"
End Select
' have user supply a path (if blank, use the current dir)
input_prompt_path = "Enter a path to search in - "
input_prompt_path = _
  input_prompt_path & "ex. C:\My Documents"
input_title_path = "Enter Search Path"
```

Listing 7.2 *(continued)*

```
this_path = InputBox(input_prompt_path, input_title_path, _
    "C:\My Documents")
' have user supply a phrase (if blank, skip this criterion)
input_prompt_text = "Enter a word or phrase to search for"
input_title_text = "Enter Search Phrase"
this_text = InputBox(input_prompt_text, input_title_text)
' validate supplied path, if one supplied
If Len(this_path) <> 0 Then
  ' test the path, first the current directory
  ' is saved, then setting the supplied path to be
  ' the current directory is tested
  this_current_directory = CurDir
  ' prepare for this to cause an error
  On Error GoTo err_in_path
  ChDir this_path
  ' back to general error routine
  On Error GoTo err_end
  ' change back to original current directory
  ChDir this_current_directory
Else
  ' if no supplied path then set variable to current dir
  this_path = CurDir
End If ' If Len(this_path) <> 0
' end of validation
' initialize myFileSearch variable
Set myFileSearch = Application.FileSearch
With myFileSearch
  .NewSearch
  .LookIn = this_path
  .SearchSubFolders = True
  .Filename = "*" & this_ext
  If Len(this_text) > 0 Then
    .TextOrProperty = this_text
  End If
  If .Execute() > 0 Then
    For Each myFile In .FoundFiles
      ' put any processing here that you need!
      MsgBox myFile
    Next
  End If
End With
```

Listing 7.2 (continued)

```
' normal ending here
Exit Sub
err_in_path:
' change back to original current directory
ChDir this_current_directory
' alert with specific message
MsgBox this_path & " is not a valid path. Try again."
Exit Sub
err_end:
' this will trap any other error
MsgBox "This error occurred: " & Err.Description
End Sub
```

First a number of variables are set. Then error trapping is turned on with this statement:

```
On Error GoTo err_end
```

err_end is a label in the code, located at the end of the routine. This line tells the routine to go to err_end if any error occurs. err_end simply displays a message saying that an error has occurred and the error's description. The code at the end of the routine looks like this:

```
err_end:
' this will trap any other error
MsgBox "This error occurred: " & Err.Description
```

Next, the type of file to search for is determined. All of the Office products return their name with the use of the Application.Name property. A Select Case construct is used with this property to determine the correct file extension. The this_ext variable holds the file extension:

```
Select Case Application.Name
  Case "Microsoft Access"
    this_ext = ".mdb"
  Case "Microsoft Excel"
    this_ext = ".xls"
  Case "Microsoft PowerPoint"
    this_ext = ".ppt"
  Case "Microsoft Word"
    this_ext = ".doc"
End Select
```

Next, the user is prompted to supply two pieces of information: one is a path to search in, and the other is a phrase to search for. These two input boxes are shown in Figures 7.2 and 7.3, respectively.

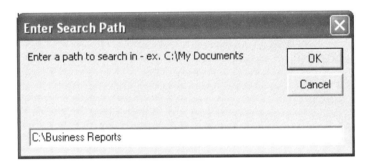

Figure 7.2 A search path is entered

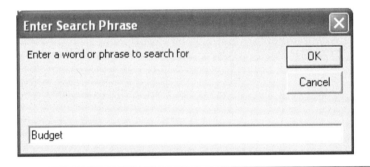

Figure 7.3 A search phrase is entered

The code that prepares and displays the input boxes is this:

```
' have user supply a path (if blank, use the current dir)
input_prompt_path = "Enter a path to search in - "
input_prompt_path = _
  input_prompt_path & "ex. C:\My Documents"
input_title_path = "Enter Search Path"
this_path = InputBox(input_prompt_path, input_title_path, _
  "C:\My Documents")
' have user supply a phrase (if blank, skip this criterion)
input_prompt_text = "Enter a word or phrase to search for"
input_title_text = "Enter Search Phrase"
this_text = InputBox(input_prompt_text, input_title_text)
```

For each input box, a prompt message and a box title are set. The first input box opens with a supplied default value ("C:\My Documents").

NOTE: Bear in mind that allowing a user to enter a path is inefficient and prone to mistakes—not to mention that many people won't even know what to do. It is wiser to provide a list box, a drop-down list, or an Explorer-like tree to choose the path from. The problem here is that the code in this example is not based on a form that allows such controls. The controls needed for a better interface (such as a list box or a tree) can only be used within a "host" or container, such as a form or a command bar. The InputBox() function does not offer this functionality.

The supplied path is validated. First it is tested for length.

```
If Len(this_path) <> 0 Then
```

If the length is greater than zero, then a test must be performed to see if it is a good path. There is no VBA built-in function to test a path, so a little extra code does the trick. First the current directory (CurDir) is stored in the this_current_directory variable. A new error trap, On Error GoTo err_in_path, is established. Then Change Directory (ChDir) is used to change to the supplied path. If this is not successful because the supplied path is not valid, then the processing is directed to the specific err_in_path trap. This error routine differs from the previous one only because it returns a specific message about the invalid directory:

```
this_current_directory = CurDir
' prepare for this to cause an error
On Error GoTo err_in_path
ChDir this_path
```

If the supplied path *is* valid, then the code is not redirected to err_in_path. Two things are left to do. One is to reestablish the general error trap, and the other is to return the system to the stored current directory:

```
' back to general error routine
On Error GoTo err_end
' change back to original current directory
ChDir this_current_directory
```

The current directory and the path to search in do not have to be the same. In fact, they have nothing to do with each other. The only reason this code stores and returns to the current directory is because it is just good programming practice. It has no effect on the file search.

Finally, if the supplied path has a zero length, then the current directory is established as the path to search in. This is not a great fix, because the current directory may be one that contains no files of interest. Still, some path needs to be supplied, so it is better than nothing.

```
Else
  ' if no supplied path then set variable to current dir
  this_path = CurDir
End If ' If Len(this_path) <> 0
```

An alternative in this routine could be to keep forcing the user to enter paths until one is determined as valid. In other words, the code could be rewritten to consider zero length to be invalid.

To continue, validation is complete; it's time to search for files. First the `myFileSearch` variable is initialized. The reason for waiting until now to initialize the variable is that there is no point in doing so until after validation:

```
' initialize myFileSearch variable
Set myFileSearch = Application.FileSearch
```

Finally, the file search is performed:

```
With myFileSearch
  .NewSearch
  .LookIn = this_path
  .SearchSubFolders = True
  .Filename = "*" & this_ext
  If Len(this_text) > 0 Then
    .TextOrProperty = this_text
  End If
  If .Execute() > 0 Then
    For Each myFile In .FoundFiles
      ' put any processing here that you need!
      MsgBox myFile
    Next
  End If
End With
```

Note that the determined file extension is appended to an asterisk to create the needed wildcard.ext pattern (such as "*.xls"). Also note that the `.TextOrProperty` property is set to the `this_text` string. This string, which was prompted with the input box shown in Figure 7.3, has not been validated. The entered string is not validated; however, the length of the entry is. As long as the length of the entry is greater than zero, then the string is used.

Two other properties are worth noting here: `FileType` and `Last-Modified`. They are coded this way:

```
.FileType = msoFileTypePowerPointPresentations
.LastModified = msoLastModifiedThisMonth
```

`FileType` can be used as an alternative to the `Filename` property. Instead of establishing a search pattern with `Filename`, `FileType` recognizes these constants:

msoFileTypeAllFiles

msoFileTypeDatabases

msoFileTypeExcelWorkbooks

msoFileTypePowerPointPresentations

msoFileTypeWordDocuments

msoFileTypeTemplates

msoFileTypeOfficeFiles

The last constant, *msoFileTypeOfficeFiles*, is the default. It is used for the pattern matching when no other `FileType` is set *and* when the `Filename` property is also not used.

I recommend using only a few of the constants—in particular the ones that apply to a typical user file type, such *msoExcelWorkbooks*. The default *msoFileTypeOfficeFiles* not only finds standard Office files but also finds templates and HTML files. It is not likely that a search would be meant to find so many file types. The same holds true for *msoFileTypeAllFiles*. This will find all files, including executables (.exe) and other files not likely to be of use to your users.

The `LastModified` property provides a useful feature in that searches can be performed with dates. It is not uncommon to forget what a file name is or where the file is stored, but to remember the file type and the fact that it was recently saved. The constants for `LastModified` are:

```
msoLastModifiedAnyTime
msoLastModifiedLastMonth
msoLastModifiedLastWeek
msoLastModifiedThisMonth
msoLastModifiedThisWeek
msoLastModifiedToday
msoLastModifiedYesterday
```

The default value is *msoLastModifiedAnyTime*.

File Dialogs

VERSION NOTE: Microsoft Office Object Library file dialogs are available only in Office XP and Office 2003.

The `FileDialog` object allows developers to present and use four different dialog boxes. These are the common Open and Save As dialogs, as well as a File Picker and a Folder Picker. The latter two are typically used as browse dialogs. Implementing these dialogs via code differs from the typical user-interface activity because these are under the control of your code.

With each of the four dialogs, the user selection(s) are available through the `SelectedItems` property. The action(s) you wish to take based on these returned selections depend on further code development. However, two of the dialogs, Open and Save As, allow instant processing by the system by using the `Execute` method.

Table 7.1 lists pertinent properties and methods of the `FileDialog` object.

The four dialogs are coded in a nearly identical manner. A good way to call them is to use a `With . . . End With` construct:

```
With Application.FileDialog(msoFileDialogSaveAs)
      ' your coding here
End With
```

or

Table 7.1 Properties and methods of the `FileDialog` object

Property/Method	Comment
AllowMultiSelect property	True/False. Allows selecting more than one item in a list. Available with the Open and File Picker dialogs.
ButtonName property	Each dialog has two buttons: an action button and a cancel button. This property sets the caption on the action button.
DialogType property	Returns the type of dialog box that is running. This is useful when a choice of action is needed based on the type of dialog.
Execute method	For the Open and Save As dialogs, forces the dialog to take the respective open or save as action immediately when the action button is clicked.
Filters property	Used for establishing which file types appear in the File of Type list in a dialog. Available for the Open and File Picker dialogs.
InitialFileName property	Sets the default path or file name: For the Open and File Picker dialogs, initializes the dialog to the supplied path. If a valid file name is included in the path, then the file is selected in the dialog. For the Folder Picker dialog, initializes the dialog to the folder. For the Save As dialog, initializes the dialog to the supplied path. If a file name is included, then the file name is automatically entered in the dialog.
SelectedItems property	Returns the selected items as a collection.
Show method	Makes the dialog visible and active.
Title property	Each dialog has a title that can be set using this property.

```
Dim fd As FileDialog
Set fd = Application.FileDialog(msoFileDialogFilePicker)
With fd
    ' your coding here
End With
```

The type of dialog to display is determined by the supplied built-in constant. These are:

msoFileDialogOpen

msoFileDialogSaveAs

msoFileDialogFilePicker

msoFileDialogFolderPicker

which represent the Open, Save As, File Picker, and Folder Picker dialogs, respectively.

Listing 7.3 shows an example of initializing and presenting the Open dialog.

Listing 7.3 Displaying the File Open dialog

```
With Application.FileDialog(msoFileDialogOpen)
  .AllowMultiSelect = True
  .ButtonName = "Open Budget(s)"
  .Filters.Clear
  .Filters.Add "Excel Files", "*.xls"
  .InitialFileName = "C:\Budget\"
  .Title = "Budget Worksheets"
  .Show
  .Execute
End With
```

The code in Listing 7.3 sets some properties and then displays the dialog. First the `AllowMultiSelect` property is set to true. This enables selecting multiple files in the dialog by holding down the Shift or Control keys. The caption of the action button is customized. The Files of Type list is first cleared with the `Clear` method of the `Filters` property. Then one file type is established: Excel files in this example. The title of the dialog is customized. Finally, the `Show` method displays the dialog. The dialog stays open until either the action button is clicked or the dialog is otherwise closed. In this example, the `Execute` method is invoked, there-

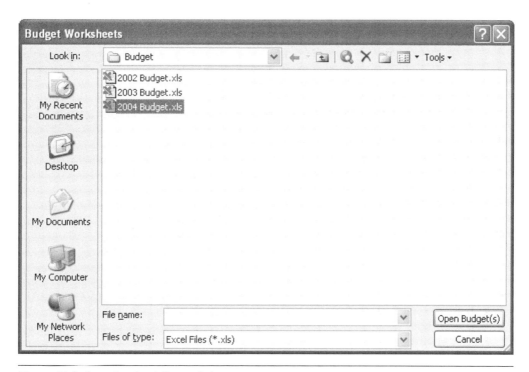

Figure 7.4 A customized Open dialog

fore opening any selected files when the action button is clicked. Figure 7.4 is a display of this dialog. It is titled, captioned, filtered, and set to the path as indicated in the Listing 7.3 code.

In the next example, shown in Listing 7.4, the File Picker dialog is displayed. The code construct is nearly identical except that there is no Execute method in the code. Execute is available only for the Open and Save As dialogs. Instead, the SelectedItems property is used to address the selected file(s).

Listing 7.4 Displaying the File Picker dialog

```
Dim fd As FileDialog
Set fd = Application.FileDialog(msoFileDialogFilePicker)
With fd
  .ButtonName = "OK"
  .AllowMultiSelect = True
  .Filters.Clear
```

Listing 7.4 *(continued)*

```
.Filters.Add "Word Files", "*.doc"
.Filters.Add "Text Files", "*.txt"
.Filters.Add "HTML Files", "*.html"
.InitialFileName = "C:\Software Survey\"
.Title = "Survey Files"
If .Show = -1 Then
  For selected_files = 1 To .SelectedItems.Count
    MsgBox .SelectedItems(selected_files)
  Next
End If
End With
```

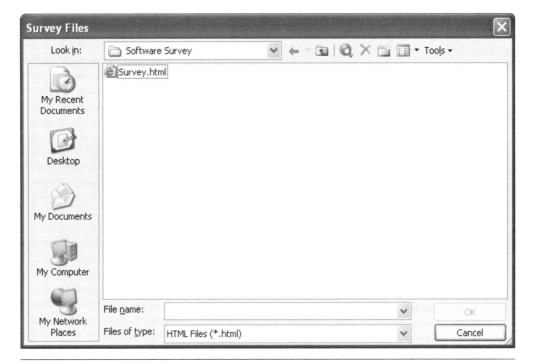

Figure 7.5 A customized File Picker dialog

The code in Listing 7.4 is similar to the code in Listing 7.3, with a few key changes. Three filters have been included for the Files of Type list: .doc, .html., and .txt. Once selections have been made in the dialog and the action button is clicked, the selections are available in the `Selected-Items` property. See Figure 7.5. In this example, a loop is established using the `Count` property, and each item is returned in a message box. Any other action depends on further code development.

Command Bars

A command bar is an object that appears as a toolbar or a menu bar. Another type of command bar is the pop-up, but that is a confusing term because most of us consider a pop-up to be a type of form (or message box, and so on) that appears as a top window following some action. With respect to command bars, however, a pop-up is either the functionality to create cascading menus on a menu bar, or it is a shortcut menu typically displayed with a right mouse click.

Custom toolbars and menu bars are quite useful in initiating relevant procedures in custom solutions. They provide an excellent means to make needed functionality easy to access while preserving screen real estate. You can set their name, position, and placement of controls, and they can be made visible or hidden as needed.

NOTE: The distinction between a toolbar and a menu bar is minor. A menu bar displays text, and a toolbar displays buttons with pictures. However, a menu bar can display text in a cascading menu, and a toolbar can display text. Both toolbars and menu bars offer built-in or custom functionality.

The `CommandBars` collection includes the command bars themselves, and each command bar has a collection of controls that are placed on it. These controls differ from standard controls not so much in their use but in the way they are addressed and implemented. Standard form-based controls have several events, such as `onClick`, `onChange`, `Before-Update`, and more. Command bar controls have but the single `On-Action` event handler.

Following is the VBA code to set up a command bar. This particular one takes a numerical input and returns a value based on a selected mathematical function. The mathematical functions are standard in VBA. This command bar is generic enough to work in any Office application, with minor modifications as pointed out later. Figure 7.6 shows the command bar when it is set up and visible.

Figure 7.6 A command bar with a combo box control and an edit control

The command bar, named "Math Functions", has just two controls: a combo box that displays a list of math functions and an edit control into which a number is typed. Once a number is entered, pressing the Tab key or the Enter key runs the code that produces the mathematical answer.

Two sections of code are provided here to make this happen. One code procedure creates the command bar. The second set of code is the event handler—it runs as a result of pressing Tab or Enter. The second set of code is set to the OnAction property of the edit control. The first procedure, which creates the command bar, is shown in Listing 7.5.

Listing 7.5 Creating a command bar

```
Sub create_commandbar()
On Error Resume Next
CommandBars("Math Functions").Delete
On Error GoTo err_end
Dim myBar As CommandBar
Dim myControl As CommandBarComboBox
Dim myEdit As CommandBarControl
Set myBar = CommandBars.Add("Math Functions")
Set myControl = myBar.Controls.Add(msoControlComboBox)
With myControl
  .Width = 100
  .AddItem "Absolute"
  .AddItem "Arctangent"
  .AddItem "Cosine"
```

Listing 7.5 *(continued)*

```
  .AddItem "Logarithm"
  .AddItem "Sine"
  .AddItem "SqRoot"
  .AddItem "Tangent"
  .Text - "SqRoot"
  .BeginGroup = True
End With
Set myEdit = myBar.Controls.Add(msoControlEdit)
With myEdit
  .Enabled = True
  .BeginGroup = True
  .OnAction = "=calc_num()"
End With
myBar.Visible = True
Exit Sub
err_end:
CommandBars("Math Functions").Delete
MsgBox "Deleted"
End Sub
```

In detail, Listing 7.5 does the following:

First an attempt is made to delete an existing Math Functions command bar. Since the command bar is re-created each time the code is run, it is prudent to remove any existing copy. The On Error Resume Next ensures that if no command bar is found to delete, the code will keep running.

```
On Error Resume Next
CommandBars("Math Functions").Delete
```

The following resets the error trap to an ending routine, then dimensions the object variables and sets myBar to a new Math Functions command bar:

```
On Error GoTo err_end
Dim myBar As CommandBar
Dim myControl As CommandBarComboBox
Dim myEdit As CommandBarControl
Set myBar = CommandBars.Add("Math Functions")
```

The following code creates a combo box on the command bar. Its width is set to accommodate the width of items in the list. The repetitive

AddItem methods create the items in the list. Finally, the Text property sets the default value to appear in the combo box—until something else is selected. The BeginGroup property inserts a separator. Its purpose is to provide a good layout in the command bar:

```
Set myControl = myBar.Controls.Add(msoControlComboBox)
With myControl
  .Width = 100
  .AddItem "Absolute"
  .AddItem "Arctangent"
  .AddItem "Cosine"
  .AddItem "Logarithm"
  .AddItem "Sine"
  .AddItem "SqRoot"
  .AddItem "Tangent"
  .Text = "SqRoot"
  .BeginGroup = True
End With
```

The following sets up the edit control, which allows typing. New here is the OnAction property, which is set to a custom function:

```
Set myEdit = myBar.Controls.Add(msoControlEdit)
With myEdit
  .Enabled = True
  .BeginGroup = True
  .OnAction = "=calc_num()"
End With
```

Finally, the command bar is set to visible:

```
myBar.Visible = True
```

The OnAction property of the edit control is set to run a function that calculates an answer based on the type of math function selected in the combo box and the actual value entered in the edit control. Listing 7.6 shows the function.

The code in Listing 7.6 performs the following steps:

1. Dimensions variables
2. Sets variables to the controls on the command bar
3. Validates if the entered value is not empty (length must be greater than zero)

Listing 7.6 The function set to the `OnAction` property of the command bar created with the code in Listing 7.5

```
Function calc_num()
Dim this_num As Double
' these four lines are used to get the values
' in the two controls of the Math Functions command bar
Dim num_function As CommandBarControl
Dim num As CommandBarControl
Set num_function = _
     CommandBars("Math Functions").Controls(1)
Set num = CommandBars("Math Functions").Controls(2)
' test if the length of the supplied number is > 0
' if not, then inform user and exit
If Len(num.Text) = 0 Then
  MsgBox "Must supply a value"
  Exit Function
End If
' test if the supplied value is a number
' if not, then inform user and exit
If Not IsNumeric(num.Text) Then
  MsgBox "Must supply a number. You supplied: " & num.Text
  Exit Function
End If
' calculate using correct math function based on selection
Select Case num_function.Text
  Case "Absolute"
    this_num = Abs(num.Text)
  Case "Arctangent"
    this_num = Atn(num.Text)
  Case "Cosine"
    this_num = Cos(num.Text)
  Case "Logarithm"
    this_num = Log(Abs(num.Text))
  Case "Sine"
    this_num = Sin(num.Text)
  Case "SqRoot"
    this_num = Sqr(Abs(num.Text))
  Case "Tangent"
    this_num = Tan(num.Text)
End Select
' display the result
MsgBox this_num
End Function
```

4. Validates that the entered value is numeric

5. Calculates a result based on the selected math function

6. Displays the result in a message box

Note that the `calc_num()` function shown in Listing 7.6 seeks out the arguments it requires to deliver its result. In particular, it assigns variables to the controls on the command bar, in order to gain the values. Typically a function receives its arguments from wherever the function is called. The difference here is that it is difficult to include the arguments in the `OnAction` property. In fact, the line of code

```
.OnAction = "=calc_num()"
```

works fine within Excel and Access. However, Word and PowerPoint need the code modified to look like this:

```
.OnAction = "calc_num"
```

Implementation of custom command bars takes planning and differs with each application. The Math Functions command bar example presented here is problematic. For example, consider what could happen in Excel. A given single workbook has the code to create the toolbar *and* has the `calc_num()` function. That workbook is open, the code is run that creates the command bar, and the math functions work as expected. Later the workbook is closed. Now another Excel workbook is opened. The Math Functions command bar is available: the command bar has become embedded in Excel itself. But the `calc_num()` function cannot be found. Using the command bar causes a bug. In other words, even though the first workbook created the command bar, Excel kept it as a global command bar even after the workbook was closed. The code it needs is available only when the first workbook is opened.

This leads to the consideration that either the `calc_num()` function must somehow be stored globally to all Excel workbooks, or the Math Function command bar must be deleted when the workbook that created it is closed. Both of these options are valid and can be implemented. Excel workbooks have a `Close` event in which the command bar can be deleted. Or the code can be made global as an add-in.

Table 7.2 presents guidelines for implementing custom command bars for each core Office application. Note that these are just guidelines. The very nature of customizing command bars makes it impossible to create a set of hard rules for implementation. Your requirements may very well necessitate another approach.

Table 7.2 Guidelines for custom command bar use in each Office application

Application	Guidelines
Word	If global functionality is needed, include the coding in Word's Normal template. For a document-specific command bar, put the code into a module created in the document. Then call the routine that creates the command bar from the document's `Open` event. Delete the command bar in the document's `Close` event.
Excel	If global functionality is needed, create an add-in that creates the command bar and includes the coding. For a workbook-specific command bar, put the code into a module created in the workbook. Then call the routine that creates the command bar from the workbook's `Activate` event. Delete the command bar in the workbook's `Deactivate` event. This setup provides a way for the toolbar to disappear when switching to another open workbook. Then it reappears when a user switches to the workbook that makes use of the custom command bar.
Access	Custom functionality is stored within each separate database. The only way to create functionality available to all databases is to create an add-in.
PowerPoint	Given the nature of PowerPoint, it is unlikely to have custom functionality that is specific to just one presentation. Consider that except for running slide shows, PowerPoint completely runs in design mode. There rarely, if ever, is a need for any functionality that would apply to a specific presentation. Custom command bars and other functionality can be saved as an add-in.

Summary

The Microsoft Office Object Library provides the ability to develop solutions with user-friendly enhancements. In addition to the file search, file dialog, and command bar objects presented in this chapter, there are also the Answer Wizard, the Office Assistant, balloon-style help, the Office Data Source Object, Web Components, and signatures. These are certainly worth becoming familiar with, as they have many practical uses in custom solutions.

CHAPTER 8

Microsoft Forms

VERSION NOTE: The material in this chapter works with all versions of Office.

The Microsoft Forms 2.0 Object Library delivers the ability to create customizable, programmable forms inside Office applications. Known interchangeably as *user forms* or just *forms*, they act as containers to hold controls and custom processes. Events, properties, and methods exist both for a form and for the controls it holds.

Forms can be used in any of the core Office products (not InfoPath). They operate the same regardless of the host product. A major purpose of user forms is to facilitate efficient data entry. For example, a business application in Excel may require several pieces of data to be entered, but into several unrelated areas of the workbook. A user form helps by putting all the entry points together in one place, thereby creating a user-friendly application.

Generally, a user makes selections in a form and then initiates an action to run a process. The process may be initiated, for example, when a command button is clicked, or when a selection is made in a drop-down list, or even just when the form is closed. Similarly, a process may run when the form is first displayed. Figure 8.1 shows a user form based on a particular business need, in this case creating an appointment with a client.

When to Use Forms Instead of Standard Screen Components

Even though forms are available to any core Office product, they are best used with Word or Excel. The reason: these two products have no alternative form creation component. (Excel does have a limited form feature for

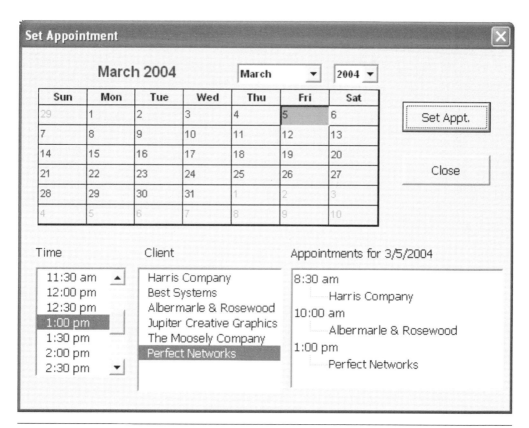

Figure 8.1 A user form

simple repetitive entry.) Access has a great form designer, and therefore gains little by using the Microsoft Forms library. Outlook, too, has form designer capabilities, although Outlook forms have a limited programming model. Outlook can make use of user forms in the situations where Outlook forms do not provide enough power. PowerPoint presentations are usually informational and therefore have little use for the interaction provided by forms.

Consider how Excel can benefit from forms. Unless specifically protected, Excel's open structure gives users the ability to enter text, numeric data, and graphics anywhere within a workbook. Even when limitations are set via workbook or worksheet protection, the means to validate data on the fly is not great.

Cells have no events to add code to. This in turn means it takes extra planning to validate entry as it occurs. Excel does have a validation feature: cells can be limited to certain types of input. However, these cells must be known ahead of time and planned for accordingly. Even so, validation is not necessarily what is needed. Often the goal is just to have input go into the correct area(s).

Worksheets do have helpful events, such as `Change` and `Calculate`, but in order to use these events, all possibilities of the worksheet have to be considered and coded for. In other words, it probably is not feasible to use the `Change` event just to report when nonnumeric data is found. The worksheet may have areas where cell contents must be numeric, but also areas where text is allowed, such as labels or column headings.

Word, too, is difficult to protect and validate effectively. Fields can be used to accept input, yet they may be missed altogether if many fields are scattered about a large document. A typical example is a contract with mostly boilerplate text and a dozen or so "fill-in-the-blank" areas in the document.

User forms are ideal for both of these situations. Forms are designed in the development phase and then used in production. The actions that display forms, make use of the entries, and then close the forms are all predeveloped before a user accesses a form.

Creating a Form

This section demonstrates the creation of two forms. The forms sit in an Excel workbook that maintains a schedule of appointments to see clients. The first form is used to facilitate easy click-through appointment setting. The form makes use of the calendar control to both set an appointment and view appointments that are already set up. Two lists—times and clients—are used with the calendar to make an appointment.

A third list shows appointments that are already established. Setting an appointment is difficult for any of us when we cannot see what appointments have already been scheduled. The form as shown in Figure 8.1 displays existing appointments for the day selected in the calendar. As new appointments are set, the list on the right of the form is updated. This list is displayed with a tree-view control, which shows the hierarchy of times and appointments.

The first step in creating a form is to select UserForm from the Insert menu in the VB Editor. See Figure 8.2. Note that although forms are handled through a separate library reference, the Office applications are "aware" of the Forms library without having to take the additional step of making the reference. In fact, the VB Editor allows you to insert a form using a standard menu item.

Next controls are added to the form. If necessary, make the Toolbox visible via the View…Toolbox menu or by clicking on the Toolbox icon. This example uses command buttons, list boxes, labels, a tree view, and the calendar. The tree-view and calendar controls are not standard items in the Toolbox, so they need to be added. First, though, let's put the standard controls on the form. Command buttons, list boxes, and labels are added to the form by clicking on the control's button in the Toolbox and then

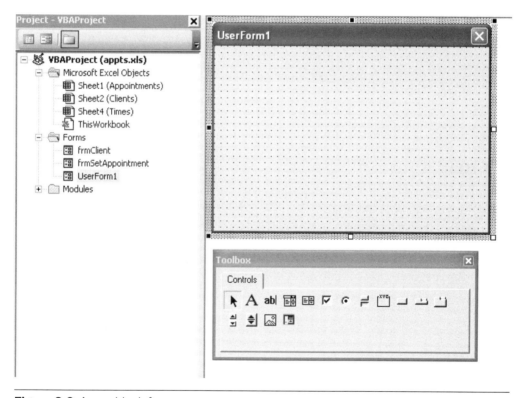

Figure 8.2 A new blank form

drawing the control on the form, or by just dragging them from the Toolbox to the form. Figure 8.3 shows the form with the command buttons, list boxes, and labels.

Now comes the task of adding the calendar and tree-view controls. First, with the mouse, *right-click* on the Toolbox. The pop-up menu should have a choice of "Additional Controls..." Click to see the additional controls. An alternate way to see the list of controls is to use the Tools...Additional Controls menu. The Tools menu selection for Additional Controls is enabled only when the Toolbox is visible. Figure 8.4 shows the Additional Controls dialog, which is quite similar to a list of references.

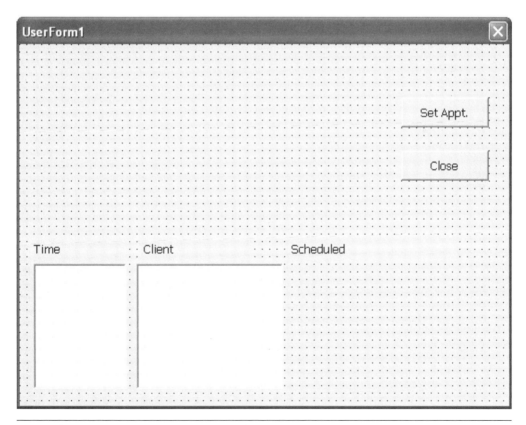

Figure 8.3 Controls are added to a user form

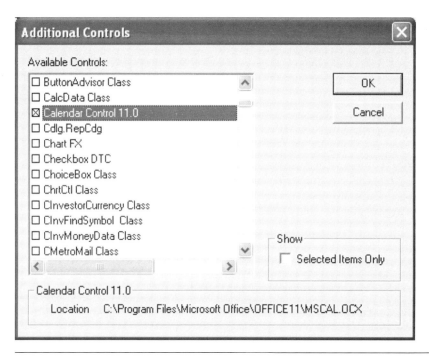

Figure 8.4 Additional controls are found in this dialog

Search your list for the *Calendar Control* and the *Microsoft TreeView Control*. Select them and click OK. They will now be available in the Toolbox. Click and draw, or drag them to the form.

NOTE: There are many controls available to use on forms. Exploring the use of the additional controls can lead to new, rewarding development!

There are several properties to set for both the form and the controls. Table 8.1 lists the object, the property, and the setting. To actually set properties, the Properties window must be visible. If it is not, then use the View... Properties menu to make it visible.

Additional properties may be set for more utility or functionality. For example, font sizes may need to be adjusted to work on different screen resolutions.

Table 8.1 Property settings for the Set Appointment form

Object	Property	Setting
User Form	Name	frmSetAppointment
	Caption	Set Appointment
Calendar Control	Name	calAppointments
Button (Close)	Name	cmdClose
	Caption	Close
	Cancel	True
Button (Set Appointment)	Name	cmdSetAppointment
	Caption	Set Appt.
Label (Time)	Name	lblTime
	Caption	Time
Label (Client)	Name	lblClient
	Caption	Client
Label (Scheduled)	Name	lblScheduled
	Caption	Scheduled
List Box (Times)	Name	lstTimes
	MultiSelect	0-fmMultiSelectSingle
List Box (Clients)	Name	lstClients
	MultiSelect	0-fmMultiSelectSingle
Tree View	Name	treeAppointments

Adding Code

Programming code for forms is entered into code modules, the same as any other VBA code. With the form present in the Visual Basic Editor, you can (1) use the View…Code menu, (2) right-click the form in the Project Explorer and select View Code, or (3) right-click the form itself and select View Code.

There are several events available for the form and for the controls. The form has Initialize and Terminate events, as well as Activate and Deactivate events. These occur in this order: Initialize, Activate, Deactivate, Terminate. Setup routines can be placed in the Initialize or Activate events, or both. Cleanup routines can be placed in Deactivate or Terminate events, or both. The goal of your development will drive how to apply these. Note that the Deactivate event fires when moving from one user form to another, but not when a form closes.

Each control has a set of events. In most cases the Click event is used to generate some action. The code module of the form contains all the code that this form uses. In other words, no external modules are used. Listing 8.1 shows the full module of the form.

Listing 8.1 The code behind the Set Appointment form

```
Private Sub UserForm_Initialize()
Dim lookup_end_row As Integer
Dim get_lookup As Integer
' clear controls on the form
Me.lstClients.Clear
Me.lstTimes.Clear
' populate the times list box
' find the size of the list, then loop through
' filling the list box with the AddItem method
With ActiveWorkbook.Worksheets("Times")
  lookup_end_row = .Cells(1, 1).CurrentRegion.Rows.Count
  For get_lookup = 1 To lookup_end_row
    Me.lstTimes.AddItem .Cells(get_lookup, 1)
  Next
End With
' populate the clients list box
' find the size of the list, then loop through
' filling the list box with the AddItem method
With ActiveWorkbook.Worksheets("Clients")
  lookup_end_row = .Cells(1, 1).CurrentRegion.Rows.Count
  For get_lookup = 1 To lookup_end_row
    Me.lstClients.AddItem .Cells(get_lookup, 1)
  Next
End With
```

Listing 8.1 *(continued)*

```
' set the calendar control to "today"
With calAppointments
   .Day = Day(Now)
   .Month = Month(Now)
   .Year = Year(Now)
End With
Me.lblScheduled.Caption = "Appointments On " & _
    Me.calAppointments
calAppointments_Click
End Sub
Private Sub calAppointments_Click()
Dim this_time As String
Dim time_node As Node
' clear the tree view
Me.treeAppointments.Nodes.Clear
' select entries and sort by time (column B)
Cells(1, 1).CurrentRegion.Select
Selection.Sort Key1:=Range("B1"), Header:=xlYes, _
    DataOption1:=xlSortTextAsNumbers
this_time = ""
Cells(2, 1).Activate
Do Until ActiveCell = ""
  ' if the date in column A matches
  ' the date in the calendar . . .
  If ActiveCell = Me.calAppointments Then
    ' add to appointment tree . . .
    ' if not a new time, then enter child client node
    If ActiveCell.Offset(0, 1) = this_time Then
      Me.treeAppointments.Nodes.Add this_time, tvwChild, _
        , ActiveCell.Offset(0, 2)
    Else
      ' if a "new" time then . . .
      ' enter new time parent, and . . .
      ' enter child client node
      this_time = ActiveCell.Offset(0, 1)
      With Me.treeAppointments.Nodes
        .Add , , this_time, this_time
        .Add this_time, tvwChild, , ActiveCell.Offset(0, 2)
      End With
    End If
  End If
```

Listing 8.1 *(continued)*

```
  ActiveCell.Offset(1, 0).Activate
Loop
' expand the tree view
For Each time_node In Me.treeAppointments.Nodes
  time_node.Expanded = True
Next
' update label of tree view control
Me.lblScheduled.Caption = _
    "Appointments for " & Me.calAppointments
Cells(1, 1).Select
End Sub
Private Sub cmdSetAppointment_Click()
' validate all required entries are made
If Me.lstClients.ListIndex < 0 Then
  MsgBox "Must Select a Client to Make Appointment For"
  Exit Sub
End If
If Me.lstTimes.ListIndex < 0 Then
  MsgBox "Must Select a Time for the Appointment"
  Exit Sub
End If
' enter the appointment on the worksheet
With ActiveWorkbook.Worksheets("Appointments")
  ' find next empty row
  .Cells(2, 1).Activate
  Do Until ActiveCell = ""
    ActiveCell.Offset(1, 0).Activate
  Loop
  ' now on the next empty row
  ActiveCell = Me.calAppointments
  ActiveCell.Offset(0, 1) = Me.lstTimes
  ActiveCell.Offset(0, 2) = Me.lstClients
End With
calAppointments_Click
End Sub
Private Sub lstClients_DblClick _
    (ByVal Cancel As MSForms.ReturnBoolean)
' select entries and sort by client, date, and time
Cells(1, 1).CurrentRegion.Select
```

Listing 8.1 (continued)

```
Selection.Sort Key1:=Range("C1"), Order1:=xlAscending, _
    Key2:=Range("A1"), Order2:=xlDescending, _
        Key3:=Range("B1"), Order3:=xlDescending, _
        Header:=xlYes, DataOption1:=xlSortTextAsNumbers
Cells(1, 1).Select
' appointment data is now sorted, so
' read down until first row for this client
' this row has latest scheduled appointment
Cells(2, 3).Activate
Do Until ActiveCell = Me.lstClients
  ActiveCell.Offset(1, 0).Activate
Loop
' prepare frmClient before displaying it
frmClient.Caption = "Detail for " & Me.lstClients
frmClient.lblLastAppt.Caption = _
    "Latest Scheduled Appointment Is On " & _
    Format(ActiveCell.Offset(0, -2), "mm/dd/yyyy") & _
    " at " & ActiveCell.Offset(0, -1)
' show the next form
frmClient.Show
End Sub
Private Sub cmdClose_Click()
  Me.Hide
End Sub
```

The module in Listing 8.1 consists of four significant procedures. A fifth procedure— cmdClose_Click—closes the form by using the Hide method:

```
Private Sub cmdClose_Click()
  Me.Hide
End Sub
```

NOTE: A form is displayed by calling the Show method and is closed by calling the Hide method.

The UserForm_Initialize procedure prepares the form just prior to its being displayed. The two list boxes—one for the times of the day and one for the list of clients—are filled from values found within the

Excel workbook. There is a worksheet with clients' names listed in column A starting in row 1. The number of clients is determined by using the `CurrentRegion` method. Then a loop is used to fill the list box using the `AddItem` method. Here is the code that fills the client list:

```
'  populate the clients list box
'find the size of the list, then loop through
' filling the list box with the AddItem method
With ActiveWorkbook.Worksheets("Clients")
  lookup_end_row = .Cells(1, 1).CurrentRegion.Rows.Count
  For get_lookup = 1 To lookup_end_row
    Me.lstClients.AddItem .Cells(get_lookup, 1)
  Next
End With
```

The calendar control is set to display the current day by applying the `Now()` function to the `Day`, `Month`, and `Year` properties:

```
With calAppointments
  .Day = Day(Now)
  .Month = Month(Now)
  .Year = Year(Now)
End With
```

The last line of the code calls another routine in the module: `cal-Appointments_Click`. This is the `Click` event of the calendar control. This event updates the display of the tree-view control. The tree-view control is used to display the set appointments for whatever date is displayed in the calendar control. In other words, anytime the calendar control is clicked, the tree view is updated to display any appointments for that day. When the form opens, it is necessary to update the tree view, and firing the calendar's `Click` event does the trick.

The `calAppointments_Click` routine clears the tree-view control and repopulates it. The goal is to not only display the appointments of the day, but also to list them in the correct time sort. The method used to accomplish this is to sort the entries on the worksheet and then populate the tree view with sequential entries that match the given day.

On the Appointments worksheet, the data is sorted by column B, which holds appointment times. Note that in order to avoid confusing sort results, the `DataOption1` parameter of the `Sort` method is set to treat the times as numbers (`xlSortTextAsNumbers`). If this were not taken into account, the times would sort as text, and the sort result would be incorrect:

```
Selection.Sort Key1:=Range("B1"), Header:=xlYes, _
    DataOption1:=xlSortTextAsNumbers
```

NOTE: The `DataOption1` parameter of the `Sort` method was introduced in Excel 2002. If you are running an older version of Excel, another method is needed to sort by time. An alternative is to create a list of dedicated times in another column and use that for the sort. The additional column used for the sort would gain real-time values by applying the `TimeValue()` function.

After the sort, the data is listed in order by time, without regard to the dates in column A. The data is examined with a loop, and when an entry in column A (the appointment dates) matches the date in the calendar control, the tree-view control is updated. The tree view will receive one or two new entries, depending on whether or not the time found in the current row has already been put into the tree view.

When the first occurrence of a time is found, the tree-view control receives a "parent" entry of the time and a "child" entry of the client name. When the time has already been entered in the tree view, the entry is just a "child" of the time already in the tree view. The `Add` method of the `Nodes` property of the tree view allows setting the hierarchical relationships. The code that accomplishes this is:

```
If ActiveCell = Me.calAppointments Then
  ' add to appointment tree . . .
  ' if not a new time, then enter child client node
  If ActiveCell.Offset(0, 1) = this_time Then
    Me.treeAppointments.Nodes.Add this_time, tvwChild, _
        , ActiveCell.Offset(0, 2)
  Else
    ' if a "new" time then . . .
    ' enter new time parent, and . . .
    ' enter child client node
    this_time = ActiveCell.Offset(0, 1)
    With Me.treeAppointments.Nodes
      .Add , , this_time, this_time
```

```
        .Add this_time, tvwChild, , ActiveCell.Offset(0, 2)
      End With
    End If
  End If
```

The `cmdSetAppointment_Click` routine is run by clicking on the Set Appt. button. This action writes the new appointment back onto the worksheet:

```
' enter the appointment on the worksheet
With ActiveWorkbook.Worksheets("Appointments")
  ' find next empty row
  .Cells(2, 1).Activate
  Do Until ActiveCell = ""
    ActiveCell.Offset(1, 0).Activate
  Loop
  ' now on the next empty row
  ActiveCell = Me.calAppointments
  ActiveCell.Offset(0, 1) = Me.lstTimes
  ActiveCell.Offset(0, 2) = Me.lstClients
End With
```

The next available row is determined and the data from the two list boxes and calendar control are inserted into the appropriate columns. Finally, the `calAppointments_Click` routine is called to update the tree-view control.

The last routine is built into the double-click event of the client list box. The `lstClients_DblClick` procedure prepares a second form for display. The purpose of the second form is to give more detail about a client. In particular the next form, named `frmClient`, displays the latest scheduled appointment and the sales history of the client.

The preparation of the `frmClient` form involves first sorting the data on the Appointments worksheet. This sort requires setting the sort ordering for all three columns—date, time, and client:

```
Selection.Sort Key1:=Range("C1"), Order1:=xlAscending, _
    Key2:=Range("A1"), Order2:=xlDescending, _
      Key3:=Range("B1"), Order3:=xlDescending, _
      Header:=xlYes, DataOption1:=xlSortTextAsNumbers
```

The purpose of the sort is to make the first record per client have the latest date and time. Therefore, the `Order2` and `Order3` parameters are both set to descending (`xlDescending`). Then the data is looped through until the client is found:

```
Do Until ActiveCell = Me.lstClients
  ActiveCell.Offset(1, 0).Activate
Loop
```

The frmClient form is updated, before actual display, to have the latest scheduled appointment sitting in the Caption property of a label on the form. Then the form is displayed. Figure 8.5 shows the frmClient form.

```
frmClient.Caption = "Detail for " & Me.lstClients
frmClient.lblLastAppt.Caption = _
    "Latest Scheduled Appointment Is On " & _
    Format(ActiveCell.Offset(0, -2), "mm/dd/yyyy") & _
    " at " & ActiveCell.Offset(0, -1)
' show the next form
frmClient.Show
```

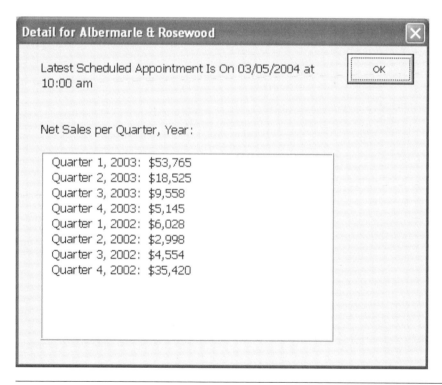

Figure 8.5 The frmClient form, displayed by double-clicking the client list in the frmSetAppointment form

The `frmClient` form has a code module of its own. As in the `frm-SetAppointment` form, the facility to close the form sits behind a button control with this procedure:

```
Private Sub cmdOK_Click()
  Me.Hide
End Sub
```

The `Initialize` event, shown in Listing 8.2, is the only other procedure of the form.

Listing 8.2 The `Initialize` event of `frmClient` queries a database

```
Private Sub UserForm_Initialize()
Dim sales As New ADODB.Connection
Dim sales_set As New ADODB.Recordset
Dim ssql As String

' clear list box
Me.lstSales.Clear

' build SQL statement to pull sales history from database
ssql = "SELECT * FROM tblSales WHERE "
ssql = ssql & " tblSales.Client=""" & _
    frmSetAppointment.lstClients & """ "
ssql = ssql & " ORDER BY Year Desc, Quarter Asc;"

' database is in same directory as this workbook
sales.Provider = "Microsoft.Jet.OLEDB.4.0"
sales.Open ActiveWorkbook.Path & "\sales.mdb"
' open recordset
With sales_set
  .ActiveConnection = sales
  .Open (ssql)
  If Not sales_set.EOF Then
    Do Until sales_set.EOF
      ' add to list box
      Me.lstSales.AddItem "Quarter " & _
          sales_set.Fields("Quarter") & ", " & _
          sales_set.Fields("Year") & ": $" & _
          Format(sales_set.Fields("Sales"), "###,###")
```

Listing 8.2 *(continued)*

```
        sales_set.MoveNext
      Loop
    End If
End With
End Sub
```

The purpose of the `Initialize` routine is to pull data from an Access database and display it on the form. ADO and SQL are used to create a recordset of data for the particular client. The SQL statement is built by passing the client name selected in the client list box on the `frmSet-Appointment` form—the client name that was just double-clicked.

NOTE: See the Appendix for resources on ADO and SQL.

The database is queried for sales data, and returns it sorted descending by year and ascending by quarter. This data populates the list box. This list box is used just to display data: no procedures are established for any events of the list box control. Overall, the form simply displays data and will stay visible until dismissed by clicking on the OK button. Table 8.2 lists the settings for the form and controls.

Table 8.2 Property settings for the Client form

Object	Property	Setting
User Form	Name	`frmClient`
	Caption	(Set via code from
		`frmSetAppointment`)
Button (OK)	Name	`cmdOK`
	Caption	`OK`
	Cancel	`True`
Label (Last Appointment)	Name	`lblLastAppt`
	Caption	(Set via code from
		`frmSetAppointment`)

Table 8.2 *(continued)*

Object	Property	Setting
Label (Client)	Name	lblClient
	Caption	Client
Label (Sales)	Name	lblSales
	Caption	Net Sales per Quarter, Year:
List Box (Sales History)	Name	lstSales
	MultiSelect	0-fmMultiSelectSingle

Form and Application Interaction

From the user interface, there is no direct access to user forms. User forms are only directly available in the VB Editor. To present forms to users requires some action outside the form itself to first display the form.

The Set Appointment form seen in Figure 8.1 is made visible by clicking a button on the Appointments worksheet. See Figure 8.6. The code behind the button is:

```
Public Sub show_appt_form()
    frmSetAppointment.Show
End Sub
```

The show_appt_form routine sits in a standard code module. The Show method of the form is necessary to display the form yet cannot be called within the form's code module.

Summary

User forms are quite useful: they are fully capable of handling all that can be achieved with VBA. The Toolbox comes with the set of standard controls, and additional controls can be added and put to good use. There are several events to which procedures can be attached. As we have seen, user forms can even maintain a logical hierarchy, in that one form can call another.

	A	B	C	D	E	F
1	**Date**	**Time**	**Client**			
2	3/5/04	10:00 am	Albermarle & Rosewood		Appointments	
3	4/10/03	9:00 am	Albermarle & Rosewood			
4	3/30/03	10:00 am	Albermarle & Rosewood			
5	3/21/03	10:30 am	Albermarle & Rosewood			
6	3/11/03	2:00 pm	Albermarle & Rosewood			
7	3/5/03	10:00 am	Albermarle & Rosewood			
8	2/9/04	9:30 am	Best Systems			
9	4/12/03	3:00 pm	Best Systems			
10	3/21/03	9:00 am	Best Systems			
11	3/11/03	9:00 am	Best Systems			
12	3/5/04	8:30 am	Harris Company			
13	8/20/03	9:00 am	Harris Company			
14	8/19/03	8:30 am	Harris Company			
15	4/22/03	8:00 am	Harris Company			
16	4/8/03	8:30 am	Harris Company			
17	3/30/03	10:00 am	Harris Company			
18	3/21/03	1:00 pm	Harris Company			

Figure 8.6 The Set Appointment form is made visible by clicking a button on the worksheet

Deciding if, when, and how to incorporate user forms into your custom applications depends on the particular requirements. User forms provide additional methods of user interaction, some of which the host application may not be able to match. User forms have the additional benefit of being application independent. Forms can be hosted in most Office applications with little modification. In Chapter 12, a case study demonstrates a sophisticated user form.

CHAPTER 9

XML and Office

VERSION NOTE: The material in this chapter is unique to Office 2003.

Office 2003 features a rich XML function set. Compared with Office XP, support for practical XML work has been enhanced with several new objects, properties, and methods. The new functionality is nearly all contained in Word and Excel. With these products are new ways to open, import, work with, export, and save XML data. There also is new functionality in Access. This chapter explores XML use as it applies to each product. Note that InfoPath is covered separately in Chapter 11.

NOTE: See Chapter 11 for information on InfoPath.

Table 9.1 contains brief descriptions of terms used throughout this chapter. This table serves as a reference for various discussion points in this chapter, because not all readers will be conversant in XML terminology.

NOTE: See the Appendix for resources on XML basics.

XML and Word 2003

WordML

Word is typically used for working with unstructured data. That is, the structure of documents is not generally as rigid as the grid of columns and rows in a database table or a spreadsheet. Paragraphs have different lengths. Text may be presented as sentences, bullet points, numbered lists,

Table 9.1 Brief descriptions of terms used in this chapter

Term	Description
Attribute	A name/value construct that can be associated with an element. For example: `<City Name="Seattle"></City>`
Element	The basic XML tag. An element has an opening and a closing tag. For example: `<City>Seattle</City>` Elements can be nested.
Map/XML Map	An Excel 2003 object used for managing XML data in a workbook.
Namespace	Used to ensure unique elements. Because element tags can be freely named, two elements may have the same name. For example, "Name" may apply to both a person's name and a city name. By associating tags with a unique namespace, the uniqueness carries through to the tag. For example: `<ns:Name>`
Node	A generic term for either an element or an attribute.
Parent/Child/ Grandparent/Grandchild	Nested XML data can be hierarchically referenced using these terms.
Repeating/Nonrepeating	Elements, or groups of elements, may or may not be repetitive in an XML file.
Schema	Describes tag-based data. Used for indicating data types, restrictions, sequence of data, and so on.
Transform/Transformation	The act of, or result of, applying an XSL/XSLT. A transformation changes the presentation of data (such as from XML to HTML).
URL/URI	Uniform Resource Locator/Uniform Resource Identifier. Used primarily in namespace declarations. URLs and URIs are unique (such as a Web site address).

Table 9.1 *(continued)*

Term	Description
Valid/Well-Formed	XML data must adhere to certain rules. It is well formed when the rules have not been broken. It is valid when it adheres to an indicated schema.
WordML	A unique XML-based language used to store and describe native Word documents. WordML itself follows XML rules.
XML	Extensible Markup Language. A tag-based standard for storing data. XML files use the .xml extension. The term is used to refer to either the data itself or the file type.
XPath	A language used for locating nodes within XML data.
XSD	Extensible Schema Definition. Schemas use the .xsd file extension. The term is used to refer to either the schema itself or the file type.
XSL/XSLT	Extensible Style Sheet Language (Transformations). XML style sheets use either the .xsl or .xslt file extension. The terms denote either the language itself or the file type.

or block quotes. There may or may not be tables. If there are tables, they may not necessarily be uniform. In a nutshell, a Word document is not expected to have a strict structure. On the other hand, a Word document contains quite a bit of formatting, even if it's just using built-in defaults.

This presents a dilemma when we attempt to save a Word document as an XML file. Although it is possible to save just the document's text wrapped in XML tags representing each paragraph, quite a bit of the document's presentation would be lost.

The answer is WordML. WordML is an XML-based language used for describing and storing Word documents. It is structured in accordance with XML syntax rules. When a standard Word document is saved as

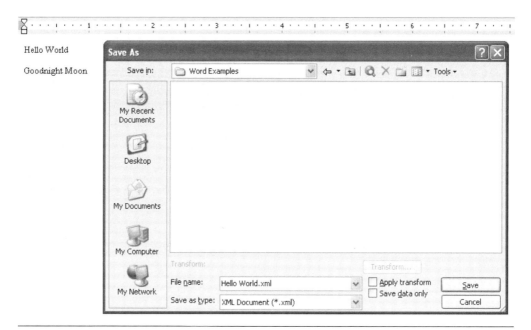

Figure 9.1 Saving a Word document as XML

Figure 9.2 A simple Word document saved as XML produces a considerable amount of WordML

```
                <w:layoutRawTableWidth />
                <w:layoutTableRowsApart />
                <w:useWord97LineBreakingRules />
                <w:dontAllowFieldEndSelect />
                <w:useWord2002TableStyleRules />
            </w:compat>
        </w:docPr>
-   <w:body>
    -   <wx:sect>
        -   <w:p>
            -   <w:r>
                    <w:t>Hello World</w:t>
                </w:r>
            </w:p>
            <w:p />
        -   <w:p>
            -   <w:r>
                    <w:t>Goodnight Moon</w:t>
                </w:r>
            </w:p>
        -   <w:sectPr>
                <w:pgSz w:w="12240" w:h="15840" />
                <w:pgMar w:top="1440" w:right="1800" w:bottom="1440" w:left="1800" w:header="720"
                    w:footer="720" w:gutter="0" />
                <w:cols w:space="720" />
            </w:sectPr>
        </wx:sect>
    </w:body>
</w:wordDocument>
```

Figure 9.3 Content is stored in the XML file below most of the WordML information

XML, an option to "Save data only" appears in the Save As dialog. See Figure 9.1. Checking the option invariably leads to warnings that the resultant XML file will not be well formed. Leaving the "Save data only" option unchecked instructs Word to use WordML to save the document.

The XML file created with WordML preserves the settings of the document within the XML file. That is, the presentation settings are stored as values within tags. A WordML file is structured such that the WordML data occupies the top of the file, and the document contents are embedded inside the body tag. In Figure 9.1, a simple Word document is being saved as XML. The document has two lines of text: "Hello World" and "Goodnight Moon". The XML created from this action is shown in Figure 9.2. (The file is opened in Internet Explorer for a user-friendly presentation.)

The XML file is mostly WordML. Scrolling down through the file, we can see the actual content nestled inside the body tags (w:body), shown here in Figure 9.3. Opening an XML file that has been saved with WordML restores the file to its original appearance.

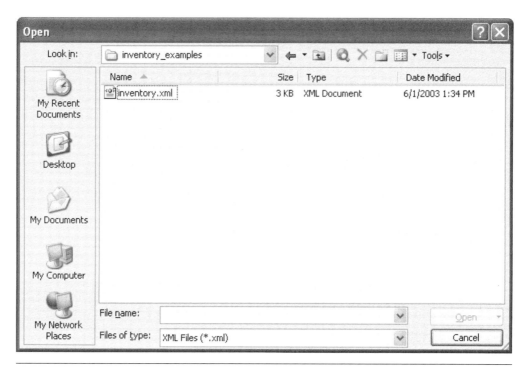

Figure 9.4 Opening an XML file

Opening Standard XML Files

Word easily opens and works with non-WordML XML files. The Open dialog has "XML Files" as one of the Files of Type settings. See Figure 9.4. Note that in the Open dialog there are no options to consider. All that is available is the open action.

During the open process, if the XML file has embedded WordML, then Word uses it to format the document. When an XML file does not have WordML, then the data appears structured. The process that Word applies when it opens the file is not particularly sophisticated. Instead, Word displays what must already be a structured file. Word simply shows the tags and the content. See Figure 9.5.

The actual inventory.xml file that appears in Figure 9.5 is shown here in Listing 9.1.

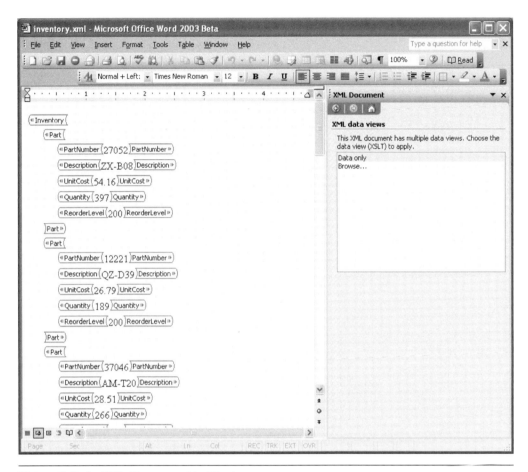

Figure 9.5 An XML file opened in Word

Listing 9.1 The inventory.xml file

```xml
<?xml version="1.0" encoding="UTF-8"?>
<Inventory>
   <Part Manufacturer="Heartland Hardware">
      <PartNumber>27052</PartNumber>
      <Description>ZX-B08</Description>
      <UnitCost>54.16</UnitCost>
      <Quantity>397</Quantity>
      <ReorderLevel>200</ReorderLevel>
   </Part>
```

Listing 9.1 *(continued)*

```
<Part Manufacturer="Heartland Hardware">
   <PartNumber>12221</PartNumber>
   <Description>QZ-D39</Description>
   <UnitCost>26.79</UnitCost>
   <Quantity>189</Quantity>
   <ReorderLevel>200</ReorderLevel>
</Part>
<Part Manufacturer="Heartland Hardware">
   <PartNumber>37046</PartNumber>
   <Description>AM-T20</Description>
   <UnitCost>28.51</UnitCost>
   <Quantity>266</Quantity>
   <ReorderLevel>300</ReorderLevel>
</Part>
<Part Manufacturer="Strong Tools and Supplies">
   <PartNumber>10958</PartNumber>
   <Description>CE-K57</Description>
   <UnitCost>49.27</UnitCost>
   <Quantity>369</Quantity>
   <ReorderLevel>500</ReorderLevel>
</Part>
<Part Manufacturer="Heartland Hardware">
   <PartNumber>27656</PartNumber>
   <Description>RS-R72</Description>
   <UnitCost>34.10</UnitCost>
   <Quantity>328</Quantity>
   <ReorderLevel>300</ReorderLevel>
</Part>
<Part Manufacturer="Heartland Hardware">
   <PartNumber>13352</PartNumber>
   <Description>BP-R59</Description>
   <UnitCost>51.67</UnitCost>
   <Quantity>121</Quantity>
   <ReorderLevel>150</ReorderLevel>
</Part>
<Part Manufacturer="Strong Tools and Supplies">
   <PartNumber>21923</PartNumber>
   <Description>VG-P07</Description>
   <UnitCost>44.62</UnitCost>
```

Listing 9.1 (continued)

```
        <Quantity>343</Quantity>
        <ReorderLevel>200</ReorderLevel>
    </Part>
    <Part Manufacturer="Strong Tools and Supplies">
        <PartNumber>35834</PartNumber>
        <Description>YY-H34</Description>
        <UnitCost>50.41</UnitCost>
        <Quantity>60</Quantity>
        <ReorderLevel>50</ReorderLevel>
    </Part>
    <Part Manufacturer="Heartland Hardware">
        <PartNumber>12532</PartNumber>
        <Description>NN-O59</Description>
        <UnitCost>58.98</UnitCost>
        <Quantity>212</Quantity>
        <ReorderLevel>200</ReorderLevel>
    </Part>
    <Part Manufacturer="Heartland Hardware">
        <PartNumber>33294</PartNumber>
        <Description>UL-I23</Description>
        <UnitCost>52.98</UnitCost>
        <Quantity>55</Quantity>
        <ReorderLevel>100</ReorderLevel>
    </Part>
    <Part Manufacturer="Heartland Hardware">
        <PartNumber>23230</PartNumber>
        <Description>RN-N17</Description>
        <UnitCost>29.67</UnitCost>
        <Quantity>277</Quantity>
        <ReorderLevel>200</ReorderLevel>
    </Part>
    <Part Manufacturer="Strong Tools and Supplies">
        <PartNumber>35864</PartNumber>
        <Description>DO-Y15</Description>
        <UnitCost>50.44</UnitCost>
        <Quantity>234</Quantity>
        <ReorderLevel>250</ReorderLevel>
    </Part>
```

Listing 9.1 *(continued)*

```
<Part Manufacturer="Strong Tools and Supplies">
    <PartNumber>37584</PartNumber>
    <Description>YQ-D02</Description>
    <UnitCost>20.28</UnitCost>
    <Quantity>120</Quantity>
    <ReorderLevel>250</ReorderLevel>
</Part>
</Inventory>
```

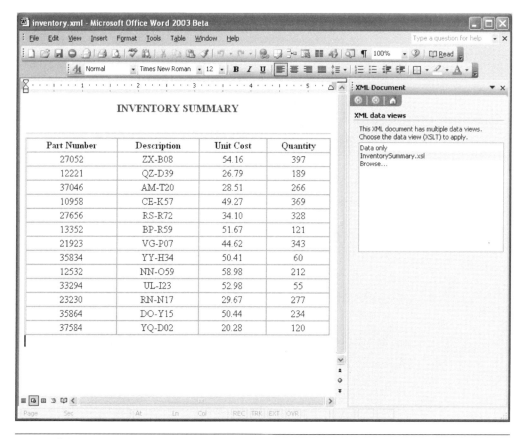

Figure 9.6 The XML data is transformed using an XSLT file

In Figure 9.5, the task pane is showing XML Document options. Within the task pane is a list of data views. This is a list of available XSLT options to apply to the open XML file. Using the Browse option, an XSLT file, InventorySummary.xsl, is found and applied. The result of this action is shown in Figure 9.6.

Listing 9.2 shows the contents of the InventorySummary.xsl file.

Listing 9.2 An XSLT file used to format the XML data

```
<?xml version="1.0"?>
<xsl:stylesheet
  xmlns:xsl="http://www.w3.org/1999/XSL/Transform"
  xmlns:ns1="http://www.solutions4office/transform"
  version="1.0">
<xsl:output method="html"/>
<xsl:template match="/">
  <HTML>
  <HEAD>
    <TITLE>Inventory Summary</TITLE>
  </HEAD>
  <BODY>
    <H1 ALIGN="CENTER">
        <font SIZE="4" COLOR="Blue">
            INVENTORY SUMMARY
        </font>
    </H1>
    <TABLE WIDTH="100%">
      <TR>
        <TH>Part Number</TH>
        <TH>Description</TH>
        <TH>Unit Cost</TH>
        <TH>Quantity</TH>
      </TR>
      <xsl:for-each select="//Inventory/Part">
      <TR>
        <TD ALIGN="Center">
            <xsl:value-of select="PartNumber"/>
        </TD>
        <TD ALIGN="Center">
            <xsl:value-of select="Description"/>
        </TD>
```

Listing 9.2 *(continued)*

```
          <TD ALIGN="Center">
              <xsl:value-of select="UnitCost"/>
          </TD>
          <TD ALIGN="Center">
              <xsl:value-of select="Quantity"/>
          </TD>
       </TR>
     </xsl:for-each>
    </TABLE>
  </BODY>
  </HTML>
</xsl:template>
</xsl:stylesheet>
```

The InventorySummary.xsl file shown in Listing 9.2 formats the XML data. The data is transformed into HTML output. HTML tags such as <HEAD>, <BODY>, and <TABLE> are evident in the code. XSL and XPath syntax are also here, used for selecting portions of the XML:

```
<xsl:for-each select="//Inventory/Part">
```

and assigning XML data to the HTML tags:

```
<xsl:value-of select="Quantity"/>
```

So far, an XML file has been opened and then an XSLT file has been applied. Programmatically, here is how this is done. Opening an XML file is accomplished the same way as opening any other Word file:

```
Documents.Open "C:\XML\inventory_examples\inventory.xml"
```

An option is to open the file with a transformation. In a single action, this opens the file and applies the transformation shown in Figure 9.6:

```
Documents.Open "C:\XML\inventory_examples\inventory.xml", _
XMLTransform:="C:\XML\inventory_examples\InventorySummary.xsl"
```

To apply a transformation to an already open XML file, the file is closed and reopened with the transformation. Listing 9.3 shows the code.

To continue, another XSLT file is added to the list of data views. The InventoryReorder.xsl file is found using the Browse feature. The XML data is once again formatted, as shown in Figure 9.7.

Listing 9.3 Applying a transformation to an open XML file

```
Sub apply_xslt_to_active_doc()
  Dim this_path As String
  this_doc_path = ActiveDocument.FullName
  this_xsl = ActiveDocument.Path & "\InventorySummary.xsl"
  ActiveDocument.Close SaveChanges:=True
  Documents.Open this_doc_path, XMLTransform:=this_xsl
End Sub
```

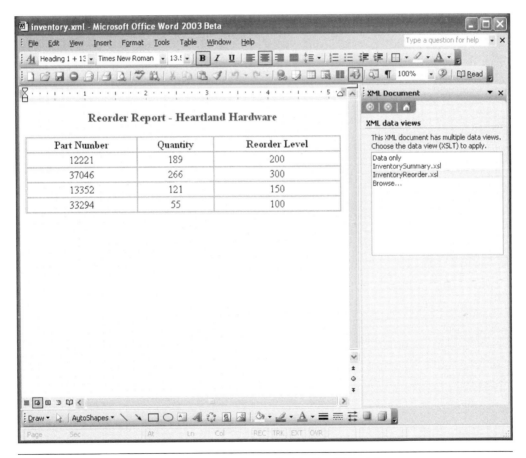

Figure 9.7 An additional transformation is applied to the XML data

The InventoryReorder.xsl file has a bit of intelligence. It filters data to one vendor, Heartland Hardware, and returns only data records in which the quantity is less than the reorder level. In other words, this report lists only those inventory items that need to be reordered from a single vendor. The InventoryReorder.xsl file is shown in Listing 9.4.

Listing 9.4 A transformation that filters and tests the XML data

```
<?xml version="1.0"?>
<xsl:stylesheet
  xmlns:xsl="http://www.w3.org/1999/XSL/Transform"
  xmlns:ns1="http://www.solutions4office/transform"
  version="1.0">
<xsl:output method="html"/>
<xsl:template match="/">
  <HTML>
  <HEAD>
    <TITLE>Inventory Reorder List</TITLE>
  </HEAD>
  <BODY>
    <H1 ALIGN="CENTER">
      <font SIZE="4" COLOR="Blue">
        Reorder Report - Heartland Hardware
      </font>
    </H1>
  <TABLE WIDTH="100%">
    <TR>
      <TH>Part Number</TH>
      <TH>Quantity</TH>
      <TH>Reorder Level</TH>
    </TR>
    <xsl:for-each select="//Inventory/Part">
      <xsl:if test="@Manufacturer='Heartland Hardware'">
        <xsl:if test="ReorderLevel>Quantity">
    <TR>
      <TD ALIGN="Center"><xsl:value-of select="PartNumber"/></TD>
      <TD ALIGN="Center"><xsl:value-of select="Quantity"/></TD>
      <TD ALIGN="Center"><xsl:value-of select="ReorderLevel"/></TD>
    </TR>
```

Listing 9.4 (*continued*)

```
        </xsl:if>
      </xsl:if>
    </xsl:for-each>
  </TABLE>
  </BODY>
  </HTML>
</xsl:template>
</xsl:stylesheet>
```

The XSLT `if` statement is used to filter the output to just the Heartland Hardware manufacturer:

```
<xsl:if test="@Manufacturer='Heartland Hardware'">
```

The @ symbol used in the test indicates that `Manufacturer` is an attribute. This can be seen back in Listing 9.1—in which every `Part` tag has the `Manufacturer` attribute. Once a part record is determined to be for this manufacturer, the next line tests to see if the `ReorderLevel` element is greater than the `Quantity` element:

```
<xsl:if test="ReorderLevel>Quantity">
```

Schemas

XML schemas (XSD files) can be applied to Word documents and to XML files. A schema is used to validate the data's structure: to ensure that required elements are in the data and to indicate the data types. The approach for applying schemas differs depending on whether Word will be displaying a standard Word document or data that is already valid as XML.

Applying a Schema to an XML File

First, here is an approach for using a schema with an XML file. Three steps occur:

1. A schema is added to Word.
2. An XML file is opened.
3. The schema is attached to the document.

Listing 9.5 shows the schema file.

Listing 9.5 The inventory_schema_2.xsd schema file

```xml
<?xml version="1.0" encoding="UTF-8"?>
<xsd:schema xmlns:xsd="http://www.w3.org/2001/XMLSchema">
 <xsd:element name="Inventory">
  <xsd:complexType>
   <xsd:sequence>
    <xsd:element ref="Part" minOccurs="0"
     maxOccurs="unbounded"/>
   </xsd:sequence>
  </xsd:complexType>
 </xsd:element>
<xsd:element name="Part">
  <xsd:complexType>
   <xsd:sequence>
    <xsd:element name="PartNumber" minOccurs="1"
       maxOccurs="1">
     <xsd:simpleType>
      <xsd:restriction base="xsd:string"/>
     </xsd:simpleType>
    </xsd:element>
    <xsd:element name="Description" minOccurs="1"
       maxOccurs="1">
     <xsd:simpleType>
      <xsd:restriction base="xsd:string"/>
     </xsd:simpleType>
    </xsd:element>
    <xsd:element name="UnitCost" minOccurs="1"
       maxOccurs="1">
     <xsd:simpleType>
      <xsd:restriction base="xsd:decimal"/>
     </xsd:simpleType>
    </xsd:element>
    <xsd:element name="Quantity" minOccurs="1"
       maxOccurs="1">
     <xsd:simpleType>
      <xsd:restriction base="xsd:integer"/>
     </xsd:simpleType>
    </xsd:element>
    <xsd:element name="ReorderLevel" minOccurs="1"
       maxOccurs="1">
     <xsd:simpleType>
      <xsd:restriction base="xsd:integer"/>
```

Listing 9.5 *(continued)*

```
    </xsd:simpleType>
   </xsd:element>
  </xsd:sequence>
 </xsd:complexType>
 </xsd:element>
</xsd:schema>
```

The schema requires that for any `Part` element, all five children elements must be present: `PartNumber`, `Description`, `UnitCost`, `Quantity`, and `ReorderLevel`. The `minOccurs` and `maxOccurs` attributes are set to 1 for all the children. This means that each child must appear once within each `Part` element (the parent). Listing 9.6 shows the XML tiny_inventory.xml file.

Listing 9.6 The tiny_inventory.xml file

```
<?xml version="1.0" encoding="UTF-8"?>
<ns:Inventory
   xmlns:ns="http://solutions4office.com/inventory/ex2">
   <ns:Part Manufacturer="Heartland Hardware">
      <ns:Description>RV-708</ns:Description>
      <ns:UnitCost>54.16</ns:UnitCost>
      <ns:Quantity>397</ns:Quantity>
      <ns:ReorderLevel>200</ns:ReorderLevel>
   </ns:Part>
   <ns:Part>
      <ns:Description>QZ-D39</ns:Description>
      <ns:UnitCost>26.79</ns:UnitCost>
      <ns:Quantity>189</ns:Quantity>
      <ns:ReorderLevel>200</ns:ReorderLevel>
   </ns:Part>
</ns:Inventory>
```

Note that the tiny_inventory.xml file has three details that will spawn validation errors: the `PartNumber` child element is missing in both `Part` elements, and the first `Part` element has an attribute (`Manufacturer`) that is not specified in the schema.

Next, the `validate_xml` routine is going to add the schema to Word, open the XML file, and attach the schema to the XML. This will result in validation errors. Listing 9.7 shows the `validate_xml` routine.

Listing 9.7 A schema and an XML file are brought together

```
Sub validate_xml()
On Error GoTo err_end
Dim example_path As String
Dim namespace As String
' change path as needed
example_path = "C:\2003_June\XML\Word\inventory_examples\"
' establish unique namespace
namespace = "http://solutions4office.com/inventory/ex2"
' add the namespace to Word
Application.XMLNamespaces.Add Path:= _
        example_path & "inventory_schema_2.xsd", _
        NamespaceURI:=namespace
' open the XML file
Documents.Open FileName:=example_path & "tiny_inventory.xml"
' attach the namespace to the document
Application.XMLNamespaces(namespace). _
        AttachToDocument (ActiveDocument)
exit_sub:
' update the task pane to display "XML Structure"
Application.TaskPanes(wdTaskPaneXMLStructure).Visible = True
Exit Sub
err_end:
' a validation error can occur
MsgBox Err.Description
Resume exit_sub
End Sub
```

In the `validate_xml` routine, two variables are used to hold the path to the files and the namespace, respectively, used to relate the schema and the XML:

```
example_path = "C:\2003_June\XML\Word\inventory_examples\"
' establish unique namespace
namespace = "http://solutions4office.com/inventory/ex2"
```

The namespace is added to the `Namespaces` collection, using the `Add` method. Note that the `Namespaces` collection belongs to Word (the `Application` object) and not to a particular document. The path and file name are supplied, as well as the `NamespaceURI`. The URI is held in the `namespace` variable:

```
Application.XMLNamespaces.Add Path:= _
        example_path & "inventory_schema_2.xsd", _
        NamespaceURI:=namespace
```

The XML file is opened using the `Open` method:

```
Documents.Open FileName:=example_path & "tiny_inventory.xml"
```

The `AttachToDocument` method is used to associate the schema with the open file. The name of the document is supplied to the `Attach-ToDocument` method. The schema is referenced by the namespace:

```
Application.XMLNamespaces(namespace). _
        AttachToDocument (ActiveDocument)
```

At the start of the routine an error trap was turned on. As expected, the validation failure is caught, and presented in the message shown in Figure 9.8.

Figure 9.8 The XML does not validate against the attached schema

Figure 9.9 shows the appearance of the open XML file with the validation errors. The task pane is set to show XML Structure. The error icons are visible within the task pane, nestled in where the errors occurred.

Figures 9.10 and 9.11 show details about the errors when the user hovers the mouse over them or right-clicks on them, respectively.

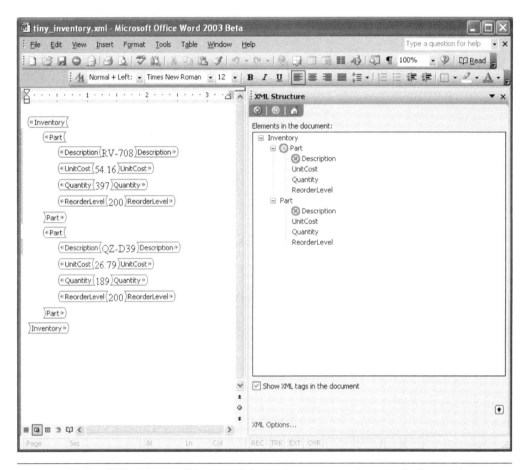

Figure 9.9 The XML did not validate, and the task pane uses icons to indicate where the errors are

Using a Schema to Mark Up a Word Document

In this next example, a schema is used to provide tags to mark up non-XML information. Bear in mind that this type of activity—turning text in a Word document into an XML file—does not always make sense. A lengthy, narrative type of Word document would not easily conform to a more rigid XML structure. To overcome this limitation, Word uses its internal WordML, as explained previously.

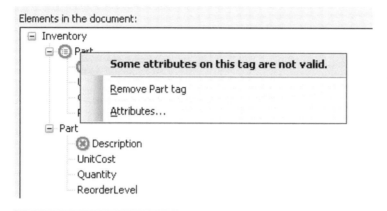

Figure 9.10 Identification of an attribute error

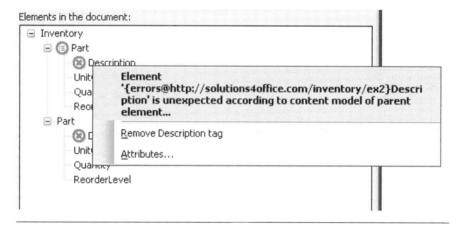

Figure 9.11 Identification of the missing `PartNumber` element. The error message actually identifies the `Description` tag as the error—because it should not be the first child element

This example, though, marks up a document that already has a structure. In particular, data that is in a Word table will be marked up with tags from a schema. First, Figure 9.12 shows the document before the processing.

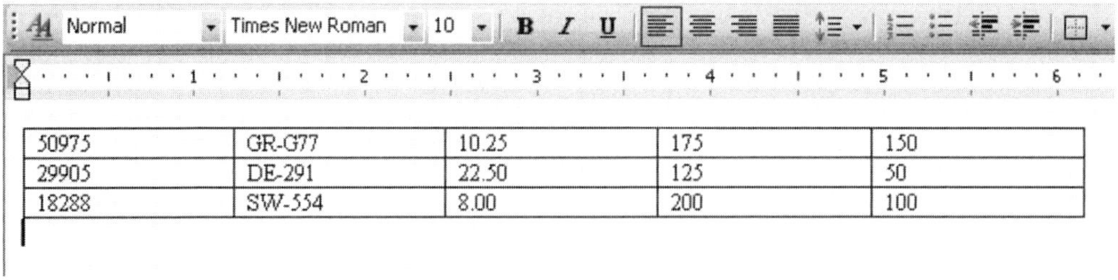

50975	GR-G77	10.25	175	150
29905	DE-291	22.50	125	50
18288	SW-554	8.00	200	100

Figure 9.12 A Word table inside a document

The markup process is automated. A VBA routine addresses the table, row, and cell objects and applies the appropriate tags. The `uses_schema_to_markup_document_table` routine is shown in Listing 9.8.

Listing 9.8 Marking up Word data with XML tags from an attached schema

```
Sub uses_schema_to_markup_document_table()
Dim example_path As String
Dim namespace As String
Dim row_count As Integer
Dim mark_up As Integer
example_path = "C:\2003_June\XML\Word\inventory_examples\"
namespace = "http://solutions4office.com/inventory/ex1"
Application.XMLNamespaces.Add Path:= _
     example_path & "inventory_schema.xsd", _
     NamespaceURI:=namespace
Application.XMLNamespaces(namespace). _
    AttachToDocument (ActiveDocument)
' already know table is 5 columns
' each row equates to "Part" element
' each column equates to a child of Part
With ActiveDocument.Tables(1)
    row_count = .Rows.Count
    For mark_up = 1 To row_count
       .Rows(mark_up).Select
       ActiveDocument.XMLNodes.Add "Part", namespace
       .Cell(mark_up, 1).Select
       ActiveDocument.XMLNodes.Add "PartNumber", ""
       .Cell(mark_up, 2).Select
       ActiveDocument.XMLNodes.Add "Description", ""
```

Listing 9.8 *(continued)*

```
        .Cell(mark_up, 3).Select
        ActiveDocument.XMLNodes.Add "UnitCost", ""
        .Cell(mark_up, 4).Select
        ActiveDocument.XMLNodes.Add "Quantity", ""
        .Cell(mark_up, 5).Select
        ActiveDocument.XMLNodes.Add "ReorderLevel", ""
    Next mark_up
    .Select
End With
Selection.Rows.ConvertToText Separator:=wdSeparateByParagraphs
Selection.Collapse wdup
MsgBox "done"
End Sub
```

In this routine, the document with the table (new_inventory.doc) is assumed to be open and is the active document. The schema is added via the namespace and then is attached to the active document:

```
example_path = "C:\2003_June\XML\Word\inventory_examples\"
namespace = "http://solutions4office.com/inventory/ex1"

Application.XMLNamespaces.Add Path:= _
    example_path & "inventory_schema.xsd", _
    NamespaceURI:=namespace

Application.XMLNamespaces(namespace). _
    AttachToDocument (ActiveDocument)
```

With the knowledge that the active document has one table with five columns of data, we use the following code to mark up the data using the Add method of the XMLNodes collection. In particular, the table is looped through based on the number of rows in the table (from the Rows.Count property). Each entire row is tagged as a Part element, then within the loop, as each individual row is being processed, each cell of the row receives the appropriate tag:

```
With ActiveDocument.Tables(1)
    row_count = .Rows.Count
    For mark_up = 1 To row_count
        .Rows(mark_up).Select
        ActiveDocument.XMLNodes.Add "Part", namespace
```

```
            .Cell(mark_up, 1).Select
        ActiveDocument.XMLNodes.Add "PartNumber", ""
            .Cell(mark_up, 2).Select
        ActiveDocument.XMLNodes.Add "Description", ""
            .Cell(mark_up, 3).Select
        ActiveDocument.XMLNodes.Add "UnitCost", ""
            .Cell(mark_up, 4).Select
        ActiveDocument.XMLNodes.Add "Quantity", ""
            .Cell(mark_up, 5).Select
        ActiveDocument.XMLNodes.Add "ReorderLevel", ""
    Next mark_up
    .Select
End With
```

Finally, the table is converted to text:

```
Selection.Rows.ConvertToText Separator:=wdSeparateByParagraphs
```

The result: the data is properly tagged, as shown in Figure 9.13.

Attributes

Attributes are not visible in tagged data in Word. Back in Figures 9.5 and 9.9, attributes are not shown, although they are present in the XML data. To view attributes, the Attributes dialog is used. See Figure 9.14. This dialog can be opened by right-clicking on a tag indicator. In Figure 9.14 the Attributes dialog is displaying attributes for the Part element, because that is the tag that received a right-click. The Part element does have the Manufacturer attribute; the name and value of the attribute are seen in the dialog.

Nodes

A node can be either an element or an attribute. XPath is used to select a node or group of nodes. In Word there is an XMLNodes collection, the XMLNode object, the SelectNodes method, and the SelectSingleNode method. Given this, some useful applications involving XPath and nodes are achievable. Listing 9.9 shows how the objects and methods are used with VBA code.

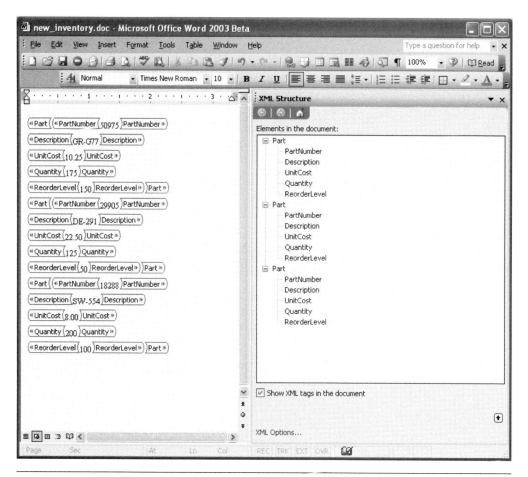

Figure 9.13 Table data has been tagged

Listing 9.9 Using XPath syntax to select XML data

```
Sub explore_nodes()
Dim xml_node As XMLNode
Dim xml_nodes As XMLNodes
With ActiveDocument
  Set xml_node = .SelectSingleNode("//Part[2]/Quantity")
  Debug.Print "The Quantity of the second Part is " & _
```

Listing 9.9 *(continued)*

```
      xml_node.Text
  Set xml_nodes = _
    .SelectNodes(("//Part[@Manufacturer='Heartland
Hardware']"))
  Debug.Print "There are " & xml_nodes.Count & _
    " Parts from Heartland Hardware"
End With
End Sub
```

Figure 9.14 Displaying attributes

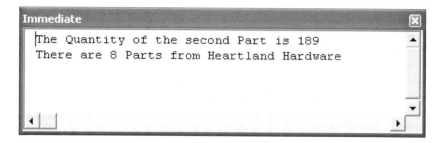

Figure 9.15 The Immediate window shows returned information about an XML file

Assuming that the XML file shown in Listing 9.1 is the active document, the `explore_nodes` routine in Listing 9.9 would return the information shown in Figure 9.15.

XML and Access 2003

Access programmatically supports three methods to address XML data. These are `ImportXML`, `ExportXML`, and `TransformXML`. There is no support for external schemas. When importing data, Access corrals the data to the standard data types it supports.

Importing XML

The `ImportXML` method is used to import XML data into an Access table. There are two parameters to the method: the path to the XML file and an indicator of how to use the incoming data. There are three options in this regard: import data and structure, import just structure, or append data. These are the same options available when importing text or importing from another Access table.

Listing 9.10 shows the salesdata.xml file.

Listing 9.10 The salesdata.xml file to be imported into Access

```
<?xml version="1.0" encoding="UTF-8"?>
<SalesData>
  <SalesRecord>
    <UnitDescription>Gizmos</UnitDescription>
```

Listing 9.10 *(continued)*

```
    <UnitsSold>45</UnitsSold>
    <PricePerUnit>14.95</PricePerUnit>
  </SalesRecord>
  <SalesRecord>
    <UnitDescription>Gadgets</UnitDescription>
    <UnitsSold>92</UnitsSold>
    <PricePerUnit>8.95</PricePerUnit>
  </SalesRecord>
  <SalesRecord>
    <UnitDescription>Spin-A-Rounds</UnitDescription>
    <UnitsSold>17</UnitsSold>
    <PricePerUnit>6</PricePerUnit>
  </SalesRecord>
  <SalesRecord>
    <UnitDescription>Time Wasters</UnitDescription>
    <UnitsSold>33</UnitsSold>
    <PricePerUnit>9.99</PricePerUnit>
  </SalesRecord>
</SalesData>
```

The salesdata.xml file is imported into Access, with the "Structure and Data" option. The code to do this is:

```
Sub import_xml_all_elements()
  Dim data_path As String
  ' change path as needed
  data_path = "C:\XML_Files\salesdata.xml"
  Application.ImportXML data_path, acStructureAndData
  MsgBox "done"
End Sub
```

The result of this import operation is shown in Figure 9.16.

The XML data is now stored in Access as standard Access data. Note that the data root of the XML file, SalesData, is not carried over. Instead, the table name is the same as the first child of the data root: SalesRecord. The element names—UnitDescription, UnitsSold, and PricePerUnit—have become the field names. The data correctly appears within the fields.

Taking this a step further, Listing 9.11 shows an altered version of the XML file. In this case new elements for SalesPerson and Territory have been added at the top. Note that while the SalesRecord elements repeat, the SalesPerson and Territory elements appear just once.

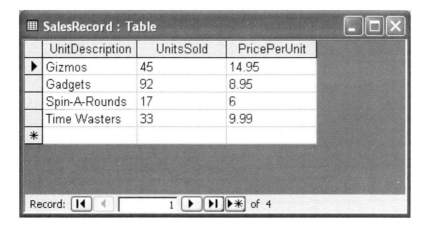

Figure 9.16 The `ImportXML` method creates a new table

Listing 9.11 The salesdata_2.xml file has additional elements

```xml
<?xml version="1.0" encoding="UTF-8"?>
<SalesData>
  <SalesPerson>Mary Smith</SalesPerson>
  <Territory>SouthWest</Territory>
  <SalesRecord>
    <UnitDescription>Gizmos</UnitDescription>
    <UnitsSold>45</UnitsSold>
    <PricePerUnit>14.95</PricePerUnit>
  </SalesRecord>
  <SalesRecord>
    <UnitDescription>Gadgets</UnitDescription>
    <UnitsSold>92</UnitsSold>
    <PricePerUnit>8.95</PricePerUnit>
  </SalesRecord>
  <SalesRecord>
    <UnitDescription>Spin-A-Rounds</UnitDescription>
    <UnitsSold>17</UnitsSold>
    <PricePerUnit>6</PricePerUnit>
  </SalesRecord>
  <SalesRecord>
```

Listing 9.11 *(continued)*

```
   <UnitDescription>Time Wasters</UnitDescription>
   <UnitsSold>33</UnitsSold>
   <PricePerUnit>9.99</PricePerUnit>
  </SalesRecord>
</SalesData>
```

The same routine is used, with just the file name changed:

```
Sub import_xml_all_elements()
  Dim data_path As String
  ' change path as needed
  data_path = "C:\XML_Files\salesdata_2.xml"
  Application.ImportXML data_path, acStructureAndData
  MsgBox "done"
End Sub
```

In this case Access has split the data into two tables. Access has sensed that the SalesRecord elements contain repeating data, and that the SalesPerson and Territory elements are not part of the repeating data. Figure 9.17 shows the result of the import.

Access will not import attributes. Listing 9.12 shows an XML file based on attributes.

Listing 9.12 The Geography.xml file is all attributes

```
<?xml version="1.0" encoding="UTF-8"?>
<Geography>
  <Country name="Canada">
    <Province Name="Ontario">
      <City name="Toronto"/>
      <City name="Thunder Bay"/>
      <City name="Wellington"/>
    </Province>
    <Province Name="Quebec">
      <City name="Montreal"/>
      <City name="Quebec City"/>
      <City name="Pierre"/>
    </Province>
  </Country>
</Geography>
```

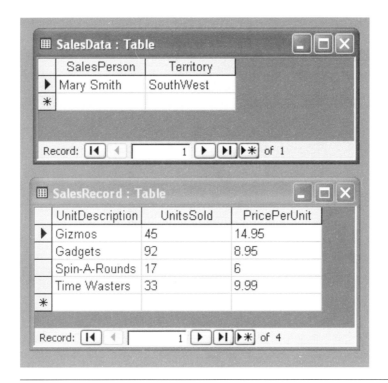

Figure 9.17 Access imports one XML file into two tables

Using this import routine:

```
Sub import_xml_all_attributes()
  Dim data_path As String
  ' change path as needed
  data_path = "C:\XML_Files\Geography.xml"
  Application.ImportXML data_path, acStructureAndData
  MsgBox "done"
End Sub
```

results in the table shown in Figure 9.18.

The table is not named after the Country element. Instead, the table is named "Province," which is the grandchild of the root element (Geography–Country–Province). The one field—City—contains no data. The conclusion here is that the ImportXML method is useful with element-based data only.

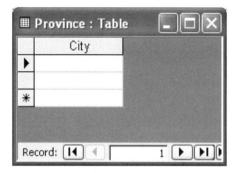

Figure 9.18 A table is created but attribute data is not imported

Exporting XML

The `ExportXML` method is used for exporting data out of Access into an XML format. Both single table/query data and multiple table/query data can be exported. An Access database named Pets.mdb is used to demonstrate. Figure 9.19 shows the Relationships window of the database, which is modeled on a veterinarian practice. There are tables for Clients, Pets,

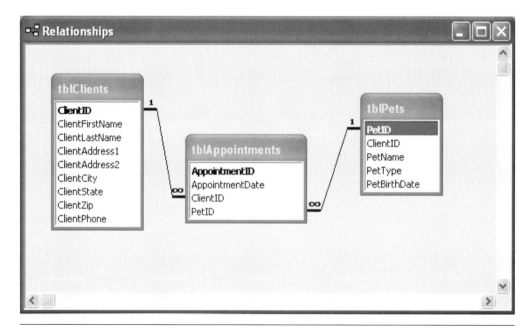

Figure 9.19 Table relationships in the Pets.mdb database

and Appointments. The tblAppointments table joins the tblClients and tblPets tables.

The `export_xml_1` routine in Listing 9.13 exports just the Clients table (tblClients). A path is supplied and two parameters are indicated. One is the name of the XML file to be created (clients.xml) and the other is the name of the schema file to be created (clients.xsd).

Listing 9.13 Exporting a single table to an XML file

```
Sub export_xml_1()
Dim output_path As String
' change path as needed
output_path = "C:\XML_Files\Example1\"
Application.ExportXML acExportTable, "tblClients", _
  output_path & "clients.xml", _
  output_path & "clients.xsd"
MsgBox "done"
End Sub
```

Figure 9.20 shows the created clients.xml file, as displayed in Internet Explorer.

The clients.xsd file has also been created. A portion of it is shown here:

```
.
.
.
<xsd:complexType>
<xsd:sequence>
<xsd:element name="ClientID" minOccurs="1"
    od:jetType="autonumber"    od:sqlSType="int"
    od:autoUnique="yes"
    od:nonNullable="yes" type="xsd:int"/>
<xsd:element name="ClientFirstName" minOccurs="0"
    od:jetType="text" od:sqlSType="nvarchar">
<xsd:simpleType>
<xsd:restriction base="xsd:string">
<xsd:maxLength value="50"/>
</xsd:restriction>
</xsd:simpleType>
</xsd:element>
.
.
.
```

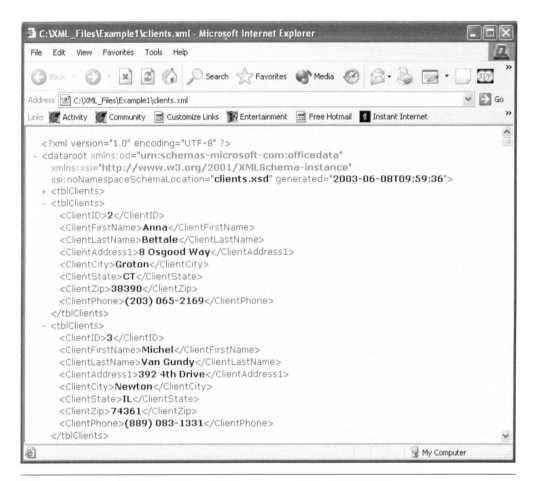

Figure 9.20 The clients.xml file, which is an export of a single table

Note how the schema file contains `jetType` and `sqlSType` attributes. In other words, this schema contains information useful for Access and SQL Server XML operations. In fact, during an import, Access will not accept schemas other than a type like this that it recognizes.

Next, a multitable export is run. The `export_xml_2` routine is shown in Listing 9.14.

Listing 9.14 Two related tables are exported to an XML file

```
Sub export_xml_2()
Dim output_path As String
' create an AdditionalData object
Dim objAD As AdditionalData
Set objAD = Application.CreateAdditionalData
' the "base" table is indicated in the ExportXML method
' so first establish the related tables for the export
With objAD
   .Add "tblAppointments"
End With
' change path as needed
output_path = "C:\XML_Files\Example2\"
Application.ExportXML acExportTable, "tblClients", _
   output_path & "clients.xml", _
   output_path & "clients.xsd", AdditionalData:=objAD
MsgBox "done"
End Sub
```

In the `export_xml_2` routine, there is a new object: `Additional-Data`. This object serves to capture export instructions, which are then applied as a parameter to the `ExportXML` method. First the object is created:

```
Dim objAD As AdditionalData
Set objAD = Application.CreateAdditionalData
```

Next, objects to be included in the export are added to the `Additional-Data` object. A key point here is that the `AdditionalData` object is being fed the names of the *related* object(s). The *main* object is specified later in the actual method call. So, in this case, tblAppointments is added to `objAD`:

```
With objAD
   .Add "tblAppointments"
End With
```

Finally, when the export method is called, the tblClients table is identified, and the method uses the `AdditionalData` parameter:

```
Application.ExportXML acExportTable, "tblClients", _
   output_path & "clients.xml", _
   output_path & "clients.xsd", AdditionalData:=objAD
MsgBox "done"
```

Figure 9.21 shows the output of this operation displayed in Internet Explorer. The key difference, compared with Figure 9.20, is that the related data (from tblAppointments) is embedded in the client data.

Finally, the export_xml_3 routine in Listing 9.15 adds the Clients and Pets tables to the AdditionalData object. The base table here is

Figure 9.21 XML output of two related tables

tblAppointments. This routine attempts to use the junction Appointments table (creating the many-to-many of Clients and Pets) to embed the client and pet data as children of each appointment.

Listing 9.15 Indicating to treat clients and pets as children of appointments

```
Sub export_xml_3()
Dim output_path As String
' create an AdditionalData object
Dim objAD As AdditionalData
Set objAD = Application.CreateAdditionalData
' the "base" table is indicated in the ExportXML method
' so first establish the related tables for the export
With objAD
  .Add "tblClients"
  .Add "tblPets"
End With
' change path as needed
output_path = "C:\XML_Files\Example3\"
Application.ExportXML acExportTable, "tblAppointments", _
  output_path & "appointments.xml", _
  output_path & "appointments.xsd", AdditionalData:=objAD
MsgBox "done"
End Sub
```

The `export_xml_3` routine creates a nonhierarchical XML data structure. The result is that all appointment data is followed with all client data, which is followed with all pet data. The relations did not transfer into the XML. Figure 9.22 shows a midsection of the XML file, displayed in Internet Explorer. As can be seen, the appointment data ends and the client data begins.

Transforming XML

Access can be used to transform XML using an XSL (XSLT) file. The `TransformXML` method takes three parameters: the path to the source XML, the path to the transformation file, and the output path. Listing 9.16 shows how this method is used.

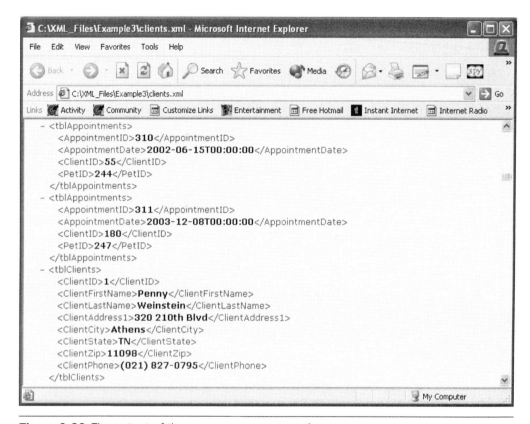

Figure 9.22 The output of the `export_xml_3` routine

Listing 9.16 Using the `TransformXML` method

```
Sub transform_xml()
Dim example_path As String
' change path as needed
example_path = "C:\XML_Files\Example4\"
 Application.TransformXML _
    example_path & "office_data.xml", _
    example_path & "office_data.xsl", _
    example_path & "office_data.html"
MsgBox "done"
End Sub
```

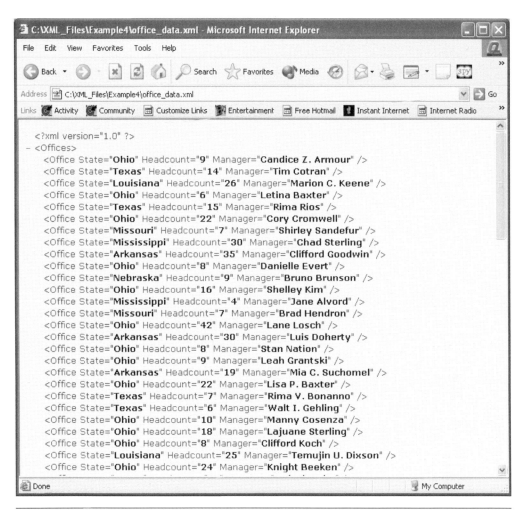

Figure 9.23 The office_data.xml file before being transformed

The office_data.xml file is shown in Figure 9.23. The root element is `Offices`. There are several `Office` elements, which have three data points as attributes: `State`, `Headcount`, and `Manager`.

The office_data.xsl file, shown in Listing 9.17, is used to transform the data.

Listing 9.17 An XSLT used to transform the office_data.xml file

```
<?xml version="1.0"?>
<xsl:stylesheet
 xmlns:xsl="http://www.w3.org/1999/XSL/Transform"
 version="1.0">
<xsl:output method="html"/>
<xsl:template match="/">
  <HTML>
  <HEAD>
  <TITLE>Office Headcounts</TITLE>
  </HEAD>
  <BODY>
  Headcounts over 25 are in <B>Bold</B><BR/><BR/>
  <TABLE WIDTH="100%" Border="1">
    <TR>
      <TH>City</TH>
      <TH>Head Count</TH>
      <TH>Manager</TH>
    </TR>
    <xsl:for-each select="Offices/Office">
    <TR>
      <xsl:choose>
      <xsl:when  test="@Headcount>25">
        <TD ALIGN="Center">
           <B><xsl:value-of select="@State"/></B></TD>
        <TD ALIGN="Center">
           <B><xsl:value-of select="@Headcount"/></B></TD>
        <TD ALIGN="Center">
           <B><xsl:value-of select="@Manager"/></B></TD>
      </xsl:when>
      <xsl:otherwise>
        <TD ALIGN="Center">
           <xsl:value-of select="@State"/></TD>
        <TD ALIGN="Center">
           <xsl:value-of select="@Headcount"/></TD>
        <TD ALIGN="Center">
           <xsl:value-of select="@Manager"/></TD>
      </xsl:otherwise>
      </xsl:choose>
    </TR>
    </xsl:for-each>
  </TABLE>
```

Listing 9.17 *(continued)*

```
   </BODY>
   </HTML>
</xsl:template>
</xsl:stylesheet>
```

The transform is accomplished by reading all the Office elements with this statement:

```
<xsl:for-each select="Offices/Office">
```

For each office, a test checks if the Headcount attribute contains a value greater than 25. If it does, then the State, Headcount, and Manager values are output with bold tags (<B> </B>) around them (which makes them appear bold). If the Headcount is 25 or less, then the three data points are output as nonbold:

```
<xsl:choose>
<xsl:when  test="@Headcount>25">
  <TD ALIGN="Center">
      <B><xsl:value-of select="@State"/></R></TD>
  <TD ALIGN="Center">
      <B><xsl:value-of select="@Headcount"/></B></TD>
  <TD ALIGN="Center">
      <B><xsl:value-of select="@Manager"/></B></TD>
</xsl:when>
<xsl:otherwise>
  <TD ALIGN="Center">
      <xsl:value-of select="@State"/></TD>
  <TD ALIGN="Center">
      <xsl:value-of select="@Headcount"/></TD>
  <TD ALIGN="Center">
      <xsl:value-of select="@Manager"/></TD>
</xsl:otherwise>
</xsl:choose>
```

When this transform is run, the office_data.html file is created, shown in Figure 9.24. The rows with Headcounts greater than 25 are bold.

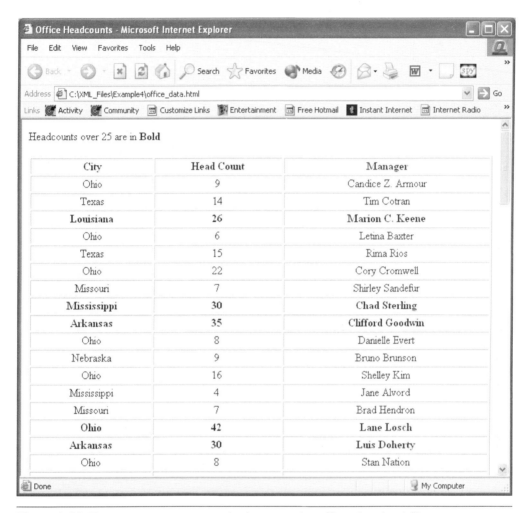

Figure 9.24 The `TransformXML` method creates the office_data.html file

XML and Excel 2003

XML Maps

In Excel, much of the processing and manipulation of XML data is managed through the use of a new object: the XML map. Maps essentially are representations of XML schema. The advantages of XML maps are that they are contained in a collection; they can individually be swapped in and out; and they have several properties and a few methods with which to manipulate data.

The `Add` method is used to add a map to the `XmlMaps` collection. The collection belongs to the `Workbook` object. A map can be culled either from a schema file or directly from an XML file. In the latter case, Excel will infer a schema from the data. In Listing 9.18, the `explore_maps` routine shows how two maps are added. The first is from a schema, and the second is directly from an XML file.

Listing 9.18 Adding maps to the `XmlMaps` collection

```
Sub explore_maps()
Dim map_count As Integer
Dim map_loop As Integer
With ActiveWorkbook
  ' delete any existing maps
  map_count = .XmlMaps.Count
  For map_loop = map_count To 1 Step -1
    .XmlMaps(map_loop).Delete
  Next map_loop
 .XmlMaps.Add("C:\XML_Files\student_grades_schema.xsd").Name _
      = "Student Grades Schema"
 .XmlMaps.Add("C:\XML_Files\student_grades.xml").Name _
      = "Student Grades XML"
End With
End Sub
```

Each add operation points to a file and names the map. The first add points to a schema (.xsd) file and names the new map as `"Student Grades Schema"`:

```
.XmlMaps.Add("C:\XML_Files\student_grades_schema.xsd").Name _
      = "Student Grades Schema"
```

The second add is directly from XML data. Excel will create a map from it but will display the message shown in Figure 9.25.

Listings 9.19 and 9.20 show the student_grades_schema.xsd and student_grades.xml files, respectively.

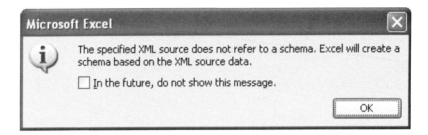

Figure 9.25 Excel warns that it will create an inferred schema

Listing 9.19 The student_grades_schema.xsd file

```
<?xml version="1.0" encoding="UTF-8"?>
<xsd:schema xmlns:xsd="http://www.w3.org/2001/XMLSchema"
   targetNamespace="http://www.solutions4office.com/students">
<xsd:element name="StudentGrades">
  <xsd:complexType>
    <xsd:sequence>
      <xsd:element name="Instructor" minOccurs="1"
          maxOccurs="1">
        <xsd:simpleType>
          <xsd:restriction base="xsd:string"/>
        </xsd:simpleType>
      </xsd:element>
      <xsd:element name="Course" minOccurs="1" maxOccurs="1">
        <xsd:simpleType>
          <xsd:restriction base="xsd:string"/>
        </xsd:simpleType>
      </xsd:element>
      <xsd:element name="Semester" minOccurs="1" maxOccurs="1">
        <xsd:simpleType>
          <xsd:restriction base="xsd:string"/>
        </xsd:simpleType>
      </xsd:element>
    <xsd:element name="Student" maxOccurs="unbounded">
      <xsd:complexType>
        <xsd:sequence>
          <xsd:element name="Name" minOccurs="1"
              maxOccurs="1">
            <xsd:simpleType>
              <xsd:restriction base="xsd:string"/>
            </xsd:simpleType>
```

Listing 9.19 *(continued)*

```
                </xsd:element>
                <xsd:element name="Midterm_Grade" minOccurs="1"
                    maxOccurs="1">
                  <xsd:simpleType>
                    <xsd:restriction base="xsd:string"/>
                  </xsd:simpleType>
                </xsd:element>
                <xsd:element name="Final_Grade" minOccurs="1"
                    maxOccurs="1">
                  <xsd:simpleType>
                    <xsd:restriction base="xsd:string"/>
                  </xsd:simpleType>
                </xsd:element>
            </xsd:sequence>
          </xsd:complexType>
      </xsd:element>
      </xsd:sequence>
    </xsd:complexType>
</xsd:element>
</xsd:schema>
```

Listing 9.20 The student_grades.xml file

```
<?xml version="1.0"?>
<StudentGrades>
<Instructor>Thomas Marrelton</Instructor>
<Course>Ancient History</Course>
<Semester>Spring 2003</Semester>
  <Student>
    <Name>Rob Albrecht</Name>
    <Midterm_Grade>B</Midterm_Grade>
    <Final_Grade>B</Final_Grade>
  </Student>
  <Student>
    <Name>Claudette Sunder</Name>
    <Midterm_Grade>B</Midterm_Grade>
    <Final_Grade>A</Final_Grade>
  </Student>
  <Student>
    <Name>Donna Davidson</Name>
    <Midterm_Grade>C</Midterm_Grade>
```

Listing 9.20 *(continued)*

```
    <Final_Grade>C</Final_Grade>
  </Student>
  <Student>
    <Name>Ann Cuttori</Name>
    <Midterm_Grade>B</Midterm_Grade>
    <Final_Grade>C</Final_Grade>
  </Student>
  <Student>
    <Name>Mark Antelman</Name>
    <Midterm_Grade>C</Midterm_Grade>
    <Final_Grade>A</Final_Grade>
  </Student>
  <Student>
    <Name>Kristie Deatrick</Name>
    <Midterm_Grade>B</Midterm_Grade>
    <Final_Grade>B</Final_Grade>
  </Student>
  <Student>
    <Name>Barry L. Hagenstick</Name>
    <Midterm_Grade>B</Midterm_Grade>
    <Final_Grade>A</Final_Grade>
  </Student>
</StudentGrades>
```

The two maps are now available to use in Excel. Either can be selected in the XML Source task pane, shown in Figure 9.26. These two maps are identical in design; they appear identical in the task pane, as well.

In the task pane is the Workbook Maps button. Clicking it displays the XML Maps dialog (see Figure 9.27). The dialog does point out a difference between the two maps. The schema file (in Listing 9.19) has a `targetNamespace` attribute. This attribute has been stored as the namespace for the map. The map based directly on the XML data does not have a namespace.

At this point at least one schema is in place in the workbook. However, no data is present. A schema can be used as a template to enter data. The fields in the XML Source task pane can be dragged onto the worksheet. Doing so will result in two possible outcomes. Dragging the `Instructor`, `Course`, or `Semester` fields to the worksheet results in single-entry cells for each of these fields. Dragging the `Student` element, or either of its children—`Midterm_Grade` or `Final_Grade`—results in a list.

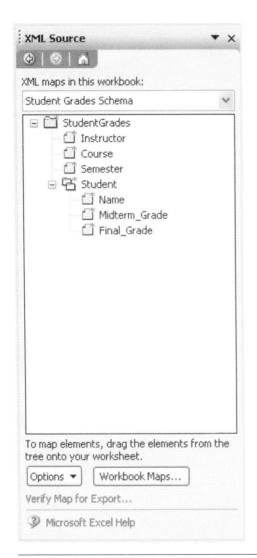

Figure 9.26 The XML Source task pane shows the XML maps

The reason for this distinction has to do with how the schema describes the structure. In Listing 9.19, the `Instructor`, `Course`, and `Semester` fields are restricted to a single instance. In particular, the `maxOccurs` attribute is set to 1. An element described in this manner can appear only once, or it is not valid:

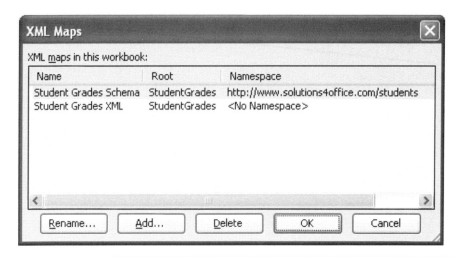

Figure 9.27 The XML Maps dialog

```
<xsd:element name="Instructor" minOccurs="1"
    maxOccurs="1">
```

On the other hand, the `Student` element has the `"unbounded"` value for the `maxOccurs` attribute. This literally means these elements can appear an endless number of times:

```
<xsd:element name="Student" maxOccurs="unbounded">
```

Excel recognizes the distinction of the `maxOccurs` attribute and acts accordingly to treat associated data as repeating or nonrepeating. The repeating elements on the worksheet are bound by a border and have an extra row at all times ready for input to append to the list. (Lists are explained in a section later in this chapter.) An asterisk is present in the "new record" row. Figure 9.28 shows the worksheet with the dragged fields.

Importing XML

XML imports are accomplished through an XML map. XML data cannot exist on a worksheet without an associated map, so it is necessary to indicate a map when importing XML. However, the map can be derived from the XML file.

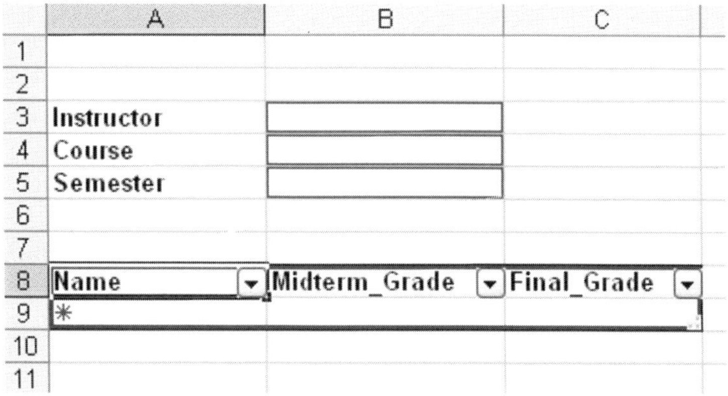

Figure 9.28 A worksheet with entry points based on the schema

The `import_xml` routine in Listing 9.21 imports XML data from a file. The XML data to be imported is in Listing 9.20, shown previously. The map is based on the structure of the XML file.

Listing 9.21 Importing XML data

```
Sub import_xml()
Dim new_worksheet As Worksheet
Dim student_grades_map As XmlMap
Application.DisplayAlerts = False
With ActiveWorkbook
' delete the Student Grades worksheet, if it exists
On Error Resume Next
Worksheets("Student Grades").Delete
On Error GoTo 0
' add new worksheet, name it Student Grades
Set new_worksheet = .Worksheets.Add
new_worksheet.Name = "Student Grades"
new_worksheet.Activate
' delete any existing maps
map_count = .XmlMaps.Count
For map_loop = map_count To 1 Step -1
  .XmlMaps(map_loop).Delete
Next map_loop
' import xml file, assign map as student_grades_map
' overwrite=true, destination is cell B2
```

Listing 9.21 *(continued)*

```
    .XmlImport "C:\XML_Files\student_grades.xml", _
    student_grades_map, True, "B2"
    End With
End Sub
```

The `import_xml` routine first deletes and then adds back the Student Grades worksheet:

```
Worksheets("Student Grades").Delete
On Error GoTo 0
' add new worksheet, name it Student Grades
Set new_worksheet = .Worksheets.Add
new_worksheet.Name = "Student Grades"
new_worksheet.Activate
```

All existing maps are deleted. This step is not required, but it ensures that the map that will be created during the import does not duplicate an existing map:

```
For map_loop = map_count To 1 Step -1
  .XmlMaps(map_loop).Delete
Next map_loop
```

Finally, the `XmlImport` method imports the data. The path to the data file is indicated. Also, a reference to the map object is included. This is a required parameter. The last two parameters indicate whether to overwrite existing data, and where to place the data on the worksheet. Although included here, the overwrite parameter serves no purpose because the routine re-creates the entire worksheet. There cannot be any data to overwrite:

```
    .XmlImport "C:\XML_Files\student_grades.xml", _
    student_grades_map, True, "B2"
```

The data lands in the worksheet as a structured list. See Figure 9.29. The result is interesting because the data has been denormalized. This may be an unwanted effect in some cases, but it is typical of the way data is kept in Excel.

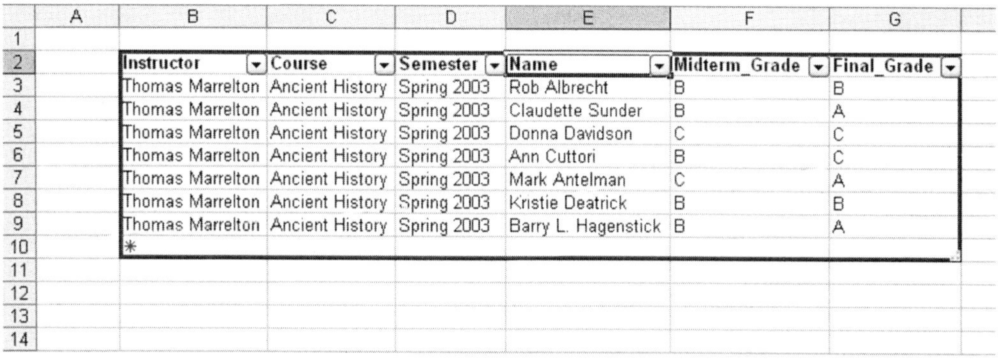

Instructor	Course	Semester	Name	Midterm_Grade	Final_Grade
Thomas Marrelton	Ancient History	Spring 2003	Rob Albrecht	B	B
Thomas Marrelton	Ancient History	Spring 2003	Claudette Sunder	B	A
Thomas Marrelton	Ancient History	Spring 2003	Donna Davidson	C	C
Thomas Marrelton	Ancient History	Spring 2003	Ann Cuttori	B	C
Thomas Marrelton	Ancient History	Spring 2003	Mark Antelman	C	A
Thomas Marrelton	Ancient History	Spring 2003	Kristie Deatrick	B	B
Thomas Marrelton	Ancient History	Spring 2003	Barry L. Hagenstick	B	A

Figure 9.29 Imported XML data appears as a list

Exporting XML

XML export is done through a map. Using the map ensures that the data is well formed; if it isn't, the export will not proceed. To clarify, even if the data on a worksheet is well formed in its own right, it must match the schema of the specified map. Taken from another perspective, the map must already be associated with data, or there will be nothing to export. The `export_xml` routine in Listing 9.22 runs an export.

Listing 9.22 Exporting XML from a worksheet

```
sub export_xml()
Dim output_file As String
With ActiveWorkbook
  output_file = .Path & "\xml_out_1.xml"
  On Error Resume Next
  Kill output_file
  .XmlMaps(1).Export (output_file)
End With
End Sub
```

Opening XML

The `OpenXML` method opens an XML file into a new workbook. There are three parameters: the path to the XML file, a style sheet indicator, and an open option indicator. There are four open options: three control how the data is opened into a workbook, and the fourth is used to allow a user to intervene and select one of the other three. The three significant option values and their meanings are as follows:

- `xlXmlLoadImportToList`—load onto the worksheet as a list
- `xlXmlLoadMapXml`—load as a schema into the XML Source task pane
- `xlXmlLoadOpenXml`—load onto the worksheet with XPath headers (as done in Excel 2002)

The `open_xml` routine in Listing 9.23 opens the office_data.xml file three times—each time with a different open option.

Listing 9.23 Options for opening an XML file

```
Sub open_xml()
  Dim data_path As String
  ' change path as needed
  data_path = "C:\XML_Files\office_data.xml"
  Workbooks.OpenXML data_path, , xlXmlLoadImportToList
  Workbooks.OpenXML data_path, , xlXmlLoadMapXml
  Workbooks.OpenXML data_path, , xlXmlLoadOpenXml
End Sub
```

Figure 9.30 shows the three open workbooks, arranged for visibility in the application space. One important point to consider is that there must be, or must have been, at least one other open workbook. The `open_xml` routine had to have been in an open workbook in order for it to have opened the other workbooks.

In Figure 9.30, the top workbook appears empty. This is the workbook that was opened as a map. The XML Source task pane shows the derived schema, because in Figure 9.30 that particular workbook is the active one. If one of the other workbooks were activated, the task pane would be empty.

Saving XML

Saving XML data is similar to exporting XML data   it is done through a map. Listing 9.24 shows how the code works.

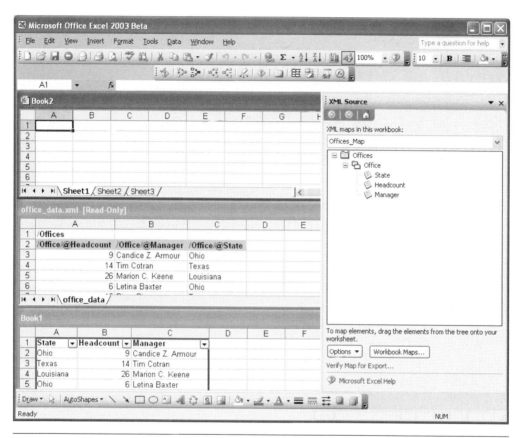

Figure 9.30 Three ways of opening an XML file

Listing 9.24 Using the `SaveAsXMLData` method

```
Sub saveas_xml()
Dim output_file As String
With ActiveWorkbook
  output_file = .Path & "\xml_out.xml"
  .SaveAsXMLData output_file, .XmlMaps(1)
End With
End Sub
```

A map may or may not be able to output the XML. The SaveAsXML-Data method will complete a save only if the XML is normalized. In Figure 9.30, in the lower-right corner, is the "Verify Map for Export" link. If the

Figure 9.31 XML data cannot be saved if denormalized

data is not normalized, as seen with the Student Grades data in Figure 9.29, the Verify Map for Export link returns the message shown in Figure 9.31.

Lists

Lists are objects, similar to ranges, but with some unique properties and methods. Lists have a conceptual association with XML data because XML placed on a worksheet becomes a list. Lists, however, can be treated independently.

Programmatically, lists are called `ListObjects`. There is a `ListObjects` collection, which belongs to the `Worksheet` object. Referring to the list seen in Figure 9.29, the `explore_lists` routine, in Listing 9.25, returns information about the `ListObjects` collection, and about the individual list.

Listing 9.25 Working with lists

```
Sub explore_lists()
Dim ws As Worksheet
Set ws = Worksheets(ActiveSheet.Name)
Debug.Print "The active worksheet has " & _
    ws.ListObjects.Count & " list(s)"
With ws.ListObjects(1)
  Debug.Print "The first list..."
  Debug.Print "   occupies " & .Range.Address
  Debug.Print "   has " & .ListColumns.Count & " columns"
  Debug.Print "   has " & .ListRows.Count & " rows"
  Debug.Print " has this map: " & .XmlMap
End With
End Sub
```

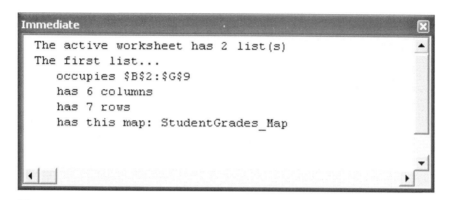

Figure 9.32 Information about a list on a worksheet

Figure 9.32 displays the output of the `explore_lists` routine.

Lists can be programmatically added and deleted. This snippet of code adds a list in the first column from rows 15 to 20, and names it as "New List":

```
Dim ws As Worksheet
Set ws = Worksheets(ActiveSheet.Name)
With ws
.ListObjects.Add(xlSrcRange, Range("$A$15:$A$20"), , _
   True).Name = "New List"
End With
```

Using the MSXML Parser to Work with XML Data

Even though Microsoft Office 2003 has a great deal of XML support built into some products, there is still quite a bit that cannot be accomplished. For example, there is no real way to code XML solutions with PowerPoint. Excel requires a map for import and export. Access cannot import attributes.

Microsoft provides a robust XML parser, called MSXML (also known as Microsoft XML Core Services). It is available as a free download from the Microsoft MSDN Web site (see the Appendix). It is implemented as a reference within the References list in the Visual Basic Editor. The MSXML Parser can be used with any product.

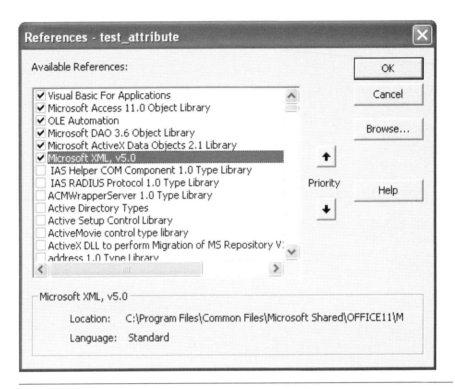

Figure 9.33 Establishing a reference to the MSXML Parser

Once downloaded and installed, a reference needs to be made, as shown in Figure 9.33.

The functionality offered by the MSXML Parser is vast, and a comprehensive discussion is beyond the scope of this book. However, to demonstrate how the parser can complement the XML functionality in Office 2003, the `get_xml_using_parser` routine in Listing 9.26 overcomes a limitation discussed earlier in the chapter. Back in the discussion on XML and Access, it was shown that Access cannot import attributes. This was clearly seen in Figure 9.18 (see page 302).

In contrast, the `get_xml_using_parser` routine reads through the same attribute-based XML file and fills an Access table with the attribute data.

Listing 9.26 Using the MSXML Parser to bring attribute data into Access

```
Sub get_xml_using_parser()
  On Error GoTo err_end
  Dim conn As ADODB.Connection
  Dim xmlobj As DOMDocument
  Dim xmlnode As IXMLDOMNode
  Dim xmlchildnode As IXMLDOMNode
  Dim xmlnodelist As IXMLDOMNodeList
  Dim xml_file As String
  Dim province_name As String
  Dim ssql As String
  ' conn . . .
  Set conn = CurrentProject.Connection
  ' set reference to XML file
  ' change path as needed
  xml_file = "C:\XML_Files\Geography.xml"
  ' load XML file into DOM object
  Set xmlobj = New DOMDocument
  xmlobj.async = False
  xmlobj.Load xml_file

  ' create node list of Provinces
  Set xmlnodelist = _
   xmlobj.selectNodes _
   ("/Geography/Country/Province")
  ' for each Province in Provinces . . .
  For Each xmlnode In xmlnodelist
    ' store province name - comes from attribute
    province_name = xmlnode.Attributes(0).Text
    ' for each city in province (a city is a child)
    For Each xmlchildnode In xmlnode.childNodes
      ' insert province and city into Access table
      ssql = "Insert Into tblGeography (Province, City) " & _
          "Values ('" & province_name & "', '" & _
          xmlchildnode.Attributes(0).Text & "')"
      conn.Execute (ssql)
    Next
  Next
  MsgBox "Data Inserted"
  Exit Sub
err_end:
  MsgBox Err.Description
End Sub
```

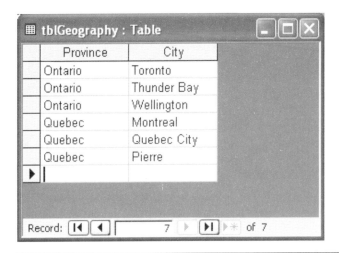

Figure 9.34 The MSXML Parser provides a way to import attribute data into Access

Briefly, the `get_xml_using_parser` routine uses objects provided by the parser (such as `IXMLDOMNode`); XPath (`"/Geography/Country/Province"`); the attributes collection (`province_name = xmlnode.Attributes(0).Text`); and ADO and SQL. Figure 9.34 shows the results of the routine, which has filled the tblGeography table with the attribute values.

Summary

Office has come a long way in support of XML functionality. Office 2003 has several new features that improve ease of use when working with XML data and technologies. The familiar user interfaces of Word, Excel, and Access make for an easy transition to working with XML. New objects, such as maps in Excel and data views in Word, remove much of the burden of implementing confusing schema and transformation processing.

Word 2003 has several new ways of working with XML. The document area displays XML element tags, attributes are exposed through a dialog, there is dynamic schema support, and so on. Excel 2003 has similar abilities and provides methods to the functionality through the new map object. Access 2003 has gained the ability to export related data; otherwise, the XML features in Access 2003 are not as sophisticated as those in Word 2003 or Excel 2003.

Although Office 2003 does have ample XML functionality, the MSXML Parser can be implemented into solutions to fill the gaps. The parser is an independent utility and can be referenced by all the Office products.

Further examples of XML coding and use are found in Chapters 14, 15, and 16. Chapter 14 demonstrates Excel's ability to read and process XML data. Chapter 15 showcases Word's XML functionality in applying a schema, manipulating XML data, and applying a transformation. Chapter 16 uses the MSXML Parser to work around Access 2003's limitations in importing related XML data. InfoPath receives a dedicated, separate overview in Chapter 11.

CHAPTER 10

Smart Tags

VERSION NOTE: The Word and Excel examples in this chapter work with the Office XP and Office 2003 versions of these products. The Access and PowerPoint examples are exclusive to Office 2003 versions.

Office XP introduced smart tag functionality in Word and Excel. Outlook also displays smart tags when Word is used as the e-mail editor. Office 2003 increases smart tag support to include Access and PowerPoint as well.

There are several uses of smart tags. Some smart tags are provided directly by the Office products. For example, when AutoCorrect identifies a typing error, the AutoCorrect options are presented in a smart tag. See Figure 10.1.

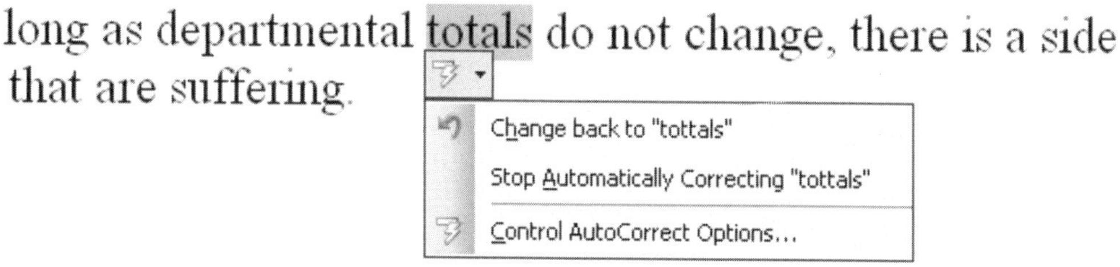

Figure 10.1 The AutoCorrect smart tag

Smart tags consist of a system of *recognizers* and *actions*. When certain terms (words or phrases) are keyed in, they are recognized, and a list of possible actions is presented. Figure 10.2 shows a list of actions that have appeared based on a recognized term. This particular term, "Budget", is recognized because the term has been included in a custom smart tag list.

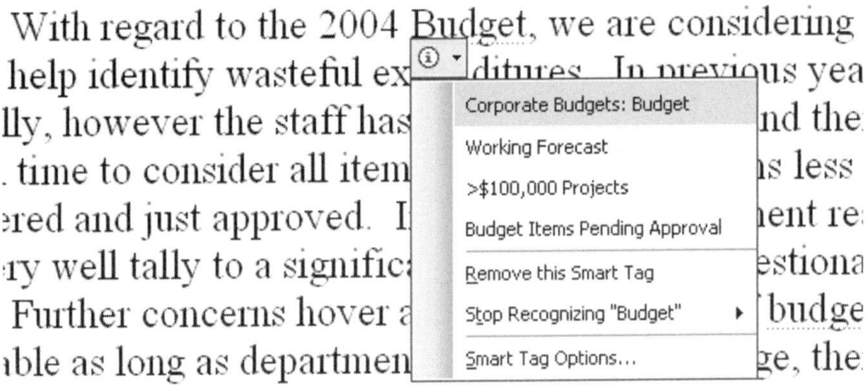

With regard to the 2004 Budget, we are considering
help identify wasteful ex〔ⓘ ▾〕ditures. In previous yea
lly, however the staff has⎢ Corporate Budgets: Budget ⎪nd the
. time to consider all item⎢ Working Forecast ⎪is less
:red and just approved. I⎢ >$100,000 Projects ⎪ient re:
·ry well tally to a signific:⎢ Budget Items Pending Approval ⎪estiona
 Further concerns hover :⎢ Remove this Smart Tag ⎪budge
ıble as long as departmen⎢ Stop Recognizing "Budget" ▸ ⎪ge, the:
⎢ Smart Tag Options... ⎪

Figure 10.2 A custom smart tag recognizes the word "Budget"

Word, Excel, and PowerPoint smart tags recognize terms, but Access
smart tags do not. In Access, a property is set to associate a database/query
field or a form control with smart tag actions. However, the field or control
displays the actions in all records—regardless of the value of the field in
any record. Figure 10.3 shows an Access query with every record displaying the indicator of smart tag actions in the CustomerType field. The value
of the field does not matter. This makes for a different approach to smart
tag use in Access. Access smart tags are discussed later in this chapter.

For developers, there is a programmable paradigm for smart tags.
Smart tags are implemented via specialized XML files. These files are
stored in a designated place in a computer's directory structure, and the
Office products incorporate the smart tags into the user interface. A typical location where smart tag source files are stored is C:\Program
Files\Common Files\Microsoft Shared\Smart Tag\Lists. This path could
be different depending on how Office was installed.

There are two approaches to smart tag development. One is to create
"simple" smart tags, in which all logic is contained in the XML file. Such
actions are limited to hyperlinks. Smart tags can also be developed to use
functionality in dynamic link library (DLL) files. Creating DLL files requires Visual Basic, C++, C#, or other appropriate development tools. As
such, DLL use with smart tags is beyond the scope of this book. See the
Appendix for resources on smart tags and DLL files.

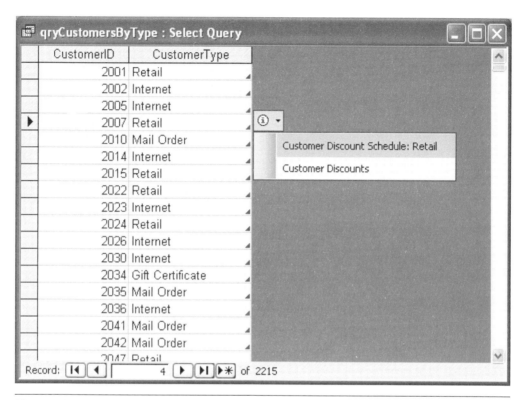

Figure 10.3 Smart tags in Access use actions only

The Smart Tag Schema

Figure 10.2 shows how the Budget smart tag works within Office. The actions—Working Forecast, >$100,000 Projects, and Budget Items Pending Approval—are derived from the Budget.XML file, stored in the smart tag directory. The Budget.XML file must follow a certain schema to be valid as the source of a smart tag's logic.

The conformance of the Budget.XML file to the smart tag schema is explained here. Figure 10.4 shows the Budget.XML file opened in Internet Explorer (Internet Explorer is used for its XML-formatting capabilities).

Taken line by line, here is how this file is assembled.

The first line contains the root element, and establishes a unique namespace with the assignment of the FL identifier. FL becomes the

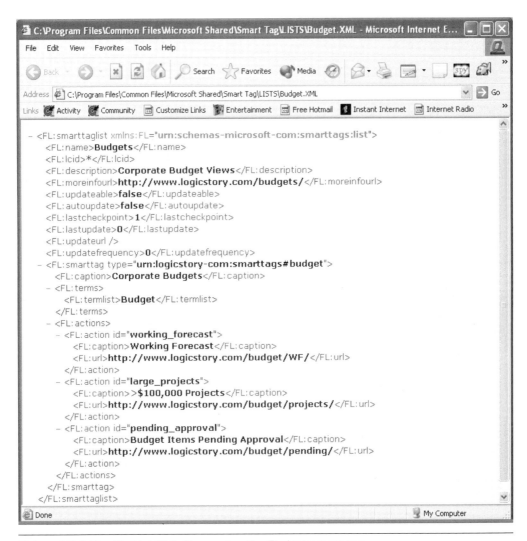

Figure 10.4 The Budget.XML file creates the Budget smart tag

"shorthand" of the namespace as applied to the rest of the file's elements. This line starts the file, and is required:

```
<FL:smarttaglist
    xmlns:FL="urn:schemas-microsoft-com:smarttags:list">
```

The next line establishes a name for the smart tag. This is required:

```
<FL:name>Budgets</FL:name>
```

Next is an optional line that identifies the locale ID. Particular values, such as 1033, can be used here. The asterisk indicates "any". If a particular locale ID is used, then the XML file must reside in a directory named as the locale ID:

```
<FL:lcid>*</FL:lcid>
```

The `description` element is required:

```
<FL:description>Corporate Budget Views</FL:description>
```

The "More Info URL" (`moreinfourl`) element lists a place to get more information about the smart tag. This is optional:

```
<FL:moreinfourl>
    http://www.logicstory.com/budgets/
</FL:moreinfourl>
```

The next six elements work in concert. They describe the update capabilities of the smart tag. For example, the logic of a smart tag may very well change periodically. Perhaps the URL for an action will change, or new actions will need to be included in the smart tag. All of the six update-related elements are optional; however, they all must be present for updates to work. The Budget smart tag does not update, and the six update elements could have been left out, but they are kept in for illustrative purposes.

The `updateable` element is simply a Boolean flag to indicate whether the smart tag is allowed to be updated. Clearly this would have to be set to true for updates to work:

```
<FL:updateable>false</FL:updateable>
```

The `autoupdate` element takes this a step further and sets a Boolean flag to indicate whether updates can be automated:

```
<FL:autoupdate>false</FL:autoupdate>
```

The `lastcheckpoint` element adheres to version numbering. An integer goes here. When checking for updates, this number is compared to the one on the server. If the server version is greater, then an update can occur. When the update occurs, the new value is written into the element:

```
<FL:lastcheckpoint>1</FL:lastcheckpoint>
```

The `lastupdate` element is a count of how many minutes have passed from 1970 through the minute of the last update. In other words, this element will hold a static number that only becomes bigger when an update occurs. The starting value is "0", since no updates have occurred in this example:

```
<FL:lastupdate>0</FL:lastupdate>
```

The `updateurl` element is the URL where updates can be found. In this example, none is entered because updates are not initiated:

```
<FL:updateurl></FL:updateurl>
```

The last of the six update-related elements is `updatefrequency`. This is an integer that specifies the number of minutes that should pass between update calls. The default is 10800—which is one week:

```
<FL:updatefrequency>0</FL:updatefrequency>
```

The remaining section of the Budget.XML file describes the list of terms to be recognized and the possible actions. The section starts with the parent `smarttag` element. This element is required. The `type` attribute contains a unique namespace:

```
<FL:smarttag type="urn:logicstory-com:smarttags#budget">
```

The required `caption` element gives a user-friendly identifier to the smart tag. The caption appears in the heading of the smart tag. Refer to Figure 10.2, where "Corporate Budgets" heads the list of actions:

```
<FL:caption>Corporate Budgets</FL:caption>
```

Next is the actual list of terms to be recognized. Terms are required, and they are separated by a comma. This particular example has just one term—Budget:

```
<FL:terms>
    <FL:termlist>Budget</FL:termlist>
</FL:terms>
```

The final portion of the XML file contains the action(s). First, a parent `actions` element is entered, then separate `action` blocks follow. Each `action` has an `id`, a `caption`, and a `URL` element. These are all required. Here is the first action, "Working Forecasts", as seen in Figure 10.2:

```
<FL:actions>
    <FL:action id="working_forecast">
        <FL:caption>Working Forecast</FL:caption>
```

```
    <FL:url>
        http://www.logicstory.com/budget/WF/
    </FL:url>
</FL:action>
```

When this action is selected in the smart tag, the Web page in the URL element is displayed in the default Web browser. The two remaining actions for the Budget smart tag are displayed here. Each action calls its indicated URL:

```
<FL:action id="large_projects">
    <FL:caption>&gt;$100,000 Projects</FL:caption>
    <FL:url>
        http://www.logicstory.com/budget/projects/
    </FL:url>
</FL:action>
<FL:actions>
    <FL:action id="pending_approval">
        <FL:caption>Budget Items Pending Approval</FL:caption>
        <FL:url>
            http://www.logicstory.com/budget/pending/
        </FL:url>
    </FL:action>
```

Note the difference in syntax for the >$100,000 action. In Figure 10.2, the greater-than symbol (>) is apparent. In an XML file, the > symbol is used for encasing tag names, so to create the symbol as a text reference, a code—>—is used. The greater-than symbol is one of five characters that require an "entity reference" to be used in place of the actual character. Table 10.1 lists the five characters and their equivalents. Many XML-based utilities compensate for the reserved characters even when not replaced with the entity reference. Also, the quote mark and apostrophe are not actually restricted characters, but since they are used in attributes, it may be deemed appropriate to use the entity references for clarity in the text portions of an XML file.

The remainder of the file is simply the closing tags for the major elements:

```
        </FL:actions>
    </FL:smarttag>
</FL:smarttaglist>
```

Table 10.1 Entity references for reserved XML characters

Symbol	Name	Entity Reference
>	greater than	`&gt;`
<	less than	`&lt;`
&	ampersand	`&amp;`
"	quote mark	`&quot;`
'	apostrophe	`&apos;`

The actions in the Budget smart tag will simply display a static Web page. However, smart tags can lead to dynamic actions by using the `{TEXT}` placeholder. This works like a variable in traditional programming. In the case of smart tags, `{TEXT}` stores the individual term that was recognized. The value can then be sent to the Web page for dynamic processing. The power of using the `{TEXT}` placeholder is demonstrated later in this chapter.

Saving and Using Smart Tag Files

Smart tag files must be saved typically in the C:\Program Files\Common Files\Microsoft Shared\Smart Tag\Lists directory. The path could differ, depending on installation or network properties. There may also be a subfolder, 1033, with additional files. The subfolder may have a different name, depending on the local language.

In Word, Excel, and PowerPoint, smart tag usage is controlled through the smart tags tab in the AutoCorrect dialog. The dialog differs slightly within each application. Figure 10.5 shows the dialog in Word. From here, smart tags are checked to include their functionality within the application or unchecked to leave the functionality out.

The Excel and PowerPoint dialogs are similar. Figure 10.6 displays the AutoCorrect dialog in PowerPoint.

In Access, smart tags are not presented on a tab in the AutoCorrect dialog but instead are presented in a separate dialog. See Figure 10.7.

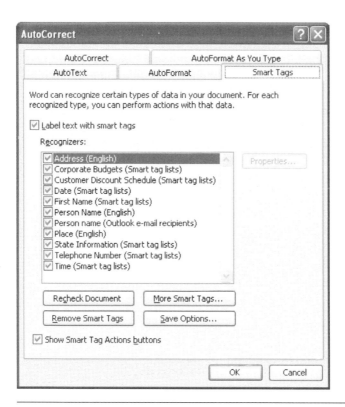

Figure 10.5 Using smart tags in Word

Using Smart Tags in Word and PowerPoint

Figure 10.5 shows smart tags available to use in a given Word session. One of these, State Information, is a custom smart tag application. The purpose of the State Information smart tag is to provide state data, and a link to a tourism site, for each of the New England states. The list of recognized terms literally is the list of six New England states: Connecticut, Maine, Massachusetts, New Hampshire, Rhode Island, and Vermont. Figure 10.8 shows the contents of the States.XML file, opened in Internet Explorer (again, IE is used for presentation).

The structure of the States.XML file adheres to the smart tag schema. This example, though, differs a bit from the preceding Budget example. The list of terms includes six entries—the states of New England. The actions

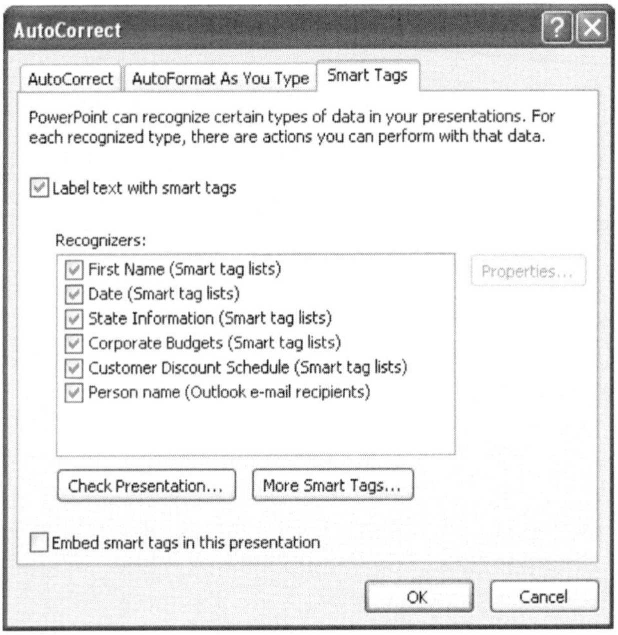

Figure 10.6 Using smart tags in PowerPoint

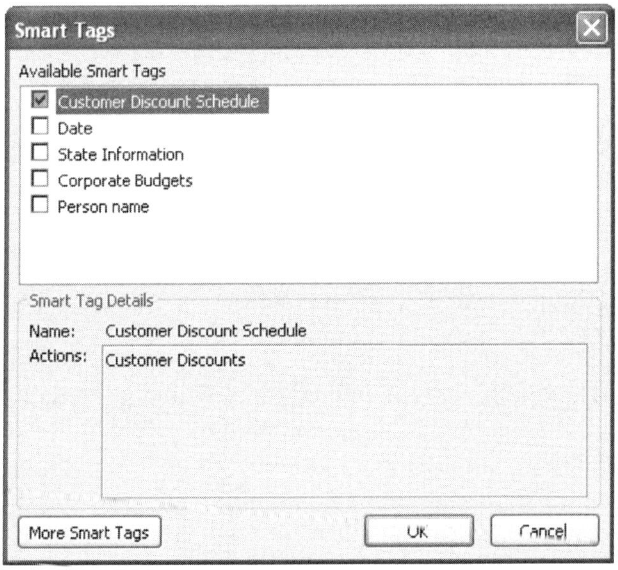

Figure 10.7 Setting smart tag usage in Access

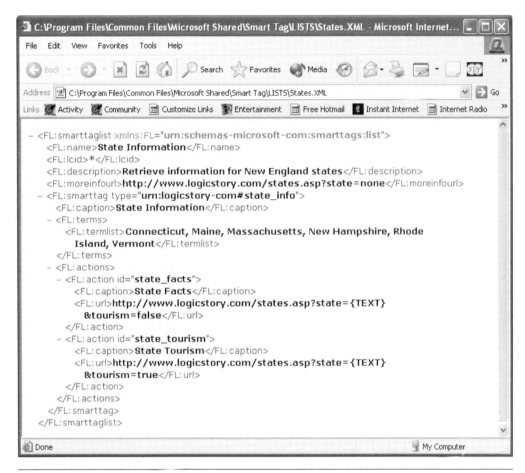

Figure 10.8 The States.XML file contains the logic for the State Information smart tag

make use of the {TEXT} placeholder. This placeholder stores the actual term that initiated the smart tag. For example, the value of {TEXT} may be "Massachusetts" or "Vermont", or any other term in the list. Being able to use the placeholder to capture and pass the term to a Web page makes for powerful Web integration.

Figure 10.9 shows the State Information smart tag being presented for the term "Vermont."

Figure 10.9 Smart tag actions for a recognized term

NOTE: In Word and PowerPoint, recognized terms display a dotted purple line underneath. In Excel, recognized terms display a small purple triangle in the lower-right corner of the cell that contains the term. In Access too, a small purple triangle appears, although technically the term is not recognized.

Two actions are presented: State Facts and State Tourism. These two actions, whether for Vermont or any other state in the list of terms, are processed at one Web address. The {TEXT} placeholder is used to pass the term to the Web address as part of the query string. In fact, the query string has two name/value pairs: one for the state name and the other to indicate whether the action is to view the state facts or the tourism information.

To be precise, this is the URL element for state facts:

```
<FL:url>
   http://www.logicstory.com/states.asp?state=
       {TEXT}&amp;tourism=false
</FL:url>
```

NOTE: This discussion assumes some knowledge of HTML and ASP coding. See the Appendix for resources.

The Web page called by the smart tag action is www.logicstory.com/states.asp. Two specifics are provided in the query string: the state and the tourism indicator:

```
?state={TEXT}&amp;tourism=false
```

Using Vermont as the example, when the State Facts action is selected, the complete URL is:

```
http://www.logicstory.com/states.asp?state=Vermont&tourism=false
```

Assuming a live Internet connection is present, the action calls up the Web browser and navigates to the URL, shown in Figure 10.10.

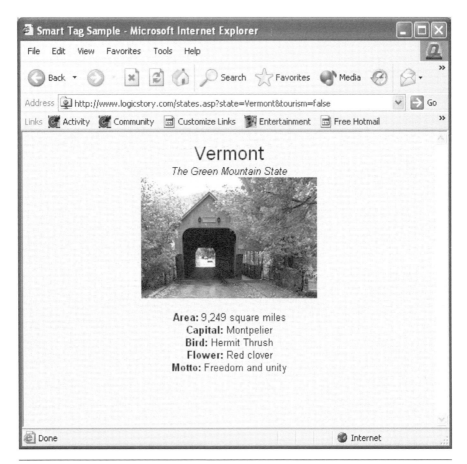

Figure 10.10 The smart tag action navigates to a Web page

Note that the Web address in the browser includes the query string created with the {TEXT} placeholder. Since a recognized term can be passed to a Web page, there are many ways to extend functionality. Using Active Server Pages (ASP) or other processing methods that can be used with Web pages, the passed term can be included in database calls, Web service interaction, and more.

In this example, the ASP page simply returns some hard-coded facts. A Select...Case construct returns the appropriate information. Listing 10.1 shows the code in the States.asp file.

Listing 10.1 An Active Server Page processes the passed smart tag term

```
<HTML>
<HEAD>
<TITLE>Smart Tag Sample</TITLE>
</HEAD>
<BODY BGColor="#EFEFEF">
<%
select case request.querystring("state")
   case "Connecticut"
      area="5,544"
      capital="Hartford"
      bird="American Robin"
      flower="Mountain laurel"
      motto="Qui Transtulit Sustinet"
      slogan="The Constitution State"
      tourism="http://www.tourism.state.ct.us/"
      map="conn.gif"
      pix="conn.jpg"
   case "Maine"
      area="33,741"
      capital="Augusta"
      bird="Chickadee"
      flower="White pine cone"
      motto="Dirigo"
      slogan="The Pine Tree State"
      tourism="http://www.visitmaine.com"
      map="maine.gif"
      pix="maine.jpg"
   case "Massachusetts"
      area="9,241"
```

Listing 10.1 *(continued)*

```
            capital="Boston"
            bird="Chickadee"
            flower="Mayflower"
            motto="Ense Petit Placidam Sub Libertate Quietem"
            slogan="The Bay State"
            tourism="http://www.mass-vacation.com"
            map="mass.gif"
            pix="mass.jpg"
        case "New Hampshire"
            area="9,283"
            capital="Concord"
            bird="Purple Finch"
            flower="Purple lilac"
            motto="Live free or die"
            slogan="The Granite State"
            tourism="http://www.visitnh.gov"
            map="newhampshire.gif"
            pix="newhampshire.jpg"
        case "Rhode Island"
            area="1,231"
            capital="Providence"
            bird="Rhode Island red"
            flower="Violet"
            motto="Hope"
            slogan="The Ocean State"
            tourism="http://www.visitrhodeisland.com"
            map="rhodeisland.gif"
            pix="rhodeisland.jpg"
        case "Vermont"
            area="9,249"
            capital="Montpelier"
            bird="Hermit Thrush"
            flower="Red clover"
            motto="Freedom and unity"
            slogan="The Green Mountain State"
            tourism="http://www.travel-vermont.com"
            map="vermont.gif"
            pix="vermont.jpg"
end select
if request.querystring("tourism")="false" then
    response.write("<Center>")
```

Listing 10.1 *(continued)*

```
  response.write("<Font Face=""Arial, Helvetica"" Size=""5"">")
  response.write(request.querystring("state") & "<BR>")
  response.write("<Font Size=""2""><I>" & slogan & "</I><BR>")
  response.write("<Img Src=" & pix & ">")
  response.write("<BR><BR>")
  response.write("<B>Area: </B>" & area & " square miles<BR>")
  response.write("<B>Capital: </B>" & capital & "<BR>")
  response.write("<B>Bird: </B>" & bird & "<BR>")
  response.write("<B>Flower: </B>" & flower & "<BR>")
  response.write("<B>Motto: </B>" & motto & "<BR>")
else
  response.redirect(tourism)
end if
%>
</BODY>
</HTML>
```

After a few standard HTML tags (`HTML`, `HEAD`, and so on), the processing portion of the ASP code uses the term found in the query string as the basis for the `Select . . . Case` construct:

```
select case request.querystring("state")
```

An `If . . . Then . . . Else` test concludes whether to return the state facts or to redirect the browser to the tourism Web site. The tourism Web sites' URLs are stored in the `tourism` variable within the `Case` statements:

```
tourism="http://www.visitrhodeisland.com"
```

The query string carries the flag for whether the action is for state facts or tourism. If `tourism=true`, then the redirect is used and the browser is sent to the appropriate URL:

```
  response.redirect(tourism)
```

When the State Facts action is selected, the ASP code outputs the HTML to create the Web page seen in Figure 10.10.

Smart tags appear and work in PowerPoint in the same manner as in Word. Note that for both of these applications, the recognized terms can be anywhere within text. That is, a term can be by itself or anywhere in a sentence, a paragraph, and so on. Excel differs in this approach, as explained in the next section.

Using Smart Tags in Excel

Smart tag functionality in Excel works in exactly the same manner as in Word and PowerPoint but with one major hitch. The terms must be separate from any other text. Therefore, even if both the Budget and the State Information smart tags presented in this chapter are active, a sentence such as "The budget for Maine is available for review" will not cause any term recognition.

Figure 10.11 shows smart tag recognition in Excel. The New England states are recognized because they each appear solo. The key to the terms being recognized is the small triangle in the bottom right of each cell. The sentence is not recognized.

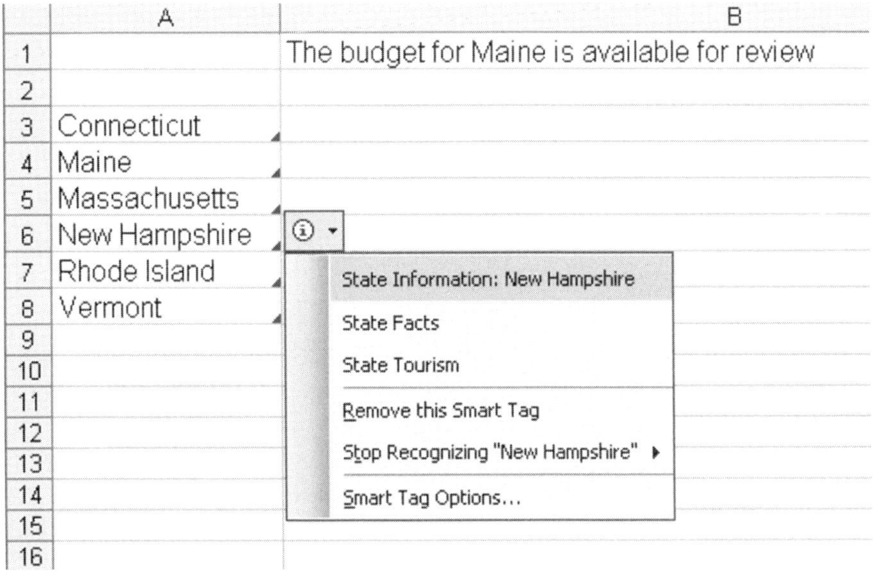

Figure 10.11 Smart tag recognition in Excel

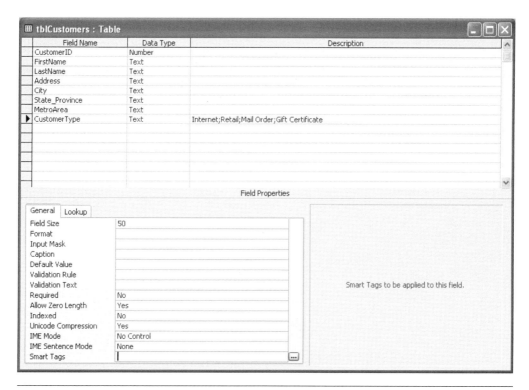

Figure 10.12 Access table fields have a Smart Tags property

Using Smart Tags in Access

Access smart tag usage is available to tables, queries, and forms. Both table and form design environments support smart tag properties at the field and control levels, respectively. Figure 10.12 displays the design for an Access table named tblCustomers.

The CustomerType field will be set to use a smart tag. The ellipsis (...) to the right of the Smart Tags property (at the bottom of the Properties pane) leads to the Smart Tags dialog, shown in Figure 10.13.

In this dialog, the Customer Discount Schedule smart tag is turned on. Once the OK button is clicked, the Smart Tags property in the table design displays the namespace for the smart tag element (the `type` attribute), as shown in Figure 10.14.

Figure 10.13 Selecting which smart tags to use

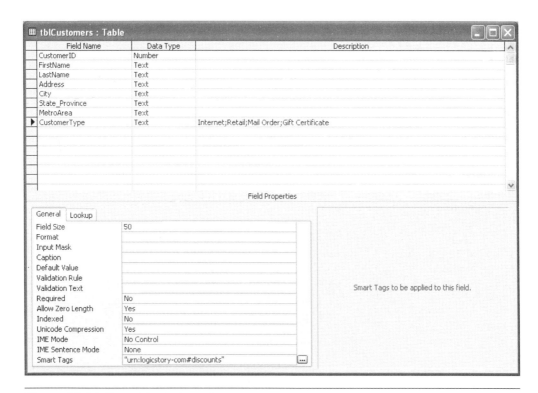

Figure 10.14 The table design after a smart tag is selected

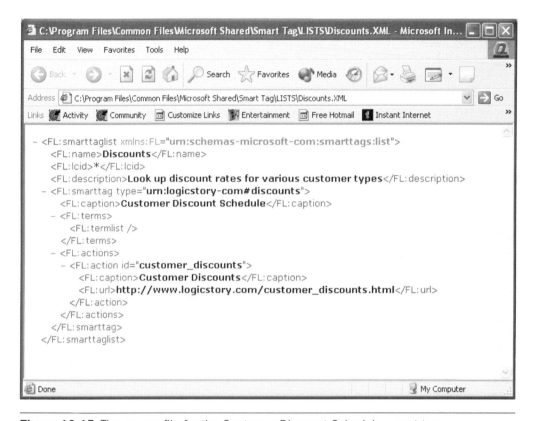

Figure 10.15 The source file for the Customer Discount Schedule smart tag

Figure 10.15 shows the Discounts.XML file displayed in Internet Explorer.

A query based on the tblCustomers table contains the CustomerID and CustomerType fields. The smart tag availability is seen as the small triangle in the lower-right corner of the CustomerType field, within each record. See Figure 10.16.

Note that the smart tag is available only where the field has an actual value (Retail, Internet, Mail Order, and so on). However, also note that the smart tag's source XML file has an empty terms list. This shows a nuance of using smart tags in Access. Access has the intelligence to avoid displaying smart tags in empty fields, yet the terms are not recognized anyway.

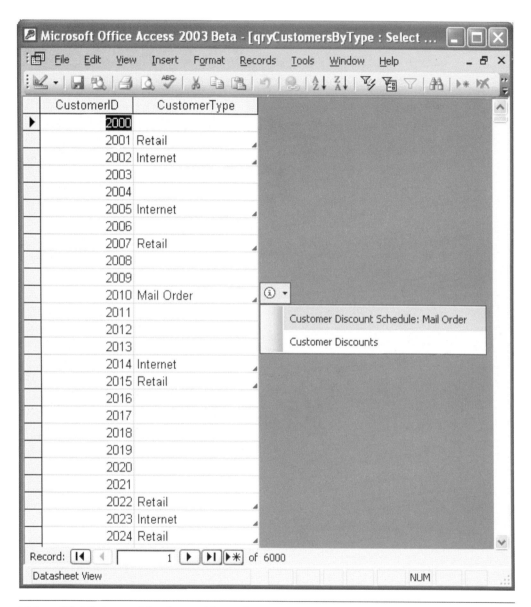

Figure 10.16 A smart tag is used in an Access query

Access smart tag use requires an approach in which the action(s) are relevant to any value found in the field. In this particular case, the action leads to a schedule of customer discounts posted on a Web page, shown in Figure 10.17. However, if any nonsensible values were present in the CustomerType field, they would just as successfully bring the focus to the Web page. The {TEXT} placeholder can be used to carry the value of the field to the Web page, where a value can be used if it makes sense to do so.

For forms, *some* controls support smart tags. The label, text box, list, and combo box have a smart tag property similar in approach to Access table fields. The controls will display the small triangle leading to the smart tag, regardless of the text. As such, as with table fields, smart tag use is best

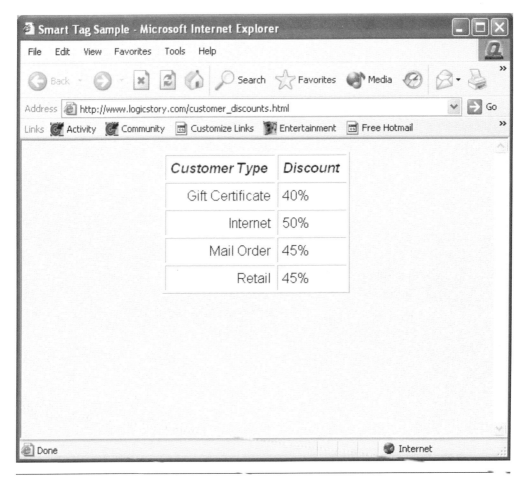

Figure 10.17 The Customer Discount Schedule leads to a relevant Web page

considered where the action(s) will apply to any possible text. Or in other words, the text in the form control should have no relevance to the action(s).

Figure 10.18 shows a form with a combo box. The combo text values—"this" and "that"—have no relevant use for the indicated smart tag of State Information (described in the previous section on Word). In this scenario, sending "this" or "that" to the Web page that processes the names of New England states would produce no usable result.

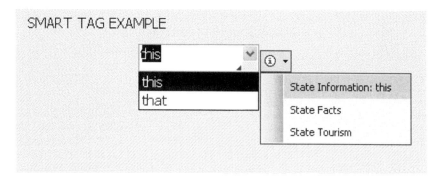

Figure 10.18 An Access form and combo box calling a smart tag action

Summary

Smart tags offer a powerful dimension to Office document creation. Due to their customizable nature and the ability to send a value to a Web page, quite a bit can be done to enhance user activities. This chapter explained how to implement smart tags in Word, PowerPoint, Excel, and Access. Access does not recognize terms and therefore requires a different approach to make the most sense of smart tag functionality.

The examples here are "simple" smart tags—they do not use DLL files. DLL interaction adds much more functionality to what smart tags can do. When smart tag DLL files are created, a programmable library (called the Microsoft Smart Tags 2.0 Type Library) is referenced. See the Appendix for resources. The examples in this chapter can interact with Web sites, a capability that in itself can be quite powerful when coupled with ASP or other Web programmable languages.

CHAPTER 11

Introduction to InfoPath

Overview

InfoPath is a hybrid product built on familiar form design tools and a comprehensive set of XML technologies and standards. As a graphical user interface (GUI) designer, InfoPath has the familiar controls (text box, list, button, and more) as well as the familiar design capabilities, such as drag-and-drop. There are new controls unique to InfoPath, which are explained in this chapter.

The purpose of InfoPath is to create distributable forms, which in turn capture structured input. In this regard, InfoPath fills a vital need of efficient data collection. Unlike other form engines, InfoPath structures data at the point of entry—because entry is guided by the constraints of a schema. Further, there are robust validation mechanisms in InfoPath that give increased control over entry.

Data entered into an InfoPath form is treated immediately as XML data and can optionally be saved to an external XML file. This feature furthers the utility of InfoPath, because data flowed through an InfoPath form essentially turns entered data into a reusable structure that other systems can work with. Saving information in an XML file is just one option. Other options include submitting the information to a Web service or a database, or using scripting code to process the information for other purposes. A filled-in form can even be e-mailed, thereby providing workflow capability.

Figure 11.1 shows an InfoPath form during design. The right side of the application contains a task pane that is currently displaying the Controls toolbox. The list of possible task panes is displayed as well.

At the start, a form can be designed based on an existing schema. This is not a strict requirement. Form design can start with a "blank," unbound form. Working with a schema, however, is comparable to designing an Access form that is bound to a record source. Using a schema as a guideline

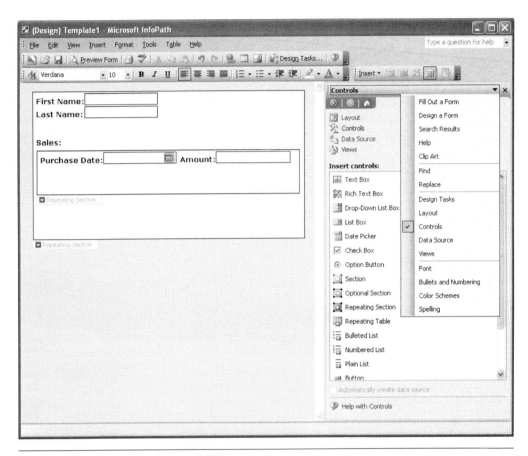

Figure 11.1 An InfoPath form being designed

will force the schema's constraints into the form. Figure 11.2 shows the same form as seen in Figure 11.1, but with the Data Source task pane in view. The schema is displayed in the task pane, and an additional dialog box is opened with particulars about one of the schema elements.

InfoPath provides a mechanism for creating *views*. Within the context of one InfoPath form, there can be multiple views. A view, therefore, is the piece of the GUI that users will work with. Figures 11.1 and 11.2 show a view being developed although it is referenced as a form. Essentially then, a "form" is really a catchall term for one or more views.

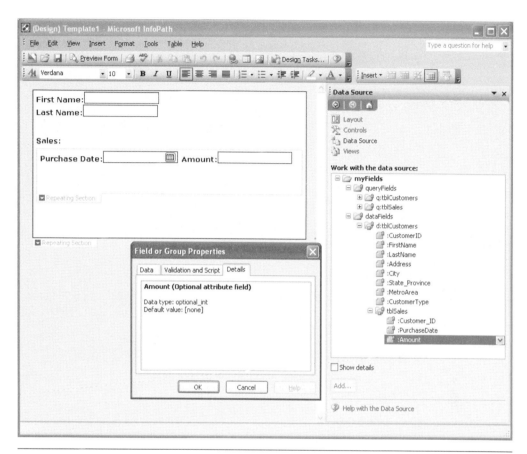

Figure 11.2 A form based on a schema

NOTE: InfoPath interaction occurs through views, which are a component of a form. However, for discussion purposes, the terms *form* and *view* are interchangeable.

InfoPath File Types

InfoPath form templates are stored in a compressed format with the .xsn extension. A form template file actually can be decompressed to individualize the underlying files. In design mode, the File menu has the Extract Form

Table 11.1 InfoPath form files

File Type/Extension	Comment
Form File (.xsn)	The compressed (CAB) file that contains all the other files.
Manifest (.xsf)	Contains information and references to all of the other files in the form solution. A master file of sorts.
Schema (.xsd)	The schema for the form. There will also be a schema for secondary data sources.
View (.xsl)	Each view in the form solution is described in a separate transformation file.
Sample Data (.xml)	Contains sample data for use in previewing the form.
Script Code (.js or .vbs)	Either a JScript or a VBScript code module.

Files item. Using this command decompresses the .xsn file into multiple files. The types of files used by InfoPath are summarized in Table 11.1.

Other files may be present as well, such as graphics, HTML, and more.

Designing Forms

When InfoPath is launched, one of the options is to design a form. There are four approaches to this: (1) create a form from a data source, (2) work with a new blank form, (3) customize a sample form, or (4) open a previously designed form in design mode. See the Design a Form task pane in Figure 11.3.

Selecting to Create an Unbound Form

Selecting to work with a new blank form sets the screen up with an empty form. The Design Tasks task pane appears and leads to further design activities. See Figure 11.4.

Figure 11.3 The Design a Form task pane

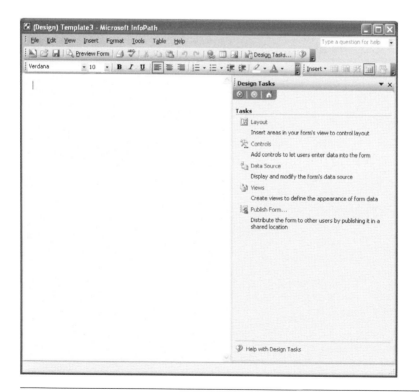

Figure 11.4 A blank form is ready for design

Figure 11.5 There are no fields integrated into this blank form

Because no schema has been specified, the Data Source displays an empty "myFields" folder. See Figure 11.5.

At this point, sections, controls, or both can be inserted into the form. The Layout option features table and section choices, and the Controls option lists a number of controls. Controls can be placed inside or outside of sections or tables. Because there is no schema, there are no constraints on how the form can be designed. Effectively, this way of working is a form-to-schema approach. By placing sections and controls, the developer is designing a schema. As the controls are placed, properties can be set, such as making entry required. With placement of controls and sections, the Data Source begins to fill up. See Figure 11.6.

A schema is actually being created. Saving the form and then using the Extract Form Files feature (under the File menu) creates the set of supporting files. One of these is the schema, shown in Figure 11.7. Note that this schema is being autogenerated by InfoPath.

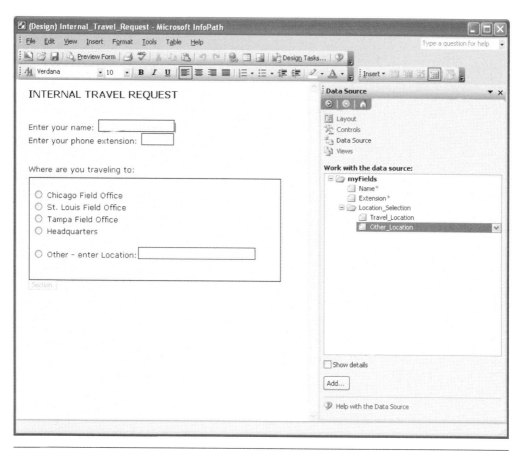

Figure 11.6 The Data Source list grows as controls are placed on the form

Selecting to Create a Bound Form

When selecting to create a form from a data source, the Data Source Setup Wizard is launched. See Figure 11.8.

Each of the data source options is explained here.

XML Schema or XML Data File

Selecting a schema or XML file brings the wizard to a pane where a path to a schema or XML file can be entered. The Browse button can be used to locate the file. See Figure 11.9.

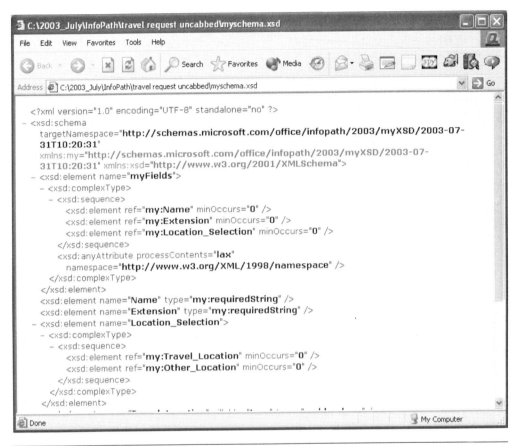

Figure 11.7 A schema is being developed by placing controls and selecting properties

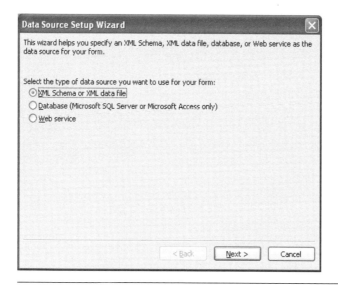

Figure 11.8 The Data Source Setup Wizard

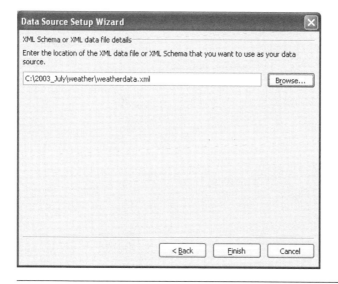

Figure 11.9 Selecting the schema or XML file

Once the file is selected and the Finish button is clicked, a blank form is presented. In the Data Source task pane, the schema is present. See Figure 11.10.

Whether a schema or an actual XML data file has been selected in the wizard, the schema appears in the task pane. In the case of a schema file, this is a simple view of the facts found in the schema. If an actual XML data file has been selected in the wizard, InfoPath derives the schema from the structure of the XML. InfoPath notifies the user that this is the case in an informational message. See Figure 11.11.

As seen in Figure 11.11, InfoPath asks whether to use the XML data as the default data in the form. This provides a way to see how the data is pre-

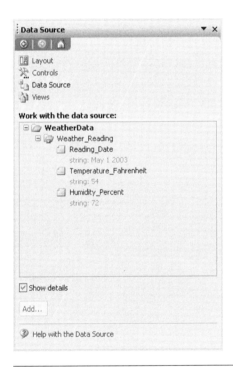

Figure 11.10 The schema is available in the Data Source task pane

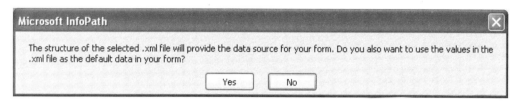

Figure 11.11 Options when using an XML file as the basis for form design

sented as the form is designed. There is a helpful Preview feature that displays how a form will actually look and function when deployed. The Preview can use data from the XML file that is the basis of the schema. One of the files found in the compressed .xsn file is sampledata.xml. This file is created whether the form is based on just a schema or on an actual XML file. The difference is whether the sampledata.xml file will contain empty tags. Listing 11.1 shows the contents of the sample data file, based on the weatherdata.xml file referenced in Figure 11.9.

Listing 11.1 The contents of the sampledata.xml file

```
<ns:WeatherData
      xmlns:ns="http://www.solutions4office.com/weather"
      xmlns:my="http://schemas.microsoft.com/office/infopath/
      2003/myXSD/2003-07-31T11:03:35">
   <ns:Weather_Reading>
      <ns:Reading_Date>
         May 1 2003
      </ns:Reading_Date>
      <ns:Temperature_Fahrenheit>
         54
      </ns:Temperature_Fahrenheit>
      <ns:Humidity_Percent>
         72
      </ns:Humidity_Percent>
   </ns:Weather_Reading>
</ns:WeatherData>
```

Database

A form can be structured on a schema derived from an Access or SQL Server database. Selecting this option in the Data Source Setup Wizard leads to a pane in the wizard where information about the database connection is entered. As shown in Figure 11.12, the first step is to select the database. Clicking the Select Database button brings up the Select Data Source dialog.

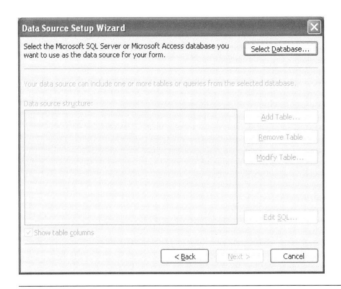

Figure 11.12 Selecting a database for the InfoPath form

The Select Data Source dialog is used to navigate to an Access database, or to use ODBC or other connectivity methods to connect to SQL Server. A connection to Access can also be made using ODBC.

After a database is selected, a list of data tables and queries is presented. See Figure 11.13.

The Data Source Setup Wizard is still open, and now the current pane of the wizard displays the selected table. This may be the only data source that is required; however, it is possible to add other tables or queries, to indicate relationships, and even to edit the assembled SQL statement.

Clicking the Add Table button brings up the Add Table or Query dialog. See Figure 11.14. Selecting a table and proceeding with the Next button

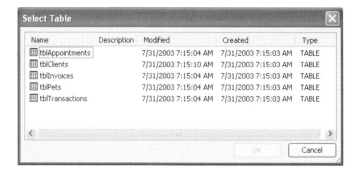

Figure 11.13 Selecting a database object

Figure 11.14 The Add Table or Query dialog

displays the Edit Relationship dialog. See Figure 11.15. Creating a relationship requires knowledge of the data. In other words, the purpose of the data should be known before a relationship is established. This concept does not apply exclusively to InfoPath but makes sense for good database design. In other words, these dialogs imitate how relationships are set when creating a database.

The Edit Relationship dialog displays relationships and can lead to further dialogs to add or delete relationships. In this example, InfoPath determined the inherent relationship without further input. The wizard now displays the two related tables, shown in Figure 11.16.

Finally, the Edit SQL button leads to a dialog where the SQL statement can be edited. See Figure 11.17.

Figure 11.15 The Edit Relationship dialog

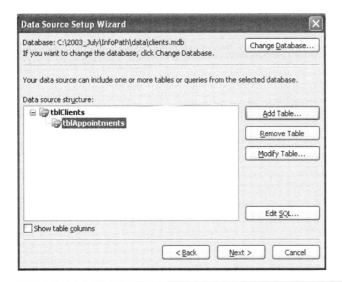

Figure 11.16 The Data Source Setup Wizard is filling in with selections

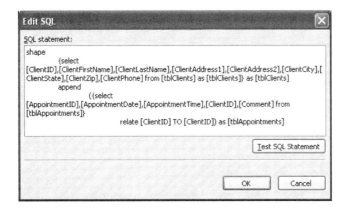

Figure 11.17 The Edit SQL dialog

The last pane of the wizard summarizes the selections and asks which view to start with. The wizard will finish by creating two views. The Query View is predesigned and serves as a query-by-form vehicle for querying the database. The Data View is a blank form waiting to be designed. Figure 11.18 shows the supplied Query View. Note that the Data Source task pane displays the fields from the database tables. These have now been turned into the schema.

Web Service

Selecting a Web service as the data source advances the Data Source Setup Wizard to a pane where the communication loop with the Web service is selected, as shown in Figure 11.19.

Proceeding with the Next button, the wizard displays an entry box for the URL to a WSDL address. It can be entered, or a search can be initiated by clicking the Search UDDI button. See Figure 11.20.

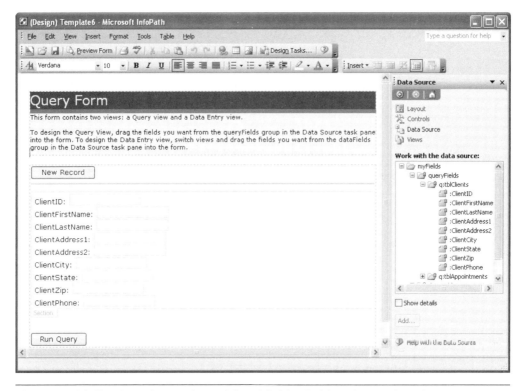

Figure 11.18 The Data Source Setup Wizard finished with a view and a schema

Figure 11.19 Selecting submit and receive options with a Web service

Figure 11.20 A Web service address is entered, or a search can be run

Clicking the Search UDDI button provides a dialog where a search is run. The search uses these criteria: (1) which UDDI database to search in, (2) which field to search in (Provider or Service), and (3) a keyword. Results are returned in a list, and a Web service can be selected. See Figure 11.21. Clicking the OK button closes the dialog and continues with the wizard.

TERMS: UDDI = Universal Description, Discovery, and Integration
WSDL = Web Service Description Language

Next in the wizard is a list of available operations provided by the Web service. See Figure 11.22.

The last screen in the Data Source Setup Wizard is a summary of selections made, shown in Figure 11.23.

After the wizard is dismissed, the fields from the Web service are in the Data Source task pane, shown in Figure 11.24.

Figure 11.21 Running a UDDI search

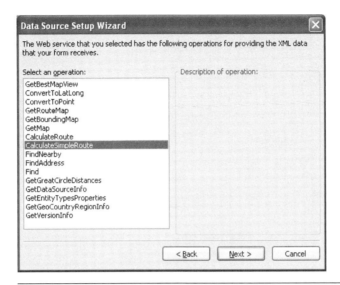

Figure 11.22 Available Web service operations

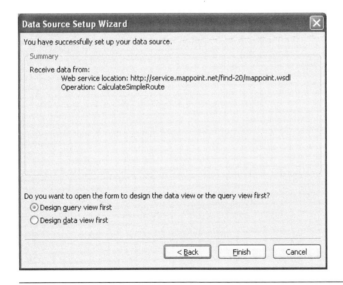

Figure 11.23 A summary of selections

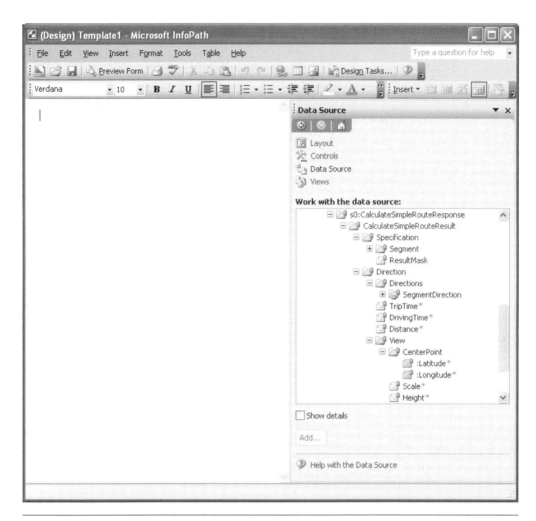

Figure 11.24 Fields from the Web service become the assumed schema in InfoPath

Design Tasks

Activities for form design are supported in the task pane and are organized around four areas: Layout, Controls, Data Source, and Views. The four key groupings are the same regardless of whether the developer is creating a new blank form, creating a bound form, or editing an existing form design. Each of these groupings is explained in this section.

Layout

The choices in the Layout pane are table configurations, for the most part. Inserting a table into the form design area does not affect the schema; however, it will force changes to the XSLT file (see Table 11.1). This makes sense because even the inclusion of a table is an attribute of a view.

Tables are used as containers for controls and text. As with Word, tables here are helpful for organizing and aligning other visual elements. Figure 11.25 shows how a table is used to align controls and text. The text is right-aligned in the left column and the controls are left-aligned in the right column. This is a common technique to visually pair up a textual instruction such as "Enter Your Name" with the actual entry box. Also in Figure 11.25, the task pane displays the Layout options.

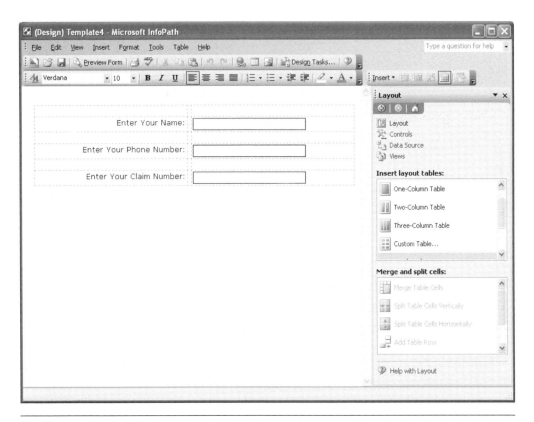

Figure 11.25 Using tables for structured layout

Controls

The Controls pane is where all the standard form controls are found, as well as a few controls unique to InfoPath. Figure 11.26 displays the pane with the available controls.

A few controls bear special mention. First consider that when controls are placed into a form's design, InfoPath updates the underlying schema and transformation files. XML schema protocol includes indicating the frequency of data sections in an XML file. In particular, the `minOccurs` and

Figure 11.26 InfoPath controls for designing forms

`maxOccurs` attributes in a schema are used to constrain the data in this way. The placement of the "optional section" and the "repeating section" (or "repeating table") controls causes InfoPath to update the schema in play. The schema update reflects the selection and placement of the controls.

Here is a step-by-step example. A repeating section is placed into an otherwise blank form. The section is considered the same as a field. It is manually renamed to `Repeating_Section_Example`. The following snippet has been inserted by InfoPath into the schema:

```
<xsd:sequence>
    <xsd:element ref="my:Repeating_Section_Example"
        minOccurs="0" maxOccurs="unbounded"/>
</xsd:sequence>
```

The placement of a repeating section has caused a schema entry that indicates repetitive data via the value of the `maxOccurs` attribute. The value of `unbounded` means that the section can repeat. If the value of `maxOccurs` were equal to 1, or if the `maxOccurs` attribute were not present, then the section could not repeat. Next, this is tested.

A regular (nonrepeating) section is inserted. The control is renamed `Regular_Section`. The schema gains this line:

```
<xsd:sequence>
    <xsd:element ref="my:Regular_Section" minOccurs="0"/>
</xsd:sequence>
```

The `maxOccurs` attribute is not present. Therefore, the section would violate validation if it were to repeat. Note too that a "Cannot be blank" setting affects the `minOccurs` attribute.

Another InfoPath-specific control is the expression box. This accepts an XPath statement, which is used to locate or manipulate specific data within the XML. See Figure 11.27.

The expression box is explained further in a later section.

Figure 11.27 XPath statements are entered into the expression box to locate data

Data Source

The Data Source pane displays a hierarchical representation of the schema. Whether built by placing controls on a blank form or derived from establishing a link with a database, XML file/schema, or Web service, the Data Source pane will display all schema elements and attributes as groups and fields. Groups indicate complex types in the schema; fields are simple types.

As an example, an XML data file is set as the data source. InfoPath derives a schema from this file. Here are the contents of the XML data file:

```
<?xml version="1.0" encoding="UTF-8"?>
<Geography>
  <Country name="Canada">
    <Province Name="Ontario">
      <City name="Toronto"/>
      <City name="Thunder Bay"/>
      <City name="Wellington"/>
    </Province>
    <Province Name="Quebec">
      <City name="Montreal"/>
      <City name="Quebec City"/>
      <City name="Pierre"/>
    </Province>
  </Country>
</Geography>
```

And shown in Figure 11.28 is the representation in the Data Source task pane.

Province, for example, is a complex type because it contains City elements. The Data Source task pane displays Province as a group (as a folder icon).

Views

Views provide the ways of making the schema useful for differing purposes. In other words, once a schema is built up or derived, it is the layout and visual appeal of the form area that users see and interact with.

Each "form" has one or more views. Multiple views are created based on the single schema, however, each view is designed with a different purpose. In production, the various views are available to users to select from a menu. A setting can override a view's appearance on the menu.

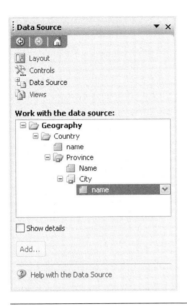

Figure 11.28 InfoPath derives a schema from XML data

Views are saved by InfoPath as XSL transformations. A separate XSLT file is created for each view.

Step-by-Step Form Design

This section shows the steps taken to create an InfoPath form. When sections or controls are placed on a form, either the developer must bind them to a group or field in the data source or, if working with an unbound form, InfoPath will build the schema automatically.

To exemplify building a form, a certain approach is taken to having a schema to work from. The new form will be based on an XML file, but just for the purpose of letting InfoPath create a schema from the file's structure. InfoPath's flexible nature is put to use here. In this example, we are not interested in any data at this point, but we do want the structure of the XML. The benefit here is that we do not need a real schema file to get started. Bear in mind that this is just one approach to form creation in InfoPath. Listing 11.2 displays the XML file.

Listing 11.2 The Orders.xml file is used to create a schema

```
<?xml version="1.0"?>
<Orders>
    <SalesPerson></SalesPerson>
    <Date></Date>
    <Order>
        <Customer></Customer>
        <PONumber></PONumber>
        <LineItem>
            <Title></Title>
            <Quantity></Quantity>
        </LineItem>
    </Order>
</Orders>
```

Note that this XML file is empty of any data. However, the elements are key to having InfoPath create a schema. The XML structure shows that the Order element has three child elements: Customer, PONumber, and LineItem. LineItem has two child elements as well: Title and Quantity.

This structure mirrors a salesperson's activities. On a given date (the Date element), any number of orders can be completed. For each single order, there is one customer and one purchase order number. The order, however, can have multiple line items—each of which comprise a book title and the quantity.

From the Design a Form task pane, the New From Data Source option is selected. Then, in the Data Source Setup Wizard, the XML Schema or XML data file option is selected. The Orders.xml file is browsed to. Finally, after the wizard finishes, the Data Source task pane displays the elements and structure from the Orders.xml file. See Figure 11.29.

Setting Properties

Because the data source is based on just an XML file with no schema, some properties need to be set. Right-clicking on the LineItem group displays a context menu. One item on the menu is Properties. Selecting Properties brings up the Field or Group Properties dialog. In this dialog is a checkbox to indicate that the LineItem group can repeat. See Figure 11.30.

Figure 11.29 A schema is in place to begin building a form

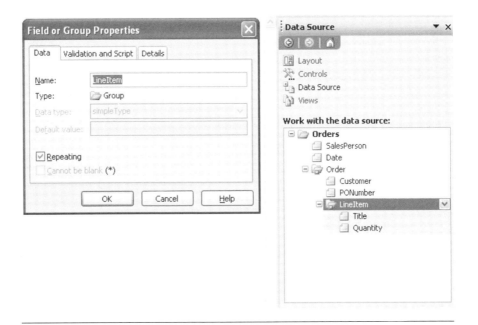

Figure 11.30 A group is set to be repeating

The same `Repeating` property is applied to the `Order` group. The `Date` field is set to the Date data type. See Figure 11.31. Also, the `Quantity` field is set to an integer.

Inserting Text and Controls

Text can be typed directly into the form. There are font properties and styles that can be applied to text—the same as in Word and other Office products. To place controls in the form, either fields (or groups) can be dragged from the Data Source task pane, or controls can be dragged from the Controls task pane, or the Insert menu can be used.

When fields or groups are dragged, the control is bound to the field (or fields, if a group was dragged). InfoPath places the logical choice of control type based on the field data type. The control type can be changed after the fact. When a control is placed first, however, the bound property must be set using the Field or Group Properties dialog shown in Figure 11.31.

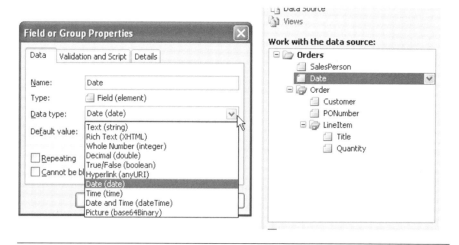

Figure 11.31 The `Date` field is set to the Date data type

For this example, two text boxes need to be inserted near the top of the form: one for the salesperson's name and one for the date. A text box is used for the name, and a date picker control is used for the date. See Figure 11.32. In the figure, the `SalesPerson` field has already been dragged over. For the `Date`, however, the Insert menu was used to insert a date picker control. Before InfoPath inserts the control, the field to bind to must be selected.

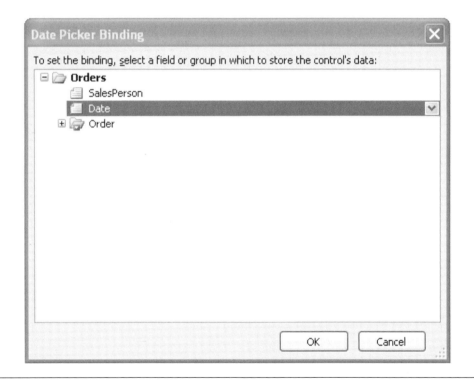

Figure 11.32 A control must be bound to be inserted

Tables and Sections

Next, the entire Order group is dragged onto the form. InfoPath offers options on how to insert the group as it is dragged. See Figure 11.33.

Figure 11.34 shows the form as it is being developed. Several controls are in the form, and they have been moved around for aesthetic value. Some borders and shading have been applied. Also note that the sections are "repeating." An expression box has also been inserted into the form.

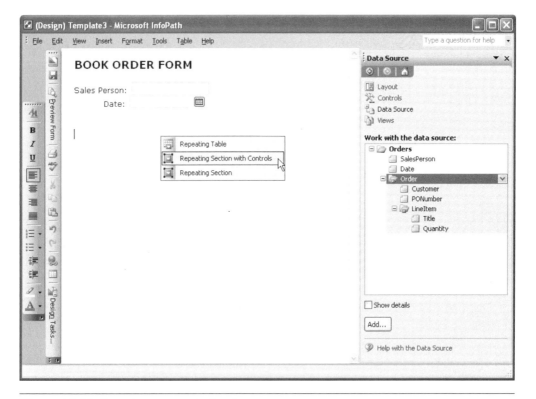

Figure 11.33 Dragging a group to the form

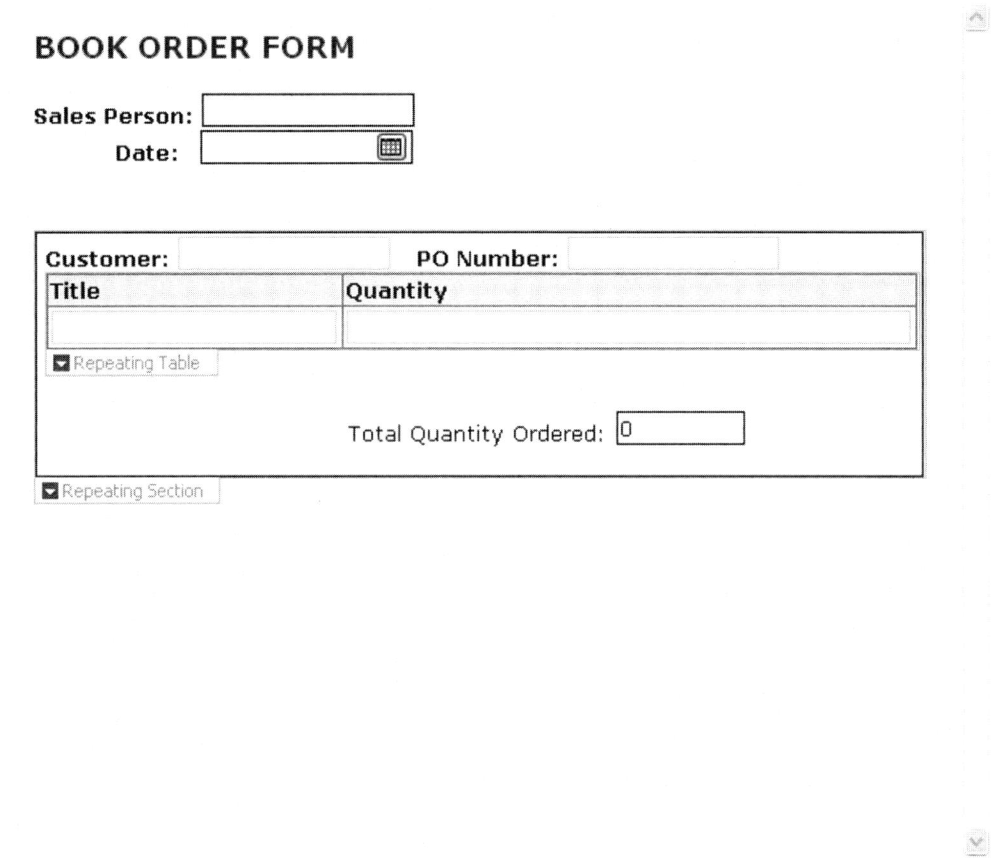

BOOK ORDER FORM

Sales Person: [   ]

Date: [📅]

Customer:	PO Number:
Title	**Quantity**

🔽 Repeating Table

Total Quantity Ordered: [0   ]

🔽 Repeating Section

Figure 11.34 The form is being developed

Expression Box

An expression box is used to enter an XPath statement. The statement usually locates information within the structure of the XML. The purpose could simply be to display an important piece of information or, more likely, to display some sort of total or average.

When an expression box control is inserted into the form, the Insert Expression Box dialog appears and is ready to accept a statement. There is a button to the right of the entry box that leads to a list of the groups and fields. A field can be selected from the list.

In this example, the purpose of the expression box is to display a running sum of quantities ordered over the whole of a single customer's order. The XPath expression for this is

```
sum(LineItem/Quantity[.!=""])
```

This statement returns the sum of the `Quantity` field, and it avoids counting blank entries (a necessary precaution to prevent an error). Figure 11.35 shows the expression being entered.

The form is now complete in its layout. When it is in production, customers' names should be in a drop-down list, removing the need to type them in. Customer information is kept in a separate XML file. To make this information available, the file is added as a secondary data source.

Secondary Data Sources

Secondary data sources are useful for populating controls with lookup information, or for interacting with other data outside of the form (a technique that would require coding). In this example, a secondary data source provides the customer list. Secondary Data Sources is an item under the Tools menu. Selecting it displays the Secondary Data Sources dialog. Using the dialog to add a new source runs the Data Source Setup Wizard explained earlier in the chapter. One difference, though, is a place to give the new data source a working name. Figure 11.36 shows the Secondary Data Sources dialog.

The source of the referenced Customers data source is shown in Listing 11.3.

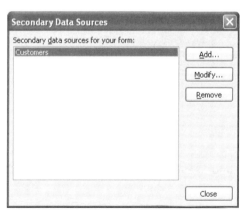

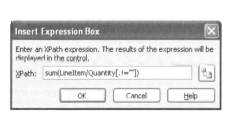

Figure 11.35 The Insert Expression Box dialog

Figure 11.36 Adding a secondary data source

Listing 11.3 The customer list is contained in an XML file

```xml
<?xml version="1.0"?>
<Customers>
    <Customer Name="Bookwares"/>
    <Customer Name="Mostly Books"/>
    <Customer Name="Smith Distributors"/>
    <Customer Name="Wholesale Foods and Books"/>
</Customers>
```

Next, the Customer text box on the form needs to be changed to a drop-down. Right-clicking on the box leads to the menu item to do this, shown in Figure 11.37.

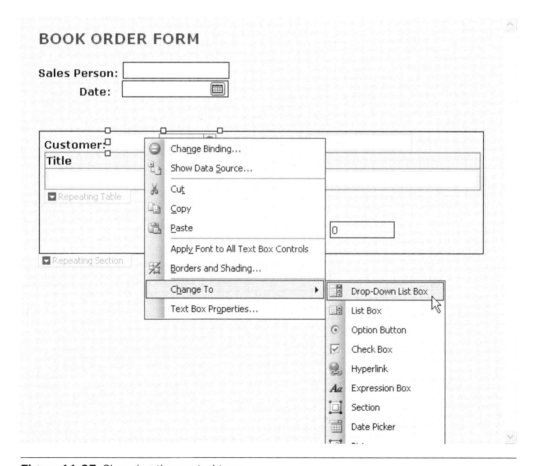

Figure 11.37 Changing the control type

Next, the properties of the drop-down need to include using the new data source to fill the list entries. See Figure 11.38.

Form Files

While in design mode, the Extract Form Files item under the File menu writes all the supportive files to a selected directory. A number of files are included for just this simple application. Figure 11.39 shows a directory filled with files.

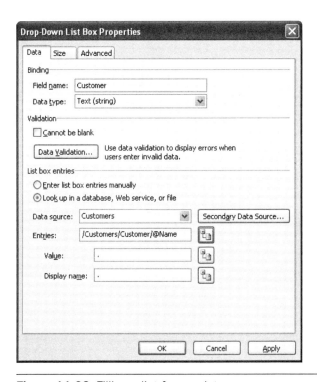

Figure 11.38 Filling a list from a data source

Figure 11.39 Files used to create this InfoPath form

This form was started without a dedicated schema. The activity in designing the form has created one, displayed in Figure 11.40.

Submitting Forms

One of the decisions involved with InfoPath development is what to do with the data collected in a form. There are four options:

- Submit to a Web service
- Submit via HTTP to a Web site
- Submit using custom scripting
- Save the production version of the filled-in form as an XML file

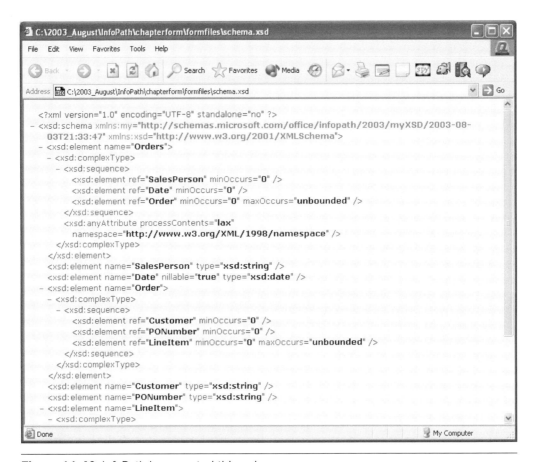

Figure 11.40 InfoPath has created this schema

While in design mode, submit selections are made in the Submitting Forms dialog, found under the Tools menu. See Figure 11.41.

The Submitting Forms dialog will vary depending on which of the three submit options is selected. In this example, the HTTP option is selected, and therefore an entry box is shown to enter the URL. It is not necessary to indicate a submit option. When a production form is filled in, it can simply be saved. This creates an XML file that contains the data from the form. Be aware of the distinction between saving the filled-in production form and saving the form design. When saving a form in production use, an XML file is created with the data. When a form in design mode is saved, the form definition is saved. This distinction is explained next.

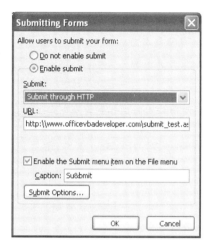

Figure 11.42 Saving or publishing a form

Figure 11.41 The Submitting Forms dialog

Saving and Publishing a Form

The first time a form is saved, InfoPath prompts whether to publish or save the form. See Figure 11.42. Selecting Save leads to a standard File Save As dialog box. Save stores the form design. However, a form should be published when ready for distribution.

Selecting Publish runs the Publishing Wizard. See Figure 11.43. The Publishing Wizard prompts where to store the production version of the form.

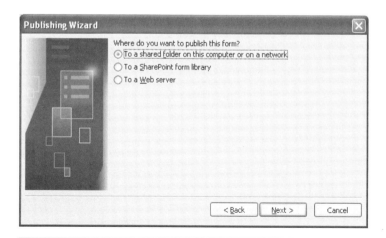

Figure 11.43 Specifying where to publish a form

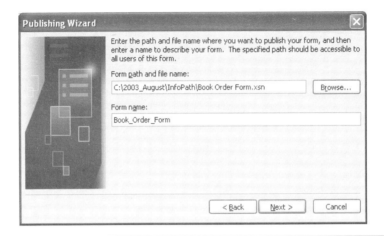

Figure 11.44 The Publishing Wizard gathers information to publish the form

Continuing with the Publishing Wizard, the saved form design and a name for the form are entered, as shown in Figure 11.44.

The Publishing Wizard finishes with a saved production version of the form in the selected location. The form is now available and can be selected in the Fill Out a Form task pane. Doing so opens the form ready for input. Figure 11.45 shows the form opened in this manner, with information filled in.

Programming InfoPath Forms

InfoPath supports programming in either JScript or VBScript. (VBA is not available in InfoPath.) The object model, properties, methods, and events stay the same regardless of which of the two scripting languages is selected. Portions of programmable code are autogenerated by InfoPath. Additional coding can be done manually.

The code is stored in a separate file, which is one of the components of the overall form file. (See Table 11.1.) The two scripting languages cannot be mixed together. The desired scripting language should be selected early in the design of a form. Once code is generated, the option to change language is not available. The scripting language is selected in the Form Options dialog (under the Tools menu), shown in Figure 11.46.

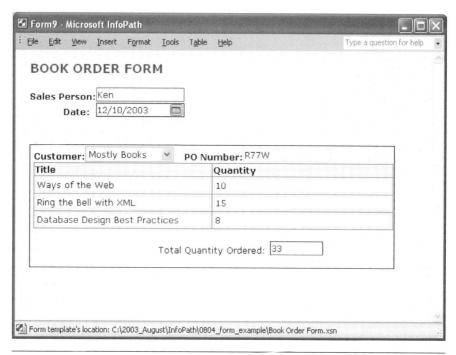

Figure 11.45 The published form is used for entering an order

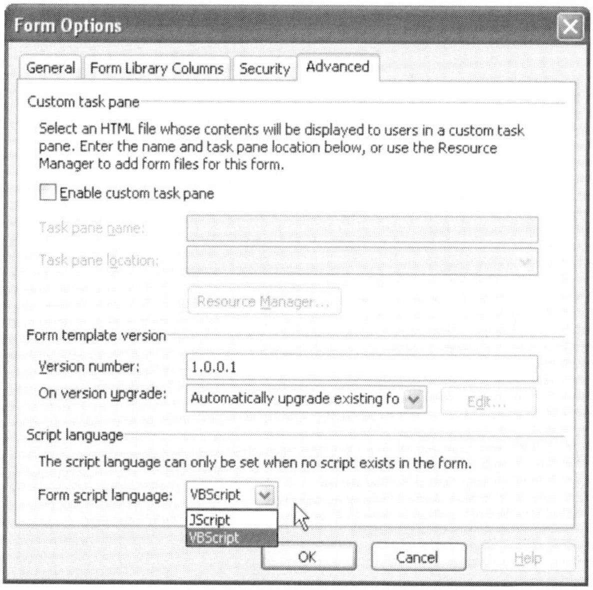

Figure 11.46 Selecting the scripting language

Overview of the Scripting Environment

The Tools menu leads to the Script Editor. Similar to the VBA environment, the Script Editor has an Object Browser, Project Explorer, Code pane, Immediate window, and so forth. Figure 11.47 shows a few of these elements.

The object model is available in the Object Browser, shown in Figure 11.48. Objects are shown along with their member properties, methods, and events. Table 11.2 has a subjective list of major objects.

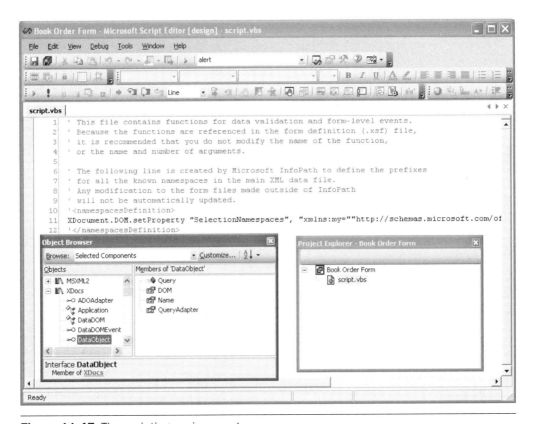

Figure 11.47 The scripting environment

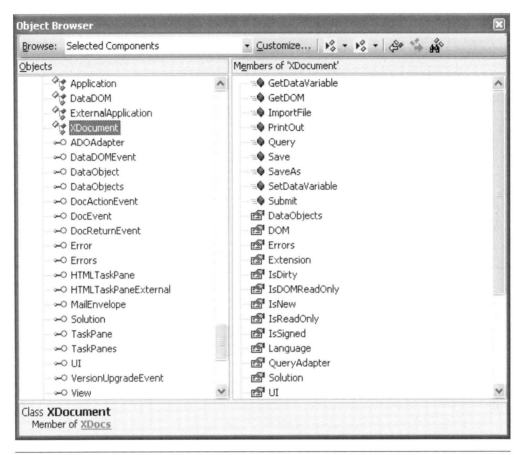

Figure 11.48 The Object Browser displays the InfoPath programmatic model

The Document Object Model

The Document Object Model (DOM) is an in-memory representation of XML data. When a form and data are active in InfoPath, then a DOM representation sits in memory. When data is entered or deleted in the form, the representative XML nodes in the DOM are added or deleted. The DOM is programmable via the robust MSXML Parser library. This library is available in the scripting environment. Figure 11.49 displays a portion of the library in the Object Browser.

Table 11.2 Major objects in InfoPath

Object	Comments
Application	Represents InfoPath. Has the Quit method. Leads to collections such as Windows and XDocuments.
XDocument/XDocuments collection	Represents the form (and underlying solution). Has several properties, methods, and events.
DataObject/DataObjects collection	Represents the secondary data sources.
DataDOM	Has events that are triggered by updates to the underlying DOM structure.
DOM (property)	This is a property of the XDocument. Through this property, the programmatic model of the MSXML Parser is applied to the DOM.
UI (property)	The UI (user interface) property provides the methods to display a message box, a modal dialog, and so on.

An in-depth treatment of programming InfoPath is itself a subject worthy of a separate book. Also, InfoPath ships with several sample forms. These all have programming examples in them, written in JScript. Minor modifications can make them usable as VBScript. For more information, see the references listed in the Appendix.

Summary

The intent of this chapter was to give a reasonable overview of InfoPath. Most of the basics were touched on. The layout, controls, and data source usage were explained and demonstrated. How a form is designed was covered in detail. The programming environment was introduced.

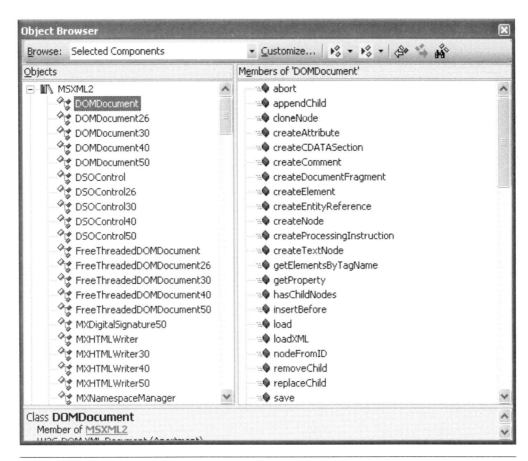

Figure 11.49 The DOM can be programmed

A single chapter cannot cover all facets of this comprehensive product. Issues such as security, menu bar customization, and deployment options have not been addressed. InfoPath is just being released and fills an emerging niche in the business place. There will doubtless be a slew of books devoted exclusively to InfoPath that will fully describe all the ins and outs of the product. The impact of InfoPath has not yet been felt, but by all reasonable assumptions, InfoPath could become a "killer app." Controlling data from entry to execution is certainly a valuable advantage.

PART III

Case Studies

CHAPTER 12

Mail Merge Magic

Using Word as a Front End to Access

VERSION NOTE: As is, this solution works with Word 2002 and Word 2003. The use of the `FileDialog` object limits the applicability to these versions. Alternative coding to work around using the `FileDialog` object will extend the solution to earlier versions of Word.

The Problem

Mail merges are a common function at this marketing company, but users have a difficult time assembling filtered sets of customer records that serve as mail merge sources. The criteria for filtering the full set of records in the customer database change constantly based on business and project needs. Users have been going into the customer database itself and creating queries that they would later select in Word during the mail merge.

A few difficulties have arisen with this approach. First, users are not trained in creating queries. Although the Query Grid in Access does make it easy to point and click through the process of creating a query, knowledge of Boolean logic, grouping, and aggregate functions is needed to correctly create queries with complex criteria. There is no confidence that the queries are correctly designed.

Second, the database is becoming cluttered with queries that are confusing, ill named, and incorrect. Last, but not least: users should not even need to open the database directly. This entire approach has been a distraction to users whose job function is not technical.

The Requirements

- The company needs an easy way to query the customer database to create mail merge source records.
- Users must have the ability to select criteria based on customer type, location, interests, and purchase patterns.
- Location selection should allow querying by metropolitan areas and/or states/provinces.
- Purchase pattern selection should allow querying by purchase frequency and/or amount spent, within a specified period of time.
- Once a query and criteria are established, the solution should allow it to be named and saved for future use.
- "Can it all be run without leaving Word?" Users don't want to learn how to make queries in Access.

Solution Tool Set and Files

- VBA
- SQL
- ADO
- Microsoft Forms
- MergeSolution.doc, mergdata.doc, Customers.mdb

NOTE: For the discussion of this case study, MergeSolution.doc is referred to as the *solution document*.

Table 12.1 Routines used in this solution

Routine	Module
cmdImportDoc_Click	frmMain
cmdShowQueryScreen_Click	frmMain
cmdSaveFile_Click	frmMain
get_list	frmQuery

Table 12.1 *(continued)*

Routine	Module
has_selections	frmQuery
populate_listbox	frmQuery
save_existing_query	frmQuery
save_new_query	frmQuery
cmdDeleteQuery_Click	frmQuery
cmdLoadQuery_Click	frmQuery
cmdQuery_Click	frmQuery
cmdSaveQuery_Click	frmQuery
UserForm_Initialize	frmQuery
cmdClose_Click	frmQuery
load_combo	frmSelectQuery
load_query	frmSelectQuery
cmdCancel_Click	frmSelectQuery
cmdLoadQuery_Click	frmSelectQuery
lstQueries_DblClick	frmSelectQuery
UserForm_Initialize	frmSelectQuery
open_conn	modDocumentCode
close_conn	modDocumentCode
create_recset	modDocumentCode
close_recset	modDocumentCode
MainForm_Show	modDocumentCode
Document_Open	ThisDocument

Notes on This Case Study

The solution demonstrated in this case study automates the creation and storage of sets of criteria to be applied against a database. Although its purpose is to help with mail merges, what it really does in this respect is to automate the creation of the source records. The solution does not actually run a mail merge. It helps prepare for the mail merge, and the user does the rest.

This case study also demonstrates sophisticated SQL statement creation via point-and-click functionality in a user form. This aspect of the solution could be adapted for any projects that require querying a database.

Consider how a mail merge works. There are source records, and there is the main document—which holds a mixture of text and inserted fields from the schema of the source records (and possibly other elements, such as graphics). The result of a merge is a set of new documents, labels, e-mail messages, or files—in which the fields have been filled with data. This solution is designed to make new documents. In addition to automating the creation of source records, the solution has features to assist with moving boilerplate text in and out of the main document. Figure 12.1 lays out the flow of the solution.

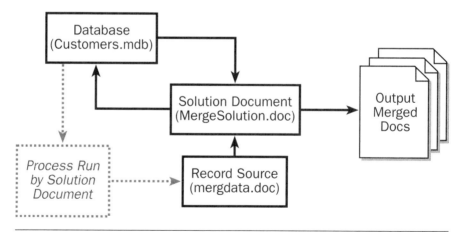

Figure 12.1 A map of the solution

The Structure of the Customers Database

All source data resides in the Customers database. The tables are shown in Figure 12.2. They are:

- **tblCustomers**—This table holds name and address information. It also has fields to categorize a customer by type (retail, mail order, and so on) and by metro area. MetroArea is a useful field, which helps to group customers by an area, but not particularly by state or province. For example, the metro area named "New York City" is applied to customers who live in the New York City area, which includes portions of New York, New Jersey, and Connecticut.
- **tblSales**—This holds purchase sums made by customers. Only two significant fields are here: PurchaseDate and Amount. Customers can have multiple records in this table.
- **tblInterests_Lookup**—This is a lookup table. Customers can be categorized with areas of interest such as gardening, travel, cooking, and so on. Each interest category has a numerical ID and a name.
- **tblInterests**—This table joins the customers and interests. The table contains only the keys of the related tables.
- **tblQueries**—This table is used for storing criteria sets that users create using the custom functionality in the solution document. As discussed later in the chapter, users make selections in a user form, which has a Save feature. Criteria selections on the form are saved in this table. The fields here match the available selections on the form. Note that this table has no relation to the other tables.

Using the Solution

The solution document serves as the front end and contains all the programming code. All functionality is run from this document; the document itself is the mail merge document. Most of the code sits in the code modules of the three user forms. An additional module, `modDocumentCode`, holds a few additional routines. Figure 12.3 shows the development environment.

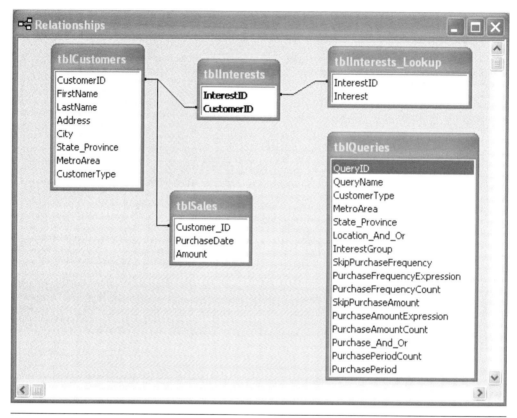

Figure 12.2 The schema of the Customers database

Listing 12.1 shows the full code found in the modDocumentCode module. This module holds commonly used routines called from other areas of the solution. Note that in the open_conn function, the Customers database is expected to be in the same directory as the document. Change the code as needed when adapting this solution.

Listing 12.1 The modDocumentCode module

```
Public conn As ADODB.Connection
Public recset As ADODB.Recordset

Public Function open_conn()
  On Error GoTo err_end
  Set conn = New ADODB.Connection
  conn.Provider = "Microsoft.Jet.OLEDB.4.0"
```

Listing 12.1 *(continued)*

```
' assumes the database is in the same directory . . .
this_path = ActiveDocument.Path
conn.Open this_path & "/Customers.mdb"
Exit Function
err_end:
MsgBox Err.Description
End Function
Public Function close_conn()
conn.Close
Set conn = Nothing
End Function
Public Function create_recset()
Set recset = New ADODB.Recordset
End Function
Public Function close_recset()
recset.Close
Set recset = Nothing
End Function
Public Sub MainForm_Show()
frmMain.Show
End Sub
```

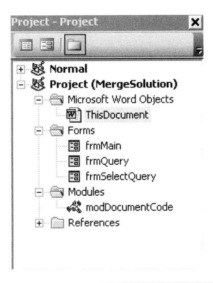

Figure 12.3 The solution document's VBA project

The Main Form

The solution document has coding in the `Document_Open` event that displays the Main form, as shown in Figure 12.4.

This form serves as a navigator to the real functionality of the solution. The Close button on the form simply closes the form; it does not close the document. This action is achieved with a single line of code in the click event of the button:

```
Me.Hide
```

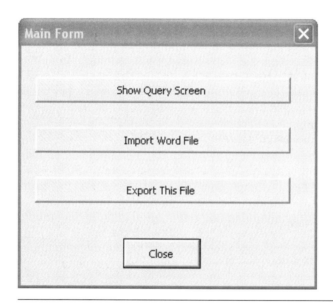

Figure 12.4 The Main form is displayed when opening the document

Setting the Keystroke Shortcut

Besides the Close button, all the other buttons run routines that eventually close the Main form. However, users often need to redisplay the form. To make this easy, a shortcut keystroke—Control+M—is set in the document. This is a manual setting done through the Tools...Customize menu. See Figure 12.5.

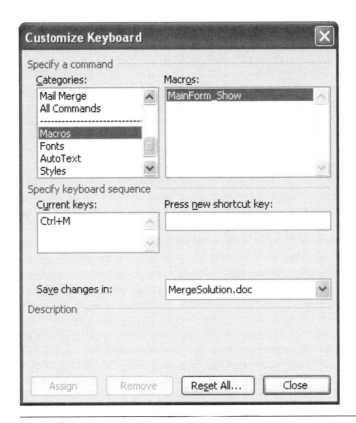

Figure 12.5 Setting a keyboard shortcut

In the Customize dialog is a button with the caption "Keyboard…", which displays the Customize Keyboard dialog. Of the various settings in this dialog, first the "Save changes in" box is set to the solution document.

This step must be done first, or else the correct routine to assign a shortcut will not be found. It is likely when this dialog is first displayed that the "Save changes in" setting displays Normal.dot. Normal is Word's general overall template, and in fact it is fairly synonymous with Word itself. The keyboard shortcut should be available only to the solution document, not to all of Word. While the "Save changes in" setting is set to Normal, only routines that are stored in Normal will be visible in the dialog.

The next step is to find the routine named `MainForm_Show`. This routine sits in the `modDocumentCode` module of the solution document. The routine simply displays the Main form using the `Show` method:

```
Public Sub MainForm_Show()
  frmMain.Show
End Sub
```

To assign the keyboard shortcut to this routine, first select Macros in the Categories list of the dialog, then select the routine itself in the Macros list.

What Happens When the Document Is Opened

The DynamicMailMerge.doc document contains the `Document_Open` procedure shown in Listing 12.2. This code belongs to the `ThisDocument` object seen in Figure 12.3.

Listing 12.2 This code runs when the document opens.

```
Private Sub Document_Open()
  ' break the connection to the merge data
  ' will be reconnected when running a query
  ActiveDocument.MailMerge.MainDocumentType = _
      wdNotAMergeDocument
  ' show Main Form
  frmMain.Show
End Sub
```

As discussed previously, the routine displays the Main form, but prior to that an important action takes place. The solution document is set to *not* be a mail merge document. When mail merge documents are opened, they seek out the source data for the merge. For this solution, the source is always a document named mergdata.doc, and the solution re-creates it with each mail merge. As such, its existence is not critical ahead of running the solution.

Further, when first installing the solution document, the source file does not exist. If the solution document were not set this way, a message such as the one shown in Figure 12.6 would appear. This message is thereby avoided and relieves users of making a confusing decision.

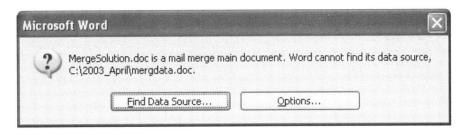

Figure 12.6 Programming ensures that this confusing message will not appear

Inserting Content from Another Document

This solution was developed to automate the creation of letters. This is one of a handful of uses for mail merges. Another common one is creating labels. However, whereas labels often use just the data coming from the source records, letter merges typically mix the source data with boilerplate text.

So functionality was built into this solution to help insert text from other Word documents. On the Main form is a button labeled "Import Word File". Clicking this button calls up the File dialog shown in Figure 12.7.

NOTE: `FileDialog` is an object available from the Office Object Library. See Chapter 7, "Common Microsoft Office Objects," for more information.

When a document is selected with this dialog, then the entire contents of the document's body (minus headers and footers) is copied into the solution document. The code that accomplishes this sits in the click event of the button. Listing 12.3 shows the code.

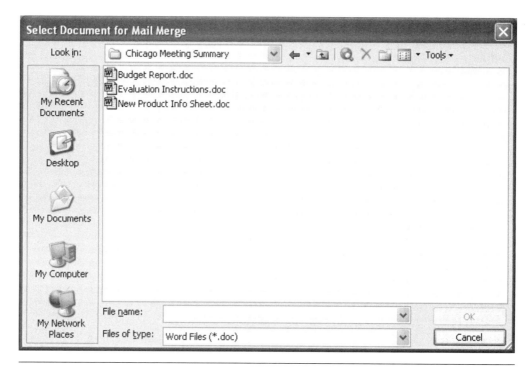

Figure 12.7 Select another Word document to copy text from

Listing 12.3 Copy the contents from a selected document into the solution document.

```
Private Sub cmdImportDoc_Click()
' imports the contents of another Word document
' to serve as the body of the mail merge
On Error GoTo err_end
Dim fd As FileDialog
Dim file_name As String
file_name = ""
Set fd = Application.FileDialog(msoFileDialogFilePicker)
With fd
  .AllowMultiSelect = False
  .Filters.Clear
  .Filters.Add "Word Files", "*.doc"
  .Title = "Select Document for Mail Merge"
```

Listing 12.3 *(continued)*

```
    If .Show = True Then
        file_name = .SelectedItems(1)
    End If
End With
' test for either Cancel button or
' OK button - but without file selected
' if Length=0 then Cancel button was clicked
' if tilde is present then no file selected
If Len(file_name) = 0 Or InStr(1, file_name, "~") > 0 Then
    Exit Sub
End If
' close form - no longer needed
Me.Hide
' clear this solution document first before
' pasting contents from other document
Selection.HomeKey Unit:=wdStory
Selection.EndKey Unit:=wdStory, Extend:=wdExtend
Selection.Delete Unit:=wdCharacter, Count:=1
' open selected document
Documents.Open file_name
' copy entire document and close it
Selection.WholeStory
Selection.Copy
ActiveWindow.Close
' paste contents into this solution document
Selection.Paste
Exit Sub
err_end:
' if unable to open doc, display the Query form
frmQuery.Show
MsgBox Err.Description
End Sub
```

In the `cmdImportDoc_Click` routine in Listing 12.3, the `fd` variable is set to the `FileDialog`—in the guise of the File Picker; then some properties are set and the dialog is displayed with the `Show` method:

```
Set fd = Application.FileDialog(msoFileDialogFilePicker)
With fd
    .AllowMultiSelect = False
```

```
.Filters.Clear
.Filters.Add "Word Files", "*.doc"
.Title = "Select Document for Mail Merge"
If .Show = True Then
   file_name = .SelectedItems(1)
End If
End With
```

The dialog is dismissed with either the OK button or the Cancel button. There are three possible outcomes: (1) a file is selected and the OK button is clicked, (2) no file is selected and the OK button is clicked, or (3) the Cancel button is clicked (regardless of whether a file is selected). A test is run to catch the second and third possibilities, because either of these needs to cause an abrupt exit from the routine. When the Cancel button is clicked, a length of zero is always returned. If the OK button is clicked without a file name, then the "owner" file name is returned. See Figure 12.8.

When a document is opened, Word creates the *owner* file in the same directory. This file is used for managing the document in a shared environment. Owner files begin with the tilde (~) character.

The second part of the test uses the `InStr()` function to look for the tilde character:

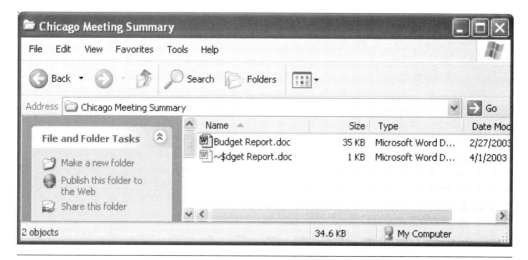

Figure 12.8 When documents are open, Word maintains associated owner files

```
If Len(file_name) = 0 Or InStr(1, file_name, "~") > 0 Then
   Exit Sub
End If
```

When the test fails, the routine continues. The dialog is dismissed with the `Hide` method and the body of the solution document is cleared:

```
Me.Hide
' clear this solution document first before
' pasting contents from other document
Selection.HomeKey Unit:=wdStory
Selection.EndKey Unit:=wdStory, Extend:=wdExtend
Selection.Delete Unit:=wdCharacter, Count:=1
```

Next the selected file is opened and its contents are copied. The file is then closed and the contents are pasted into the solution document:

```
Documents.Open file_name
' copy entire document and close it
Selection.WholeStory
Selection.Copy
ActiveWindow.Close
' paste contents into this solution document
Selection.Paste
```

Saving the Content from the Solution Document

The routine behind the Import Word File button on the Main form essentially performs the opposite function of the routine behind the Export This File button. That is, one imports text into the solution document and the other saves the text back out into a Word file. However, there is a key difference. The import routine is simply a help to users. It automates what is usually done manually by opening a file and using copy and paste features.

In contrast, the export functionality works differently—it's not the same as just doing a Save As from the Word interface. Nothing prevents the solution document from being saved or saved as. Simply saving the file is expected and encouraged, especially given that users can type into it or import text with the import routine.

Performing a Save As, however, has a drawback: the VBA project will be saved along with the new document. The functionality behind the Export button was developed specifically to allow users to save *the text only* from the solution document into a new document—without the VBA code.

This is accomplished with the `cmdSaveFile_Click` routine, shown in Listing 12.4.

Listing 12.4 Displaying the Save As dialog

```
Private Sub cmdSaveFile_Click()
' saves the body of this document into a new document,
' However . . .
' does so without saving the programming code!
On Error GoTo err_end
Dim fd As FileDialog
Dim file_name As String
' get new file name from dialog
file_name = ""
Set fd = Application.FileDialog(msoFileDialogSaveAs)
With fd
  .AllowMultiSelect = False
  .Title = "Save Document"
  If .Show = True Then
    file_name = .SelectedItems(1)
  End If
End With
' if no selection . . .
If Len(file_name) = 0 Then Exit Sub
Me.Hide
' copy body of "this" document
Selection.WholeStory
Selection.Copy
' add new document and reference it by its window
Documents.Add
this_window_doc = ActiveWindow.Document
' paste into new document
Windows(this_window_doc).Activate
ActiveWindow.Selection.Paste
' save and close new document
ActiveDocument.SaveAs FileName:=file_name
ActiveDocument.Close
' at this point the entire merge doc is selected,
' so deselect . . .
Selection.Collapse
Exit Sub
err_end:
MsgBox Err.Description
End Sub
```

In this routine, the `FileDialog` is set as a Save As dialog. Some properties are set and the dialog is displayed. In the `cmdImportDoc_Click` shown in Listing 12.3, the test for file selection and the Cancel button had to include the possibility that the OK button might be clicked without a file being selected in the dialog. In contrast, with the `FileDialog` serving as a Save As dialog, it is not possible to click the Save button until a file is selected or a file name is typed in. Therefore, the test simply checks for zero length, which indicates that the Cancel button was clicked:

```
Set fd = Application.FileDialog(msoFileDialogSaveAs)
With fd
  .AllowMultiSelect = False
  .Title = "Save Document"
  If .Show = True Then
    file_name = .SelectedItems(1)
  End If
End With
' if no selection . . .
If Len(file_name) = 0 Then Exit Sub
```

In Figure 12.9, the dialog is shown as it is initially displayed. The Save button is disabled. It remains so until a file is selected or a name is typed in.

Proceeding with the Save As, the dialog is dismissed with the `Hide` method. Then the `WholeStory` method is used to select the body of the solution document, which is then copied.

A new document is added, and a reference is added to the window it appears in. Using the window reference, the new document is activated and the contents are pasted into the document. The new document is saved using the supplied name from the dialog, and the file is closed:

```
Me.Hide
' copy body of "this" document
Selection.WholeStory
Selection.Copy
' add new document and reference it by its window
Documents.Add
this_window_doc = ActiveWindow.Document
' paste into new document
Windows(this_window_doc).Activate
ActiveWindow.Selection.Paste
' save and close new document
ActiveDocument.SaveAs FileName:=file_name
ActiveDocument.Close
```

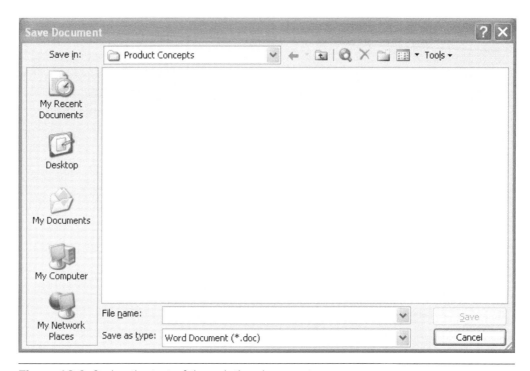

Figure 12.9 Saving the text of the solution document

At this point, the text in the solution document is still completely selected, so it is necessary to deselect. This is done by collapsing the `Selection` object:

```
Selection.Collapse
```

The Query Form

The Query form contains the bulk of the solution's functionality. In addition to initiating the process to create the source set of data for the merge, it also handles creating criteria (later transferred into an SQL statement), saving a set of criteria, and loading previously saved criteria. Clicking the Show Query Screen button on the Main form displays the Query form, as shown in Figure 12.10.

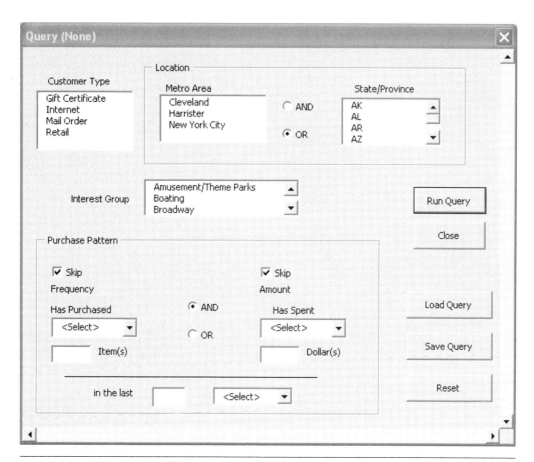

Figure 12.10 The Query form

The Query form contains several controls, some of which require particular property settings. Figure 12.11 shows the Query form in design mode.

Following the numerical annotations in Figure 12.11, Table 12.2 shows the key settings. For all objects, the Name property is in the second column. Other required properties are listed in the third column.

A few key points about the form and the controls need mentioning. First, the caption of the form itself changes when the form is run. This is evident by comparing the form design in Figure 12.11 with the form as run, seen in Figure 12.10. The form caption will further change if and when a saved query is loaded. This is explained later.

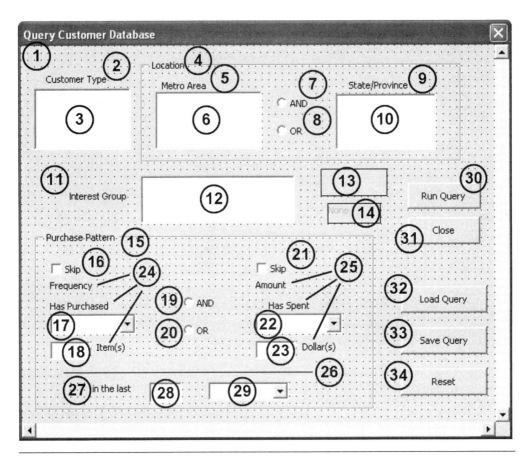

Figure 12.11 The Query form in design mode

Table 12.2 Initial property settings for the Query form

Number	Object	Properties and Settings
1	frmQuery (Form)	Caption = Query Customer Database Scroll Bars = Both
2	lblCustomerType (Label)	Caption = Customer Type
3	lstCustomerTypes (List Box)	Column Count = 1 Multi Select= Select Multi
4	grpLocation (Frame)	Caption = Location

Table 12.2 *(continued)*

Number	Object	Properties and Settings
5	`lblMetroArea` (Label)	Caption = Metro Area
6	`lstMetroAreas` (List Box)	Column Count = 1 Multi Select= Select Multi
7	`optLocationAnd` (Option Button)	Caption = AND
8	`optLocationOr` (Option Button)	Caption = OR
9	`lblStateProvince` (Label)	Caption = State/Province
10	`lstStatesProvinces` (List Box)	Column Count = 1 Multi Select= Select Multi
11	`lblInterestGroup` (Label)	Caption = Interest Group
12	`lstInterests` (List Box)	Bound Column = 1 Column Count = 2 Column Widths = 0 pt; 1.45 pt Multi Select= Select Multi
13	`lblQueryName` (Label)	Border Style = Single Visible = False
14	`lblQueryID` (Label)	Border Style = Single Visible = False
15	`grpPurchasePattern` (Frame)	Caption = Purchase Pattern
16	`chkSkipFrequency` (Checkbox)	Caption = Skip
17	`cmbExpressionsFrequency` (Combo Box)	Column Count = 1
18	`txtFrequencyCount` (Text Box)	
19	`optPurchaseAnd` (Option Button)	Caption = AND

Table 12.2 *(continued)*

Number	Object	Properties and Settings
20	optPurchaseOr (Option Button)	Caption = OR
21	chkSkipAmount (Checkbox)	Caption = Skip
22	cmbExpressionsAmount (Combo Box)	Column Count = 1
23	txtAmountCount (Text Box)	
24	lblFrequency (Label) lblHasPurchased (Label) lblItems (Label)	Caption = Frequency Caption = Has Purchased Caption = Item(s)
25	lblAmount (Label) lblHasSpent (Label) lblDollars (Label)	Caption = Amount Caption = Has Spent Caption = Dollar(s)
26	lblLine (Label)	Caption = _____
27	lblLast (Label)	Caption = in the last
28	txtPeriodCount (Text Box)	
29	cmbPeriods (Combo Box)	Column Count = 1
30	cmdRunQuery (Command Button)	Caption = Run Query
31	cmdClose (Command Button)	Caption = Close
32	cmdLoadQuery (Command Button)	Caption = Load Query
33	cmdSaveQuery (Command Button)	Caption = Save Query
34	cmdReset (Command Button)	Caption = Reset

There are four list boxes on the form: `lstCustomerTypes`, `lst-MetroAreas`, `lstStatesProvinces`, and `lstInterests`. Of the four, three consist of a single column. The fourth list box, `lstInterests`, contains a two-column list. The first column is the bound column, and it is not visible because its width is set to zero. The list is drawn from the `tblInterests_Lookup` table (see Figure 12.2). The table's first column, `InterestID`, is the key needed for building the SQL statement. The second column holds the descriptive names of various interests. These are the values that appear in the list box.

The `lblQueryName` and `lblQueryID` label controls, numbers 13 and 14 respectively in Figure 12.11, are not visible when the form is displayed. These labels are not meant for users to see. Instead, they are used as placeholders for some of the form's functionality. In particular, these labels are used to hold the name and ID of any loaded or saved query that is currently residing on the form. This is explained further later in this section.

What Happens When the Query Form Is Displayed

Clicking the Show Query Screen button on the Main form displays the Query form. The form's initialization routine runs the first time the form is displayed. The `UserForm_Initialize` routine is shown in Listing 12.5.

Listing 12.5 The initialization routine of the Query form

```
Private Sub UserForm_Initialize()
On Error GoTo err_end
Dim ssql As String
Dim groups_array()
Dim interests_count As Integer
Dim interests_loop As Integer
open_conn
create_recset

' populate Customer Types list box
populate_listbox "CustomerType", "lstCustomerTypes", _
    conn, recset
' populate Metro Areas list box
populate_listbox "MetroArea", "lstMetroAreas", _
    conn, recset
```

Listing 12.5 *(continued)*

```
' populate States/Provinces list box
populate_listbox "State_Province", "lstStatesProvinces", _
    conn, recset

' populate Interest Groups list box
' this is a double-column list, so it is handled differently
' the list box is populated using an array that is set
' to the List property
ssql = "Select InterestID, Interest"
ssql = ssql & " from tblInterests_Lookup Order By Interest"
recset.Open (ssql), conn, adOpenStatic
recset.MoveLast
interests_count = recset.RecordCount
ReDim groups_array(interests_count, 2)
recset.MoveFirst
For interests_loop = 0 To interests_count - 1
  groups_array(interests_loop, 0) = recset.Fields(0)
  groups_array(interests_loop, 1) = recset.Fields(1)
  recset.MoveNext
Next interests_loop
Me.lstInterests.List = groups_array()
close_recset
close_conn

With Me
  ' populate combo boxes with these selections . . .
  With .cmbExpressionsFrequency
    .AddItem "At least"
    .AddItem "Exactly"
    .AddItem "More than"
    .Value = "<Select>"
  End With
  With .cmbExpressionsAmount
    .AddItem "At least"
    .AddItem "Exactly"
    .AddItem "More than"
    .Value = "<Select>"
  End With
```

Listing 12.5 *(continued)*

```
With .cmbPeriods
    .AddItem "day(s)"
    .AddItem "month(s)"
    .AddItem "year(s)"
    .Value = "<Select>"
End With

' other initial form settings . . .
.optLocationOr = True
.optPurchaseAnd = True
.chkSkipAmount = True
.chkSkipFrequency = True
.Caption = "Query (None)"
.lblQueryID = ""
.lblQueryName = ""
End With
Exit Sub
err_end:
MsgBox Err.Description
End Sub
```

The purpose of the initialization is to set the form to an initial blank state, and to get the latest values for the list boxes and combo boxes. The values for these lists come from the Customers database. To accomplish this, a connection to the database needs to be started. Since the database is actually referenced from multiple procedures, the ADO database access code is stored as a function named open_conn. This function is in the modDocumentCode module, as shown earlier in Listing 12.1.

Once the database connection is made with the call to open_conn, another shared function, create_recset is called to create a Recordset object. Then the three list boxes that are single column (lstCustomerTypes, lstMetroAreas, lstStatesProvinces) are populated with calls to the populate_listbox routine. This routine, shown in Listing 12.6, takes four parameters: the field name from the database (the table is hard-coded in the routine), the name of the list box, the ADO connection object, and the ADO recordset object. The call takes the form of:

```
populate_listbox "CustomerType", "lstCustomerTypes", _
    conn, recset
```

Listing 12.6 shows the `populate_listbox` routine. In a nutshell, this routine runs a Group By query against the tblCustomers table and then uses the `Add` method to populate the list box with the results of the returned recordset.

Listing 12.6 The `populate_listbox` routine fills a list box with values from the database.

```
Private Sub populate_listbox(fieldname As String, _
    listboxname As String, conn As ADODB.Connection, _
    recset As ADODB.Recordset)
' populates the three list boxes that are single column -
' Customer Types, Metro Areas, and States/Provinces
On Error GoTo err_end
Dim ssql As String
ssql = "Select " & fieldname & " From tblCustomers"
ssql = ssql & " Group By " & fieldname
ssql = ssql & " Having " & fieldname & " Is Not Null"
ssql = ssql & " Order By " & fieldname & " Asc"
recset.Open (ssql), conn, adOpenForwardOnly
Do While Not recset.EOF
  Me.Controls(listboxname).AddItem recset.Fields(0)
  recset.MoveNext
Loop
recset.Close
Exit Sub
err_end:
MsgBox Err.Description
End Sub
```

Back in the form's initialization, the interest groups list box (`lst-Interests`) is populated using different code, because it is the only double-column list box. To fill this list box, the database is queried for all values in the tblInterests_Lookup table. This table has two fields: InterestID and Interest. The values in these fields are fed into an array, and then the `List` property of the list box is set to the array:

```
ssql = "Select InterestID, Interest"
ssql = ssql & " from tblInterests_Lookup Order By Interest"
recset.Open (ssql), conn, adOpenStatic
recset.MoveLast
```

```
interests_count = recset.RecordCount
ReDim groups_array(interests_count, 2)
recset.MoveFirst
For interests_loop = 0 To interests_count - 1
  groups_array(interests_loop, 0) = recset.Fields(0)
  groups_array(interests_loop, 1) = recset.Fields(1)
  recset.MoveNext
Next interests_loop
Me.lstInterests.List = groups_array()
```

The combo boxes and option buttons on the form are then set to given values. For example, this populates the combo box used in creating purchase pattern frequency criteria:

```
With .cmbExpressionsFrequency
  .AddItem "At least"
  .AddItem "Exactly"
  .AddItem "More than"
  .Value = "<Select>"
End With
```

NOTE: The initial setting of the Query form occurs just once during the initialization routine. Values are queried from the database only the first time the form is displayed. Subsequent calls to open the form do not seek out new database values.

This is a subjective approach. The disadvantage is that there may be new values, such as a new interest group in the database. However, the odds are not great that this is an issue, because the form will be initialized the next time it is called after opening the solution document—perhaps the next business day.

On the other hand, the benefit of not reinitializing the form with each display is that entered or loaded criteria will stay on the form throughout the time the solution document is open. This is very useful as users tweak the criteria.

If initialization is desired every time the form is displayed, then the form's `Activate` event is the target for putting code to run upon each display.

Making Selections on the Query Form

The choices offered on the Query form mirror the structure of the data in the Customers database. Criteria can be selected on customer type, location, interests, and purchase patterns.

Selections of location criteria can include one or both of metro areas and states/provinces. When both types of location criteria are selected, these can be treated with either an AND or an OR operator.

Selections of purchase pattern criteria can include one or both of frequency (how many purchases made) or amount spent. When both types of purchase pattern criteria are selected, these can be treated with either an AND or an OR operator. Regardless of whether one or both purchase pattern criteria types are used, they share a date range criteria selection.

In Figure 12.12, a previously saved query has been loaded into the Query form. The query name is *"NYC Metro Retail Customers Broadway Purchased 1x in Past Year"*. This name appears in the title bar of the form (the caption of the form). A single customer type—Retail—is selected. A single metro area—New York City—is selected. Remember that metro area is a subjective category used to group customers based on proximity to a city. In addition to customers in New York City, those in surrounding suburbs, including northern New Jersey and southwestern Connecticut, are New York City metro area customers.

In this query, also, customers must be included in the Broadway interest group and must have purchased at least one item in the past year. To sum this up, this query is equivalent to the plain-English statement *"Show me all customers in the New York City area who like Broadway and have purchased at least one item in the past year."* In fact, the query's name is a shortened version of this statement.

Saving a Query

Clicking the Save Query button runs the process to append a record to the tblQueries table in the Customers database. This table does not actually hold SQL or any type of query code or statements, but instead it contains a column for each control on the Query form. Figure 12.13 shows the design of this table.

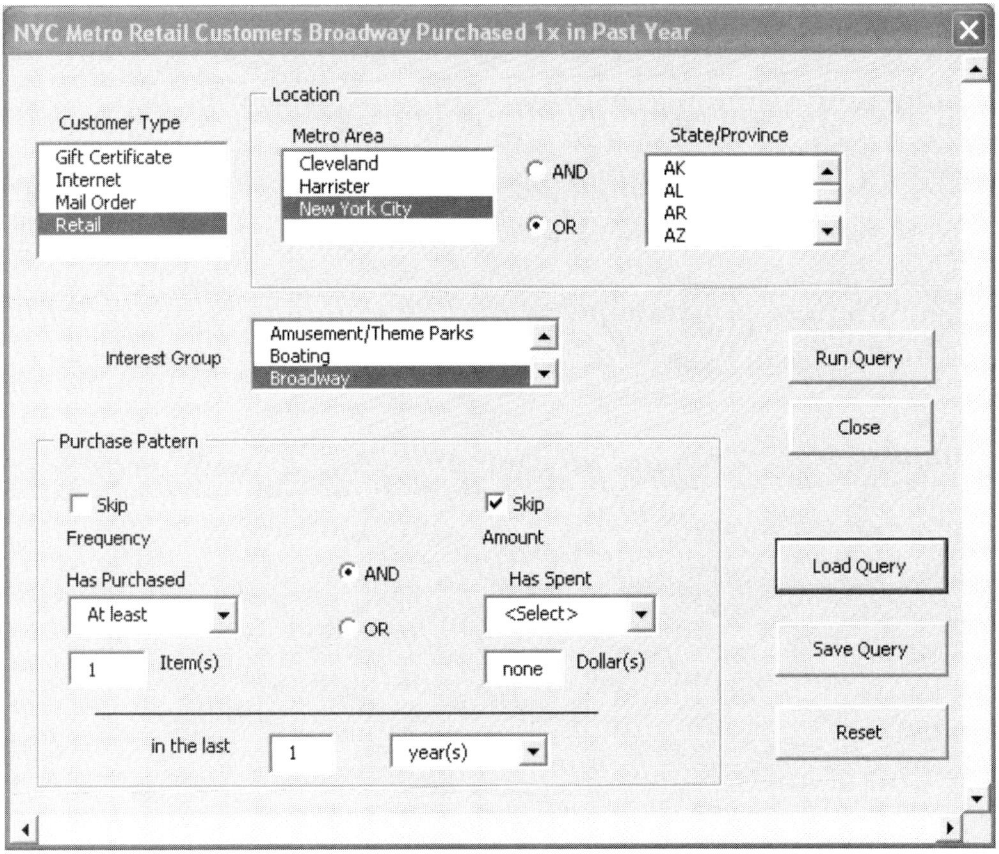

Figure 12.12 The Query form with selected criteria

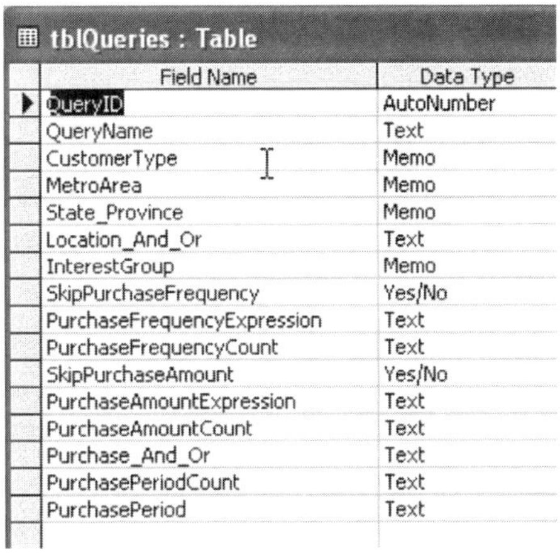

tblQueries : Table

Field Name	Data Type
QueryID	AutoNumber
QueryName	Text
CustomerType	Memo
MetroArea	Memo
State_Province	Memo
Location_And_Or	Text
InterestGroup	Memo
SkipPurchaseFrequency	Yes/No
PurchaseFrequencyExpression	Text
PurchaseFrequencyCount	Text
SkipPurchaseAmount	Yes/No
PurchaseAmountExpression	Text
PurchaseAmountCount	Text
Purchase_And_Or	Text
PurchasePeriodCount	Text
PurchasePeriod	Text

Figure 12.13 The tblQueries table in design mode

In Figure 12.14, a query has been designed that asks *"Show me mail order or Internet customers who have spent at least 200 dollars in the past 3 years."* Since this is a new query, the form's title bar does not display a name yet. The query needs to be saved (or loaded) for a name to appear. Continuing in Figure 12.14, the Save Query button has already been clicked, which displays an input box to enter a name for the query. An appropriate name has been entered.

The click event of the Save Query button is shown in Listing 12.7.

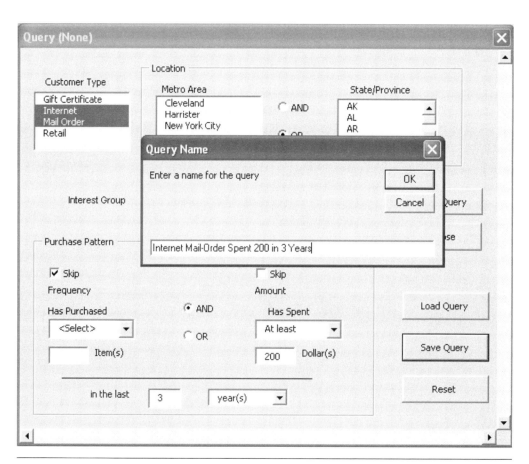

Figure 12.14 A query being saved

Listing 12.7 Preparing to save a query

```
Private Sub cmdSaveQuery_Click()
Dim query_name As String
query_name = InputBox("Enter a name for the query", _
    "Query Name", Me.lblQueryName.Caption)
If Len(query_name) = 0 Then
  MsgBox "No name entered!  Cannot save query!"
  Exit Sub
End If
' clean up apostrophes
query_name = Replace(query_name, "'", "''")

' is this a previously saved query?
If IsNumeric(Me.lblQueryID) Then
  save_existing_query query_name
Else
  save_new_query query_name
End If
End Sub
```

The `cmdSaveQuery_Click` routine seen in Listing 12.7 does not actually save the query. Instead, it validates that a name was entered into the input box. If a name has been entered, then the `Replace()` function is used to double up any apostrophes. This is necessary to avoid a failure for the SQL Insert that will shortly occur.

Next is the determination of whether this is a new query being saved for the first time, or if this is a previously saved query that is being updated. The `txtQueryID` text box is tested for a value. This text box, as well as the `txtQueryName` text box, are not visible to the user but are used for this very purpose of managing queries on the form. If a previously saved query had been loaded (explained shortly), then the two hidden text boxes would have values. Look back to Figure 12.11 to see the text boxes in design mode.

Consider that if an existing query is being updated, then its key value (the QueryID column in tblQueries) must be known. If this is an existing query, then the key value is in the invisible `txtQueryID` text box. Testing for this value determines which route to take in saving the query—treat as existing or treat as new—which in turn calls the appropriate routine:

```
If IsNumeric(Me.lblQueryID) Then
  save_existing_query query_name
Else
  save_new_query query_name
End If
```

The two routines that actually put data into the database are shown in Listing 12.8.

Listing 12.8 Routines used for saving queries

```
Sub save_existing_query(query_name As String)
' this is an SQL update of a previously saved
' query that is currently loaded on the form
On Error GoTo err_end
Dim crit As String ' criteria
Dim ssql As String
' prepare ADO
open_conn
' assemble SQL Insert
ssql = "UPDATE tblQueries SET QueryName = '" & _
    query_name & "', "
crit = get_list("lstCustomerTypes")
ssql = ssql & "CustomerType='" & crit & "', "
crit = get_list("lstMetroAreas")
ssql = ssql & "MetroArea='" & crit & "', "
crit = get_list("lstStatesProvinces")
ssql = ssql & "State_Province='" & crit & "', "
If Me.optLocationAnd = True Then
  ssql = ssql & "Location_And_Or='And', "
Else
  ssql = ssql & "Location_And_Or='Or', "
End If
crit = get_list("lstInterests")
ssql = ssql & "InterestGroup='" & crit & "', "
If Me.chkSkipFrequency = True Then
  ssql = ssql & "SkipPurchaseFrequency = True, "
Else
  ssql = ssql & "SkipPurchaseFrequency = False, "
End If
ssql = ssql & "PurchaseFrequencyExpression='" & _
    Me.cmbExpressionsFrequency & "', "
```

Listing 12.8 *(continued)*

```
If Len(Me.txtFrequencyCount) = 0 Then
  ssql = ssql & "PurchaseFrequencyCount='none', "
Else
  ssql = ssql & "PurchaseFrequencyCount='" & _
      Me.txtFrequencyCount & "', "
End If
If Me.chkSkipAmount = True Then
  ssql = ssql & "SkipPurchaseAmount = True, "
Else
  ssql = ssql & "SkipPurchaseAmount = False, "
End If
ssql = ssql & "PurchaseAmountExpression='" & _
    Me.cmbExpressionsAmount & "', "
If Len(Me.txtAmountCount) = 0 Then
  ssql = ssql & "PurchaseAmountCount='none', "
Else
  ssql = ssql & "PurchaseAmountCount='" & _
      Me.txtAmountCount & "', "
End If
If Me.optPurchaseAnd = True Then
  ssql = ssql & "Purchase_And_Or='And', "
Else
  ssql = ssql & "Purchase_And_Or='Or', "
End If
If Len(Me.txtPeriodCount) = 0 Then
  ssql = ssql & "PurchasePeriodCount='none', "
Else
  ssql = ssql & "PurchasePeriodCount='" & _
    Me.txtPeriodCount & "', "
End If
ssql = ssql & "PurchasePeriod='" & Me.cmbPeriods & "' "
ssql = ssql & " Where QueryID=" & Me.lblQueryID
conn.Execute (ssql)
Me.lblQueryName = query_name
Me.Caption = query_name
MsgBox "Query Saved"
Exit Sub
err_end:
MsgBox Err.Description
End Sub
```

Listing 12.8 *(continued)*

```
Sub save_new_query(query_name As String)
' this is an SQL append of the new query
' that is currently on the form
On Error GoTo err_end
Dim crit As String ' criteria
Dim ssql As String
' prepare ADO
open_conn
create_recset
' assemble SQL Insert
ssql = "Insert Into tblQueries (" & _
    "QueryName, CustomerType, " & _
    "MetroArea, State_Province, Location_And_Or, " & _
    "InterestGroup, SkipPurchaseFrequency, " & _
    "PurchaseFrequencyExpression, " & _
    "PurchaseFrequencyCount, SkipPurchaseAmount, " & _
    "PurchaseAmountExpression, PurchaseAmountCount, " & _
    "Purchase_And_Or, PurchasePeriodCount, " & _
    "PurchasePeriod) Values ('" & query_name & "', "
' CUSTOMER TYPES
crit = get_list("lstCustomerTypes")
ssql = ssql & "'" & crit & "', "
' METRO AREAS
crit = get_list("lstMetroAreas")
ssql = ssql & "'" & crit & "', "
' STATES-PROVINCES
crit = get_list("lstStatesProvinces")
ssql = ssql & "'" & crit & "', "
' LOCATION AND/OR
If Me.optLocationAnd = True Then
  ssql = ssql & "'And', "
Else
  ssql = ssql & "'Or', "
End If
' INTEREST GROUPS
crit = get_list("lstInterests")
ssql = ssql & "'" & crit & "', "
' SKIP PURCHASE FREQUENCY
If Me.chkSkipFrequency = True Then
  ssql = ssql & True & ", "
Else
  ssql = ssql & False & ", "
End If
```

Listing 12.8 *(continued)*

```
' PURCHASE FREQUENCY EXPRESSION
ssql = ssql & "'" & Me.cmbExpressionsFrequency & "', "
' PURCHASE FREQUENCY COUNT
If Len(Me.txtFrequencyCount) = 0 Then
  ssql = ssql & "'none', "
Else
  ssql = ssql & "'" & Me.txtFrequencyCount & "', "
End If
' SKIP PURCHASE AMOUNT
If Me.chkSkipAmount = True Then
  ssql = ssql & True & ", "
Else
  ssql = ssql & False & ", "
End If
' PURCHASE AMOUNT EXPRESSION
ssql = ssql & "'" & Me.cmbExpressionsAmount & "', "
' PURCHASE AMOUNT COUNT
If Len(Me.txtAmountCount) = 0 Then
  ssql = ssql & "'none', "
Else
  ssql = ssql & "'" & Me.txtAmountCount & "', "
End If
' PURCHASE AND/OR
If Me.optPurchaseAnd = True Then
  ssql = ssql & "'And', "
Else
  ssql = ssql & "'Or', "
End If
' PURCHASE PERIOD COUNT
If Len(Me.txtPeriodCount) = 0 Then
  ssql = ssql & "'none', "
Else
  ssql = ssql & "'" & Me.txtPeriodCount & "',"
End If
' PURCHASE PERIOD
ssql = ssql & "'" & Me.cmbPeriods & "')"
conn.Execute (ssql)
' now get the new saved query id and store it on form
recset.Open ("Select Max(QueryID) from tblQueries"), _
    conn, adOpenStatic
Me.lblQueryID = recset.Fields(0)
recset.Close
```

Listing 12.8 *(continued)*

```
' store the query name in the form and as the form caption
Me.lblQueryName = query_name
Me.Caption = query_name
Exit Sub
err_end:
MsgBox Err.Description
End Sub
```

Both the save_existing_query and save_new_query routines make calls to the get_list() function, shown in Listing 12.9.

Listing 12.9 The get_list and has_selections functions are used to concatenate lists.

```
Private Function get_list(list_box_name As String) _
      As String
' purpose - concatenate selection in multi-select list box
' into one string with the pipe character (|) serving as
' the separator
On Error GoTo err_end
Dim ctrl As Control
Dim selected_loop As Integer
get_list = "none"
Set ctrl = Me.Controls(list_box_name)
If has_selections(ctrl) = True Then
  get_list = ""
  For selected_loop = 0 To ctrl.ListCount - 1
    If ctrl.Selected(selected_loop) = True Then
      get_list = get_list & ctrl.List(selected_loop) & "|"
    End If
  Next selected_loop
  ' remove last pipe character (|)
  get_list = Left(get_list, Len(get_list) - 1)
End If
Exit Function
err_end:
MsgBox Err.Description
End Function
```

Listing 12.9 *(continued)*

```
Private Function has_selections(list_box As ListBox) _
    As Boolean
' returns true if any items in a list are selected
has_selections = False
Dim selected_test As Integer
For selected_test = 0 To list_box.ListCount - 1
   If list_box.Selected(selected_test) = True Then
      has_selections = True
   End If
Next selected_test
End Function
```

The `get_list()` function accepts a list box as an argument and will concatenate all selected values. At the start, the function sets itself to return "none". Then `get_list()` passes the list box to the `has_selections()` function, which determines if any values in the list box are selected. If `has_selections()` returns true, then `get_list()` moves ahead to create a concatenated string.

The resultant string represents the values in the list box, separated with the pipe character (|):

```
get_list = "none"
Set ctrl = Me.Controls(list_box_name)
If has_selections(ctrl) = True Then
  For selected_loop = 0 To ctrl.ListCount - 1
    If ctrl.Selected(selected_loop) = True Then
      get_list = get_list & ctrl.List(selected_loop) & "|"
    End If
  Next selected_loop
```

A line of cleanup is needed, because the string ends with a pipe, so it is removed:

```
get_list = Left(get_list, Len(get_list) - 1)
```

In practice, for example, if a handful of states were selected in the state/province list box, `get_list()` would return a string such as this:

```
Alabama|Florida|Georgia|Mississippi|Texas
```

The `save_existing_query` and `save_new_query` routines perform a similar function. The former updates an existing record, and the latter creates a new record. In either case, the record structure is the same. However, the Update and Insert SQL operations use statements that are different enough to code separate routines to create the necessary SQL.

The query shown in Figure 12.12 is being saved for the first time. The `save_new_query` routine will generate the following SQL statement. Bear in mind that this is the SQL used to put values into the table, but the values themselves are not an SQL statement:

```
Insert Into tblQueries (QueryName, CustomerType, MetroArea,
State_Province, Location_And_Or, InterestGroup,
SkipPurchaseFrequency, PurchaseFrequencyExpression,
PurchaseFrequencyCount, SkipPurchaseAmount,
PurchaseAmountExpression, PurchaseAmountCount, Purchase_And_Or,
PurchasePeriodCount, PurchasePeriod) Values
('Internet or Retail Spent 200 in 3 Years',
'Internet|Mail Order', 'none', 'none', 'Or', 'none', True,
'<Select>', 'none', False, 'At least', '200', 'And',
'3','year(s)')
```

Note that the QueryID field is not addressed in the SQL Insert. The field's data type is AutoNumber, and as such will automatically increment to the next highest value. However, after the Insert is complete, this number has to be assigned to the `txtQueryID` text box on the Query form. So, near the end of the `save_new_query` routine, a query is run to get the `Max()` value of this field, which is then assigned to the text box:

```
recset.Open ("Select Max(QueryID) from tblQueries"), _
    conn, adOpenStatic
Me.lblQueryID = recset.Fields(0)
recset.Close
```

When a previously saved and loaded query is saved again, the `save_existing_query` routine produces an Update SQL statement:

```
UPDATE tblQueries SET QueryName =
'Internet or Retail Spent 200 in 3 Years',
CustomerType='Internet|Mail Order', MetroArea='none',
State_Province='none', Location_And_Or='Or',
InterestGroup='none', SkipPurchaseFrequency = True,
PurchaseFrequencyExpression='<Select>',
```

```
PurchaseFrequencyCount='none', SkipPurchaseAmount = False,
PurchaseAmountExpression='At least', PurchaseAmountCount='200',
Purchase_And_Or='And', PurchasePeriodCount='3',
PurchasePeriod='year(s)'  Where QueryID=17
```

In this case the SQL must use the QueryID, because this is the key to the record being updated.

With either type of save operation, the `Execute` method is used to run it:

```
conn.Execute (ssql)
```

Loading a Query

Clicking the Load Query button displays the Load Query form, `frm-SelectQuery`, shown in Figure 12.15.

The Load Query form serves as a pop-up from the Query form. It simply displays saved queries and allows one to be selected and loaded into the Query form. The one list box on the form, `lstQueries`, has two columns, with the first being set to a width of zero so it will not appear. The list box is populated from the tblQueries table in the database. Only the QueryID and QueryName fields are fed to the list box. Since the list is multi-column, an array is first populated, and then the array is assigned to the `List` property of the list box. This activity occurs in the initialization routine of the form.

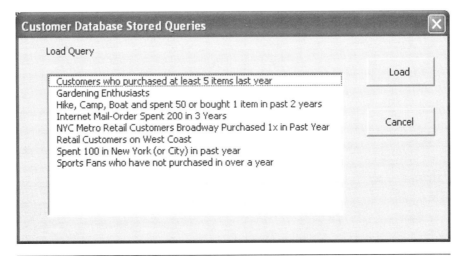

Figure 12.15 Selecting a query to be loaded into the Query form

The entire code module of the `frmSelectQuery` is shown in Listing 12.10.

Listing 12.10 The functionality behind the Load Query form

```
Private Sub load_list(recset As ADODB.Recordset, _
    ctrl_name As String, field_name As String)
On Error GoTo err_end
' populate list boxes on frmQuery . . .
Dim deselct As Integer
Dim ctrl As Control
Dim loop1 As Integer
Dim loop2 As Integer
' set reference to passed list box
Set ctrl = frmQuery.Controls(ctrl_name)
' clear the list box by deselecting all items
For deselct = 0 To ctrl.ListCount - 1
 ctrl.Selected(deselct) = False
Next deselct
' When the query was saved, if nothing in the list box was
' selected, then the phrase "none" was stored in the db.
' However, if there were selection(s) in the list, then
' the values were concatenated with the pipe character (|)
' serving as the separator.
' This snippet breaks the concatenation apart and
' loops to find each value in the list box, which then
' is toggled back to a selected state.
If recset.Fields(field_name) <> "none" Then
  data_array = Split(recset.Fields(field_name), "|")
  For loop1 = 0 To ctrl.ListCount - 1
    For loop2 = 0 To UBound(data_array)
      If Trim(ctrl.List(loop1)) = _
         Trim(data_array(loop2)) Then
         ctrl.Selected(loop1) = True
      End If
    Next loop2
  Next loop1
End If
Exit Sub
err_end:
MsgBox Err.Description
End Sub
```

Listing 12.10 *(continued)*

```
Private Sub load_query()
' purpose - to set up frmQuery with the selections
' of the selected query
On Error GoTo err_end
' prepare ADO
open_conn
create_recset
' Users see a list of query names, but the bound column
' holds the QueryID, which is the key in the db table
ssql = "Select * from tblQueries "
ssql = ssql & " Where QueryID=" & Me.lstQueries
recset.Open (ssql), conn, adOpenStatic
' there are 4 list boxes which are loaded in a
' similar fashion, so the load_list routine handles this
load_list recset, "lstCustomerTypes", "CustomerType"
load_list recset, "lstMetroAreas", "MetroArea"
load_list recset, "lstStatesProvinces", "State_Province"
load_list recset, "lstInterests", "InterestGroup"
' filling the rest for frmQuery based on data
' in the recordset . . .
With frmQuery
  If recset.Fields("Location_And_Or") = "And" Then
    .optLocationAnd = True
  Else
    .optLocationOr = True
  End If
  .chkSkipFrequency = False
  If recset.Fields("SkipPurchaseFrequency") = True Then _
    .chkSkipFrequency = True
  .cmbExpressionsFrequency = _
    recset.Fields("PurchaseFrequencyExpression")
  .txtFrequencyCount = _
    recset.Fields("PurchaseFrequencyCount")
  If recset.Fields("Purchase_And_Or") = "And" Then
    .optPurchaseAnd = True
  Else
    .optPurchaseOr = True
  End If
  .chkSkipAmount = False
  If recset.Fields("SkipPurchaseAmount") = True Then _
    .chkSkipAmount = True
```

Listing 12.10 *(continued)*

```
  .cmbExpressionsAmount = _
     recset.Fields("PurchaseAmountExpression")
  .txtAmountCount = recset.Fields("PurchaseAmountCount")
  .txtPeriodCount = recset.Fields("PurchasePeriodCount")
  .cmbPeriods = recset.Fields("PurchasePeriod")
  .lblQueryID = recset.Fields("QueryID")
  .lblQueryName = recset.Fields("QueryName")
  .Caption = Me.lstQueries.Column(1)
End With
' close ADO
close_recset
close_conn
MsgBox "Query Loaded"
Exit Sub
err_end:
MsgBox Err.Description
End Sub
Private Sub cmdCancel_Click()
  Me.Hide
  End Sub
Private Sub cmdLoadQuery_Click()
  load_query
  Me.Hide
End Sub
Private Sub lstQueries_DblClick _
  (ByVal Cancel As MSForms.ReturnBoolean)
  ' double-clicking on a query name loads it
  load_query
  Me.Hide
End Sub
Private Sub UserForm_Initialize()
On Error GoTo err_end
Dim query_array()
' prepare ADO
open_conn
create_recset
' populate query list . . .
' the list box that displays query names is a 2 column list
' so the list box is populated using an array that is set
' to the List property
ssql = "Select QueryID, QueryName"
```

Listing 12.10 *(continued)*

```
ssql = ssql & " from tblQueries Order By QueryName"
recset.Open (ssql), conn, adOpenStatic
recset.MoveLast
' query_count holds the number of saved queries in the db,
' so redimension the array to this size
query_count = recset.RecordCount
ReDim query_array(query_count, 2)
recset.MoveFirst
' populate the array . . .
For fill_list = 0 To query_count - 1
  query_array(fill_list, 0) = recset.Fields(0)
  query_array(fill_list, 1) = recset.Fields(1)
  recset.MoveNext
Next fill_list
' fill the list box with the array
Me.lstQueries.List = query_array()
' close ADO
close_recset
close_conn
Exit Sub
err_end:
MsgBox Err.Description
End Sub
```

The `MultiSelect` property of the `lstQueries` list box is set to `Single`, because only one query can be loaded at a time. Clicking on a query name and then clicking the Load button, or just double-clicking on a query name, will run the process of loading the query into the Query form. The `load_query` routine handles this operation.

In the `load_query` routine, an ADO connection and recordset are initiated, and then the database is queried based on the QueryID, which is hidden from view but is the bound column of the list box:

```
ssql = "Select * from tblQueries "
ssql = ssql & " Where QueryID=" & Me.lstQueries
recset.Open (ssql), conn, adOpenStatic
```

The purpose of the `load_query` routine is to set values of the controls on the Query form. On the Query form are the four list boxes—all which allow multi-selected values. A list box's multiple values, if any, have been stored as a single concatenated string, which uses the pipe character to separate the values in the string. The strings must now be split apart. The list boxes are one by one sent to the `load_list` routine. This routine was developed just to handle the values for the list boxes:

```
load_list recset, "lstCustomerTypes", "CustomerType"
load_list recset, "lstMetroAreas", "MetroArea"
load_list recset, "lstStatesProvinces", "State_Province"
load_list recset, "lstInterests", "InterestGroup"
```

A value of "none" had been stored if no values in the list box were selected when the query was saved, but if that is not the case, then the `Split()` function is used to break apart the concatenation. The `Split()` function returns an array, named `data_array`.

A nested loop structure is used to match the values in the array with the full set of values in the list box. The outer loop iterates up to the size of the full list in the list box, and the inner loop iterates up to the size of the array. When a match is found, the `Selected` property is set to true:

```
If recset.Fields(field_name) <> "none" Then
  data_array = Split(recset.Fields(field_name), "|")
  For loop1 = 0 To ctrl.ListCount - 1
    For loop2 = 0 To UBound(data_array)
      If Trim(ctrl.List(loop1)) = _
         Trim(data_array(loop2)) Then
         ctrl.Selected(loop1) = True
      End If
    Next loop2
  Next loop1
End If
```

Continuing on with the `load_query` routine, the rest of the controls on the Query form are set with the saved values. For example, this snippet sets the state of the two option buttons inside the purchase pattern frame:

```
If recset.Fields("Purchase_And_Or") = "And" Then
  .optPurchaseAnd = True
Else
  .optPurchaseOr = True
End If
```

Finally, three key values are set. The invisible label controls on the form are given the ID and name of the query, and the form's title bar is updated with the name of the query:

```
.lblQueryID = recset.Fields("QueryID")
.lblQueryName = recset.Fields("QueryName")
.Caption = Me.lstQueries.Column(1)
```

Deleting a Query

Functionality to delete queries from the database was not initially built into this solution. During testing, users quickly adapted to just changing the criteria of a loaded query and then renaming it when the Save button was clicked. If the Save button is clicked when a loaded query is on the form, the input box still appears to enter a name. In this condition, the input box is already populated with the query's name. The name is retrieved from the invisible `txtQueryName` control on the form. However, the name can be changed in the input box. The query is still stored from where it came in the database because the key is the QueryID—which does not change.

The end result is that the query's name has been updated. This approach was adequate for the solution. A dedicated Delete feature could be added. It would be as simple as just running a Delete query based on the QueryID.

Resetting the Query Form

Clicking the Reset button runs a simple routine that clears all values from the controls on the form, and then calls the form's initialization routine to populate the controls with the initial values, as shown in Listing 12.11.

Listing 12.11 Resetting the Query form

```
Private Sub cmdReset_Click()
' restores to blank form
With Me
  .lstCustomerTypes.Clear
  .lstMetroAreas.Clear
  .lstStatesProvinces.Clear
  .lstInterests.Clear
  .cmbExpressionsFrequency.Clear
  .cmbExpressionsAmount.Clear
  .cmbPeriods.Clear
  .txtFrequencyCount = ""
```

Listing 12.11 *(continued)*

```
  .txtAmountCount = ""
  .txtPeriodCount = ""
End With
' call initialize routine to repopulate lists and combos
UserForm_Initialize
End Sub
```

Running a Query

Running a query creates the record source and prepares the solution document for mail merge work. The result is to leave the solution document in a state such that the record source is "attached," and the merge fields are available. Clicking the Run Query button on the Query form runs the cmdRunQuery_Click routine, which performs these steps:

- Validate the input.
- Create an SQL statement based on the criteria on the form.
- Create a set of records using the SQL and associate these records with the solution document.

The cmdRunQuery_Click routine is the real guts of the solution. It is shown in its entirety in Listing 12.12, followed by discussion of key points.

Listing 12.12 Creating the record source for a mail merge

```
Private Sub cmdRunQuery_Click()
On Error GoTo err_end
Dim ctrl As Control
Dim crit_flag As Boolean
Dim area_flag As Boolean
Dim interest_flag As Boolean
Dim purchase_frequency_flag As Boolean
Dim purchase_amount_flag As Boolean
Dim selected_loop As Integer
Dim ssql As String
Dim cust_crit As String ' customer criteria
Dim interest_crit As String ' interest criteria
```

Listing 12.12 *(continued)*

```
Dim purchase_crit As String ' purchase criteria
Dim this_path As String
Dim rec_count As Integer
Dim merge_field_count As Integer
Dim newdoc As String
Dim field_names As Integer
Dim field_data As Integer

' !!!   Validation Section   Validation Section  !!!
' validate purchase frequency criteria, if used
If Me.chkSkipFrequency = False Then
  If cmbExpressionsFrequency = "<Select>" Or _
       (Not IsNumeric(txtFrequencyCount)) Then
    MsgBox "Missing or incorrect " & _
        "Purchase Frequency Criteria"
    Exit Sub
  Else
      purchase_frequency_flag = True
  End If
End If
' validate purchase amount criteria, if used
If Me.chkSkipAmount = False Then
  If cmbExpressionsAmount = "<Select>" Or _
       (Not IsNumeric(txtAmountCount)) Then
    MsgBox "Missing or incorrect " & _
        "Purchase Amount Criteria"
    Exit Sub
  Else
      purchase_amount_flag = True
  End If
End If
' validate purchase period, if used
If Me.chkSkipAmount = False Or _
   Me.chkSkipFrequency = False Then
  If (Not IsNumeric(Me.txtPeriodCount)) Or _
    Me.cmbPeriods = "<Select>" Then
    MsgBox "Missing or incorrect " & _
       "Purchase Period Criteria"
    Exit Sub
  End If
End If
' !!! End Validation Section   End Validation Section  !!!
```

Listing 12.12 *(continued)*

```
' to facilitate building SQL string . . .
' cust_crit holds criteria for customer type, metro area,
'        and state/province
' interest_crit holds criteria for interest groups
' purchase_crit holds criteria for purchase patterns

' flags are also used:
' crit_flag -- to indicate whether there are any criteria
'              for customer type, metro area, or
'              state/province
' area_flag -- to indicate whether the AND/OR between
'              metro area and state/province is used
' interest_flag -- to indicate any interest groups
' purchase_frequency_flag -- to indicate criteria for
'              purchase frequency
' purchase_amount_flag -- to indicate criteria for
'              purchase amount
crit_flag = False
cust_crit = ""
' CUSTOMER TYPES    CUSTOMER TYPES    CUSTOMER TYPES
' if specific customer types are used,
' then must cycle through the list,
' and build the SQL with the selected list items
Set ctrl = Me.lstCustomerTypes
If has_selections(ctrl) = True Then
  cust_crit = cust_crit & "CustomerType In ("
  For selected_loop = 0 To ctrl.ListCount - 1
    If ctrl.Selected(selected_loop) = True Then
      cust_crit = cust_crit & "'" & _
        ctrl.List(selected_loop) & "', "
    End If
  Next selected_loop
' strip last comma and space, and append closing parenthesis
cust_crit = Left(cust_crit, Len(cust_crit) - 2) & ")"
crit_flag = True
End If
' METRO AREA / STATE    METRO AREA / STATE
' Since metro areas and states have a dedicated
' And/Or indicator, first must determine
' that at least one of these criteria points are used
If has_selections(Me.lstMetroAreas) = True Or _
   has_selections(Me.lstStatesProvinces) = True Then
```

Listing 12.12 *(continued)*

```
' if specific metro areas are used,
' then must cycle through the list,
' and build the SQL with the selected list items
Set ctrl = Me.lstMetroAreas
If has_selections(ctrl) = True Then
  ' crit_flag indicates whether this is a continuation
  ' of the SQL Where clause
  If crit_flag = True Then
     cust_crit = cust_crit & " AND ("
  Else
     cust_crit = cust_crit & "("
  End If
  cust_crit = cust_crit & "MetroArea In ("
  For selected_loop = 0 To ctrl.ListCount - 1
    If ctrl.Selected(selected_loop) = True Then
      cust_crit = cust_crit & "'" & _
        ctrl.List(selected_loop) & "', "
    End If
  Next selected_loop
  ' strip last comma & space and append close parenthesis
  cust_crit = Left(cust_crit, Len(cust_crit) - 2) & ")"
  crit_flag = True
  area_flag = True
End If
' if specific states/provinces are used,
' then must cycle through the list,
' and build the SQL with the selected list items
Set ctrl = Me.lstStatesProvinces
If has_selections(ctrl) = True Then
  ' crit_flag indicates whether this is a continuation
  ' of the SQL Where clause
  ' must also use the area_flag to determine
  ' if AND/OR is used, based on whether
  ' metro areas are used
  If area_flag = False And crit_flag = True Then
     cust_crit = cust_crit & " AND ("
  End If
  If area_flag = False And crit_flag = False Then
     cust_crit = cust_crit & "("
  End If
  If area_flag = True Then
    If Me.optLocationAnd = True Then
```

Listing 12.12 *(continued)*

```
        cust_crit = cust_crit & " AND "
      Else ' must be an Or
        cust_crit = cust_crit & " OR "
      End If
    End If
    cust_crit = cust_crit & "State_Province In ("
    For selected_loop = 0 To ctrl.ListCount - 1
      If ctrl.Selected(selected_loop) = True Then
        cust_crit = cust_crit & "'" & _
          ctrl.List(selected_loop) & "', "
      End If
    Next selected_loop
    ' strip last comma & space and append close parenthesis
    cust_crit = Left(cust_crit, Len(cust_crit) - 2) & ")"
    crit_flag = True
  End If
  cust_crit = cust_crit & ")"
End If
interest_crit = ""
' INTEREST GROUPS    INTEREST GROUPS    INTEREST GROUPS
' if specific interest groups are used,
' then must cycle through the list,
' and assemble selected list items into SQL
interest_flag = False
Set ctrl = Me.lstInterests
If has_selections(ctrl) = True Then
  interest_flag = True
  interest_crit = " tblInterests.InterestID In ("
  For selected_loop = 0 To ctrl.ListCount - 1
    If ctrl.Selected(selected_loop) = True Then
      interest_crit = interest_crit & _
        ctrl.List(selected_loop) & ", "
    End If
  Next selected_loop
interest_crit = _
  Left(interest_crit, Len(interest_crit) - 2) & ")"
crit_flag = True
End If
purchase_crit = ""
```

Listing 12.12 *(continued)*

```
' PURCHASE PATTERNS   PURCHASE PATTERNS   PURCHASE PATTERNS
If purchase_frequency_flag = True Or _
   purchase_amount_flag = True Then
   purchase_crit = purchase_crit & " ("
  If purchase_frequency_flag = True Then
    purchase_crit = purchase_crit & _
       "Count(PurchaseDate)" & _
      Choose(Me.cmbExpressionsFrequency.ListIndex + 1, _
      "<=", "=", ">") & Abs(Me.txtFrequencyCount)
  End If
  If purchase_amount_flag = True Then
    ' get the AND/OR operator
    If purchase_frequency_flag = True Then
      If Me.optPurchaseAnd = True Then
         purchase_crit = purchase_crit & " AND "
      Else
         purchase_crit = purchase_crit & " OR "
      End If
    End If
    purchase_crit = purchase_crit & "Sum(Amount)" & _
      Choose(Me.cmbExpressionsAmount.ListIndex + 1, _
      "<=", "=", ">") & Abs(Me.txtAmountCount)
  End If
  purchase_crit = purchase_crit & ")"
End If
' build SELECT part of SQL
ssql = "SELECT FirstName, LastName, Address, City, " & _
   "State_Province, MetroArea, CustomerType"
' if purchase frequency is used . . .
If purchase_frequency_flag = True Then
  ssql = ssql & ", Count(PurchaseDate) AS CountOfPurchaseDate"
End If
' if purchase amount is used . . .
If purchase_amount_flag = True Then
  ssql = ssql & ", Sum(Amount) AS SumOfAmount"
End If
' if interests are used . . .
If interest_flag = True Then
  ssql = ssql & ", Interest "
End If
```

Listing 12.12 *(continued)*

```
'if both interests and purchase patterns are not used . . .
If purchase_frequency_flag = False And _
    purchase_amount_flag = False And _
    interest_flag = False Then
  ssql = ssql & " From tblCustomers "
End If
' if purchase patterns are used, but interests are not . . .
If (purchase_frequency_flag = True Or _
    purchase_amount_flag = True) And _
    interest_flag = False Then
  ssql = ssql & " FROM tblCustomers INNER JOIN " & _
  "tblSales ON tblCustomers.CustomerID = " & _
  "tblSales.Customer_ID "
End If
' if interests are used but purchase patterns are not . . .
If (purchase_frequency_flag = False And _
    purchase_amount_flag = False) And _
    interest_flag = True Then
  ssql = ssql & " FROM (tblCustomers INNER JOIN " & _
  "tblInterests ON tblCustomers.CustomerID = " & _
  "tblInterests.CustomerID) INNER JOIN " & _
  "tblInterests_Lookup ON tblInterests.InterestID = " & _
  "tblInterests_Lookup.InterestID "
End If
' if interests are used and purchase patterns are used . . .
If (purchase_frequency_flag = True Or _
    purchase_amount_flag = True) And _
    interest_flag = True Then
  ssql = ssql & " FROM tblInterests_Lookup INNER JOIN " & _
  "((tblCustomers INNER JOIN tblSales ON " & _
  "tblCustomers.CustomerID = tblSales.Customer_ID) " & _
  "INNER JOIN tblInterests ON " & _
  "tblCustomers.CustomerID = tblInterests.CustomerID) " & _
  "ON tblInterests_Lookup.InterestID = " & _
  "tblInterests.InterestID"
End If
' if purchase patterns are not used, then there is no "
' Group By, and the location and interest criteria "
' is in the Where clause
If purchase_frequency_flag = False And _
    purchase_amount_flag = False Then
```

Listing 12.12 *(continued)*

```
    If crit_flag = True Then
        ssql = ssql & " Where "
        If Len(cust_crit) > 0 And Len(interest_crit) > 0 Then
          ssql = ssql & cust_crit & " And " & interest_crit
        End If
        If Len(cust_crit) > 0 And Len(interest_crit) = 0 Then
          ssql = ssql & cust_crit
        End If
        If Len(cust_crit) = 0 And Len(interest_crit) > 0 Then
          ssql = ssql & interest_crit
        End If
    End If
Else ' purchase patterns are selected, and so
        ' there is a Group By section -
        ' the Where clause gets the criteria of the
        ' purchase period (example: the last 60 days)
        ' and also if interest groups are used, the
        ' InterestIDs are in the Where clause;
        ' the rest of criteria now go in the
        ' Having section
    ssql = ssql & " Where "
    ssql = ssql & " PurchaseDate Between Now()-"
    ssql = ssql & Abs(Me.txtPeriodCount) * _
        Choose(Me.cmbPeriods.ListIndex + 1, 1, 30, 365)
    ssql = ssql & " And Now() "
    If Len(interest_crit) > 0 Then
      ssql = ssql & " AND " & interest_crit
    End If
    ssql = ssql & " GROUP BY FirstName, LastName, " & _
        "Address, City, State_Province, MetroArea, " & _
        "CustomerType "
    If interest_flag = True Then
      ssql = ssql & ", Interest "
    End If
    ssql = ssql & " Having "
    If crit_flag = True Then
      If Len(cust_crit) > 0 Then
        ssql = ssql & cust_crit & " And " & purchase_crit
      Else
        ssql = ssql & purchase_crit
      End If
    End If
End If
```

Listing 12.12 *(continued)*

```
End If
' Complete SQL statement is now assembled
' break link to any data source by
' changing status of document type
ActiveDocument.MailMerge.MainDocumentType = _
    wdNotAMergeDocument
' prepare ADO
open_conn
create_recset
' open recordset based on assembled SQL
recset.Open (ssql), conn, adOpenStatic
If recset.EOF Then
  MsgBox "No Records Returned! Try different criteria."
  Exit Sub
Else
  ' get count of fields in recordset set
  ' need this in creating merge source
  merge_field_count = recset.Fields.Count
  ' A mail merge requires a merge source - which is
  ' a set of records. The source can be various
  ' file types - Access, text, etc. For this solution
  ' another Word document is used. This file is hard-coded
  ' as mergdata.doc and is created in the same directory
  ' as the solution. Change as needed.
  newdoc = ActiveDocument.Path & "\mergdata.doc"
  ' add new document
  Documents.Add
  ' insert a header row, with a tab as the separator
  ' Chr(9) is the tab character
  For field_names = 0 To merge_field_count - 2
    Selection.TypeText recset.Fields(field_names).Name
    Selection.TypeText Chr$(9)
  Next field_names
  ' the last header name . . .
  Selection.TypeText _
    recset.Fields(merge_field_count - 1).Name
  ' insert a paragraph and move down
  Selection.InsertParagraphAfter
  Selection.MoveDown Unit:=wdParagraph
```

Listing 12.12 *(continued)*

```
  ' insert merge data from recordset
  Do Until recset.EOF
  For field_data = 0 To merge_field_count - 2
    If Not IsNull(recset.Fields(field_data)) Then
      Selection.TypeText Trim(recset.Fields(field_data))
    End If
    Selection.TypeText Chr$(9)
  Next field_data
  ' the last field . . .
  If Not IsNull(recset.Fields(merge_field_count - 1)) Then
    Selection.TypeText _
      Trim(recset.Fields(merge_field_count - 1))
  End If
  ' insert paragraph and move down for next record
  Selection.InsertParagraphAfter
  Selection.MoveDown Unit:=wdParagraph
  recset.MoveNext
  Loop
End If
' release ADO
close_recset
close_conn
' the Kill command will cause an error if the file
' is not present, so reset error trap
On Error Resume Next
Kill newdoc
' error trap back to original setting . . .
On Error GoTo err_end
' save and close document with the merge source records
ActiveDocument.SaveAs FileName:=newdoc
ActiveDocument.Close SaveChanges:=wdDoNotSaveChanges
' change status of "this" document back to a Merge type
' and designate the source as the Word document just created
With ActiveDocument.MailMerge
  .MainDocumentType = wdFormLetters
  .OpenDataSource Name:=newdoc
End With
Me.Hide
Exit Sub
err_end:
MsgBox Err.Description
End Sub
```

Validation

The three combo boxes on the Query form initially display "<Select>" as a reminder for users to make a selection. Making a selection is not required for all queries; however, it is required for cases where either the skip frequency or skip amount checkboxes are unchecked.

The validation examines the state of the checkboxes, and if they are unchecked, then the presence of either the "<Select>" value or a nonnumeric value in a supporting text box is tested. The combo boxes do not operate alone in setting criteria. Each is conceptually linked with a text box to create a valid statement. For example, "has purchased at least 4 items" is determined by the combo box selection (at least) and the text box entry (4).

Therefore, if the checkbox is unchecked (false), the validity of the statement is tested. Here, for example, is the validation for purchase frequency:

```
If Me.chkSkipFrequency = False Then
  If cmbExpressionsFrequency = "<Select>" Or _
       (Not IsNumeric(txtFrequencyCount)) Then
    MsgBox "Missing or incorrect " & _
        "Purchase Frequency Criteria"
    Exit Sub
  Else
      purchase_frequency_flag = True
  End If
End If
```

SQL

The bulk of the `cmdRunQuery_Click` routine creates the SQL statement needed to get the records for the merge record source. The process of creating the SQL is a bit complex, requiring several decisions, such as:

- If both the metro area and state/province lists have selections, then correctly apply the AND/OR operator between them.

  Or

- If any part of the criteria string has been created, then append "AND" to the string so far before concatenating more criteria.

  Or

- If purchase patterns are used, then Group By and Having clauses must be built.

The SQL string is assembled in sections, and then a final concatenation puts it together just prior to applying it to the Customers database. The subsections use variables to hold the criteria strings, as well as flags that are used in decisions about how to assemble the SQL. The flags are Boolean—either true or false. These variables and flags are:

- **crit_flag**—set to true if there are criteria such as customer type
- **area_flag**—set to true if any metro area(s) are used
- **interest_flag**—set to true if any interest groups are used
- **purchase_frequency_flag** and **purchase_amount_flag**—either is set to true if the particular type of purchase pattern behavior is used
- **cust_crit**—holds the portion of the SQL Where clause about customers
- **interest_crit**—holds the portion of the SQL Where clause about interest groups
- **purchase_crit**—holds the portion of the SQL Where clause about purchase patterns

The routine assembles the Select part and the Where part of the SQL separately. The controls on the form are examined, and various testing and concatenation occur. The flag variables are used in assembling both parts. For example, this snippet shows purchase_frequency_flag and purchase_amount_flag being used to create the purchase pattern criteria:

```
purchase_crit = ""
' PURCHASE PATTERNS  PURCHASE PATTERNS  PURCHASE PATTERNS
If purchase_frequency_flag = True Or _
   purchase_amount_flag = True Then
   purchase_crit = purchase_crit & " ("
  If purchase_frequency_flag = True Then
     purchase_crit = purchase_crit & _
        "Count(PurchaseDate)" & _
        Choose(Me.cmbExpressionsFrequency.ListIndex + 1, _
        "<=", "=", ">") & Abs(Me.txtFrequencyCount)
  End If
```

Here is another snippet, which shows the flags being used in the creation of the Select . . . From part of the SQL:

```
If (purchase_frequency_flag = True Or _
    purchase_amount_flag = True) And _
    interest_flag = False Then
  ssql = ssql & " FROM tblCustomers INNER JOIN " & _
  "tblSales ON tblCustomers.CustomerID = " & _
  "tblSales.Customer_ID "
End If
```

The logic used to create the entire SQL statement is shown in Figure 12.16.

Record Source Creation

Once the SQL statement is complete, the remaining tasks of linking the solution document with a set of source records begin. First the solution document is set to *not* be a mail merge document:

```
ActiveDocument.MailMerge.MainDocumentType = _
    wdNotAMergeDocument
```

Next, using the SQL statement, the records are pulled from the database into a recordset—that is, if any records are returned:

```
open_conn
create_recset
' open recordset based on assembled SQL
recset.Open (ssql), conn, adOpenStatic
If recset.EOF Then
  MsgBox "No Records Returned! Try different criteria."
  Exit Sub
Else
```

The merge_field_count variable holds the count of fields in the recordset. The field names themselves become the headers of the merge source records. First a variable, newdoc, is set to the concatenation of the solution path and the mergdata.doc file name; then a new Word document is added. The new document (unsaved at this point) will become the record source. It receives the field names, one by one, each separated with a tab. In particular, the field_names loop does not handle the last field,

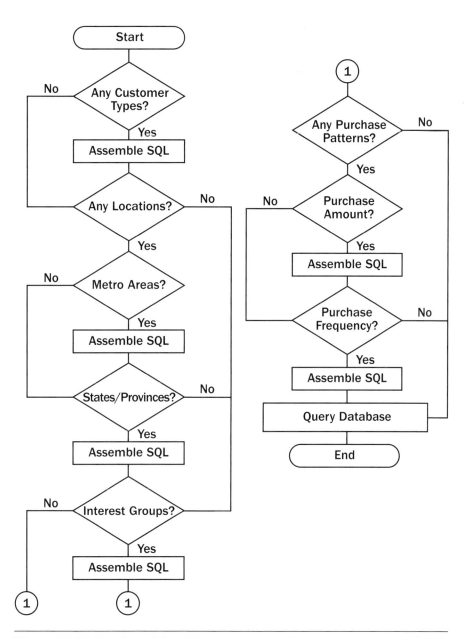

Figure 12.16 The flow of the SQL statement creation

because the loop ends each iteration with the insertion of a tab character. So the last field is just appended with a separate line:

```
merge_field_count = recset.Fields.Count
.
.
.
newdoc = ActiveDocument.Path & "\mergdata.doc"
' add new document
Documents.Add
' insert a header row, with a tab as the separator
' Chr(9) is the tab character
For field_names = 0 To merge_field_count - 2
  Selection.TypeText recset.Fields(field_names).Name
  Selection.TypeText Chr$(9)
Next field_names
' the last header name . . .
Selection.TypeText _
  recset.Fields(merge_field_count - 1).Name
```

A paragraph is entered, and the insertion point is moved down, then the recordset data is inserted into the document. As with the headers previously, a loop handles the insertion of data points followed by a tab—for all fields except the last. Then the last field is inserted with a separate statement. All of this occurs within an outer Do . . . Until loop, which is moving through the recordset:

```
Selection.InsertParagraphAfter
Selection.MoveDown Unit:=wdParagraph
.
.
.
Do Until recset.EOF
For field_data = 0 To merge_field_count - 2
  If Not IsNull(recset.Fields(field_data)) Then
    Selection.TypeText Trim(recset.Fields(field_data))
  End If
  Selection.TypeText Chr$(9)
Next field_data
' the last field . . .
If Not IsNull(recset.Fields(merge_field_count - 1)) Then
  Selection.TypeText _
    Trim(recset.Fields(merge_field_count - 1))
End If
```

```
' insert paragraph and move down for next record
Selection.InsertParagraphAfter
Selection.MoveDown Unit:=wdParagraph
recset.MoveNext
Loop
```

The completed record source document needs to be saved. This file will be named mergdata.doc. It's likely there already is a mergdata.doc in the target directory. If so, it needs to be replaced with the new one. The `Kill` statement is used, but first the error trap needs to be altered for this. If the `Kill` does not find the file, an error occurs. Using `On Error Resume Next` ensures that the routine will not stop for this error. However, just after the `Kill` statement, the error trap is set back to its original state.

Finally, the document with the merge records is saved and closed. The `newdoc` variable is used for the name. This variable contains the path with the mergdata.doc file name:

```
On Error Resume Next
Kill newdoc
' error trap back to original setting . . .
On Error GoTo err_end
' save and close document with the merge source records
ActiveDocument.SaveAs FileName:=newdoc
ActiveDocument.Close SaveChanges:=wdDoNotSaveChanges
```

The last significant action is to now associate the merge record source with the solution document. The solution document is reset back to being a mail merge document—set to handle letters. The `OpenDataSource` method associates the record source:

```
With ActiveDocument.MailMerge
  .MainDocumentType = wdFormLetters
  .OpenDataSource Name:=newdoc
End With
```

The result of this processing is shown in Figure 12.17. The solution document now has an associated record source. The Mail Merge toolbar is active, and the Insert Merge Field dialog displays the available fields.

The mergdata.doc file, sitting in the same directory as the solution document, contains the source records, shown in Figure 12.18. The document contains tab-delimited data.

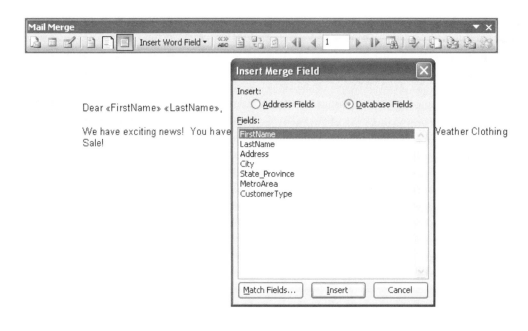

Figure 12.17 The solution document has a record source and is ready for mail merge

FirstName   →   LastName   →   Address•City → State_Province→ MetroArea   →   CustomerType¶
Kam → Cushman   →   380·Cabrillo·Road   →   Beverly·Hills → CA →   →   Retail¶
John·F.→Schatz→128·190th·Drive→ShermanWA →   →   Retail¶
Liz·A. → Mattick→357·Oregon·Street   →   Fridley→OR →   →   Retail¶
Carol → Rusche→382·Paradise   →   Sandy→ OR →   →   Retail¶
Monique   →   Mattick→1·Hanshaw·Way→Lakeland   →   WA →   →   Retail¶
Joyce→ Deporter→4·Harvard   →   Short·Hills   →   CA →   →   Retail¶
Oliver→ Estabrook   →   132·Harvard·Street   →   Slate·Hill   →   CA →   →   Retail¶
Dominick·T → Elberfeld   →   2·Pier·Street   →   Fircrest→WA →   →   Retail¶
Mia → Fujita→ 182·Alice·Street→Moorhead   →   CA →   →   Retail¶
Janice→ Bramlet→102·Smythetown·Road → East·Greenbush→WA →   →   Retail¶
Hugh → Infante→309·Pennock·Way   →   Arnold→OR →   →   Retail¶
Nuchine→Andrews   →   6·Airport·Way → St·Thomas   →   OR →   →   Retail¶
Karth → Weinstein   →   347·Glenkirk·Street   →   Southborough → CA →   →   Retail¶
Ebony→ Buhead→4·Romero·Road→Butler→ CA →   →   Retail¶
Tracie → Delaro→140·Arlington·Way   →   Westbury   →   CA →   →   Retail¶

Figure 12.18 The source records for the merge are in mergdata.doc

Summary

This case study exemplifies bridging the gap between user needs and technical prowess for getting the job done. Conceptually, users are creating SQL statements with this solution, but in a way that is familiar to them. By interacting with a familiar paradigm (a form), users unknowingly build sophisticated queries from straightforward ideas.

This study also brings to light the issue of user interaction with a database such as Access. One of the requirements for this project was to provide functionality such that users would not have to open the database and use the Query Grid. By providing the methods to avoid direct database manipulation, this solution allows users to stay on the business side of things.

This case study shows the powerful advantages of user forms. The solution provides complete point-and-click interaction, and it's the deployment of user forms that makes this work. Displaying the Main form from the solution document's Open event ensures that the entire session a user spends preparing records for a mail merge is run via the forms. Only when direct entry is required does a user need to steer away from using a form.

The solution provided in this case study can certainly be adapted for other uses. Although built around the need to enhance mail merges, a core piece of the solution involves automating database queries.

CHAPTER 13

Dynamic Data Delivery

*How to Automate Copying Data from Excel
to PowerPoint Chart Datasheets*

VERSION NOTE: This solution runs in all versions of PowerPoint and Excel.

The Problem

Business activity is periodically presented to upper management as a PowerPoint presentation. Each slide of the presentation displays one or more charts, as well as any supporting text or other visual aids.

Analysts who prepare the presentation use an Excel workbook for summarizing the data. Excel is used because of the significant number-crunching, and stores of data are kept on a dedicated worksheet. When the preliminary work in Excel is finished, there is no easy way to bring the data into PowerPoint—that is, to specifically populate the datasheets of the charts on the PowerPoint slides.

Transferring the data manually is problematic. It requires making entries into the datasheet of each chart on each slide (see Figure 13.1). Doing this work by hand is not acceptable because of the labor and time involved and because of the errors caused by having to enter the data repeatedly.

Setting up links between the Excel and PowerPoint files is not feasible. The files are often copied onto laptops or distributed to disconnected networks in satellite offices. Also, only the PowerPoint files must be brought to meetings; the Excel file is often left behind. When linking the files has been attempted, broken links have been discovered at the worst moments (like during a meeting!).

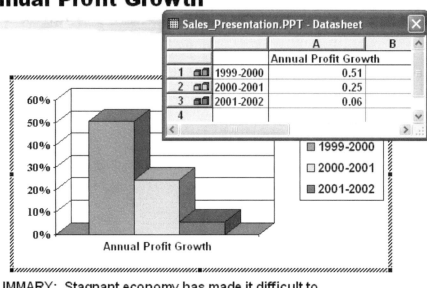

Figure 13.1 A chart and datasheet on a PowerPoint slide

The Requirements

- Provide an Excel workbook that structurally and functionally supports the particular sales data analysis.
- Provide a PowerPoint presentation file that mirrors the work done in the Excel workbook.
- Automate copying the chart series data from the Excel workbook to the chart datasheets in the PowerPoint presentation.

Solution Tool Set and Files

- VBA
- Sales_Data.xls (Excel)
- Sales_Presentation.ppt (PowerPoint)

Notes on This Case Study

The Excel workbook and PowerPoint presentation mirror each other. For each worksheet there is a related slide. A worksheet may have one or more charts, and the related slide has the same number of charts. Object naming plays a major role in this solution. Because the particular charts are predefined, the names are hard-coded for efficiency.

For this case study, the framework of a book distribution company has been used. The data behind this example represents revenue, sales, costs, returns, and income. This activity is segmented into typical book categories, such as westerns, mysteries, and cookbooks. The term *returns* used here is familiar to those in publishing, but perhaps not to others. Returns are unsold books that are returned from bookstores and other markets back through the distribution channel.

The purpose of this solution is to help analysts copy financial data. *Formatting* the data and charts in Excel is not necessary. PowerPoint files are to be formatted, because they will be used for business presentations, but the formatting aspect is not part of the solution. Formatting of the PowerPoint files is done manually after the automated data copy.

Excel Workbook Development

Let's first consider the Excel workbook. Each worksheet has been re-named to reflect its purpose. See Figure 13.2. There is one sheet with just data, and that sheet is aptly named "Data". The Data sheet holds raw data and summarizes it by time period and category. See Figures 13.3 and 13.4. In a typical production environment, the Data sheet is populated through queries into Oracle, SQL Server, or some other database product.

Figure 13.2 Worksheets are appropriately named

	A	B	C	D	E	F	G	H
1		Year	Q		Westerns	Romance	Science Fiction	Mysteries
2		2000	Q1	Revenue	17	51	3.5	6
3		2000	Q1	Marketing Cost	3	4.5	0.5	2
4		2000	Q1	Other Costs	2	3.5	1	1.5
5		2000	Q1	Net Sales	12	43	2	2.5
6		2000	Q1	Returns	4.5	6.5	2	0.25
7		2000	Q1	Net After Returns	7.5	36.5	6	2.25
8		2000	Q2	Revenue	21	55	5	6.5
9		2000	Q2	Marketing Cost	3.5	5	1.5	2
10		2000	Q2	Other Costs	2	4	2	2
11		2000	Q2	Net Sales	15.5	46	1.5	2.5
12		2000	Q2	Returns	5	7	1	1.25
13		2000	Q2	Net After Returns	10.5	35	0.5	1.25
14		2000	Q3	Revenue	18.5	58	5.5	6.5
15		2000	Q3	Marketing Cost	3.5	5	1.25	2
16		2000	Q3	Other Costs	2.5	4.25	2	2
17		2000	Q3	Net Sales	12.5	48.75	2.25	2.5
18		2000	Q3	Returns	4.5	8.25	0.5	1
19		2000	Q3	Net After Returns	8	40.5	1.75	1.5

Figure 13.3 Raw data on the Data worksheet

		Westerns	Romance	Science Fic	Mysteries	Cookbook	Travel Guid	Childrens
2001	Total Revenue	85.5	220.75	16.5	27.5	8.5	5.5	91.25
2001	Total Marketing	13	17	5	9.5	1.5	0.5	14
2001	Total Other Costs	11	17	5.75	5.75	2.5	1.75	8
2001	Total Net Sales	61.5	186.75	5.75	12.25	4.5	3.25	69.25
2001	Total Returns	16.75	21	4.25	4.5	2	0.5	20
2001	Total Net after Returns	44.75	165.75	1.5	7.75	2.5	2.75	49.25

		Westerns	Romance	Science Fic	Mysteries	Cookbook	Travel Guid	Childrens
2002	Total Revenue	89.75	213.75	20.5	30.5	10	6.5	101.25
2002	Total Marketing	12.5	13.5	6	12	2.5	0.75	12
2002	Total Other Costs	13.5	16.75	7.25	7.75	3.5	1.75	12
2002	Total Net Sales	63.75	183.5	7.25	10.75	4	4	77.25
2002	Total Returns	21	20	3.5	2.5	2	1.25	20
2002	Total Net after Returns	42.75	163.5	3.75	8.25	2	2.75	57.25

Figure 13.4 Summarized data on the Data worksheet

The rest of the Excel workbook contains dedicated worksheets that each supports a perspective of business reporting. For example, the "Marketing_As_Percent" worksheet contains a chart as well as the data from which the chart is created. See Figure 13.5.

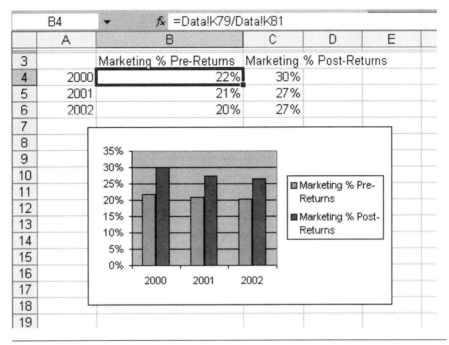

Figure 13.5 Typical structure of a worksheet used in the application

The purpose of the Marketing_As_Percent worksheet is to show how much was spent on marketing in relation to (1) income before returns and (2) income after returns. Recall that returns lower income; therefore, the marketing percentage rises when the returns are accounted for.

Charts are based on data. In this workbook, each chart's data sits in an area next to the chart. Even so, the cells in these data areas only reference data back on the Data sheet. For example, as seen in Figure 13.5, the active cell (B4) displays the value 22%. However, the formula bar shows the real content of the cell as =Data!K79/Data!K81. All raw data is on the Data worksheet.

The chart data areas do play a key role, however. The calculated values in the cells of these areas are what populate the datasheets for the charts on the PowerPoint slides. An important point emerges here. The charts on the PowerPoint slides are not "copies" of the charts on the Excel worksheets. Instead, when the process is run, the *data* from Excel will populate the datasheets in PowerPoint. Figure 13.6 shows this flow.

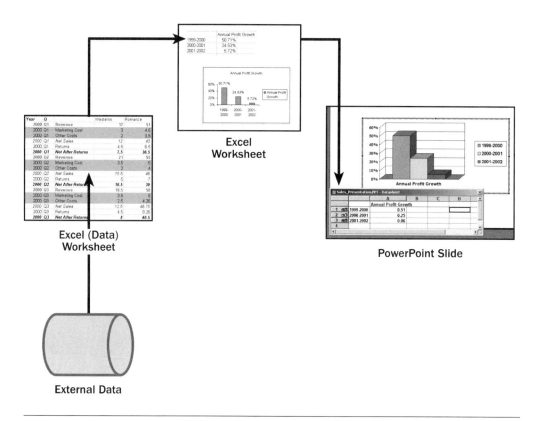

Figure 13.6 How data flows through the solution

In the Excel workbook, the data areas next to each chart are given names and therefore can be addressed as named ranges. The names used are descriptive of the data. The data area on the Marketing_As_Percent worksheet is appropriately named `Marketing_Percentage`. The Insert...Name...Define menu displays the Define Name dialog, shown in Figure 13.7. In the dialog are definitions of the named ranges. The `Marketing_Percentage` name references the area of data on the Marketing_As_Percent worksheet: `=Marketing_As_Percent!$A$3:$C$6`.

Let's examine another worksheet, Category_Profit_1. This sheet summarizes the profit for four book categories. Each category on this sheet has a data area and a chart. Consistent with all data areas, the ones on this sheet are named and contain formulas that reference values on the Data sheet. The Category_Profit_1 worksheet is shown in Figure 13.8.

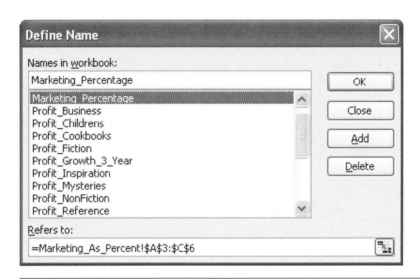

Figure 13.7 The Define Name dialog

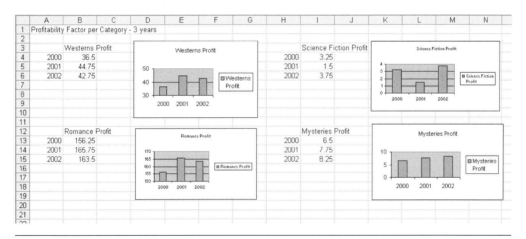

Figure 13.8 A worksheet with four charts

In summary, three assertions exist:

1. All real data is kept on the Data worksheet.

2. Each Excel chart is based on data in a nearby named range, which references the Data worksheet. The Excel charts serve as visual aids to

financial analysts and are not what appear in final reporting. Therefore, the Excel charts are not highly formatted. They are used, however, to formulate results and determine the need for investigating unusual attributes of the data. In other words, the purpose of the charts in Excel is to allow analysts to prepare supporting information to go with the final charts in PowerPoint.

3. Later, PowerPoint is updated with data, not actual charts.

There are two ways to set up the named range areas. One way is to define the names in the Define Name dialog seen in Figure 13.7. However, a fast, two-step method is simply to (1) select the area and (2) type the name in the "Name box". See Figure 13.9.

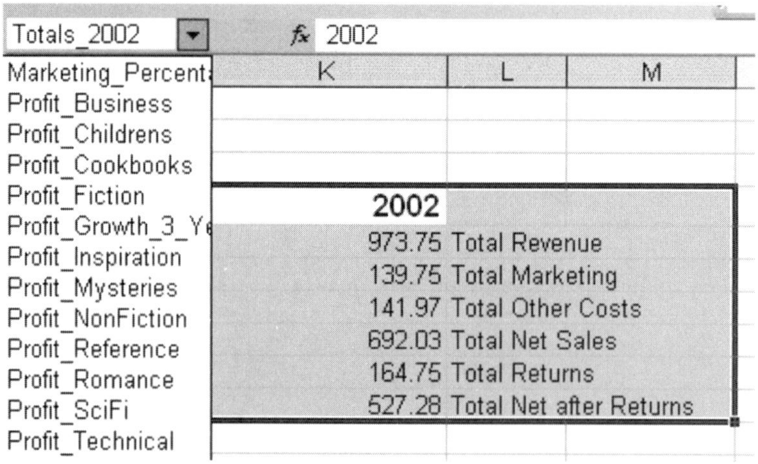

Figure 13.9 A selected area can be named using the Name box

When finished, the Excel workbook contains a Data sheet and other worksheets that each contains one or more charts, and a named range for each chart's data. No VBA coding is in the Excel workbook. In fact, VBA should be avoided in the Excel workbook because in the routine discussed later, PowerPoint opens the Excel workbook. If there is code in the workbook, then the routine may stop and prompt about enabling macros.

PowerPoint Presentation Development

The PowerPoint file mirrors the Excel file. For each worksheet, there is a slide. For each Excel chart, there is a PowerPoint chart. The PowerPoint file is created from scratch in the normal user-interface way. Slides are added, and the appropriate number of charts are added using the Insert menu or the Insert Chart button on the Standard toolbar.

In Excel, it's easy to change worksheet tab names manually, as well as give names to the ranges of data. In PowerPoint, there is no way to change slide names except with the help of VBA coding. In the PowerPoint file, it is necessary to control the names of both the slides and the charts. The charts also are named with the help of VBA.

NOTE: In the Excel workbook, it's necessary to establish the range names of the data, but not the names of the charts. In the PowerPoint presentation, it's necessary to establish the names of the charts. The PowerPoint charts have dedicated datasheets, which are accessible through the `.Datasheet` property. This is the peer of the Excel range, but it has no name property.

A routine is used to name the PowerPoint slides, and a second routine is used to name the charts on the slides. Yet another routine that does the actual copying of data requires four parameters: the Excel range name, the Excel worksheet name, the PowerPoint slide name, and the name of the PowerPoint chart. At this point, the Excel worksheet names and range names are established. Now it's time to name the PowerPoint objects.

Changing the Names of the Slides

The `change_slide_names` routine, shown in Listing 13.1, loops through the PowerPoint slides and allows the user to change their names.

Listing 13.1 Cycling through PowerPoint slides and changing their names

```
Sub change_slide_names()
On Error GoTo err_end
Dim sld As Slide
Dim current_name As String
```

Listing 13.1 *(continued)*

```
Dim current_slide_index As Integer
Dim new_slide_name As String
For Each sld In ActivePresentation.Slides
  ' get the current name
  current_name = sld.Name
  ' get the slide index number
  current_slide_index = sld.SlideIndex
  ' navigate to the slide using the index number
  ActiveWindow.View.GotoSlide Index:=current_slide_index
  ' prompt for a new slide name
  new_slide_name = InputBox$("The current slide name is " _
    & current_name, "Change Slide Name?")
  ' remove any leading/trailing spaces
  new_slide_name = Trim(new_slide_name)
  ' if the length is > 0, then change the slide name
  If Len(new_slide_name) > 0 Then
    sld.Name = new_slide_name
  End If
Next
Exit Sub
err_end:
MsgBox Err.Description
End Sub
```

The change_slide_names routine dimensions a variable, sld, to a Slide object. Then using a For Each...Next loop, each slide is processed. Each slide's name and position (index number) are stored in variables. While the loop iterates, the value in the current_slide_index variable is applied to the GotoSlide method of Active-Window.View. This forces the PowerPoint interface to display the slides one by one as they are manipulated:

```
For Each sld In ActivePresentation.Slides
  ' get the current name
  current_name = sld.Name
  ' get the slide index number
  current_slide_index = sld.SlideIndex
  ' navigate to the slide using the index number
  ActiveWindow.View.GotoSlide Index:=current_slide_index
```

While a slide is visible, an input box prompts for a new name while displaying the current name. The following snippet of code produces the input box prompt shown in Figure 13.10:

```
new_slide_name = InputBox$("The current slide name is " _
    & current_name, "Change Slide Name?")
```

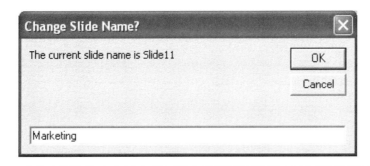

Figure 13.10 Prompting to change the name of a slide

Only a valid response is used to change the name of the slide, by giving the Name property the new name:

```
If Len(new_slide_name) > 0 Then
    sld.Name - new_slide_name
  End If
```

A similar routine was developed to change only the name of the *current* slide—whichever slide is visible in the user interface. This routine, shown in Listing 13.2, leaves out the looping portion and works with just a single slide. This routine is useful for cases in which only one slide needs to have its name changed.

Listing 13.2 Changing the name of the single current slide

```
Sub change_single_slide_name()
On Error GoTo err_end
Dim sld As Slide
Dim current_name As String
Dim new_slide_name As String
Set sld = ActiveWindow.View.Slide
```

Listing 13.2 *(continued)*

```
' get the current name
current_name = sld.Name
' prompt for a new slide name
new_slide_name = InputBox$("The current slide name is " _
    & current_name, "Change Slide Name?")
' remove any leading/trailing spaces
new_slide_name = Trim(new_slide_name)
' if the length is > 0, then change the slide name
If Len(new_slide_name) > 0 Then
    sld.Name = new_slide_name
End If
Exit Sub
err_end:
MsgBox Err.Description
End Sub
```

Changing the Names of Shapes

The other necessary action involving names is to change the names of the PowerPoint charts. Chart names are used as arguments that are passed to a subroutine, so they have to be known ahead of time. The routine shown in Listing 13.3 cycles through all the shapes on the active slide. In turn, each shape is selected and an input box is presented for changing the name.

Listing 13.3 Changing shape names on an individual slide

```
Sub change_shape_names()
On Error GoTo err_end
Dim sh As Shape
Dim current_name As String
Dim new_shape_name As String
For Each sh In ActiveWindow.View.Slide.Shapes
  sh.Select
  current_name = sh.Name
  new_shape_name = _
    InputBox$("The selected shape's name is " _
    & current_name, "Change Shape Name?")
  ' remove any leading/trailing spaces
  new_slide_name = Trim(new_slide_name)
```

Listing 13.3 *(continued)*

```
 ' if the length is > 0, then change the shape name
 If Len(new_shape_name) > 0 Then
    sh.Name = new_shape_name
 End If
Next
Exit Sub
err_end:
MsgBox Err.Description
End Sub
```

Note that the routine in Listing 13.3 cyclically selects *every* shape—whether or not that shape is a chart. Other types of shapes may need to be updated—for example, naming a text box so it can be addressed in code—so the routine selects all shapes, one by one. The selected shape is identified by the selection handles appearing around the shape. See Figure 13.11.

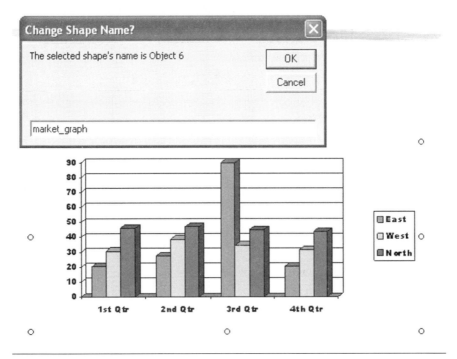

Figure 13.11 A shape is selected and its name can be changed

Updating the PowerPoint Charts

With all PowerPoint slides and charts appropriately named, the routine that copies the data from Excel to PowerPoint can be run. Actually, there are two routines: the first one, accessible from the Macro dialog in the user interface, calls the second one. The `update_charts` routine, shown in Listing 13.4, is available for users to run in the user interface because it is not explicitly qualified as `Private`. See Figure 13.12.

Listing 13.4 The `update_charts` routine

```
Sub update_charts()
On Error GoTo err_end
' dimension an object variable for the Excel workbook
Dim xl As Object
this_path = ActivePresentation.Path
```

Figure 13.12 The routines that users can run using the Macro dialog box

Listing 13.4 *(continued)*

```
' set the reference to the workbook
' workbook is assumed to be in the same directory
' change if necessary
Set xl = GetObject(this_path & "/Sales_Data.xls")
'
copy_data "Marketing_Percentage", _
    "Marketing_As_Percent", "Marketing", "market_graph", xl
copy_data "Profit_Growth_3_Year", _
    "Profit Growth Annual", "Annual", "annual_graph", xl
copy_data "Sales_Returns_Year", _
    "Returns as Percentage of Net", "Returns", _
        "returns_graph", xl
copy_data "Profit_Westerns", _
    "Category_Profit_1", "Category_1", "westerns_graph", xl
copy_data "Profit_Romance", _
    "Category_Profit_1", "Category_1", "romance_graph", xl
copy_data "Profit_SciFi", _
    "Category_Profit_1", "Category_1", "scifi_graph", xl
copy_data "Profit_Mysteries", _
    "Category_Profit_1", "Category_1", "mysteries_graph", xl
'
copy_data "Profit_Cookbooks", "Category_Profit_2", _
    "Category_2", "cookbooks_graph", xl
copy_data "Profit_Travel", "Category_Profit_2", _
    "Category_2", "travel_graph", xl
copy_data "Profit_Childrens", "Category_Profit_2", _
    "Category_2", "childrens_graph", xl
copy_data "Profit_Young_Adult", "Category_Profit_2", _
    "Category_2", "youngadult_graph", xl
'
copy_data "Profit_Business", "Category_Profit_3", _
    "Category_3", "business_graph", xl
copy_data "Profit_Reference", "Category_Profit_3", _
    "Category_3", "reference_graph", xl
copy_data "Profit_Inspiration", "Category_Profit_3", _
    "Category_3", "inspirational_graph", xl
copy_data "Profit_Technical", "Category_Profit_3", _
    "Category_3", "technical_graph", xl
'
```

Listing 13.4 *(continued)*

```
copy_data "Profit_Fiction", "Category_Profit_4", _
   "Category_4", "fiction_graph", xl
copy_data "Profit_NonFiction", "Category_Profit_4", _
   "Category_4", "nonfiction_graph", xl

xl.Close
Set xl = Nothing
MsgBox "All Charts Updated"
Exit Sub
err_end:
MsgBox Err.Description
End Sub
```

In the `update_charts` routine, an object variable, `xl`, is declared and then set to the Excel workbook. In this case study, the Excel workbook is assumed to be in the same directory and named Sales_Data.xls:

```
Dim xl As Object
this_path = ActivePresentation.Path
' set the reference to the workbook
' workbook is assumed to be in the same directory
' change if necessary
Set xl = GetObject(this_path & "/Sales_Data.xls")
```

The remainder of the routine passes arguments to the `copy_data` routine. That routine requires five arguments: range name, worksheet name, slide name, PowerPoint chart name, and the `xl` object. The `update_charts` routine calls the `copy_data` routine in this manner:

```
copy_data "Marketing_Percentage", _
   "Marketing_As_Percent", "Marketing", "market_graph", xl
```

At the end of the `update_charts` routine, the `xl` object is released, and the user is notified of completion:

```
xl.Close
Set xl = Nothing
MsgBox "All Charts Updated"
```

The `copy_data` routine, shown in Listing 13.5, handles the bulk of the work to populate the datasheets in PowerPoint.

Listing 13.5 The `copy_data` routine

```
Private Sub copy_data(range_name As String, _
     sheet_name As String, slide_name As String, _
     graph_name As String, xl As Object)
On Error GoTo err_end
Dim slide_index As Long
Dim data_array(10, 10)
Dim sh As Shape
Dim mygraph As Object
Dim row_count As Integer
Dim column_count As Integer
Dim data_rows As Integer
Dim data_columns As Integer
Dim d_range As Object
slide_index = _
   ActivePresentation.Slides(slide_name).SlideIndex
ActiveWindow.View.GotoSlide (slide_index)
Set d_range = xl.worksheets(sheet_name).Range(range_name)
With d_range
  row_count = .Rows.Count
  column_count = .Columns.Count
End With
For data_rows = 0 To row_count - 1
  For data_columns = 0 To column_count - 1
    data_array(data_rows, data_columns) = _
        d_range.Cells(data_rows + 1, data_columns + 1)
  Next data_columns
Next data_rows
Set d_range = Nothing
For Each sh In ActivePresentation.Slides(slide_name).Shapes
   If sh.Name = graph_name Then
      Set mygraph = _
          sh.OLEFormat.Object.Application.DataSheet
      mygraph.Cells.Clear
      For data_rows = 1 To row_count
        For data_columns = 1 To column_count
          mygraph.Cells(data_rows, data_columns) = _
            data_array(data_rows - 1, data_columns - 1)
        Next data_columns
      Next data_rows
   End If
Next
```

Listing 13.5 *(continued)*

```
Set mygraph = Nothing
Exit Sub
err_end:
Set mygraph = Nothing
MsgBox Err.Description
End Sub
```

To start, the `copy_data` routine is declared `Private`; therefore, it does not appear in the Macro dialog seen in Figure 13.12. This routine must be called only by the `update_charts` routine. Several variables are dimensioned at the start; a few are notable:

```
Dim slide_index As Long
Dim data_array(10, 10)
Dim sh As Shape
Dim mygraph As Object
```

The `slide_index`, `sh`, and `mygraph` variables are used to manage the positional order of a slide, the shapes on a slide, and the actual chart being manipulated in code, respectively. The use of the term *graph* in the `mygraph` variable name is just subjective naming. MS Graph is the engine behind the PowerPoint charts.

The `data_array` array is fixed to a 10×10 size. The purpose of the array is to temporarily hold series data found in Excel—in each successive named range. The 10×10 size is larger than what is needed for any data areas used in this case study. When this solution is adapted to other uses, however, it may be necessary to size the array differently, or use dynamic array sizing.

NOTE: The configuration of this process calls for Excel data to go into the array, and then for the array to feed a datasheet. Why not just directly populate the datasheet from the Excel range? During the procedure, both the Excel range and the PowerPoint datasheet are available to manipulate. The answer is that during testing, this straightforward method put an additional strain on memory and caused performance problems. Having both the `Range` object (through automation) in play along with the datasheet (an embedded OLE object) proved problematic. In fact, it was the debugging of this problem that brought to light the idea to use the interim array. The resultant process has only one of the objects in memory at a time.

The `slide_index` variable receives the `SlideIndex` value of the slide that was passed to the routine. Then the active window is changed to display the slide as its chart, or charts, are updated. This piece of the process is not necessary. A slide does not have to be the current one in view to be manipulated. However, this approach does show the user that something is occurring. Without this screen activity, it could appear that nothing is happening or that the system has frozen. Calling up each slide to be current in the view alleviates this problem. Of course, depending on how many actual slides there are, this solution may have dubious value:

```
slide_index = _
    ActivePresentation.Slides(slide_name).SlideIndex
ActiveWindow.View.GotoSlide (slide_index)
```

The `d_range` object variable is used to access the Excel range passed to the procedure. Its row count and column count are obtained, and then nested loops are used to populate the `data_array` array. As stated, the `data_array` array will not be completely filled with quality data, and further in the routine only pertinent data is extracted back out of the array. The `d_range` object is set to nothing after the array is filled:

```
Set d_range = xl.worksheets(sheet_name).Range(range_name)
With d_range
  row_count = .Rows.Count
  column_count = .Columns.Count
End With
For data_rows = 0 To row_count - 1
  For data_columns = 0 To column_count - 1
    data_array(data_rows, data_columns) = _
        d_range.Cells(data_rows + 1, data_columns + 1)
  Next data_columns
Next data_rows
Set d_range = Nothing
```

Now that the data is held in the array, next comes populating the datasheet. For the current slide, a `For Each...Next` loop cycles through all shapes on the slide. When the shape that matches the passed name is found, the `mygraph` object variable is set to the shape's datasheet. The datasheet is cleared, and a nested looping structure populates it from the array:

```
For Each sh In ActivePresentation.Slides(slide_name).Shapes
   If sh.Name = graph_name Then
      Set mygraph = _
          sh.OLEFormat.Object.Application.DataSheet
```

```
      mygraph.Cells.Clear
      For data_rows = 1 To row_count
        For data_columns = 1 To column_count
          mygraph.Cells(data_rows, data_columns) = _
            data_array(data_rows - 1, data_columns - 1)
        Next data_columns
      Next data_rows
  End If
Next
```

Summary

The procedures illustrated in this case study automate some of the work analysts need to do when preparing final reports for management. The key part of this solution is the copying of data from Excel worksheets to the datasheets behind PowerPoint charts.

This case study only points out how to copy the data. There are further avenues of development that can be explored. For example, the chart types and formats could also be applied to the PowerPoint charts by first reading those properties from the Excel charts. In practice, this addition did not have much benefit. As long as a chart first received manual formatting, it made sense to just apply the formatting directly to the PowerPoint charts. Remember, the only real purpose of the Excel charts here is for quick feedback to the analysts in preparing the supporting information of the report.

However, in adapting these techniques to your own solution, you may very well wish to incorporate additional functionality. Another possibility is that all data, chart formatting, and supporting text descriptions be housed in Excel, and the entire PowerPoint presentation be created on the fly via VBA code.

CHAPTER 14

Charting XML Data

Using Excel to Create Graphical Data Representation

VERSION NOTE: This case study is designed to work with all versions of Excel.

The Problem

A publishing company had decided to pilot-test a few sales programs. Certain key cities were selected, and presentations were made to key customers. The salespeople ended their presentations by asking the customers to grade the sales programs. A grade could be an A, B, C, or D.

Results were sent to headquarters, where they were combined into one large XML file. Management has requested a graphical summary of the results, broken out by program, region, and city. This will yield numerous charts. The problem is that tallying the data and creating the charts by hand takes too long. An automated solution is needed.

The Requirements

- Grading consists of five data points: program name, region, city, grade, and date.
- At any time, an automated process can be run to create charts based on available results.
- The chart format is 3D Pie, with grade percentage labels, and the program, region, and city in the title.
- The range of dates that the results are based on should be in the header of the worksheet containing the charts.

Solution Tool Set and Files

- VBA
- XML
- The MSXML Parser
- Grade_Reporter.xls, grades.xml, grades.xsd

Table 14.1 Routines used in this solution

Routine	Module
`create_charts`	`modChartCode`
`read_in_xml_grades`	`modChartCode`
`msxml_read_in_xml_grades`	`modChartCode`
`Workbook_Open`	`ThisWorkbook`

Notes on This Case Study

This case study features the automation of multiple chart creation. The `ChartWizard` method handles the chart creation. Some additional parameters are applied to each chart to control size and position.

The series data for the charts comes from an XML file. New features of Microsoft Office Excel 2003 are used to import the XML data. However, Excel 2003 installation is not complete throughout the firm, so an additional routine is included for users of older versions of Excel.

XML Data

The results of sales presentations are graded. There are five data points in the data: program name, region, city, grade, and presentation date. The data is stored in XML format. The root element is named `Grades`. Within the root are `Record` elements, which in turn have the five children elements. A business decision has been made to leave out customer names to ensure lack of bias. Listing 14.1 shows a portion of the XML file.

Listing 14.1 The grades are kept in an XML file.

```xml
<?xml version="1.0"?>
<Grades xmlns:xsi="http://www.w3.org/2001/XMLSchema-instance"
    xsi:noNamespaceSchemaLocation="grades.xsd">
  <Record>
    <Program>CoopAds</Program>
    <Region>East</Region>
    <City>Philadelphia</City>
    <Grade>B</Grade>
    <Date>3/2/2003</Date>
  </Record>
  <Record>
    <Program>CoopAds</Program>
    <Region>East</Region>
    <City>Philadelphia</City>
    <Grade>C</Grade>
    <Date>3/4/2003</Date>
  </Record>
  <Record>
    <Program>CoopAds</Program>
    <Region>East</Region>
    <City>Philadelphia</City>
    <Grade>A</Grade>
    <Date>3/6/2003</Date>
  </Record>
```

At Startup

The Grade_Reporter.xls file contains the custom programming of the solution. Upon opening the workbook, the workbook's Open event simply activates the main sheet (Chart Setup) and forces the display to the top of the sheet by activating the first cell. It is not likely that any other part of this sheet is in the view, but just in case, the cell activation is used. The complete opening code is presented here:

```
Private Sub Workbook_Open()
  Sheets("Chart Setup").Activate
  Cells(1, 1).Activate
End Sub
```

The Chart Setup worksheet is not particularly stylized in any way, but it provides access to a few key parameters used in making charts. As shown in Figure 14.1, this worksheet contains some values and a button.

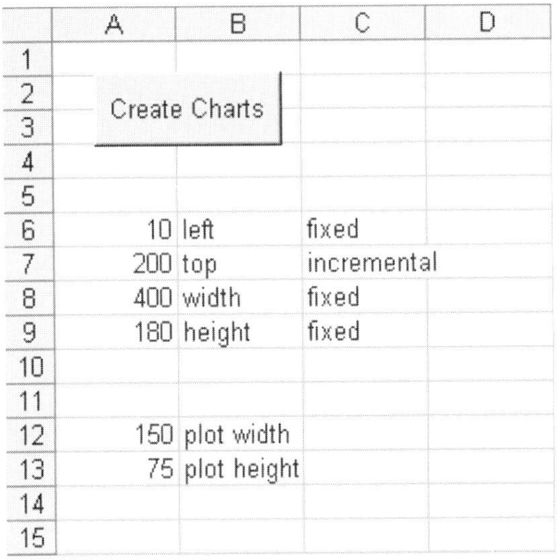

Figure 14.1 The Chart Setup worksheet

The Create Charts button runs the solution. It calls the `create_charts` routine, shown in Listing 14.2. An alternative is just to call the `create_charts` routine from the `Workbook_Open` routine. In that configuration, just opening the workbook would run the whole solution and make the charts. The advantage of building in an intermediate jumping point is to allow users to change the chart parameters listed on the Chart Setup worksheet. The effect of these parameters is explained later in this chapter.

The Solution Code

This solution contains one main routine, which calls one of two other routines dedicated to importing the XML data, depending on the version of Excel in use. All three routines are shown in Listing 14.2. The code is a bit lengthy. After the full listing, sections of code functionality are explained.

Listing 14.2 The solution code

```
Sub create_charts()
On Error GoTo err_end
Dim l, t, w, h
Dim chart_top
Dim plotwidth, plotheight
Dim date_min, date_max
Dim date_window As String
Dim date_format As Integer
Dim end_row As Integer
Dim row_resize As Integer
Dim chart_count As Integer
Dim this_city As String
Dim this_program As String
Dim city_start_row As Integer
Dim city_end_row As Integer
Dim new_rows As Integer
Dim cur_row As Integer
Dim cur_col As Integer
Dim chart_title As String
' turn off screen activity
Application.ScreenUpdating = False
' Store chart size values
With Worksheets("Chart Setup")
  ' left, top, width, height of the charts
  l = .Cells(6, 1)
  t = .Cells(7, 1)
  w = .Cells(8, 1)
  h = .Cells(9, 1)
  ' plot width and height
  plotwidth = .Cells(12, 1)
  plotheight = .Cells(13, 1)
End With
' turn off alerts
Application.DisplayAlerts = False
' feedback to user
Application.StatusBar = "Setting up Worksheets"
' delete the Charts and Data worksheets -
' insert new ones
With ActiveWorkbook
  On Error Resume Next
  .Sheets("Charts").Delete
  .Sheets("Data").Delete
```

Listing 14.2 *(continued)*

```
  ' reset error trap
  On Error GoTo err_end
  Worksheets.Add.Move after:=Worksheets(Worksheets.Count)
  ActiveSheet.Name = "Charts"
  Worksheets.Add.Move after:=Worksheets(Worksheets.Count)
  ActiveSheet.Name = "Data"
End With
' feedback to user
Application.StatusBar = "Reading Grades Data"
' read grade data from grades.xml, and insert into Data sheet
' if this is Excel 2003 or greater, then use built-in XML
methods
' else if an earlier version, use MSXML
If Application.Version >= 11 Then
    read_in_xml_grades
Else
    msxml_read_in_xml_grades
End If
' prepare header message
Sheets("Data").Activate
' use SpecialCells to find the last data row
Selection.SpecialCells(xlLastCell).Select
end_row = ActiveCell.Row - 1
' convert dates from text to real dates
For date_format = 2 To end_row
  Cells(date_format, 5) = CDate(Cells(date_format, 5))
Next date_format
' use Min and Max to get the earliest and latest dates
date_min = _
    Application.Min(Range(Cells(2, 5), Cells(end_row, 5)))
date_max = _
    Application.Max(Range(Cells(2, 5), Cells(end_row, 5)))
' date_window variable holds the complete header message
date_window = "For the period " & _
    Format(date_min, "mm/dd/yy") & " - " & _
    Format(date_max, "mm/dd/yy")
' feedback to user
Application.StatusBar = "Setting up Header"
' prepare the header on the Charts worksheet
Worksheets("Charts").Activate
```

Listing 14.2 (continued)

```
With ActiveSheet.PageSetup
    .LeftHeader = "&""Arial,Bold""&14Program Results" & _
        Chr$(13) & "by Region and Office"
    .RightHeader = date_window
End With
' to prevent charts from straddling page breaks,
' resize the sheet rows to the same height as the charts
For row_resize = 1 To 100
  ActiveSheet.Rows(row_resize).RowHeight = t
Next
' remove grid lines from the Charts sheet
ActiveWindow.DisplayGridlines = False
' sort the data by program, region, and city (columns A, B, C)
Sheets("Data").Activate
Range("A1:E" & end_row).Sort Key1:=Range("A2"), _
    Order1:=xlAscending, Key2:=Range("B2"), _
    Order2:=xlAscending, Key3:=Range("C2"), _
    Order3:=xlAscending, Header:=xlYes
chart_count = 0
' get first city and program
Cells(2, 3).Activate
this_city = ActiveCell
this_program = ActiveCell.Offset(0, -2)
city_start_row = ActiveCell.Row
' loop down through worksheet until no more data
While ActiveCell <> ""
   ' loop down while the city and the program are the same
   While ActiveCell = this_city And _
       ActiveCell.Offset(0, -2) = this_program
       ActiveCell.Offset(1, 0).Activate
   Wend
   ' now on a new city and/or new program,
   ' store ending row of previous city-program combo, and
   ' store new city and program names
   city_end_row = ActiveCell.Offset(-1, 0).Row
   this_city = ActiveCell
   this_program = ActiveCell.Offset(0, -2)
   ' increment region count
   chart_count = chart_count + 1
   ' feedback to user
   Application.StatusBar = "Processing data set " & chart_count
```

Listing 14.2 (continued)

```
' put in 10 blank rows, this creates space for calculations
For new_rows = 1 To 10
    ActiveCell.EntireRow.Insert
Next new_rows
' XML import lands data as text, needs to be converted
' to number format so calculations will work
Range(ActiveCell, _
  Cells(ActiveCell.Row + 8, ActiveCell.Column + 1)) _
 .NumberFormat = "##"
' insert formulas
' for each break in data (a change in the city-program combo)
' a summary section is created
' The charts plot the percentage of total for each grade, so
' a separate count is needed for each grade (A, B, C, D),
' and a count of the total is needed.
' The CountIf function is used
' for calculating counts based on grades.
' Then a calculation returns each grade's
' percentage of the total
' Step 1 - put in labels
With ActiveCell
  .Value = "A"
  .Offset(1, 0).Value = "B"
  .Offset(2, 0).Value = "C"
  .Offset(3, 0).Value = "D"
  .Offset(4, 0).Value = "Total"
  .Offset(5, 0).Value = "A"
  .Offset(6, 0).Value = "B"
  .Offset(7, 0).Value = "C"
  .Offset(8, 0).Value = "D"
End With
' Step 2 - Count by Grade
ActiveCell.Offset(0, 1).Formula = _
    "=CountIf(D" & city_start_row & _
      ":D" & city_end_row & ",""A"")"
ActiveCell.Offset(1, 1).Formula = _
    "=CountIf(D" & city_start_row & _
      ":D" & city_end_row & ",""B"")"
ActiveCell.Offset(2, 1).Formula = _
    "=CountIf(D" & city_start_row & _
      ":D" & city_end_row & ",""C"")"
```

Listing 14.2 *(continued)*

```
ActiveCell.Offset(3, 1).Formula = _
    "=CountIf(D" & city_start_row & _
        ":D" & city_end_row & ",""D"")"
ActiveCell.Offset(4, 1).Formula = _
    "=Sum(D" & city_end_row + 1 & _
        ":D" & city_end_row + 4 & ")"
' Step 3 - Grade Percentage of Total
ActiveCell.Offset(5, 1).Formula = _
    "=D" & city_end_row + 1 & "/D" & city_end_row + 5
ActiveCell.Offset(6, 1).Formula = _
    "=D" & city_end_row + 2 & "/D" & city_end_row + 5
ActiveCell.Offset(7, 1).Formula = _
    "=D" & city_end_row + 3 & "/D" & city_end_row + 5
ActiveCell.Offset(8, 1).Formula = _
    "=D" & city_end_row + 4 & "/D" & city_end_row + 5
' get the active cell's coordinates before the next operation
cur_row = ActiveCell.Row
cur_col = ActiveCell.Column
' format as percentage
Range(ActiveCell.Offset(5, 1), _
    ActiveCell.Offset(8, 1)).Select
Selection.NumberFormat = "0%"
' restore to the real active cell, the format operation just
' completed left the active cell on an offset cell
Cells(cur_row, cur_col).Select
' now add the chart for this site
' first prepare the chart title of the form . . .
' Program at Region-City
chart_title = ActiveCell.Offset(-1, -2) & " at " & _
  ActiveCell.Offset(-1, -1) & "-" & ActiveCell.Offset(-1, 0)
Sheets("Charts").Activate
' need to preserve t as incremental value, so use
' chart_top variable for the actual top value of each chart
If chart_count = 1 Then
  chart_top = 1
Else
  chart_top = t * chart_count - t
End If
' feedback to user
Application.StatusBar = "Creating Chart # " & chart_count
```

494   **Chapter 14   Charting XML Data**

Listing 14.2 *(continued)*

```
   ' add chart object using established size and position
   ActiveSheet.ChartObjects.Add(l, chart_top, w, h).Select
   Application.CutCopyMode = False
   ' The ChartWizard method is used to produce the chart -
   ' The data source is set to the summary section created on
   ' the Data sheet. The chart type, legend, and title
   ' are all set here.
   ActiveChart.ChartWizard Source:= _
      Range("Data!C" & cur_row + 5 & ":Data!D" & cur_row + 8), _
      Gallery:=xl3DPie, Format:=7, PlotBy:=xlColumns, _
      CategoryLabels:=1, SeriesLabels:=0, HasLegend:=1, _
      Title:=chart_title
   ActiveSheet.ChartObjects(chart_count).Activate
   ' the inner plot area is resized . . .
   ActiveChart.PlotArea.Select
   Selection.Width = plotwidth
   Selection.Height = plotheight
   ' this releases the chart and reactivates the workbook window
   Windows(ActiveWorkbook.Name).Activate
   ' back to the Data sheet - where processing was last left,
   ' just above the summary section
   Sheets("Data").Activate
   Cells(cur_row, cur_col).Select
   ' get past the 10 rows of the summary section
   ActiveCell.Offset(10, 0).Activate
   ' starting on next chart, store start row
   city_start_row = ActiveCell.Row
Wend ' end of outer loop
' at end, leave user viewing charts
Sheets("Charts").Activate
Cells(1, 1).Activate
Application.StatusBar = ""
MsgBox "done"
Exit Sub
err_end:
MsgBox Err.Description
End Sub
Sub read_in_xml_grades()
  Dim gr_map As XmlMap
  Dim xmlfile As String
```

Listing 14.2 *(continued)*

```
  Dim xmlschema As String
  Dim map_delete As Integer
  If ActiveWorkbook.XmlMaps.Count > 0 Then
    For map_delete = ActiveWorkbook.XmlMaps.Count To 1 Step -1
      ActiveWorkbook.XmlMaps(map_delete).Delete
    Next
  End If
  xmldata = ActiveWorkbook.Path & "\grades.xml"
  xmlschema = ActiveWorkbook.Path & "\grades.xsd"
  ' create a map based on the schema file
  Set gr_map = ActiveWorkbook.XmlMaps.Add(xmlschema, "Grades")
  ' import XML into Data worksheet
  ActiveWorkbook.XmlImport xmldata, gr_map, True, "Data!A1"
  ' import treats data as list, so apply unlist method
  Worksheets("Data").ListObjects(1).Unlist
End Sub
Sub msxml_read_in_xml_grades()
  ' the MSXML Parser is used for copying the grades data
  ' onto the Data sheet
  ' A reference must be made to the parser
  ' using the Tools . . . References menu
  Sheets("Data").Activate
  ' set object variables needed for working with the XML
  Dim xmlsource As DOMDocument
  Dim xmlnode As IXMLDOMNode
  Dim recordcount As Integer
  ' open the XML file . . .
  Set xmlsource = New DOMDocument
  xmlsource.async = False
  xmlsource.Load ActiveWorkbook.Path & "\grades.xml"
  recordcount = 1
  ' put headers in row 1
  Set xmlnode = xmlsource.documentElement.childNodes(1)
  For readxml = 1 To xmlnode.childNodes.Length
    Cells(recordcount, 1) = xmlnode.childNodes(0).nodeName
    Cells(recordcount, 2) = xmlnode.childNodes(1).nodeName
    Cells(recordcount, 3) = xmlnode.childNodes(2).nodeName
    Cells(recordcount, 4) = xmlnode.childNodes(3).nodeName
    Cells(recordcount, 5) = xmlnode.childNodes(4).nodeName
  Next
```

Listing 14.2 *(continued)*

```
' read through XML file, and insert data into
' successive worksheet rows
' the incremental recordcount variable is used to indicate
' the row number
For Each xmlnode In xmlsource.documentElement.childNodes
  For readxml = 1 To xmlnode.childNodes.Length
    recordcount = recordcount + 1
    Cells(recordcount, 1) = xmlnode.childNodes(0).Text
    Cells(recordcount, 2) = xmlnode.childNodes(1).Text
    Cells(recordcount, 3) = xmlnode.childNodes(2).Text
    Cells(recordcount, 4) = xmlnode.childNodes(3).Text
    Cells(recordcount, 5) = xmlnode.childNodes(4).Text
  Next
 Next
End Sub
```

Preparing the Workbook

One of the first actions taken in the create_charts subroutine is to store the chart parameter values from the Chart Setup worksheet. The variables l, t, w, and h are used for the Left, Top, Width and Height properties, respectively. Two more variables, plotwidth and plotheight, are used for the dimensions of the inner plot area of a chart:

```
With Worksheets("Chart Setup")
  ' left, top, width, height of the charts
  l = .Cells(6, 1)
  t = .Cells(7, 1)
  w = .Cells(8, 1)
  h = .Cells(9, 1)
  ' plot width and height
  plotwidth = .Cells(12, 1)
  plotheight = .Cells(13, 1)
End With
```

Figure 14.2 displays how these parameters are used.

It's important to note that these are just a few of the many parameters that can be manipulated. Other settings such as label placement, 3-D angling, colors, fonts, chart type, and more are programmable. As is, the solution uses defaults for many of these settings.

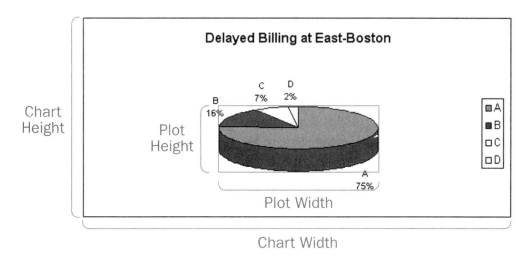

Figure 14.2 User-controllable chart parameters

As part of the solution, certain worksheets are deleted and then added back. This activity normally prompts the user, as seen in Figure 14.3. Setting the DisplayAlerts property to false removes the prompt:

```
Application.DisplayAlerts = False
```

Another user-friendly utility is the inclusion of messages in the status bar. These are placed in various strategic places in the code. Here they are displayed sequentially for convenience, although they are not placed near each other in the full routine:

```
Application.StatusBar = "Setting up Worksheets"
Application.StatusBar = "Reading Grades Data"
Application.StatusBar = "Setting up Header"
```

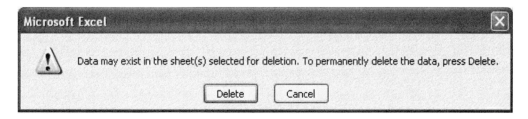

Figure 14.3 Set DisplayAlerts to false to avoid this warning

```
Application.StatusBar = "Processing data set " & chart_count
Application.StatusBar = "Creating Chart # " & chart_count
Application.StatusBar = ""
```

The final setting of the `StatusBar` property sets it to a zero-length string, which serves to clear it.

The key reason for sending messages to the status bar is that near the start of the `create_charts` routine, the screen refresh is turned off:

```
Application.ScreenUpdating = False
```

If the screen refresh were left on, the effect would be jumpy motion as the routine cycled between the Data and Chart worksheets. By turning off the screen refresh, no activity is visible. However, the status bar is not affected by the `ScreenUpdating` property. The messages appear in the status bar and users are assured the process is running.

The Charts and Data worksheets are deleted and then added back in. The `Delete` method will cause an error if one of the worksheets is not in the workbook, so the error trap is reset to resume with the next statement after the delete. In this case, the failure of the delete doesn't matter. If there is no sheet to delete, the result is the same: the worksheet is gone before being re-added.

Immediately after the `Delete` method is applied to the two worksheets, the error trap is reset to its original setting. Then the two worksheets are added back to the workbook. Each is placed at the end and named:

```
With ActiveWorkbook
  On Error Resume Next
  .Sheets("Charts").Delete
  .Sheets("Data").Delete
  ' reset error trap
  On Error GoTo err_end
  Worksheets.Add.Move after:=Worksheets(Worksheets.Count)
  ActiveSheet.Name = "Charts"
  Worksheets.Add.Move after:=Worksheets(Worksheets.Count)
  ActiveSheet.Name = "Data"
End With
```

Bringing the Data into the Workbook

This solution is structured such that the data must be imported into the Data worksheet. The data in the XML file has to end up sitting in the first five columns of the worksheet—with each row holding the data found in each Record element. Figure 14.4 shows how the data must appear after the import.

The solution provides two ways of importing the XML data. If Excel 2003 or later is installed, the XmlImport method is used. For older versions, the MSXML Parser is used. The Excel version is tested, and then the appropriate routine is called:

```
If Application.Version >= 11 Then
    read_in_xml_grades
Else
    msxml_read_in_xml_grades
End If
```

	A	B	C	D	E
1	Program	Region	City	Grade	Date
2	CoopAds	East	Baltimore	A	3/9/2003
3	CoopAds	East	Baltimore	A	3/9/2003
4	CoopAds	East	Baltimore	A	3/9/2003
5	CoopAds	East	Baltimore	A	3/9/2003
6	CoopAds	East	Baltimore	A	3/9/2003
7	CoopAds	East	Baltimore	B	3/17/2003
8	CoopAds	East	Baltimore	B	3/17/2003
9	CoopAds	East	Baltimore	D	3/17/2003
10	CoopAds	East	Baltimore	D	3/17/2003
11	CoopAds	East	Baltimore	B	3/17/2003
12	CoopAds	East	Baltimore	D	3/20/2003
13	CoopAds	East	Baltimore	B	3/20/2003
14	CoopAds	East	Baltimore	B	3/20/2003
15	CoopAds	East	Baltimore	B	3/20/2003
16	CoopAds	East	Baltimore	D	3/20/2003
17	CoopAds	East	Baltimore	A	4/1/2003
18	CoopAds	East	Baltimore	A	4/1/2003

Figure 14.4 The XML data must import in this manner

Using XmlImport

The XmlImport method requires a map to facilitate the import. A map object will be added, but first any current map objects are deleted. If this were not done, the workbook would fill up with an additional map each time the process was run. The read_in_xml_grades subroutine in Listing 14.2 takes care of this:

```
If ActiveWorkbook.XmlMaps.Count > 0 Then
  For map_delete = ActiveWorkbook.XmlMaps.Count To 1 Step -1
    ActiveWorkbook.XmlMaps(map_delete).Delete
  Next
End If
```

After the delete operation, a map is added using the schema in the grades.xsd file. The Add method requires the name of the root element, Grades in this case:

```
xmlschema = ActiveWorkbook.Path & "\grades.xsd"
' create a map based on the schema file
Set gr_map = ActiveWorkbook.XmlMaps.Add(xmlschema, "Grades")
```

The grades.xsd file is shown in Listing 14.3. The grades.xml file, already shown in Listing 14.1, refers to the grades.xsd file.

Listing 14.3 The grades.xsd schema file

```
<?xml version="1.0" encoding="UTF-8"?>
<xsd:schema xmlns:xsd="http://www.w3.org/2001/XMLSchema">
  <xsd:element name="Grades">
    <xsd:complexType>
      <xsd:sequence>
        <xsd:element ref="Record" minOccurs="0"
          maxOccurs="unbounded"/>
      </xsd:sequence>
    </xsd:complexType>
  </xsd:element>
  <xsd:element name="Record">
    <xsd:complexType>
      <xsd:sequence>
        <xsd:element name="Program" minOccurs="0">
          <xsd:simpleType>
            <xsd:restriction base="xsd:string"/>
          </xsd:simpleType>
        </xsd:element>
```

Listing 14.3 (continued)

```
          <xsd:element name="Region" minOccurs="0">
            <xsd:simpleType>
              <xsd:restriction base="xsd:string"/>
            </xsd:simpleType>
          </xsd:element>
          <xsd:element name="City" minOccurs="0">
            <xsd:simpleType>
              <xsd:restriction base="xsd:string"/>
            </xsd:simpleType>
          </xsd:element>
          <xsd:element name="Grade" minOccurs="0">
            <xsd:simpleType>
              <xsd:restriction base="xsd:string"/>
            </xsd:simpleType>
          </xsd:element>
          <xsd:element name="Date" minOccurs="0"
              type="xsd:dateTime"/>
        </xsd:sequence>
      </xsd:complexType>
    </xsd:element>
</xsd:schema>
```

After the map is completed, the XmlImport method is applied. It takes four parameters: the path to the data, the map, a Boolean value whether to overwrite existing data (it doesn't matter in this case), and where to place the data. The data is to be placed on the Data worksheet starting in the first cell, A1:

```
ActiveWorkbook.XmlImport xmldata, gr_map, True, "Data!A1"
```

The XmlImport method places the data in the correct layout required by the solution. However, XmlImport treats the data as a list (a ListObject). See Figure 14.5.

So, the Unlist method is applied to the ListObject:

```
Worksheets("Data").ListObjects(1).Unlist
```

The result is the clean set of data ready to be used by the solution, just as seen in Figure 14.4.

	A	B	C	D	E
1	Program ▼	Region ▼	City ▼	Grade ▼	Date ▼
2	CoopAds	East	Philadelphia	B	3/2/2003
3	CoopAds	East	Philadelphia	C	3/4/2003
4	CoopAds	East	Philadelphia	A	3/6/2003
5	CoopAds	East	Philadelphia	A	3/2/2003
6	CoopAds	East	Philadelphia	A	3/2/2003
7	FlexCredit	East	Philadelphia	A	3/2/2003
8	FlexCredit	East	Philadelphia	A	3/2/2003
9	FlexCredit	East	Philadelphia	A	3/2/2003
10	FlexCredit	East	Philadelphia	A	3/2/2003
11	FlexCredit	East	Philadelphia	A	3/2/2003
12	FlexCredit	East	Providence	C	3/2/2003
13	FlexCredit	East	Providence	C	3/2/2003
14	FlexCredit	East	Providence	D	3/2/2003
15	FlexCredit	East	Providence	C	3/2/2003
16	FlexCredit	East	Providence	C	3/2/2003
17	Net45	North	Cleveland	A	3/2/2003
18	Net45	North	Cleveland	A	3/2/2003
19	Net45	North	Cleveland	A	3/2/2003
20	Net45	North	Cleveland	A	3/2/2003
21	Net45	North	Cleveland	A	3/2/2003
22	FlexCredit	South	Dallas	A	3/2/2003
23	FlexCredit	South	Dallas	A	3/2/2003

Figure 14.5 The `XmlImport` method treats imported data as a list

Using the MSXML Parser to Import

For earlier versions of Excel, the MSXML Parser is used to facilitate the import of the XML data. As such, a reference to it needs to be set. See Figure 14.6. Any version will suffice.

NOTE: See the Appendix for resources on the MSXML Parser.

Two DOM (Document Object Model) variables are dimensioned: one is used to manage the XML file itself, the other is used to reference nodes within the file:

```
Dim xmlsource As DOMDocument
Dim xmlnode As IXMLDOMNode
```

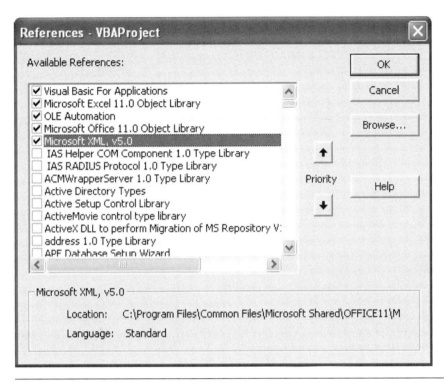

Figure 14.6 Setting a reference to the MSXML Parser

The xmlsource variable points to the XML file after it is loaded with the Load method:

```
xmlsource.Load ActiveWorkbook.Path & "\grades.xml"
```

The names of the child elements (Program, City, and so on) need to be inserted into the first row of the Data worksheet. The xmlnode variable is set to the first Record element. That is, the xmlsource.document-Element is the Grades element (the root element), and the first child node of the root is Record. See Listing 14.1 to follow this explanation in the data.

The children of Record need to be addressed. xmlNode is now set to Record, so the childNodes property of xmlNode is examined. A For...Next loop is used—set to the number of children elements—returned by the Length property:

```
recordcount = 1
' put headers in row 1
Set xmlnode = xmlsource.documentElement.childNodes(1)
For readxml = 1 To xmlnode.childNodes.Length
  Cells(recordcount, 1) = xmlnode.childNodes(0).nodeName
  Cells(recordcount, 2) = xmlnode.childNodes(1).nodeName
  Cells(recordcount, 3) = xmlnode.childNodes(2).nodeName
  Cells(recordcount, 4) = xmlnode.childNodes(3).nodeName
  Cells(recordcount, 5) = xmlnode.childNodes(4).nodeName
Next
```

NOTE: In XML DOM verbiage, the `Length` property returns a count, not an actual length.

To get the actual headings, the `nodeName` property is used:

```
Cells(recordcount, 4) = xmlnode.childNodes(3).nodeName
```

At this point, the headings have been inserted into the first row of the Data worksheet. A `For Each...Next` loop is used to insert the data. This loop sequentially addresses all `Record` elements in the file. Then an inner loop reads through each child of the `Record`. Here the `Text` property is used to access the actual data. The worksheet cells receive the data:

```
For Each xmlnode In xmlsource.documentElement.childNodes
  For readxml = 1 To xmlnode.childNodes.Length
    recordcount = recordcount + 1
    Cells(recordcount, 1) = xmlnode.childNodes(0).Text
    Cells(recordcount, 2) = xmlnode.childNodes(1).Text
    Cells(recordcount, 3) = xmlnode.childNodes(2).Text
    Cells(recordcount, 4) = xmlnode.childNodes(3).Text
    Cells(recordcount, 5) = xmlnode.childNodes(4).Text
  Next
Next
```

Processing the Data for Use in Charts

The grades data is now in the workbook, on the Data worksheet. One of the requirements is to provide the range of dates in the grades data. To accomplish this, the `SpecialCells` method is used to populate the `end_row` variable with the last significant data row:

```
Selection.SpecialCells(xlLastCell).Select
end_row = ActiveCell.Row - 1
```

At this point Excel does not recognize the dates in the XML data as real dates. To be precise, the grades.xml file *does* reference the grades.xsd schema, which indicates that Date elements are to be treated as dates:

```
<xsd:element name="Date" minOccurs="0" type="xsd:dateTime"/>
```

However, as a result of this, Excel formats the cells in column E with a custom date type, but the data itself is being treated as text.

To override this behavior, the CDate() function is applied to the dates in column E:

```
For date_format = 2 To end_row
  Cells(date_format, 5) = CDate(Cells(date_format, 5))
Next date_format
```

Next the Min() and Max() functions are used to get the earliest and latest dates in the fifth column. Finally, a message is assembled with this information and stored in the date_window variable. A format is applied here as well:

```
date_min = _
    Application.Min(Range(Cells(2, 5), Cells(end_row, 5)))
date_max = _
    Application.Max(Range(Cells(2, 5), Cells(end_row, 5)))
' date_window variable holds the complete header message
date_window = "For the period " & _
    Format(date_min, "mm/dd/yy") & " - " & _
    Format(date_max, "mm/dd/yy")
```

The Charts worksheet is activated, and the header receives values for the left and right sides (there are three header and footer sections: left, middle, and right). The left header side is set to a generic message, and the right side is set to the message stored in the date_window variable:

```
Worksheets("Charts").Activate
With ActiveSheet.PageSetup
    .LeftHeader = "&""Arial,Bold""&14Program Results" & _
        Chr$(13) & "by Region and Office"
    .RightHeader = date_window
End With
```

The first 100 rows on the Charts worksheet are resized to the value stored in the variable t. This value is used in calculating the Top property of charts as they are created. By setting the row size to this value, the placement of charts on the Charts worksheet will not straddle natural page breaks.

Because the `Height` and `Top` properties are user-controllable, these settings may force charts to fall across the page breaks. In fact, this is more likely to happen than not. By changing the row sizes to the value of variable `t`, this makes sure that the top of each chart starts at the top of a row. This in turn forces page breaks to occur only at the top of charts:

```
For row_resize = 1 To 100
  ActiveSheet.Rows(row_resize).RowHeight = t
Next
```

Adjusting the settings and seeing how the page breaks are controlled is explained later in the chapter.

Choosing 100 as the number of rows to resize is arbitrary. In production, the number of charts created topped out at around 70. The routine now continues working the Data worksheet. The data is sorted by program name, region, and city:

```
Sheets("Data").Activate
Range("A1:E" & end_row).Sort Key1:=Range("A2"), _
    Order1:=xlAscending, Key2:=Range("B2"), _
    Order2:=xlAscending, Key3:=Range("C2"), _
    Order3:=xlAscending, Header:=xlYes
```

A variable is used to count charts as they are created:

```
chart_count = 0
```

The first data points (on row 2), program and city, are stored. Also, the row that this city starts on is stored:

```
Cells(2, 3).Activate
this_city = ActiveCell
this_program = ActiveCell.Offset(0, -2)
city_start_row = ActiveCell.Row
```

The major processing loop is established as a `While . . . Wend` construct. The `While` condition here is a test for the active cell being non-empty.

```
While ActiveCell <> ""
```

Within the large loop, a smaller loop reads down the worksheet as long as both the program and the city have not changed:

```
While ActiveCell = this_city And _
    ActiveCell.Offset(0, -2) = this_program
    ActiveCell.Offset(1, 0).Activate
Wend
```

Once the active cell is on a row where either the program or city has changed, the row number of one row above needs to be stored in the `city_end_row` variable. The `Offset` property is used to return the row number. Also here, the new city and program names of the current row are stored. Either both of these have new values or just one has a new value; but what is important is that the combination is new:

```
city_end_row = ActiveCell.Offset(-1, 0).Row
this_city = ActiveCell
this_program = ActiveCell.Offset(0, -2)
```

The chart count is incremented:

```
chart_count = chart_count + 1
```

Ten new rows are inserted below the active row. These are necessary for calculations used to summarize the data for this program-city combination:

```
For new_rows = 1 To 10
    ActiveCell.EntireRow.Insert
Next new_rows
```

Nine of these rows will hold calculations. The tenth just serves as a cosmetic visual separation in the data. The nine rows need to have their format changed. When the ten rows are inserted, they take on the format of the row of the active cell. Therefore in the new rows, column D is formatted as text—which will cause the formulas not to work. The nine rows are converted to a numerical format prior to the calculations being inserted:

```
Range(ActiveCell, _
  Cells(ActiveCell.Row + 8, ActiveCell.Column + 1)) _
  .NumberFormat = "##"
```

Figure 14.7 displays the area of ten rows and how they appear after labels and calculations are inserted. First, note that the reason rows were inserted here is because the program-and-city combination (columns A and C) above the ten rows differs from the combination below.

	A	B	C	D	E
3829	Delayed Billing	East	Boston	A	5/17/2003
3830	Delayed Billing	East	Boston	A	5/17/2003
3831	Delayed Billing	East	Boston	A	5/17/2003
3832			A	170	
3833			B	35	
3834			C	15	
3835			D	5	
3836			Total	225	
3837			A	76%	
3838			B	16%	
3839			C	7%	
3840			D	2%	
3841					
3842	Delayed Billing	East	Hartford	D	3/14/2003
3843	Delayed Billing	East	Hartford	D	3/14/2003
3844	Delayed Billing	East	Hartford	D	3/14/2003
3845	Delayed Billing	East	Hartford	D	3/14/2003

Figure 14.7 The summary for a program and city

The charts display percentages of a total. For example, there are four possible grades. If the total number of presentations is 100, and each grade received a count of 25, then the percentage of each grade is 25%. The count of each grade's occurrence needs to be tallied, as does the total tally regardless of grade. With this information then, each grade's percentage of the total can be calculated using this formula:

Count of individual grade / total count of all grades

In the nine rows, going down column C, labels are placed: A, B, C, D, Total, A, B, C, and D. In column D are the formulas. Referring to Figure 14.7, Table 14.2 shows the formulas.

The first four rows use the CountIf() function to filter the count to just each respective grade. In these formulas, the range D3607:D3831 is the arbitrary area of that particular combination of program and city. The insertion of these row numbers was accomplished with the use of the city_start_row and city_end_row variables. For example, the formula to calculate the count of an individual grade follows this form in the programming code:

Table 14.2 Formulas inserted into the Data worksheet

Cell	Formula	Corresponding Label in Column C	Comment
D3832	`=COUNTIF(D3607:D3831,"A")`	A	Total count of A grade
D3833	`=COUNTIF(D3607:D3831,"B")`	B	Total count of B grade
D3834	`=COUNTIF(D3607:D3831,"C")`	C	Total count of C grade
D3835	`=COUNTIF(D3607:D3831,"D")`	D	Total count of D grade
D3836	`=SUM(D3832:D3835)`	`Total`	Total count of all grades
D3837	`=D3832/D3836`	A	A's percentage of total
D3838	`=D3833/D3836`	B	B's percentage of total
D3839	`=D3834/D3836`	C	C's percentage of total
D3840	`=D3835/D3836`	D	D's percentage of total

```
ActiveCell.Offset(0, 1).Formula = _
    "=CountIf(D" & city_start_row & _
        ":D" & city_end_row & ",""A"")"
```

In the particular case shown in Figure 14.7, `city_start_row` = 3607 and `city_end_row` = 3831. Of course, the values of these variables change throughout the looping of the routine.

The fifth row of the calculated area contains the total of the individual grade counts. The sixth through ninth rows calculate each grade's percentage of the total by dividing individual count by the total count.

The four cells that received the formula to determine grade percentage need to be formatted as percentages. The charts need to show the numerical values in the percent format. This format can be applied either here or on the chart. It is applied here:

```
Range(ActiveCell.Offset(5, 1), _
    ActiveCell.Offset(8, 1)).Select
Selection.NumberFormat = "0%"
```

The `Select` method used in the preceding formatting action has moved the active cell. Prior to inserting formulas, the active cell's original coordinates were stored, and now the active cell is set back to where it was:

```
Cells(cur_row, cur_col).Select
```

The title for the chart is determined from the data. The `Offset` method is used to address the correct data points to put together the string used in the title:

```
chart_title = ActiveCell.Offset(-1, -2) & " at " & _
    ActiveCell.Offset(-1, -1) & "-" & ActiveCell.Offset(-1, 0)
```

Creating the Charts

Now the activity returns to the Charts worksheet. From wherever the code is in the loop's iterations, the chart needs to be inserted in the vertical position that coordinates with how the rows were previously resized. When this is the first chart, the `Top` property is simply 1; however, for all charts from number two to the end, the `Top` property is calculated.

```
Sheets("Charts").Activate
' need to preserve t as incremental value, so use
' chart_top variable for the actual top value of each chart
If chart_count = 1 Then
  chart_top = 1
Else
  chart_top = t * chart_count - t
End If
```

The `chart_top` variable is calculated using the established `Top` property and the current chart number. For example, if `t` equals 200 and the tenth chart is being processed, then the top property will equal 1800.

Because earlier, the rows were resized to t (200 in this case), this forces the chart to start at the top of a row. A proof of this is that 1800 divided by 200 returns an integer (9) with no decimal. The tenth chart's Top property is set to 1800, which is the position where the tenth row starts.

With the established and calculated parameters, a Chart object is added to the worksheet:

```
ActiveSheet.ChartObjects.Add(l, chart_top, w, h).Select
```

A Chart object is just a placeholder. The ChartWizard method is used to actually create the chart into the Chart object. The source data is set to the associated area of formulas on the Data worksheet, the chart type is a 3D Pie (xl3DPie), and the chart_title variable is given to the Title property:

```
ActiveChart.ChartWizard Source:= _
    Range("Data!C" & cur_row + 5 & ":Data!D" & cur_row + 8), _
    Gallery:=xl3DPie, Format:=7, PlotBy:=xlColumns, _
    CategoryLabels:=1, SeriesLabels:=0, HasLegend:=1, _
    Title:=chart_title
```

The plot area is selected and handed the width and height:

```
ActiveSheet.ChartObjects(chart_count).Activate
' the inner plot area is resized . . .
ActiveChart.PlotArea.Select
Selection.Width = plotwidth
Selection.Height = plotheight
```

This next line gives the focus back to the worksheet (and takes it away from the Chart object):

```
Windows(ActiveWorkbook.Name).Activate
```

The processing activity once again turns to the Data worksheet. The Offset and Activate methods are used to move past the ten inserted rows. This places the active cell on a row with a new program-and-city combination. The city_start_row variable receives this row number, and the loop wraps back to its start:

```
    Sheets("Data").Activate
    Cells(cur_row, cur_col).Select
    ' get past the 10 rows of the summary section
    ActiveCell.Offset(10, 0).Activate
    ' starting on next chart, store start row
    city_start_row = ActiveCell.Row
Wend ' end of outer loop
```

Applying Variations of the `Top` and `Height` Properties

When the processing is finished, the Chart worksheet is filled with charts. See Figure 14.8. The page breaks do not break across any charts, thanks to the value in the variable `t` being the source of both the row size and the `Top` property of the charts. The value of `t` also affects how many charts appear on a page. In the example in Figure 14.8, `t` is set to 200 and the `Height` property is set to 180. The setting of 200 creates three charts on the page, and the value of 180 puts a little room between the charts.

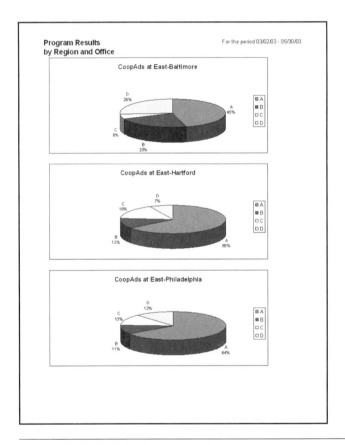

Figure 14.8 Multiple charts have been created

By applying different values of the `Top` and `Height` properties, the number of charts that will print per page can be controlled. These values are entered on the Chart Setup worksheet, seen back in Figure 14.1.

There are no hard and fast numbers to provide here, because the page size, orientation, and margin settings all affect what goes on a page. However, most systems are likely to be configured in a similar manner. With that assumption, setting the `Top` and `Height` to 400 produces one chart per page. See Figure 14.9.

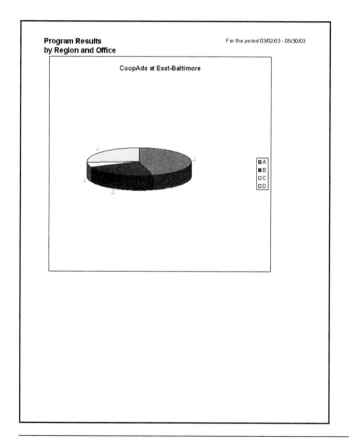

Figure 14.9 Using the `Top` and `Height` properties to produce one chart per page

Additionally, by setting `Height` to be a smaller number than `Top` allows control over how much space is in between charts. In Figure 14.10, with a `Top` of 300 and a `Height` of 200, a page holds two charts with ample room between for notes to be typed in.

The ability to control the plot width and plot height is also available through entry on the Chart Setup worksheet. These values may have to be changed to create correct chart formatting as the other parameters are changed. For example, with the settings used to create the charts in Figure 14.10, the plot width was reset to 225 and the plot height was reset to 125.

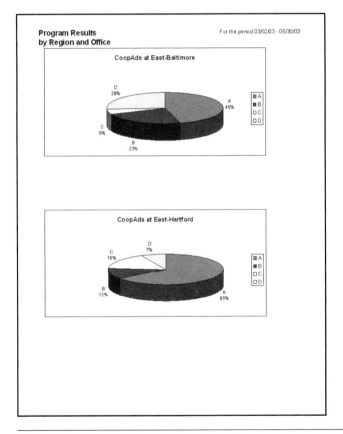

Figure 14.10 Manipulating the `Top` and `Height` properties allows control over chart placement

Summary

This case study explains importing XML data, applying formulas to summarize the data, and creating multiple charts in an automated fashion. Some approaches used in this chapter, such as the coordination of chart sizing with page breaks, enable users to create impressive reports. The solution offers two paths to import the XML data, depending on the version of Excel being used. The MSXML Parser is key to sophisticated XML processing with older versions of Excel.

CHAPTER 15

Repurposing XML Content

*Using Word to Turn Raw XML Data
into Meaningful Results*

VERSION NOTE: This case study requires Word 2003.

The Problem

According to company policy, departments must report how they fare in three areas: budget, training, and absences. Departments have goals in these three areas. Deviation from the goals—whether exceeding them, falling short, or coming in on target—is the basis for reporting.

For budget performance, the reporting consists of simply stating where each department stands with respect to its annual budget: Is the department under budget (which yields a negative percentage) or over budget (which yields a positive percentage)? In other words, when a department is –10% on budget, this means it has used less than its allotted amount of year-to-date funds. Therefore, the department is doing well on budget by having a negative percentage result.

For training reporting, goals are set for how many days of training staff in the aggregate should receive in a month; for absence reporting, how many days staff in the aggregate are expected to be out (using sick time, vacation time, and so on). The reportable results are the percent change between the goals and the actuals. The calculation is

(Goal – Actual)/Goal

For training, a lower numeric result is better than a higher one. In other words, if a department is given a goal of four training days in a month and five are used, then staff received a good amount of training, which is viewed favorably. The formula returns –0.25 from the calculation of ((4 – 5)/4). If a department has four days of training allotted for the month and none is used, then the formula returns 1.0: ((4 – 0)/4). This is not a good result.

For absenteeism, a higher numeric result is better than a lower one. If six days are expected to go to staff not being in and eight days is the actual, then the formula returns –0.33, from the calculation $((6 - 8)/6)$. On the other hand, if six is the goal and only three days of absenteeism occur in the given month, then 0.5 is returned, from $((6 - 3)/6)$.

Monthly, each department appends its results to a dedicated departmental XML file. Each XML file contains up to a year of data. The problem is that while any department's activity is easy to see, senior management needs a combined view of the results from all departments. This report is difficult for the administrative staff to assemble manually. XML is great for storing the data, but the structure makes it difficult to manually extract the data from the files.

The Requirements

- Create a combined view of departmental activity grouped by the three reportable areas: budget, training, and absence.
- The view must show the combined results for a single selected month.
- The department with the best result in each subject area should be highlighted.
- The combined view should be pleasingly formatted, and it should retain its formatting when posted to the company intranet.

Solution Tool Set and Files

- VBA
- XML Schema (XSD)
- XML Transformation (XSLT)
- Word 2003 XML capabilities
- scorecard.dot (a Word template)
- accounting_scorecard.xml
- legal_scorecard.xml
- sales_scorecard.xml
- scorecard.xsd
- scorecard.xsl

Table 15.1 Routines used in this solution

Routine	Module
`transform_scorecard`	`Module1`
`get_scorecard_data`	`Module1`
`process_xml`	`Module1`

Notes on This Case Study

In production, an assistant working for senior management creates a new document based on a template that is marked up with empty elements. See Figure 15.1. The document will end up being filled with the combined department data.

Three departments publish activity data: Legal, Accounting, and Sales. The application, the reportable results, and the process are all known by the same name: *scorecard.* The name of the Word template is scorecard.dot.

The Structure of the Source XML Files

Each of three departments publishes its scorecards in an XML file. Each of the three files follows exactly the same layout. Therefore, Listing 15.1 displays one of these files, legal_scorecard.xml.

The departmental XML files are structured such that the file represents a single year, and then there is a child element for each of the 12 months. Within each month are child elements for budget, training, and absence.

The Year and Month elements use attributes for the actual values:

```
<Year year="2003">
  <Month Num="1">
```

The Budget element contains two child elements: Amount and Qualifier. The pertinent data point is Amount. This is actually a precalculated percentage of variance from the annual budget, year-to-date. The full annual budget data is not contained in the XML data, therefore the Amount data point—although precalculated—is treated here as raw data.

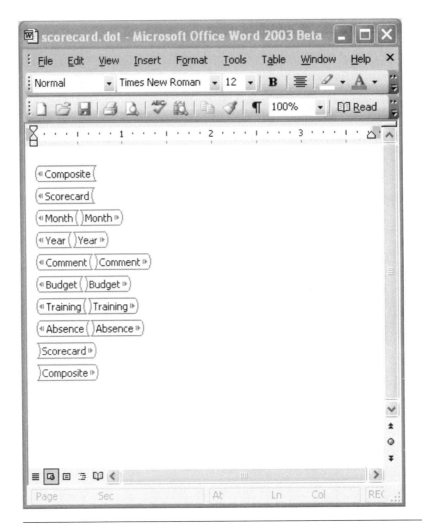

Figure 15.1 The Word template with XML tags ready to be filled with data

Both the Training and the Absence elements contain the same three child elements: Goal, Actual, and Qualifier. The goals are preset numbers determined by management. The actuals are what has transpired.

The root element of the XML files is performance_rankings— which contains the dept attribute, which holds the name of the department:

```
<performance_rankings dept="Legal">
```

Listing 15.1 The legal_scorecard.xml file

```xml
<?xml version="1.0" encoding="UTF-8"?>
<performance_rankings dept="Legal">
  <Year year="2003">
    <Month Num="1">
      <Budget>
        <Amount>11</Amount>
        <Qualifier>Percent</Qualifier>
      </Budget>
      <Training>
        <Goal>6</Goal>
        <Actual>6</Actual>
        <Qualifier>Days</Qualifier>
      </Training>
      <Absence>
        <Goal>3</Goal>
        <Actual>2</Actual>
        <Qualifier>Days</Qualifier>
      </Absence>
    </Month>
    <Month Num="2">
      <Budget>
        <Amount>12</Amount>
        <Qualifier>Percent</Qualifier>
      </Budget>
      <Training>
        <Goal>6</Goal>
        <Actual>3</Actual>
        <Qualifier>Days</Qualifier>
      </Training>
      <Absence>
        <Goal>3</Goal>
        <Actual>6</Actual>
        <Qualifier>Days</Qualifier>
      </Absence>
    </Month>
    <Month Num="3">
      <Budget>
        <Amount>4</Amount>
        <Qualifier>Percent</Qualifier>
      </Budget>
```

Listing 15.1 *(continued)*

```
      <Training>
        <Goal>6</Goal>
        <Actual>2</Actual>
        <Qualifier>Days</Qualifier>
      </Training>
      <Absence>
        <Goal>3</Goal>
        <Actual>3</Actual>
        <Qualifier>Days</Qualifier>
      </Absence>
    </Month>
    .
    .
    .

    <Month Num="12">
      <Budget>
        <Amount>2</Amount>
        <Qualifier>Percent</Qualifier>
      </Budget>
      <Training>
        <Goal>2</Goal>
        <Actual>2</Actual>
        <Qualifier>Days</Qualifier>
      </Training>
      <Absence>
        <Goal>16</Goal>
        <Actual>14</Actual>
        <Qualifier>Days</Qualifier>
      </Absence>
    </Month>
  </Year>
</performance_rankings>
```

The Structure of the XML Schema

One of the requirements is to combine the assorted department information into one view. The view also is based on XML. A schema has been created that describes how the combined XML file is to be structured. Listing 15.2 shows the scorecard.xsd file.

Listing 15.2 The schema that describes the combined department data

```xml
<?xml version="1.0" encoding="UTF-8"?>
<xsd:schema xmlns:xsd="http://www.w3.org/2001/XMLSchema">
  <xsd:element name="Composite">
    <xsd:complexType>
      <xsd:sequence>
        <xsd:element ref="Scorecard"
               minOccurs="1" maxOccurs="1"/>
      </xsd:sequence>
    </xsd:complexType>
  </xsd:element>
  <xsd:element name="Scorecard">
    <xsd:complexType>
      <xsd:sequence>
        <xsd:element name="Month" type="xsd:string"
               minOccurs="0"/>
        <xsd:element name="Year" type="xsd:integer"
               minOccurs="0"/>
        <xsd:element name="Comment" type="xsd:string"
               minOccurs="0"/>
        <xsd:element name="Budget">
          <xsd:complexType>
            <xsd:sequence>
              <xsd:element name="Department" minOccurs="0">
                <xsd:complexType mixed="true">
                  <xsd:sequence>
                    <xsd:element name="Variance"
                           type="xsd:decimal" minOccurs="0">
                    </xsd:element>
                  </xsd:sequence>
                </xsd:complexType>
              </xsd:element>
            </xsd:sequence>
          </xsd:complexType>
        </xsd:element>
        <xsd:element name="Training">
          <xsd:complexType>
            <xsd:sequence>
              <xsd:element name="Department" minOccurs="0">
                <xsd:complexType mixed="true">
                  <xsd:sequence>
```

Listing 15.2 *(continued)*

```
                    <xsd:element name="Variance"
                            type="xsd:decimal" minOccurs="0">
                    </xsd:element>
                  </xsd:sequence>
                </xsd:complexType>
              </xsd:element>
            </xsd:sequence>
          </xsd:complexType>
        </xsd:element>
        <xsd:element name="Absence">
          <xsd:complexType>
            <xsd:sequence>
              <xsd:element name="Department" minOccurs="0">
                <xsd:complexType mixed="true">
                  <xsd:sequence>
                    <xsd:element name="Variance"
                            type="xsd:decimal" minOccurs="0">
                    </xsd:element>
                  </xsd:sequence>
                </xsd:complexType>
              </xsd:element>
            </xsd:sequence>
          </xsd:complexType>
        </xsd:element>
      </xsd:sequence>
    </xsd:complexType>
  </xsd:element>
</xsd:schema>
```

The schema describes a root named `Composite`, which contains a hierarchical `Scorecard` complex type:

```
<xsd:element name="Composite">
  <xsd:complexType>
    <xsd:sequence>
      <xsd:element ref="Scorecard"
              minOccurs="1" maxOccurs="1"/>
    </xsd:sequence>
```

The `Scorecard` element contains simple and complex types. First there are simple elements for the month, year, and a comment:

```
<xsd:element name="Month" type="xsd:string"
      minOccurs="0"/>
<xsd:element name="Year" type="xsd:integer"
      minOccurs="0"/>
<xsd:element name="Comment" type="xsd:string"
      minOccurs="0"/>
```

The Comment element is not filled with data from the source department XML files. Comments are added manually after the other elements are filled. This is explained further later in the chapter.

The Budget, Training, and Absence elements are all described in an identical manner. Here is the schema for the Budget element:

```
<xsd:element name="Budget">
  <xsd:complexType>
    <xsd:sequence>
      <xsd:element name="Department" minOccurs="0">
        <xsd:complexType mixed="true">
          <xsd:sequence>
            <xsd:element name="Variance"
                    type="xsd:decimal" minOccurs="0">
            </xsd:element>
          </xsd:sequence>
        </xsd:complexType>
      </xsd:element>
    </xsd:sequence>
  </xsd:complexType>
</xsd:element>
```

Within the Budget (or Training, or Absence) element are two children: Department and Variance. The Department element, while a complex type (meaning that there are subchildren), will itself also hold data. Therefore, the mixed attribute is necessary so the resultant XML will validate:

```
<xsd:element name="Department" minOccurs="0">
  <xsd:complexType mixed="true">
```

Within the Department element is the child Variance element, which will hold a real (decimal) number:

```
<xsd:element name="Variance"
        type="xsd:decimal" minOccurs="0">
```

The Structure of the Word Template

The template contains XML tags but no data. An automated process will fill the tags with data from the source department XML files. VBA code does this; it is contained in the code module of the scorecard.dot Word template.

How the Template Was Created

The template was based on the scorecard.xsd schema file. Some of the elements of the schema have been placed in the template, but not all. The rest are filled in by the automated process. The finished template was shown earlier, in Figure 15.1. The template was created by taking a blank

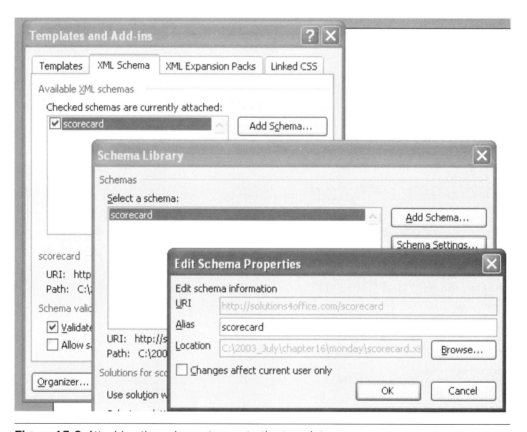

Figure 15.2 Attaching the schema to create the template

Word document and attaching the schema. Figure 15.2 shows a cascaded view of some of the dialogs used for managing schemas.

Once the schema is available in the XML Structure task pane, elements are manually added to the document body from the task pane. Figure 15.3 shows this in progress. The tags can be moved around in the document body; in fact, it was necessary to do so to create the layout seen in Figure 15.1. When the user drags and drops elements from the task pane into the document body, Word arranges them a certain way. Then the user has to rearrange them manually.

The VBA code is completely contained in the template. Listing 15.3 shows the contents of the single code module. There are three routines in the module: `transform_scorecard`, `get_scorecard_data`, and `process_xml`.

The workings of the VBA code are explained in the next section.

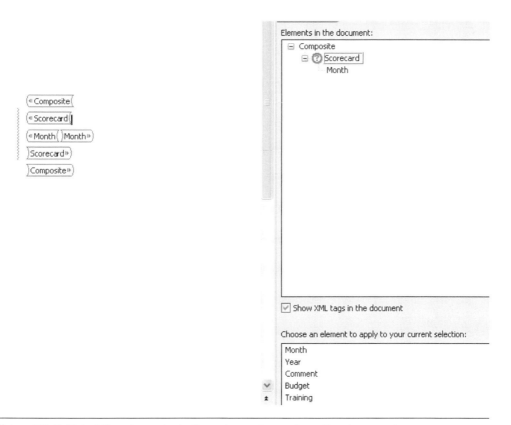

Figure 15.3 Using the elements in the schema to mark up the document

Listing 15.3 The VBA code in the scorecard.dot Word template

```
Sub transform_scorecard()
' change path as needed
ActiveDocument.TransformDocument _
  Path:="C:\2003_July\Scorecard\scorecard.xsl", _
  DataOnly:=True
End Sub
Sub get_scorecard_data()
On Error GoTo err_end
Dim this_doc As String
Dim schema_path As String
Dim xml_file_path As String
Dim namespace As String
Dim xml_node As xmlnode
Dim month_num As Integer
Dim month_input As Variant
Dim month_flag As Boolean
month_flag = False
' which month to process?
Do Until month_flag = True
  month_input = InputBox _
    ("Enter the number of the month (ex. for March, enter 3")
  ' validate month number entry
  If IsNull(month_input) = True Or _
    (Not IsNumeric(month_input)) Then
    MsgBox "For the month, must enter a number between 1 - 12"
  Else
    ' is a number, but must be between 1 and 12
    If Int(month_input) < 1 Or Int(month_input) > 12 Then
      MsgBox "The month number must be between 1 - 12"
    Else
      month_flag = True
    End If
  End If
Loop
month_num = Int(month_input)
' keep reference to this document
this_doc = ActiveDocument.Name
' change path as needed
schema_path = "C:\2003_July\Scorecard\scorecard.xsd"
namespace = "http://solutions4office.com/scorecard"
Application.XMLNamespaces.Add Path:= _
    schema_path, NamespaceURI:=namespace, Alias:=namespace
```

Listing 15.3 *(continued)*

```
Application.XMLNamespaces(namespace). _
    AttachToDocument (ActiveDocument)
' insert month and year into document
Set xml_node = Documents(this_doc).XMLNodes(1) _
    .SelectSingleNode("//Month")
xml_node.Range.Text = Choose(month_num, "January", "February", _
    "March", "April", "May", "June", "July", "August", _
    "September", "October", "November", "December")
Set xml_node = Documents(this_doc).XMLNodes(1) _
    .SelectSingleNode("//Year")
xml_node.Range.Text = 2003
' open and process XML files
' change path as needed
xml_file_path = "C:\2003_July\Scorecard\"
process_xml xml_file_path & "legal_scorecard.xml", _
    month_num, this_doc
process_xml xml_file_path & "sales_scorecard.xml", _
    month_num, this_doc
process_xml xml_file_path & "accounting_scorecard.xml", _
    month_num, this_doc
MsgBox "done"
Exit Sub
err_end:
  MsgBox Err.Description
End Sub
Sub process_xml(xmlfile As String, _
    month_num As Integer, this_doc As String)
Dim xml_node As xmlnode
Dim xml_node_2 As xmlnode
Dim month_node As xmlnode
Dim new_node As xmlnode
Dim vrnc As Single ' variance
Dim goal As Single
Dim actual As Single
Dim dept As String
Documents.Open FileName:=xmlfile
' get dept name from source
Set xml_node = ActiveDocument.XMLNodes(1) _
    .SelectSingleNode("/performance_rankings")
dept = xml_node.Attributes(1).Text
' PROCESS BUDGET
' work with Budget element
```

Listing 15.3 *(continued)*

```
Set xml_node = Documents(this_doc).XMLNodes(1) _
    .SelectSingleNode("//Budget")
' add new child element named Department to Budget element
Set new_node = xml_node.ChildNodes _
    .Add(Name:="Department", namespace:="")
' new Department element is given a value
new_node.Range.Text = dept
' work with the latest added child Department element
Set xml_node_2 = Documents(this_doc).XMLNodes(1) _
    .SelectSingleNode("//Budget/Department[position()=last()]")
' add new child element named Variance to Department element
Set new_node = xml_node_2.ChildNodes _
    .Add(Name:="Variance", namespace:="")
' work with the specified month in the source XML
Set month_node = ActiveDocument.SelectSingleNode _
    ("/performance_rankings/Year/Month[@Num='" & _
    month_num & "']/Budget")
' get the variance for the budget
vrnc = month_node.ChildNodes(1).Range.Text
' new Variance element is given value = Variance in source XML
new_node.Range.Text = vrnc
' PROCESS TRAINING
' work with Training element
Set xml_node = Documents(this_doc).XMLNodes(1) _
    .SelectSingleNode("//Training")
' add new child element named Department to Training element
Set new_node = xml_node.ChildNodes _
    .Add(Name:="Department", namespace:="")
' new Department element is given a value
new_node.Range.Text = dept
' work with the latest added child Department element
Set xml_node_2 = Documents(this_doc).XMLNodes(1) _
    .SelectSingleNode("//Training/Department[position()=last()]")
' add new child element named Variance to Department element
Set new_node = xml_node_2.ChildNodes _
    .Add(Name:="Variance", namespace:="")
' work with the specified month in the source XML
Set month_node = ActiveDocument.SelectSingleNode _
    ("/performance_rankings/Year/Month[@Num='" & _
    month_num & "']/Training")
' calculate difference between goal and actual
```

Listing 15.3 *(continued)*

```
goal = CSng(month_node.ChildNodes(1).Range.Text)
actual = CSng(month_node.ChildNodes(2).Range.Text)
' new Variance element is given calculated value
' test for 0 before doing division
If goal = 0 Then
  new_node.Range.Text = 0
Else
  new_node.Range.Text = Round(CStr((goal - actual) / goal), 2)
End If
' PROCESS ABSENCE
' work with Absence element
Set xml_node = Documents(this_doc).XMLNodes(1) _
    .SelectSingleNode("//Absence")
' add new child element named Department to Absence element
Set new_node = xml_node.ChildNodes _
    .Add(Name:="Department", namespace:="")
' new Department element is given a value
new_node.Range.Text = dept
' work with the latest added child Department element
Set xml_node_2 = Documents(this_doc).XMLNodes(1) _
    .SelectSingleNode("//Absence/Department[position()=last()]")
' add new child element named Variance to Department element
Set new_node = xml_node_2.ChildNodes _
    .Add(Name:="Variance", namespace:="")
' work with the specified month in the source XML
Set month_node = ActiveDocument.SelectSingleNode _
    ("/performance_rankings/Year/Month[@Num='" & _
    month_num & "']/Absence")
' calculate difference between goal and actual
goal = CSng(month_node.ChildNodes(1).Range.Text)
actual = CSng(month_node.ChildNodes(2).Range.Text)
' new Variance element is given calculated value
' test for 0 before doing division
If goal = 0 Then
  new_node.Range.Text = 0
Else
  new_node.Range.Text = Round(CStr((goal - actual) / goal), 2)
End If
' close XML file
ActiveDocument.Close SaveChanges:=False
End Sub
```

Locking the Code Project

The template code is vulnerable in production if left unprotected. Therefore, in the template, the code is password-protected. The protection is set in the Project Properties dialog under the Tools menu in the VBA editor. See Figure 15.4. A password is entered (the password is "solution"). There is an option to lock the project for viewing. In other words, the code can be protected yet viewable, or it can be protected against even viewing.

If or when the code needs to be edited, the code is "opened" with the password. See Figure 15.5.

Figure 15.4 Setting protection for the VBA code

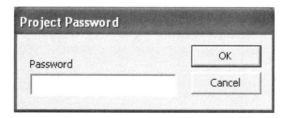

Figure 15.5 A password must be entered to view or edit the code

Saving the Template

All functionality was put into a Word document. The final procedure to make this a template was simply to save the document as a template. This was done in the Save As dialog by choosing "Document Template" in the "Save as type" drop-down. When saving as a template, Word automatically saves to the dedicated template directory. See Figure 15.6.

Using the Template

First, a document is created based on the template. This is accomplished in the New Document task pane. The scorecard.dot template may be listed in recently used templates, or it can otherwise be browsed to.

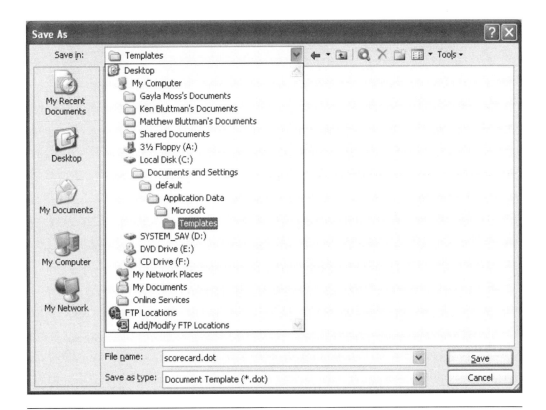

Figure 15.6 Saving a document as a template

Running the Routine to Extract the XML

Once a new document has been created based on the scorecard template, the first action is to run the `get_scorecard_data` routine from the Macros dialog. See Figure 15.7. Starting the routine could have been automated, but this approach lets the user control the order in which the document is filled. For example, the header or footer might be changed, or text could be typed below the tags. The user might enter information into the `Comment` tag. Such changes are likely to be made after the document has been filled with data, but our solution allows the user to do this first.

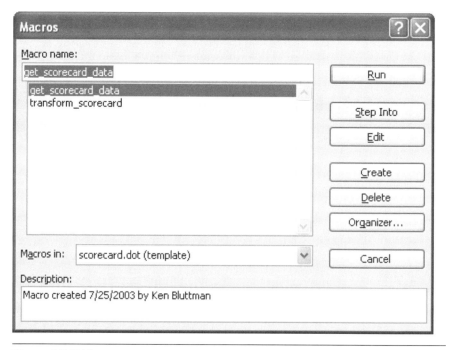

Figure 15.7 The `get_scorecard_data` routine begins the processing

Next a month must be selected. A prompt appears, asking for a number between 1 and 12. See Figure 15.8. The user keys in a number.

Here is the code snippet, taken from Listing 15.3, that displays the prompt and validates the entry:

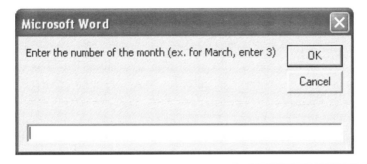

Figure 15.8 A number for a month is entered

```
Do Until month_flag = True
  month_input = InputBox _
    ("Enter the number of the month (ex. for March, enter 3")
  ' validate month number entry
  If IsNull(month_input) = True Or _
    (Not IsNumeric(month_input)) Then
    MsgBox "For the month, must enter a number between 1 - 12"
  Else
    ' is a number, but must be between 1 and 12
    If Int(month_input) < 1 Or Int(month_input) > 12 Then
      MsgBox "The month number must be between 1 - 12"
    Else
      month_flag = True
    End If
  End If
Loop
```

Once a valid number between 1 and 12 has been entered, the schema for the XML to be assembled is attached to the new document. Bear in mind that many of the elements described in the schema are already in the document as empty tags.

```
' change path as needed
schema_path = "C:\2003_July\Scorecard\scorecard.xsd"
namespace = "http://solutions4office.com/scorecard"
Application.XMLNamespaces.Add Path:= _
    schema_path, NamespaceURI:=namespace, Alias:=namespace
Application.XMLNamespaces(namespace). _
    AttachToDocument (ActiveDocument)
```

The `SelectSingleNode` method is used to target the `Month` tag in the document. Then the `Choose()` function is used to return the name of the month from the supplied month number. The month's name is added to the `Month` element via the `Range.Text` property. The same procedure is used to insert the year into the `Year` element, only in this case the value of 2003 is hard-coded:

```
Set xml_node = Documents(this_doc).XMLNodes(1) _
    .SelectSingleNode("//Month")
xml_node.Range.Text = Choose(month_num, "January", "February", _
    "March", "April", "May", "June", "July", "August", _
    "September", "October", "November", "December")
Set xml_node = Documents(this_doc).XMLNodes(1) _
    .SelectSingleNode("//Year")
xml_node.Range.Text = 2003
```

The remainder of the `get_scorecard_data` routine passes the XML file names and other needed information to the `process_xml` routine:

```
' open and process XML files
' change path as needed
xml_file_path = "C:\2003_July\Scorecard\"
process_xml xml_file_path & "legal_scorecard.xml", _
    month_num, this_doc
process_xml xml_file_path & "sales_scorecard.xml", _
    month_num, this_doc
process_xml xml_file_path & "accounting_scorecard.xml", _
    month_num, this_doc
```

Referring to Listing 15.1, the department name is stored as an attribute to the root element of the department's XML file. This department name needs to be used. The `process_xml` routine opens the XML file and uses the `SelectSingleNode` method to target the root element. Then the department name is found as the text of the first (and only) attribute. The department name is stored in the *dept* variable:

```
Documents.Open FileName:=xmlfile
' get dept name from source
Set xml_node = ActiveDocument.XMLNodes(1) _
    .SelectSingleNode("/performance_rankings")
dept = xml_node.Attributes(1).Text
```

Three subsections of code each work to process the budget, training, and absence data, respectively.

For budget data, first a node variable is set to the Budget element:

```
Set xml_node = Documents(this_doc).XMLNodes(1) _
    .SelectSingleNode("//Budget")
```

Next a new Department element is added to the Budget element. It's given the stored name of the department as its text value. A key point here is that the Department element being added already exists in the schema. Also, in the schema, the mixed attribute is what allows the text here to be entered for this otherwise complex element:

```
Set new_node = xml_node.ChildNodes _
    .Add(Name:="Department", namespace:="")
' new Department element is given a value
new_node.Range.Text = dept
```

The newly added Department element now receives its own child element: Variance. There is one little hurdle to get over. As this entire process loops for each department, a Department element is added. The child Variance element that is about to be added must go to the *correct* Department element. This is accomplished by using the XPath *position()* and *last()* functions to isolate the Department element that was also just added. Then the Variance element is added as a child node:

```
Set xml_node_2 = Documents(this_doc).XMLNodes(1) _
    .SelectSingleNode("//Budget/Department[position()=last()]")
' add new child element named Variance to Department element
Set new_node = xml_node_2.ChildNodes _
    .Add(Name:="Variance", namespace:="")
```

The Variance element needs to receive its value from the source XML file. The XML source file is currently open and is the active document for the moment. Using the month number (the month_num variable), an XPath expression isolates the correct node—where the Num attribute of the Month element in the source matches the supplied month number. Once found, the value is transferred via the vrnc variable:

```
Set month_node = ActiveDocument.SelectSingleNode _
    ("/performance_rankings/Year/Month[@Num='" & _
    month_num & "']/Budget")
' get the variance for the budget
vrnc = month_node.ChildNodes(1).Range.Text
' new Variance element is given value = Variance in source XML
new_node.Range.Text = vrnc
```

The training and absence data is carried over in the same fashion. Minor adjustments to the code subsections are necessary, though. For example, like the preceding XPath statement that isolates the last added De-partment element under the Budget element, a similar one isolates the last Department element added under the Absence element:

```
Set xml_node_2 = Documents(this_doc).XMLNodes(1) _
    .SelectSingleNode("//Absence/Department[position()=last()]")
```

Also, there is a key difference with regard to variance. For the budget data, the variance is a straight copy from the Amount element in the source XML. For training and absence, a formula is used to calculate the variance. The source XML has goal and actual values. The formula to calculate the variance is ((goal - actual)/goal). Because goal can be zero, a test must be in place to avoid division by zero. This is in the VBA code. If goal equals zero, then "0" is inserted into the new document as the variance. If goal is not zero, then the formula is applied and the result is rounded off to two decimal places. Prior to the calculation, the XML values are converted to single number types with the CSng() function (necessary for the calculation), and then the result is converted back to a string with the CStr() function:

```
goal = CSng(month_node.ChildNodes(1).Range.Text)
actual = CSng(month_node.ChildNodes(2).Range.Text)
' new Variance element is given calculated value
' test for 0 before doing division
If goal = 0 Then
  new_node.Range.Text = 0
Else
  new_node.Range.Text = Round(CStr((goal - actual) / goal), 2)
End If
```

So far, one XML file has been processed. The new document based on the template is starting to fill up, as shown in Figure 15.9.

The process loops through the three source department XML files. When complete, the document is filled with the data, per the design of the schema. Within each reportable area—budget, training, and absence—is each department, as children, with each having its own variance child. See Figure 15.10.

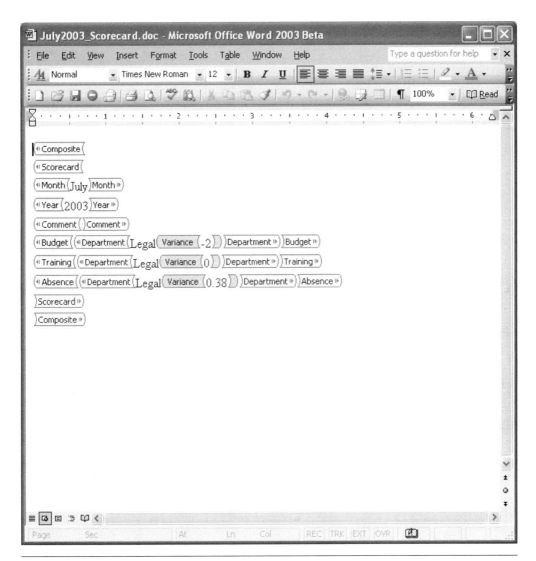

Figure 15.9 The new document is filling up with data from the source XML files

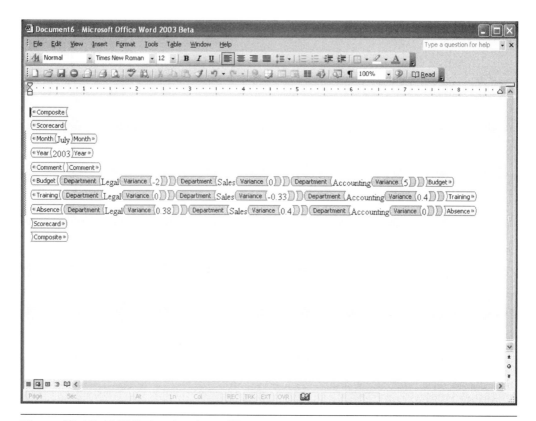

Figure 15.10 All XML data has been filled into the new document

Adding the Comments

At this point the results are visible on the screen. There is an empty Comment element that will accept typing. Making use of the Comment element is optional. If used, the comments will appear in the transformed view (coming up next). If left out, the transform will still run. Figure 15.11 shows a comment entered into the document.

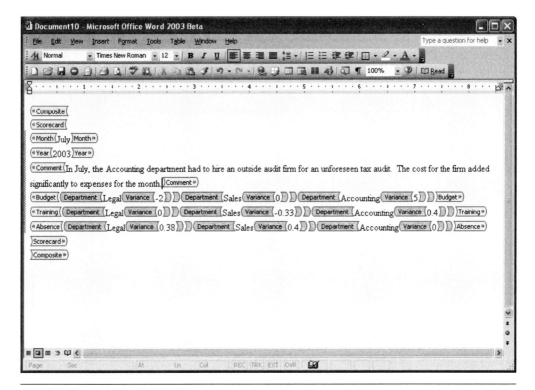

Figure 15.11 Manual comments are typed into the `Comment` element

Running the Transformation

After comments are added, the `transform_scorecard` routine can be run from the Macros dialog, shown in Figure 15.12.

The routine is just a line of code that applies the saved XSL(T) file:

```
Sub transform_scorecard()
' change path as needed
ActiveDocument.TransformDocument _
  Path:="C:\2003_July\Scorecard\scorecard.xsl", _
  DataOnly:=True
End Sub
```

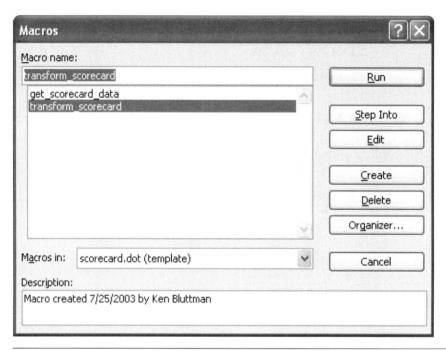

Figure 15.12 Running the transformation

The result of the transform is shown in Figure 15.13. For each category, the best results are highlighted.

The transform is accomplished with the scorecard.xsl file, shown in Listing 15.4.

Listing 15.4 The XSLT in the scorecard.xsl file transforms the data in the document

```
<?xml version="1.0"?>
<xsl:stylesheet
xmlns:xsl="http://www.w3.org/1999/XSL/Transform"
  xmlns:sc="http://www.solutions4office/scoretransform"
  version="1.0">
<xsl:output method="html"/>
<xsl:template match="/">
  <HTML>
  <HEAD>
    <TITLE>ScoreCard</TITLE>
  </HEAD>
```

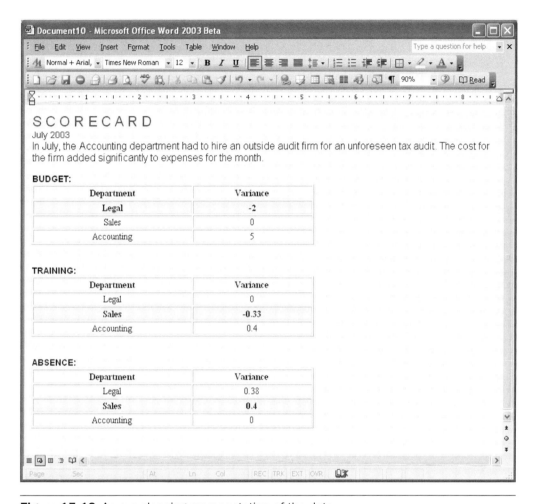

Figure 15.13 An eye-pleasing representation of the data

Listing 15.4 *(continued)*

```
<BODY>
<font Face="Arial, Helvetica">
<font SIZE="5" COLOR="Blue">
  S C O R E C A R D
</font>
<BR></BR>
<font SIZE="3">
  <xsl:value-of select="concat(//Month, ' ', //Year)"/>
</font>
```

Listing 15.4 *(continued)*

```
<BR></BR>
<font SIZE="4">
  <xsl:value-of select="//Comment"/>
</font>
<BR></BR><BR></BR>
<xsl:variable name="budget_best">
  <xsl:for-each select="//Budget/Department/Variance">
    <xsl:sort data-type="number" order="ascending"/>
    <xsl:if test="position()=1">
      <xsl:value-of select="."/>
    </xsl:if>
  </xsl:for-each>
</xsl:variable>
<xsl:variable name="training_best">
  <xsl:for-each select="//Training/Department/Variance">
    <xsl:sort data-type="number" order="ascending"/>
      <xsl:if test="position()=1">
        <xsl:value-of select="."/>
      </xsl:if>
  </xsl:for-each>
</xsl:variable>
<xsl:variable name="absence_best">
  <xsl:for-each select="//Absence/Department/Variance">
    <xsl:sort data-type="number" order="descending"/>
      <xsl:if test="position()=1">
        <xsl:value-of select="."/>
      </xsl:if>
  </xsl:for-each>
</xsl:variable>
<B>BUDGET:</B>
<TABLE WIDTH="60%" Border="1">
  <TR>
    <TH>Department</TH>
    <TH>Variance</TH>
  </TR>
  <xsl:for-each select="//Budget/Department">
  <TR>
   <xsl:choose>
     <xsl:when test="./Variance=$budget_best">
     <TD BGColor="Yellow" ALIGN="Center"><B>
      <xsl:value-of select="text() |* [not(self::Variance)]"/>
     </B></TD>
```

Listing 15.4 *(continued)*

```
        <TD BGColor="Yellow" ALIGN="Center"><B>
          <xsl:value-of select="./Variance"/>
        </B></TD>
        </xsl:when>
        <xsl:when test="./Variance!=$budget_best">
        <TD ALIGN="Center">
          <xsl:value-of select="text() |* [not(self::Variance)]"/>
        </TD>
        <TD ALIGN="Center"><xsl:value-of select="./Variance"/></TD>
        </xsl:when>
      </xsl:choose>
    </TR>
    </xsl:for-each>
</TABLE>
<BR></BR><BR></BR>
<B>TRAINING:</B>
<TABLE WIDTH="60%" Border="1">
  <TR>
    <TH>Department</TH>
    <TH>Variance</TH>
  </TR>
  <xsl:for-each select="//Training/Department">
  <TR>
   <xsl:choose>
     <xsl:when test="./Variance=$training_best">
     <TD BGColor="Yellow" ALIGN="Center"><B>
      <xsl:value-of select="text() |* [not(self::Variance)]"/>
     </B></TD>
     <TD BGColor="Yellow" ALIGN="Center"><B>
        <xsl:value-of select="./Variance"/>
     </B></TD>
     </xsl:when>
     <xsl:when test="./Variance!=$training_best">
     <TD ALIGN="Center">
        <xsl:value-of select="text() |* [not(self::Variance)]"/>
     </TD>
     <TD ALIGN="Center"><xsl:value-of select="./Variance"/></TD>
     </xsl:when>
   </xsl:choose>
  </TR>
  </xsl:for-each>
</TABLE>
```

Listing 15.4 *(continued)*

```
<BR></BR><BR></BR>
<B>ABSENCE:</B>
<TABLE WIDTH="60%" Border="1">
  <TR>
    <TH>Department</TH>
    <TH>Variance</TH>
  </TR>
  <xsl:for-each select="//Absence/Department">
  <TR>
   <xsl:choose>
     <xsl:when test="./Variance=$absence_best">
     <TD BGColor="Yellow" ALIGN="Center"><B>
      <xsl:value-of select="text() |* [not(self::Variance)]"/>
     </B></TD>
     <TD BGColor="Yellow" ALIGN="Center"><B>
       <xsl:value-of select="./Variance"/>
     </B></TD>
     </xsl:when>
     <xsl:when test="./Variance!=$absence_best">
     <TD ALIGN="Center">
       <xsl:value-of select="text() |* [not(self::Variance)]"/>
     </TD>
     <TD ALIGN="Center"><xsl:value-of select="./Variance"/></TD>
     </xsl:when>
   </xsl:choose>
  </TR>
  </xsl:for-each>
 </TABLE>
 </font>
 </BODY>
 </HTML>
</xsl:template>
</xsl:stylesheet>
```

The transformation blends HTML with values from the marked-up document. First, the word "SCORECARD" appears in large type and expanded. This is straight HTML:

```
<font SIZE="5" COLOR="Blue">
  S C O R E C A R D
</font>
```

The purpose of the transformation is to provide a new view of the data. Throughout much of the XSLT code, the `select` attribute targets an element or elements in the document. The `value-of` element inserts data into the new view. XPath expressions are used to locate nodes in the document. Using all these together, along with a concatenation, the month and year are assembled and inserted into the new view:

```
<xsl:value-of select="concat(//Month, ' ', //Year)"/>
```

The comment is inserted. If there is any actual comment, it will appear; otherwise nothing will show up:

```
<xsl:value-of select="//Comment"/>
```

One requirement is to highlight the best score within each area. This is accomplished by targeting all the nodes within a certain document level, such as `Budget/Department/Variance`. There are three data points here. The three data points are sorted, and then a test isolates the first in the sort. Using the `select` attribute, the best data point is stored in a variable. The block of code begins by declaring the variable, then it sequentially applies the filter to the particular nodes, sorts them, and finally tests for first position.

```
<xsl:variable name="budget_best">
    <xsl:for-each select="//Budget/Department/Variance">
      <xsl:sort data-type="number" order="ascending"/>
      <xsl:if test="position()=1">
        <xsl:value-of select="."/>
      </xsl:if>
    </xsl:for-each>
  </xsl:variable>
```

The `budget_best` variable stores the best value found in the variance grandchildren of the `Budget` element (`Budget–Department–Variance`). The same process is applied to the training data and the absence data. The budget and training data is sorted ascending, and the first value is the best result. Absence variance data is sorted descending. Based on the reasoning used in calculating training and absence results, the lowest value is best for training, and the highest value is best for absence.

When this part of the processing is finished, three variables are populated: `budget_best`, `training_best`, and `absence_best`.

The transformation creates tables to showcase the data. Each begins with HTML that labels the data and sets the table headings:

```
<B>BUDGET:</B>
<TABLE WIDTH="60%" Border="1">
  <TR>
    <TH>Department</TH>
    <TH>Variance</TH>
```

Once again, the *select* attribute is used to target a portion of the data. The *for-each* element of the XSLT prepares to process each element within the filtered data set:

```
<xsl:for-each select="//Budget/Department">
```

The `choose` element is used here to handle processing the two different possibilities: processing the best result, or processing a different result. The purpose of this block of code is to test for the best value by comparing each element in the filtered set with the value stored in the variable. One of the elements will match the variable (to be precise, the child `Variance` has to match). When the match is found, the code will highlight the row in yellow and apply a bold font; otherwise, no color or font change is applied.

With just two possibilities, the VBA approach would be to use an `If...Else...End If` construct. In the XSLT language, there is an *if* statement (the `if` element), but it has no "else" counterpart. In XSLT, *if* can apply a process only when the test is true. To test more than one possibility, such as here, where true and false each lead to different processing, the *choose* element, along with the appropriate number of *when* elements, is used.

To summarize, this next block of code isolates a set of nodes, then loops through each, testing for a match where the variance matches the variable holding the best value. All the nodes are output as HTML table rows (the <TR> and <TD> tags); however, the row that contains the best result receives a bold font and a yellow highlight:

```
<xsl:for-each select="//Budget/Department">
<TR>
 <xsl:choose>
   <xsl:when test="./Variance=$budget_best">
```

```
<TD BGColor="Yellow" ALIGN="Center"><B>
 <xsl:value-of select="text() |* [not(self::Variance)]"/>
</B></TD>
<TD BGColor="Yellow" ALIGN="Center"><B>
  <xsl:value-of select="./Variance"/>
</B></TD>
</xsl:when>
<xsl:when test="./Variance!=$budget_best">
<TD ALIGN="Center">
  <xsl:value-of select="text() |* [not(self::Variance)]"/>
</TD>
<TD ALIGN="Center"><xsl:value-of select="./Variance"/></TD>
</xsl:when>
 </xsl:choose>
</TR>
</xsl:for-each>
```

Note within the preceding code block that the inequality test is performed with the ! = operator. Also the complex line:

```
<xsl:value-of select="text() |* [not(self::Variance)]"/>
```

makes sure that the first column in the table displays just the department name, instead of the department name and the variance.

As throughout this case study, the processing of the training and absence data is similar or identical to how the budget data is processed. The same holds true for the transformation.

Saving the New View

The completed document is saved as an HTML file by the user, whenever he or she is ready; the save is not automated. The file can then be deployed to the company intranet. As a Web page, it can be seen in Internet Explorer. The formatting stays intact, as shown in Figure 15.14.

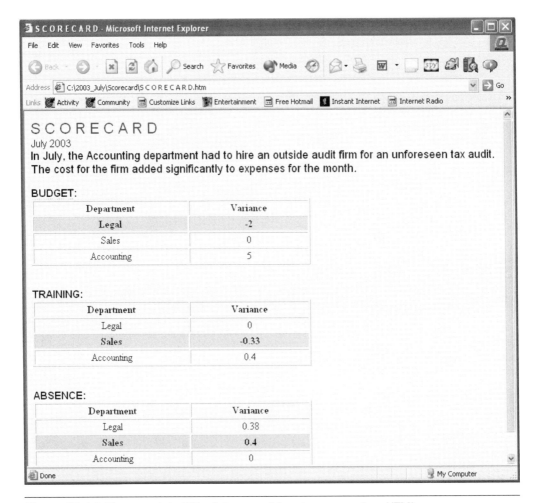

Figure 15.14 The completed Word document has been saved as HTML

Summary

This case study shows how the new XML features in Word 2003 solve a real business problem. While the structured XML format is great for data storage, there must also be ways to work with the data. Schemas and transformations complement the data by providing the muscle to manipulate the data in a meaningful way.

Word plays a key role in running a content reuse application such as that shown here. The implementation of XML use in Word 2003 enables users to enter information within the XML tags, or in other areas of the document. This functionality meets the requirement of keyed entry of the XML Comments, as well as entry into the header, footer, or other areas outside of the XML tags.

CHAPTER 16

Applying Saved InfoPath Data

Overcoming XML Processing Limitations

VERSION NOTE: This case study works with Access 2000, Access 2002, and Access 2003.

The Problem

Order information has been collected with InfoPath forms. After users have filled out the forms, they have saved their data as InfoPath XML files (per the standard Save action in InfoPath). Using the InfoPath form ensures that the numerous created data files are structurally identical.

The problem now is how to work with the data. The schema and form design are such that there are data relationships in the XML files. In particular, each file is generated by one worker, and that file holds orders for one or more customers. For each of these customers, the file holds one or more line items that make up their order.

This data needs to land in Access. Using the XML import method in Access does not keep the data related, but rather breaks it up into unrelated tables. Another process needs to be developed to bring the data into Access and keep the relations intact.

The Requirements

- The solution must have an automated process that will read data out of multiple XML files.
- The process must populate related tables in Access and, of course, keep the data relationships intact.

Solution Tool Set and Files

- InfoPath
- Access
- VBA
- The MSXML Parser
- Order_Processor.mdb
- Multiple XML files—each holding customer order information

Table 16.1 The routine used in this solution

Routine	Module
open_and_process_infopath_xml	modProcessXML

Notes on This Case Study

This case study is based partly on a hypothetical situation and partly on a pervasive existing one. At the time of this writing, InfoPath is not a released product. The problem presented here, at least concerning InfoPath, has not actually occurred in a production environment.

However, InfoPath does create XML files. The issue of how to process XML files is current and real. Presumably, this issue will have wider impact as InfoPath is used in business. InfoPath performs flawlessly at its main intended function: structured data input. As InfoPath and XML gain in popularity, new problems will arise—such as the ones addressed in this case study. How will all this XML data be processed? Just creating XML data has no value. A main benefit of XML is its reusability.

In fairness, InfoPath forms can be processed in other ways, using the Submit functionality. In practice this mode of processing will be the norm just some of the time. Certainly in some business environments, XML files will be popping up everywhere.

This case study explains how to use the MSXML Parser to manipulate the XML data according to the requirements (which are quite real in regard to getting stored XML data into an application). The fact that Access is the destination serves the purpose of this "instructional" case study. Access could be replaced here with any product. The power of the parser can be integrated into any of the Office products.

The InfoPath Form

Chapter 11, "Introduction to InfoPath," illustrated the development of an InfoPath form. The purpose of the form is to capture orders for books from book dealers. The form is shown in Figure 16.1, filled in with order information.

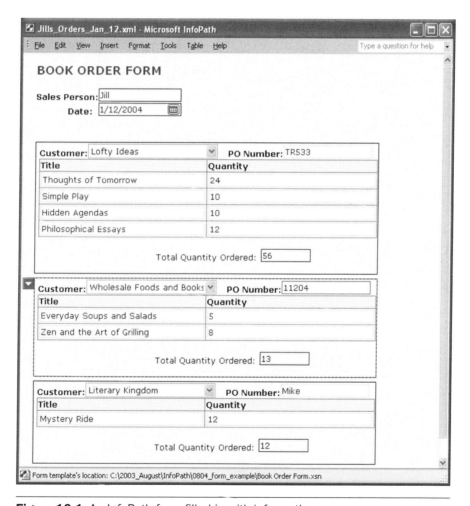

Figure 16.1 An InfoPath form filled in with information

The form displays relational data. There is a single salesperson and date. Then there are multiple customers. Further, each customer has ordered one or more book titles.

The data in this form has been saved as an XML file. The standard Save As dialog is used to enter the file name and target a directory, and InfoPath creates the XML file.

XML Created with InfoPath

Figure 16.2 shows an XML file created by InfoPath and viewed in Internet Explorer. The data relations are intact. There are single `SalesPerson` and `Date` elements. Then there are multiple `Order` elements. Each of these contains a single `Customer` and `PONumber` element. Also, each `Order` element contains multiple `LineItems`; each of these contains a `Title` and `Quantity`.

Figure 16.2 XML created by InfoPath

The Related Access Tables

The data needs to be inserted into two Access tables that have a one-to-many relationship. The SalesPerson and OrderDate data points are fields in the tblOrders table. The tables, tblOrders and tblLineItems, are related with the OrderKey field. OrderKey is the key for tblOrders and is the foreign key in tblLineItems. See Figure 16.3.

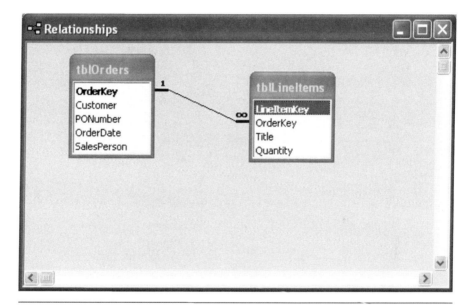

Figure 16.3 Related Access tables to be filled with the XML data

Access is able to import XML data without any programming. When the Get External Data item is selected from the File menu and an XML file is selected for input, the Import XML dialog appears. See Figure 16.4.

The dialog displays a field representation of the data to be imported. Proceeding with the import produces three tables. See Figure 16.5. The data is imported, but not in a useful manner, because the relationships are lost. For example, there is no way to know which titles in the LineItems table belong to which customer in the Order table.

Figure 16.4 The Import XML dialog

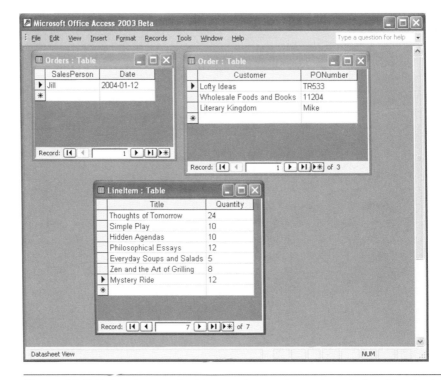

Figure 16.5 Using the standard Import feature loses the relationships in the XML data

Using the MSXML Parser to Import the Data

A developed process is necessary to correctly import the data into the specified tables and maintain relational information while doing so. The MSXML Parser library has all the functionality needed to handle this task. With regard to the requirement to read through multiple files, the File-Search object is used to identify the XML files and process them via a loop. Listing 16.1 contains the complete code solution.

Listing 16.1 The `open_and_process_infopath_xml` routine

```
Sub open_and_process_infopath_xml()
On Error GoTo err_end
' ADO variables
Dim conn As ADODB.Connection
Set conn = CurrentProject.Connection
Set recset = New ADODB.Recordset
' DOM variables
Dim xml_file As DOMDocument
Dim slsperson As IXMLDOMElement
Dim order_date As IXMLDOMElement
Dim orders As IXMLDOMNodeList
Dim order As IXMLDOMElement
Dim lineitems As IXMLDOMNodeList
Dim lineitem As IXMLDOMNode
Set xml_file = New DOMDocument
' other variables
Dim ssql As String
Dim book_title As String
Dim order_quantity As Integer
Dim this_order_key As Integer
Dim file_count As Integer
Dim getlines As Integer
Dim myFileSearch As FileSearch
Set myFileSearch = Application.FileSearch
' clear Access tables
ssql = "Delete * From tblLineItems"
conn.Execute (ssql)
ssql = "Delete * From tblOrders"
conn.Execute (ssql)
```

Listing 16.1 *(continued)*

```
' work with XML files in specified directory
With myFileSearch
  .NewSearch
  ' change path as necessary
  .LookIn = "C:\Book Orders"
  .SearchSubFolders = False
  .Filename = "*.xml"
  If .Execute() > 0 Then
    file_count = .Execute()
    For Each myfile In .FoundFiles
      ' open XML file with parser
        xml_file.async = False
        xml_file.Load myfile
          ' isolate salesperson
        Set slsperson = _
          xml_file.selectSingleNode("//SalesPerson")
      ' isolate order date
        Set order_date = _
          xml_file.selectSingleNode("//Date")
      ' create node list of all orders in the file
        Set orders = xml_file.selectNodes("//Order")
      ' for each order in the file, write a record in tblOrders
        For Each order In orders
          ssql = "Insert Into tblOrders (Customer, PONumber, "
          ssql = ssql & "OrderDate, SalesPerson)"
          ssql = ssql & " Values ("
          ssql = ssql & "'" & order.childNodes(0).Text & "', "
          ssql = ssql & "'" & order.childNodes(1).Text & "', "
          ssql = ssql & "#" & order_date.Text & "#, "
          ssql = ssql & "'" & slsperson.Text & "')"
          conn.Execute (ssql)
          ' get the new order key
          ' it has just been written to the orders table
          ' so getting the max of OrderKey returns the key number
          ' needed for the detail table
          ssql = "Select Max(OrderKey) From tblOrders"
          ' open a recordset with the SQL statement
          ' it will have one record with one field
          ' which is the OrderKey just created
          recset.Open ssql, conn, adOpenKeyset
```

Listing 16.1 *(continued)*

```
            ' store the OrderKey and close the recordset
            this_order_key = recset.Fields(0)
            recset.Close
            ' Using the OrderKey,
            ' populate the LineItems table
            ' with the details of the order
            ' this loop starts at 2 (the 3rd child
            ' in a zero-based collection) because the first 2
            ' children are the Customer and PONumber - which have
            ' been processed above in the first SQL Insert.
            ' The line items are children of the LineItem element;
            ' there can be any number of LineItem elements
            For getlines = 2 To order.childNodes.length - 1
              book_title = _
                  order.childNodes(getlines).childNodes(0).Text
              order_quantity = _
                  order.childNodes(getlines).childNodes(1).Text
              ssql = "Insert Into tblLineItems "
              ssql = ssql & "(OrderKey, Title, Quantity)"
              ssql = ssql & " Values ("
              ssql = ssql & this_order_key & ", "
              ssql = ssql & "'" & book_title & "', "
              ssql = ssql & order_quantity & ")"
              conn.Execute (ssql)
          Next
        Next
      Next
    End If
End With
MsgBox file_count & " files processed"
Exit Sub
err_end:
MsgBox "This error occurred:  " & Err.Description
End Sub
```

In order for this routine to run, two external libraries must be referenced. In the Access code module, the Tools menu leads to the References dialog, shown in Figure 16.6.

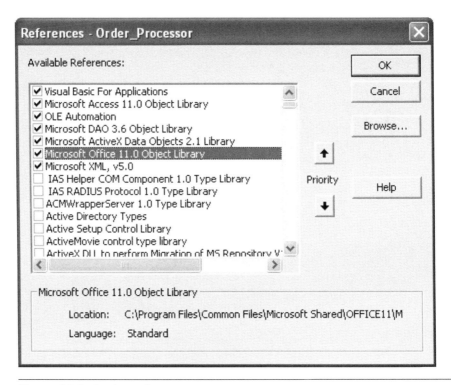

Figure 16.6 Setting references

It is necessary to have references to the Microsoft Office Object Library (11.0, 10.0, or 9.0) and Microsoft XML (v5, or earlier). The Microsoft ActiveX Data Objects (ADO) Library is likely referenced by default, but if not, a reference is needed to this as well. Any version number of ADO will suffice.

The routine begins by establishing several variables. Of note here are the parser library variables. The object types from the parser library are nodes, elements, and so on, types that mirror how XML data is structured in the Document Object Model (DOM). The DOM is an in-memory representation of XML data:

```
Dim xml_file As DOMDocument
Dim slsperson As IXMLDOMElement
Dim order_date As IXMLDOMElement
Dim orders As IXMLDOMNodeList
Dim order As IXMLDOMElement
Dim lineitems As IXMLDOMNodeList
Dim lineitem As IXMLDOMNode
```

Also, the `FileSearch` object, from the Office library, is used:

```
Dim myFileSearch As FileSearch
Set myFileSearch = Application.FileSearch
```

For the purpose of this demonstration, the two Access tables are cleared. In actual use the data would be processed further after it landed in the tables. The data could be archived or used in some other appropriate manner. Here, the data is just erased and rewritten each time the process is run:

```
' clear Access tables
ssql = "Delete * From tblLineItems"
conn.Execute (ssql)
ssql = "Delete * From tblOrders"
conn.Execute (ssql)
```

The `FileSearch` object finds the XML files in a specified directory. An assumption is made here that all needed XML files from the InfoPath form have been saved to a dedicated directory. If any files are found, a `For Each...Next` construct is used to process each file in a sequential manner:

```
With myFileSearch
  .NewSearch
  ' change path as necessary
  .LookIn = "C:\Book Orders"
  .SearchSubFolders = False
  .Filename = "*.xml"
  If .Execute() > 0 Then
    file_count = .Execute()
    For Each myfile In .FoundFiles
```

In turn, each XML file is opened:

```
xml_file.Load myfile
```

XPath is used to find the salesperson and date. These are stored in variables:

```
    ' isolate salesperson
     Set slsperson = _
       xml_file.selectSingleNode("//SalesPerson")
    ' isolate order date
     Set order_date = _
       xml_file.selectSingleNode("//Date")
```

A node list that contains all the orders is created. Each order will be processed in turn. Here, *order* is a single node, and *orders* is a list of nodes. These variables have already been set as the appropriate DOM types (node and node list):

```
Set orders = xml_file.selectNodes("//Order")
' for each order in the file, write a record in tblOrders
For Each order In orders
```

A SQL Insert statement is assembled. This writes a record to the tblOrders table. The salesperson and order date are already stored in variables. The Customer and PONumber data points are children of the Order element. Therefore, since this loop is processing an "Order," the Customer and PONumber are pulled from the array of child elements. The first child (index 0) is the Customer, and the second child (index 1) is the PONumber. For each of these, the Text property is accessed to get the actual value.

```
ssql = "Insert Into tblOrders (Customer, PONumber, "
ssql = ssql & "OrderDate, SalesPerson)"
ssql = ssql & " Values ("
ssql = ssql & "'" & order.childNodes(0).Text & "', "
ssql = ssql & "'" & order.childNodes(1).Text & "', "
ssql = ssql & "#" & order_date.Text & "#, "
ssql = ssql & "'" & slsperson.Text & "')"
conn.Execute (ssql)
```

The related data is to be written into the tblLineItems table. It is necessary to get the value of the primary key in the tblOrders table. The primary key, OrderKey, is an AutoNumber type. Because the record was just written to this table, the key is simply the highest value found in the field. The Max() function is used to get the highest value of the OrderKey field, out of all records in the table. A SQL statement (Select Max(OrderKey) From tblOrders) is used to open a recordset. The recordset returns just one record with the one field. This is the needed value, and it is stored in the this_order_key variable:

```
ssql = "Select Max(OrderKey) From tblOrders"
' open a recordset with the SQL statement
' it will have one record with one field
' which is the OrderKey just created
recset.Open ssql, conn, adOpenKeyset
' store the OrderKey and close the recordset
this_order_key = recset.Fields(0)
recset.Close
```

Next, the line items will be written into the tblLineItems table. For each Order element, the first and second child elements are the Customer and PONumber, respectively. The third child is the first line item. There may be one or more line items. A loop is established that iterates from the third item to the total count of children of the Order element. The loop is offset by one to work with the zero-based indexing.

Within each succession of this loop, the book title and quantity are found. These two items are children of the LineItem element (and are grandchildren of the Order element).

```
For getlines = 2 To order.childNodes.length - 1
  book_title = _
    order.childNodes(getlines).childNodes(0).Text
  order_quantity = _
    order.childNodes(getlines).childNodes(1).Text
```

A SQL Insert is assembled using the OrderKey (stored in the this_order_key variable), the book title, and the quantity.

```
ssql = "Insert Into tblLineItems "
ssql = ssql & "(OrderKey, Title, Quantity)"
ssql = ssql & " Values ("
ssql = ssql & this_order_key & ", "
ssql = ssql & "'" & book_title & "', "
ssql = ssql & order_quantity & ")"
conn.Execute (ssql)
```

This loop repeats for each line item. Three loops are in play; working from inside of the nest out, these are: line items, orders, and the XML files themselves. When all processing is finished, a message is displayed, as shown in Figure 16.7.

The two Access tables are filled and related, as shown in Figure 16.8. Each record in the tblOrders table has one or more records in the tblLineItems table.

Figure 16.7 Processing has completed

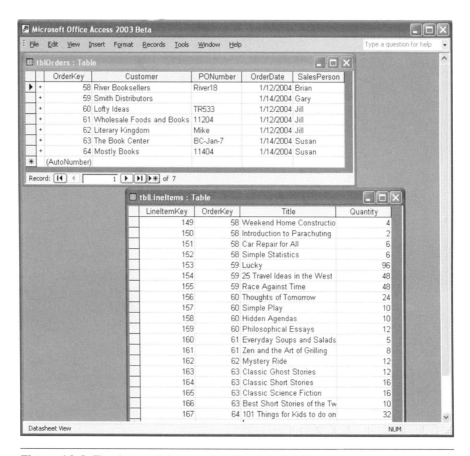

Figure 16.8 The Access tables maintain related data

Summary

Both InfoPath and Access have been used to address a larger problem of how to manage the data stored in XML files. The ability of XML to easily store data relationships within nested tags is great for content management. Applying the content, though, requires planning. This case study demonstrated how it is still a likely necessity to creatively manipulate data even when stored in an XML structured format.

Resources

This appendix lists Web sources and books, organized by major subject areas. Quite a few of these listings apply to more than one subject. I cannot vouch for the validity of the Web addresses; they may change, disappear, or become outdated. Books, too, are updated or go out of print. Such is the nature of information in the fast-paced world of software.

Also, at the time this list was assembled, there were no books yet published on Microsoft Office 2003. It's likely that many of the titles listed here will be updated for the latest release of Office.

XML Resources

Web Sources

An understanding of XML and related technologies (schemas, transformations, XPath, DOM, and so on) is essential for working with XML structured data. The World Wide Web Consortium deserves special mention here, because it is the organization that oversees the creation of XML standards:

- World Wide Web Consortium
  http://www.w3.org

Other XML sites include:

- Top XML
  http://www.topxml.com
- Perfect XML
  http://www.perfectxml.com
- The Microsoft XML Developer Center
  http://msdn.microsoft.com/xml

This URL leads to Microsoft's XML parser download page:

- *http://msdn.microsoft.com/library/default.asp?url=
  /downloads/list/xmlgeneral.asp*

Books

- *Essential XML Quick Reference,* by Aaron Skonnard and Martin Gudgin, Addison-Wesley, 2002
- *XSLT Programmer's Reference,* 2nd Edition, by Michael Kay, Wrox Press, 2001
- *XSLT Developer's Guide,* by Chris von See and Nitin Keskar, McGraw-Hill/Osborne, 2002
- *XML Programming with VB and ASP,* by Mark Wilson and Tracey Wilson, Manning Publications, 2000

Office Development

Web Sources

Some of these sites are about Office in general; others are product-specific:

- Microsoft's Office MSDN page
  http://msdn.microsoft.com/office
- Office Zealot
  http://www.officezealot.com
- The Access Web
  http://www.mvps.org/access
- The MS Word MVP FAQ Site
  http://www.mvps.org/word
- Excel VBA
  http://www.excelvba.com
- Office VBA Developer
  http://www.officevbadeveloper.com

Books

- *Alison Balter's Mastering Microsoft Access 2002 Desktop Development,* by Alison Balter, Sams Publishing, 2002
- *Access 2002 Desktop Developer's Handbook,* by Paul Litwin et al., Sybex, Inc., 2001
- *Excel 2002 Power Programming with VBA,* by John Walkenbach, M&T Books, 2001
- *Excel 2002 VBA Programmer's Reference,* by Stephen Bullen et al., Wrox Press, 2001
- *Word 2000 VBA Programmer's Reference,* by Duncan Mackenzie et al., Wrox Press, 1999
- *Programming Microsoft Outlook 2000,* by Gordon Padwick and Ken Slovak, Sams Publishing, 2000

ASP/VBScript/JavaScript/HTML

Web Sources

- Four Guys From Rolla
  http://www.4guysfromrolla.com
- ASP 101
  http://www.asp101.com
- W3 Schools
  http://www.w3schools.com

Books

- *Instant ASP Scripts,* by Greg Buczek, McGraw-Hill, 1999
- *VBScript Programmer's Reference,* by Susanne Clark et al., Wrox Press, 1999
- *Pure JavaScript,* by R. Allen Wyke et al., Sams Publishing, 1999

Microsoft Technologies

There is detailed information about many subject areas on Microsoft's Web site. In particular, these two sections—the MSDN and the Knowledge Base—are search enabled and lead to numerous documents and downloads geared for developers. A wealth of information is available here on topics such as SharePoint, data access, Web service development, .Net development, and much more:

- The Microsoft Developer Network (MSDN)
  http://msdn.microsoft.com
- Microsoft Help and Support/Knowledge Base
  http://support.microsoft.com

Technical Education/Support/Peer-to-Peer Discussion

- Microsoft Help and Support/Knowledge Base
  http://support.microsoft.com
- DevX
  http://www.devx.com
- Tek-Tips
  http://www.tek-tips.com
- W3 Schools
  http://www.w3schools.com
- Technology Basics
  http://www.technologybasics.com

Index

Note: Page numbers followed by *f* and *t* indicate figures and tables, respectively.

A

absolute reference, in Excel, 85

Access

  `AllForms` collection in, 130–132

  `AllQueries` collection in, 128–130

  `AllReports` collection in, 132–133

  `AllTables` collection in, 128–130

  `Application` object in, 125

  `CurrentData` object in, 126–128

  `CurrentProject` object in, 130, 131*f*

  custom command bars in, 249*t*

  customization in, 121

  Database window in, 123, 124*f*

  dependencies in, 141–145

  development in, 121–123

  `DoCmd` object in, 141

  `Forms` collection in, 133–136

  Forms library and, 252

  `ImportXML` method in, 297, 299*f*

  `Modules` collection in, 138–141

  `Reports` collection in, 137–138

  smart tags in, 9–10

    display of, 342

    recognizers and actions in, 332, 333*f*

    settings for, 338, 340*f*

    using, 348–353, 350*f*

  XML in, 7, 8*f*, 297–311, 557, 557*f*, 558*f*

    exporting, 302–307, 302*f*, 304*f*, 306*f*, 308*f*

    importing, 297–301, 301*f*

  XML attributes in, 300, 302*f*, 326–328, 328*f*

  XSLT in, 7, 307–311, 309*f*, 312*f*

Access database. *See* database

`AccessObject` object, dependency methods of, 143

Access table. *See* table

actions, in smart tags, 331–332, 332*f*, 333*f*

  XML for, 336–338

`Activate` event, for user form, 258

`Activate` method, 18, 82

`ActiveDocument` object, in Word, 16–18, 17*f*

`ActiveExplorer` method, in Outlook, 194*t*

`ActiveInspector` method, in Outlook, 194*t*

`ActivePrinter` property, in Word, 15–16

Active Server Pages (ASP), smart tags processed with, 344–346

`ActiveWindow` method, in Outlook, 194*t*

ActiveX Data Objects (ADO)

  in Access development, 121–123

  reference to

    in Access, 562, 562*f*

    in Excel chart, 92–93, 93*f*

    in mail merge, 61–62, 62*f*

`AddItem` method, in Excel, 262

`AdditionalData` object, in Access XML export, 302–303

`AddMembers` method, for Outlook distribution list, 219

`Add` method

  in Excel

    for charts, 91, 110

    for sheets, 73, 74*t*

    of `Workbook` collection, 71–72

    for XML maps, 313

  in PowerPoint

    of `Application` object, 149

    for shapes, 158–166, 160*t*–161*t*

    of `Slides` collection, 154

  for Word tables, 31